VOLUME 2
Recent American History
1945 to the Present

THE DORSEY SERIES IN HISTORY

VOLUME 2

Recent American History

1945 to the Present

Ralph F. de Bedts
Old Dominion University

1973
THE DORSEY PRESS   *Homewood, Illinois   60430*
IRWIN-DORSEY INTERNATIONAL   *London, England   WC2H 9NJ*
IRWIN-DORSEY LIMITED   *Georgetown, Ontario   L7G 4B3*

First Printing, October, 1973

ISBN 0-256-01414-0
Library of Congress Catalog Card No. 73–84298
Printed in the United States of America

To my dear wife,
Elizabeth Seelinger de Bedts,
who as a professional librarian
is doubly aware—if such
be possible—of the constraints
of authorship, and who remains
generously understanding

Preface

*"Who-so-ever, in writing a modern history,
shall follow truth too near the heels, it may
haply strike out his teeth."*

    Sir Walter Raleigh, in the preface to
    A *History of the World.*

THE AUTHOR is cautiously aware of the above warning uttered by that very modern individual, Sir Walter Raleigh. Nevertheless, every scholar of recent history must make tentative judgments, secure only in the knowledge that changes will inevitably affect contemporary evaluations.

I, like most other historians, think of 1933 and the New Deal as a definite watershed for recent United States history. The promotion of the general welfare took on new interpretations, and the enactments of the period soon gave evidence of complete integration into a somewhat transformed society. The evidence is far from complete as to the acceptance of 1945 and the beginning of the postwar era as another significant dividing line, which is the starting point for the second part of this work.

The events of recent and contemporary history are increasingly fascinating to students. Modern scholarship can speak to them of society's stresses and changes coming out of such other-generational events as the Great Depression, the New Deal, and World War II. In the years of greater American global involvement since the war, they are aware of the increased weight given to foreign relations while remaining keenly curious concerning the more recent social changes within their own shorter generational era. I hope that my emphasis upon political, diplomatic, economic, and social history will further stimulate their healthy regard for the complexities of recent American history.

I would like to acknowledge the valuable and constructive aid of several readers of this manuscript. The author is indebted to Peter d'A. Jones, of the University of Illinois, Chicago Circle Campus; Lawrence S. Kaplan, of Kent State University; Jack Tager, of the University of Massachusetts, Amherst; and Theodore A. Wilson, of the University of Kansas, for the many helpful suggestions offered and accepted; for judicious weighing of emphases; and for the flagging of errors. Any errors that remain are my unshared responsibility. I wish also to thank my secretary during several years of my tenure as Chairman of the Department of History, Pamela Ogram, whose keen editorial eye and speedy typewriter were indispensable.

Norfolk, Virginia   RALPH F. DE BEDTS
September 1973

Acknowledgments

THE MAPS on pages 14, 125, 133, 138, 158, and 160 are from *American Epoch*, Vol. III, 3d ed., by Arthur S. Link, William B. Catton, and William M. Leary, Jr. Copyright © 1955, 1967 by Arthur S. Link. Copyright © 1963 by Arthur S. Link and William B. Catton. Reprinted by permission of Alfred A. Knopf, Inc.

The maps on pages 90 and 304 are from Gilbert C. Fite and Norman A. Graebner, *Recent United States History*. Copyright © 1972, The Ronald Press Company, New York.

The map on page 234 is from Richard Hofstadter, William Miller, and Daniel Aaron, *The United States*, 3d ed., © 1972. Reprinted by permission of Prentice-Hall, Inc., Englewood Cliffs, N.J.

The charts on pages 312 and 313 are from *Modern America*, by Walter T. K. Nugent. Houghton Mifflin Company, 1973. Reprinted by permission of the publishers.

Contents

Introduction

IN 1945, the year this volume commences, the greatest world war of all times ended. It accounted for some 340,000 Americans dead and more than 700,000 wounded. The Russians lost between 6 and 7 million soldiers killed (plus 10 to 12 million civilians dead); the Germans listed more than 3 million military dead; the Japanese, some 1.2 million military dead. At the conclusion of the war and these staggering statistics, only the United States and Russia stood forth as great world powers. And only the United States, by virtue of its economic capacities and resources and its undamaged industrial might, could be classed as a superpower. The United States and Russia maintained their status as allies down to the war's last day, even though their relations had been badly strained at times by a variety of factors during the conflict. In subduing Japan in the closing months of the war, the United States chiefs of staff had counted upon Russian armies to take care of the large Japanese forces on the Asiatic mainland. Russia had agreed at Yalta that three months after defeat of the German armies she would join in the Allied Pacific efforts. The date Stalin subsequently gave at the Potsdam Conference for Russian entry was August 8. But two days before the Russian armies were due to move against the Japanese, the United States exploded on Hiroshima with awesome results the first terrible new weapon of the atomic age. On August 9, as the Russian armies clashed with Japan's forces in Manchuria, the second atomic bomb was dropped on Nagasaki. On the following day the Japanese cabinet decided to surrender and did so on August 14, although the formal ceremony took place on board the battleship *Missouri* in Tokyo Bay on September 2, 1945.

In the years following the war, many postsurrender studies indicated

1

that Japan had been on the absolute edge of collapse. Claims were made that neither Russian entry nor the atomic bomb had been necessary, so close were the Japanese to complete strangulation. The U.S. Navy admitted it was reduced to such targets as local ferryboats in Japanese coastal waters. Although the armies might readily have elected to fight on in the face of an American invasion, Japan's predicament and the nature of the atomic bomb prompted historical inquiry as to whether the bomb was dropped with other than military considerations in mind. Historians exploring this possibility have considered American irritation with Russian moves and an American wish to hold some power over the Soviets as possible motivation. Why, they ask for example, were the known Japanese peace feelers not taken into account? Other similar puzzles and perhaps feelings of guilt over the first use of atomic weapons spurred on such inquiry, and it raised many questions not fully answered. The United States and Russia squared off in hostile fashion in the events and attitudes of the Cold War as subsequently described herein, and historical scholarship increasingly looked to the war years and the early postwar years to explain the directions and workings of American foreign policy in the recent past.

Domestically, the war—as wars commonly do—accelerated many changes in American society. Many old attitudes changed under the stresses and necessities of war years. The family structure would never be quite the same again. Women entered the work force in numbers; and in spite of the demobilization of millions of men, the female sex was to assume a more permanent and steadily increasing role in the labor force and even in the armed services. American youth, for better or worse, was rendered more independent of family authority and of the household itself by newfound economic freedom and the sharpened awareness of new places seen and new cultures experienced. The accelerated mobility of families and separated individuals alike was a factor of change. A small wave of population moved out of many Southern states and the Appalachian border states and packed themselves into such large cities as Los Angeles, Chicago, Detroit, and Akron. The American demographic swing from rural to urban areas accelerated violently. Many blacks who were a part of the process found heightened racism in the industrial cities of the North. There they found increased antagonism from whites who considered their jobs threatened by the influx, and who often reacted violently when blacks sought to avail themselves of decent housing in previously all-white neighborhoods. Riots occurred in such places as Detroit, Los Angeles, and in New York's Harlem during the war years. But blacks had a new militancy themselves. The idea of participating in a war fought to preserve democratic traditions made blacks more conscious than ever of the gulf between American ideals and American practice. Their added political importance in large urban areas put additional weight behind their early pressures for equality. While blacks made only minor progress toward this goal in the war years, their heightened awareness and their new political and economic opportunities were the bases for the full-fledged Negro Revolution of the 1960s.

The war also left the country more conservative ideologically than it had been in the 1930s. People were tired of the turmoil of the war years and of the many changes wrought by the Great Depression and the New Deal. There was also an increased economic concentration in the large corporations that had been the chief recipients of war contracts and had benefitted from the slackening of antitrust impulses during the combat years. "Dollar-a-year" businessmen, fresh from the economic controls of mobilization duties, remained a new and powerful force within or allied with the governmental structure and its agencies. The armed forces, concerned with their intraservice rivalries and what they considered their global postwar roles to be, figured on millions of men rather than the few hundred thousand of prewar days. To fulfill their anticipated role, they expected to receive more planes, more ships, and more equipment. They found ready allies in the business community and Congress and in the support of public opinion. Growing from this combination of factors and fanned by the fears of American-Soviet confrontation was the powerful alliance that President Eisenhower later warned his countrymen about as "the military-industrial complex."

Into these responsibilities and complexities of the postwar years Harry S. Truman was catapulted on the sudden death of Franklin Roosevelt April 12, 1945. Roosevelt evidently had intended to press on with many of the social reform concepts of New Deal days, as his 1944 platform and campaign of that year indicated. Truman, adding several ideas of his own, was nevertheless hard pressed to move even small distances toward such goals in the face of frequently hostile Congresses. In the after-the-war years, the United States moved to a total global involvement, obsessively preoccupied with its fears, real and imaginary, of Communist expansion and rivalry, and with the reactions such apprehensions called into being. Cold War attitudes and actions were to dominate Americans domestically and in foreign policies for the next generation.

1

The Early Years of the Truman Presidency

Harry S. Truman

PERHAPS no Vice President ever assumed the presidency of the United States in the grip of such excruciating timing as did Harry S. Truman in the wake of Roosevelt's death on April 12, 1945. He had only been Vice President a matter of weeks, with little or no chance to gain familiarity with Roosevelt's closest advisers or with the rush of top-secret events. He had little or no experience in foreign policy and affairs of state either as a Senator from Missouri or in any other capacity, yet the crucial matters of the war's final weeks in Europe and the gravely important decisions involved could not wait. Forces must be transferred for the final onslaught against the Japanese, and an incomprehensible and awesome atomic weapon approached readiness. To face these enormous responsibilities, the nation received neither a statesman or administrator of any stature nor even a leading senatorial figure, but rather an average political figure of typical Middle-America makeup and background.

Truman was born on May 8, 1884 in the village of Lamar in the southwestern part of Missouri to John A. and Martha Ellen Truman, both of whom had also been born in the same region. Truman's grandparents had migrated westward from Virginia and Kentucky to the western Missouri area, and the family represented in many ways the sturdy and unpretentious frontier folk whose world was that of farms and small towns. The boy (whose middle initial, S., never actually stood for anything) was deeply influenced by his mother. Her Baptist faith did not preclude gaiety and music, but it put a strong emphasis on

4

a sacred sense of duty and the inner-directed discipline of character necessary for duty's performance. An illness at ten years of age and the necessity for wearing glasses led the boy away from outdoor sports and into the world of books. He read mainly history, from Plutarch and Carlyle through the American Civil War and into the American presidency. He also found time to become proficient at the piano, even to the point of brief consideration of a career as a musician.

The Truman family made several moves in and around the Jackson County area, but finally settled down for good in Independence, just a few miles south of Kansas City. The years after Harry's graduation from Independence High School were spent in a variety of jobs, including bank clerk and construction timekeeper. He also had to manage the family farm, due to his father's inability and disinterest, and later moved into the job of politics via his father's introduction. When the United States entered World War I, Truman's National Guard outfit became the 129th Field Artillery of the 35th Division. Battery D, which Truman commanded, saw continual action in Europe, and Truman emerged from the war with the rank of major. The command experience added the vital ingredient necessary to his personal self-confidence. His girl friend of long standing, Bess Wallace, became his wife on his return from the war.

A large-scale haberdashery enterprise in Kansas City failed when the postwar recession hit the farm areas. Although his partner had to choose bankruptcy, Truman paid off every debt, even though some took many years. Minor experience in county politics and a friendship with Boss Pendergast's brother, Mike, brought an offer of Pendergast's Kansas City machine support for the office of County Judge. (In Missouri, this was an administrative officer of county government rather than a judicial position.) Truman won a hard race and ran an efficient and very honest county government. Although he was not the top choice of the Tom Pendergast organization as a senatorial candidate, because of his limited loyalty to the machine and his early New Dealism, the offer came to him in 1934 when more conservative choices declined to run against the incumbent Republican. The next six years were to be quietly, and perhaps colorlessly, spent in the mutually attractive inner circles of the U.S. Senate, where he consistently supported party politics. He readily won reelection in 1940 on his own, even though the Pendergast machine was wrecked by Tom Pendergast's conviction for income tax fraud. He achieved national prominence in his second term by chairing a special committee to investigate defense effort expenditures. Although the Truman Committee, as it came to be called, did not deliberately seek gaudy headlines, its tenacious digging into the exorbitant profits, shoddy materials, Big Business favoritism, and fat lobbyist commissions that made up a sizeable part of the nation's

defense program brought the Missouri Senator into favorable focus before millions of citizens. This publicity, plus his border-state geography
and party discipline, made Harry S. Truman—whose loyalty might also
have been more dependable than that of the mercurial Henry Wallace—
a candidate for the vice presidency in 1944.

Truman exhibited an astonishing capacity for growth within the office
of President. In many ways he was the average citizen—plainspoken
and slangy in his speech, direct and disliking pretense in manner,
friendly and self-confident in attitude. With sometimes too much loyalty
to party ties and old friends, he surrounded himself with a "Missouri
Gang" that made an unsavory name for some of its members in graft
and corruption. His short temper resulted in some impulsive public statements that he—and his supporters, who were many—wished had never
been said. The little sign kept on his desk—"The Buck Stops Here"—
testified to his willingness in making decisions, although several hard-line
advisers strongly influenced the controversial "tough" line which Truman
was to take in postwar foreign policy. His domestic record was not
outstanding in comparison with the brilliant one that preceded it. But
in view of the political circumstances—and especially in comparison
with that of his successor's—it was a thoroughly presentable record
during the course of which he fought many bitter and lonely battles.
The war's end brought with it the first of many domestic problems.

Demobilization and Reconversion

The American armed forces tradition up to World War II had always
been in the image of the citizen-soldier and a citizen-army. From the
times of colonial wars, the citizen took his musket down from its pegs
over the fireplace to meet national or local threats. As soon as the danger
passed, the musket went immediately back to its usual position and
its user to his normal occupation. The later stages of World War II
and the early postwar months were very much in the same tradition,
with a swelling public and congressional outcry that saw the armed
forces threatened, in Truman's words, more with disintegration than
demobilization.

Chief of Staff Marshall began to consider the problems of demobilization as early as December 1942. In September 1944 a formal program
was announced by the War Department which allotted points to service-
men based upon such factors as months of service, combat duty, decorations, and number of dependent children. An original point score of
85 was set up as a minimal number necessary for discharge among
the 12.3 million men and women in the armed services, and particularly

for the 7.6 million stationed overseas. With the surrender of Japan, the War Department again lowered the "point system" for immediate discharge as well as providing for the release of most men over the age of 35. General MacArthur, however, released one of his many famous unauthorized statements in which he announced he would require only 200,000 troops instead of the 500,000 originally estimated for the occupation of Japan. Coming as it did at a time when the War Department had decided that postwar forces should be scaled upward from 1.2 million to 2.5 million, it merely added fuel to the fire that servicemen's families and organized interest groups were already building under their Congressmen. Deluged under congressional complaint, the Pentagon reduced the points needed for discharge three times in the last month of 1945. This left more men available for discharge overseas than the shipping could possibly accommodate. In spite of converting ten aircraft carriers, six battleships, and twenty-six cruisers into troopships, many men still waited overseas. Because of lack of replacements, the War Department then had to announce that the ensuing three-month discharge period would have to be lengthened to six months in order to carry out various overseas requirements. This news, together with blundering remarks by new Secretary of War Robert Patterson while on a Pacific tour, touched off troop demonstrations and revolts. These made headlines around Christmas, 1945 and January 1946. Although they were prevalent around the world, most of them were in the Pacific theatre, and the largest of these was in the Philippines. Some 230,000 men in the latter islands could not understand why more troops should be there than were deemed necessary for the occupation of Japan.

Many of the demonstrators gathered merely to sign petitions or send collective telegrams to Congress. Some 20,000 men in Manila did force a confrontation with their commander for explanations, and 4,000 troops were turned back at bayonet point when they attempted to do the same at Frankfort-on-the-Main in Germany. In nearly all cases, the men were treated very leniently and the incidents deliberately forgotten. In addition to the obvious factor of homesickness, the men were poorly informed as to the time and difficulty involved in converting battleships into troopships, or why American troops were needed for European occupation duty. Conflicting statements from administration officials engendered suspicion in many minds, and alleged favoritism of officers over enlisted men provided additional factors that bred wide resentment. By June 30, 1946, nine months after V-J Day, the American Army was reduced from 8 million to 1.8 million men, perhaps the last time the United States was to follow its traditional eagerness to demobilize.

The return of the veteran of World War II differed from that of any other war in American history in the generosity and sympathy of official policy. In June 1944 Roosevelt signed the far-reaching Service-men's Readjustment Act, more popularly known as the GI Bill of Rights.[1] All those with more than 90 days' service and an honorable discharge were entitled to monetary assistance for secondary or college education, to loans through the Veterans' Administration for the purchase of homes, farms, or businesses, and to unemployment benefits up to a year if they could not find a job. The economy absorbed most applicants, but the unique education benefits from government were widely used. By 1956, when the schooling subsidies expired, nearly 8 million veterans had received all or a part of their education at government expense. They were paid as much as $500 per year for tuition and books, plus subsistence for single and married men at $50 and $75 per month. This was later raised to $75 and $105. All told, the federal government disbursed about $14.5 billion in this program. Although much of it went to the veteran's individual subsistence, enough reached colleges and universities to make it the most influential measure in the long history of government aid to education. Those veterans who were disabled and required special education and training were provided for under the terms of an act passed in March 1943. Those requiring extensive medical or psychiatric care were accommodated in special facilities, and the expansion of Veterans' Administration hospitals provided continued care for service-connected disabilities.

President Truman and his advisers spent considerable time thinking of the problems of reconversion. The great difficulties of post–World War I and the Great Depression of the 1930s were a constant reminder. Truman had set up such a program before V-J Day. It included phasing out and cancellation of war contracts, and instituting measures hopefully to stabilize wages, prices, and rents. Wartime controls on production were to be reduced to the barest minimum deemed necessary. Some aspects of reconversion proved to be no trouble at all, such as the well-planned transition of servicemen from war to peace. Although the overall change of society and the economy was accomplished with far less disruption and turmoil than had been the case after World War I, there was bitter political infighting between Congress and the President and between labor and management over the reconversion of the nation's economy. Very few people liked OPA (Office of Price Administration), but most were willing to grant its necessity in keeping a lid on rental prices and scarce items during wartime. With the coming of V-J Day, the clamor to remove all controls grew to overwhelming proportions. Although those on fixed incomes (which now would include the many veterans on education subsistence amounts) could see they would be

---

[1] GI meant "government issue," and was used to refer to any standard equipment, whether bayonets, shirts, or Spam. Soon enlisted men used the term to refer to themselves.

severely hurt by an inflationary removal of all controls, many business-men and farmers were holding up commodities in the expectation of much higher market prices and an end to price controls. The outgoing Congress voted an extension of OPA only until July 1, 1946, during which time it was able to hold down the cost-of-living index to a mere 3 percent increase. Congress debated the further extension of price con-trols as pressure mounted. Even the consumer, sharing an unprecedented reservoir of $136.4 billion dammed up in personal savings accounts and government bonds, was wildly eager to pay double the usual price for scarce nylons, beef, automobiles, or apartments. The business community mounted a fierce and extensive campaign for the removal of all controls and a return to a "free" economy. Various groups in society were urged to petition their Congressmen. Business conventions sent indignant en-dorsements to the President, demanding that he "save the free enterprise system." Millions were spent in advertising the theme of an end to controls. Central to the business protest voice was the National Associa-tion of Manufacturers, whose lobbyists took the position that the removal of all controls would bring about such a production spurt that all the pent-up demand for goods would quickly be satisfied. As soon as busi-ness had reached a profitable level, the NAM contended, prices could be scaled down and the black market driven out of competition. Presi-dent Truman, government officials, and scattered groups of labor, house-wives, and consumer organizations labored to show that prices would shoot upward immediately and not come down, since then labor's de-mands for wage raises to meet such advances in the price level would result only in additional price raises to cover wage demands. The two would take turns pushing each other up and up, with the consumer forever far behind.

In midsummer Truman vetoed a toothless OPA substitute bill. Prices immediately moved upward. By July 25, when a slightly more favorable bill was hastily passed, the price index had already climbed a startling 25 percent. Using the ineffective new law, Truman reimposed ceilings on beef, but livestock dealers refused to bring their beef to market. The volume of complaints from both sides caused the administration to abandon its control efforts in October, and Truman was forced to announce the end of all major controls except those on rents and sugar. By that time the price index had climbed nearly 32 percent. Trumans' prediction had been correct—the NAM's, dead wrong; but the consumer bore the brunt of the fray. Both those who wanted controls taken off earlier and those who deplored the letting loose of the inflationary kite combined their dislike of Truman. The year 1946 brought him to a new low in popularity polls and presented him with a Republican-domi-nated Congress in the off-year elections.

Truman's popularity with labor also deteriorated in the wake of a wave of postwar strikes. Working men were bent upon forcing a wage raise that would take the place of the overtime pay that had been in their weekly envelopes throughout most of the war years. They were mortally afraid of a postwar depression, sure that inflation would cut back their actual buying power, and grimly convinced that industry's profits in defense production had been more than ample to permit a rise in wage scales. Management, concerned with the difficulties of reconversion, could not agree. With industry eager to step up civilian production and consumers with their hands full of cash waiting to buy, labor considered the time ripe to press its demands. At the end of 1945, General Motors workers went on a strike that extended into March 1946. In January of that year, electrical equipment workers embarked on a two-month strike, the steel industry suffered a four-week shutdown, and the meat packers and others instituted strikes to begin the worst strike year in history. One of the most serious work stoppages occurred when John L. Lewis ordered his United Mineworkers to strike the soft-coal mines on April 1.

While the industries dependent upon soft coal were shut down, months of fruitless negotiation in an earlier strike between the railway brotherhoods and the nation's rail systems came to an impasse. A governmental arbitration board had worked out an increase acceptable to the carriers and most of the unions, with further work-rule changes subject to continued negotiation. But two powerful unions—the Brotherhood of Locomotive Engineers and the Brotherhood of Railway Trainmen— refused to go on any further with negotiations and called for a strike beginning May 18, later postponed to May 25. A blazingly angry Truman told the two union leaders that he intended to take over the railroads in the name of the government. The speech he delivered to the nation as the deadline approached was one of the most stinging denunciations ever delivered by a President, even after toning down by Press Secretary Charley Ross and speech writer Clark Clifford. Before Congress the next day, Truman angrily demanded legislation enabling him to draft recalcitrant workers into the Army and then let the Army run the trains. The strike settlement was signed in the middle of the speech and the proposed bill, although whooped through the House, was quietly sidetracked by the Senate. It averted a near catastrophe, but its constitutionality was obviously doubtful. John L. Lewis and his miners' domain proved a tougher nut to crack for, as Lewis loftily but accurately noted, "You can't mine coal with bayonets." The desperate Truman administration fostered an arbitration board decision that gave the union much of its demands. But when Lewis sought to advance his stature in rivalry with other labor leaders by reopening the contract in November, Truman cracked down hard. Lewis and the Mineworkers' Union were the object of an injunction, adjudged in contempt of court, and saddled with a fine of several hundred thousand dollars. Truman showed that, while he was sympathetic to labor's needs, he also insisted that labor live up to its responsibilities. When labor's demands threatened the entire national interest, there was no doubt in Truman's mind as to priorities. And Truman's successful putting down of the tough and wily John L. Lewis may have marked the beginning of President Truman entirely on his own rather than in the massive shadow of FDR.

Hopeful Moves toward Peace

After less than a month in office, President Truman was able to announce "a solemn but glorious hour," the defeat of Germany. V-E Day was proclaimed on the morning of May 8, 1945. In his speech to the nation Truman chose to exaggerate somewhat by announcing that "the forces of Germany have surrendered to the United Nations." In actuality, that organization was still in the final stages of its formation. One of Truman's first official acts on becoming President at Roosevelt's death April 12 was to announce that the United Nations Charter meeting scheduled in only two more weeks at San Francisco would go on as planned. The idea of an international body that hopefully could eliminate war from the world had been one of Roosevelt's strongest hopes. Based upon the more workable aspects of the League of Nations, it had gradually been hammered out in such conferences as the Atlantic Charter in 1941, the Moscow Declaration of 1943, and the Bretton Woods and Dumbarton Oaks meetings in 1944. At Yalta in February 1945 final plans for its adoption were agreed upon, and delegates from 50 nations gathered in San Francisco on April 25, 1945 to complete the plans drawn up by the larger powers at previous sessions.

Much of the conflict behind the scenes revolved around the United States' objection to seating the delegates from the Polish government. Washington and London took for granted that the phrases such as "all democratic elements" regarding the makeup of Poland's government meant those chosen in Western, democratic-style elections. The Russians interpreted the same phrase as meaning "all those who have not actively opposed the Soviet Union." President Truman sharply upbraided Ambassador Molotov on this topic, much to the anger and discomfiture of the latter. The Soviets finally saw fit to bring 20 of the Polish exile government from London to Moscow for conferences. They wound up imprisoning 16 of the group for anti-Soviet practices, and installing the other 4—including Premier Mikolajczyk of the London Poles—in the new Polish government. The Russians, in turn, objected to the seating of delegates from Argentina because of her outright collaboration with the Nazis during the war. With Latin American pressure rising for the

United States to arrange somehow for their hemispheric colleague to be seated, the Soviet's grudging acceptance of Argentina made a potential trade for the American and British reluctant acquiescence of the Polish compromise government. With severe damage to the entire concept of a United Nations as a very real prospect, the joint acceptance of the Argentine and Polish delegates was quickly established.

After two months of further debates and negotiations, the United Nations Charter emerged. Like its League of Nations forebear,[2] it was composed of the victorious coalition. Unlike that body, its 50 participants included nations representing most of mankind. In less than two decades the number of participating nations moved up to an amazing 111. In structure, it had four main elements. These were (1) the Security Council of eleven members, five of which (United States, Great Britain, Soviet Russia, France, China) were permanent members, with the other six elected by the General Assembly for two-year terms; (2) a General Assembly, in which all member states were represented regardless of size or population; (3) the Secretariat, composed of a Secretary-General and an international staff to administer the institution; and (4) an International Court of Justice, modeled after the World Court, as the United Nations' judicial arm.

The function of the United Nations was to ease international tensions, to discuss problems that might lead to international rivalry or threaten the peace of the world, and to limit the growth of armaments. Primary responsibility for the avoidance of conflict rested in the Security Council which, unlike the League's upper body, could employ the armed forces of General Assembly members to keep the peace. However, the fact that such measures required an affirmative vote from all permanent members of the Council gave each of them a veto over such action. This potential paralysis was eased some years later by the assumption of the right to undertake such deterrent measures by the General Assembly instead. The UN included a variety of agencies. Some, like the United Nations Relief and Rehabilitation Administration (UNRRA), were created before (1943) the United Nations itself, as temporary wartime needs. Some were specialized agencies that far predated the UN, such as the International Labor Organization (ILO). Others, like the United Nations Educational, Scientific, and Cultural Organization (UNESCO), were among the many new agencies that were created to undertake studies in a variety of fields under the guidance of the UN's 18-member Social and Economic Council. The charter also created a Trusteeship Council, which was to administer trust territories put under UN jurisdiction. Unlike previous American attitudes toward the League of Nations,

---

[2] Although the League of Nations was quite defunct, for all practical purposes, before World War II even started, it did not declare itself officially dissolved until 1946.

Congress and the public wholeheartedly supported the new United Nations. The Senate on July 2, 1945 voted its approval 89 to 2, with only Republican Senators Langer of North Dakota and Shipstead of Minnesota voting in opposition. President Truman, who had appeared before the Senate to recommend ratification of the UN Charter, received news of its approval while he was at Potsdam conferring with the other two members of the Big Three.

Potsdam

The new President had been temporarily content to let Edward R. Stettinius, Jr., continue as Secretary of State while the United Nations Charter meeting progressed at San Francisco, since Stettinius had played a large and enthusiastic role in the preceding 18 formative months of the new organization. Following the successful completion of the UN Charter, however, Truman chose to appoint Stettinius as U.S. Ambassador to the United Nations and replace him with his own man. His choice was the former Senator from South Carolina, James F. Byrnes. Officially, Truman gave as part of his reasons for change the need to have an elected politician in the presidential line of succession rather than someone who had never held elective office. Unofficially, his reasons were understandable enough. He particularly wished to be brought up to date on the inside workings of the Yalta conference and what it might entail for the future. Both Stettinius and Byrnes were present, but the latter was a known quantity and the former unknown to Truman. The President had looked up to the South Carolinian when they were both members of the Senate. His great charm, quick wit, and persuasive powers were well known. Additionally, there was an undoubted feeling of guilt on Truman's part, since Byrnes had asked Truman to put his name in nomination for the vice presidency at the 1944 convention, only to see this plum go to the surprised Missourian instead.

Byrnes' appointment as Secretary of State was unanimously and quickly confirmed by the Senate out of deference to a former admired colleague, yet there were many quiet reservations when Byrnes was formally sworn into office on July 3, 1945. He had no knowledge and no experience of foreign affairs, with the possible exception of his listener's role at Yalta. Many feared that his outstanding senatorial qualifications of compromise and expediency would result in a weakening of those applications of American principle considered necessary. In actuality, Byrnes was to find that such congressional cloakroom talents were of limited use in dealing with sovereign and intransigent nations. Byrnes' record as administrator of the Office of Economic Stabilization and "Assistant President" of Domestic Affairs for Roosevelt revealed

Central and Eastern Europe: Territorial Changes, 1939–1947

a sure capacity for administration and organization. His opening speech as Secretary of State also showed a willingness to recognize a variety of ideologies as a world reality, and the strong desire to work through the new United Nations to achieve a world of peace and harmony. Yet the handicap that was to limit Byrnes as Secretary of State was to be found within the man himself. His attitude toward the President was clearly one of "there but for the grace of God go I." Although not actually true, the holding of this view manifested itself in everything from a bitter and caustic tongue to the occasional impression that the President's and Secretary's role were reversed. Such a relationship could expand neither Byrnes' efficacy nor his tenure.

The presidential party left in early July for the Big Three meeting in Germany with a tremendous secret: the atomic weapon so long in development would be exploded while they were in conference. The site agreed upon for the talks was Potsdam, the German city made famous by Frederick II of Prussia, some 45 miles southwest of Berlin. The meetings would be held in the former palace of the German Crown Prince. To precede the conference, Truman had dispatched Harry Hopkins to Moscow in May to talk privately to Marshal Stalin regarding American concern over deteriorating Soviet-American relations. Hopkins indicated that the gravest matter for American concern was the Russian failure to implement the Yalta agreements in the manner that the United States was led to expect. Stalin, in turn, had bitter and suspicious questions to ask regarding American intentions toward Poland and why Argentina had been admitted to the United Nations. He also pointed out that Lend-Lease had been suddenly and "brutally" cut off and, although it had been resumed, the United States was not to assume that such pressures would bring about Soviet capitulation. Stalin suspiciously insisted to Hopkins that the Yalta agreements referred to the reconstruction of the Polish government, and that this could only mean that the existing government must form the basis of any new one. Besides, the Marshal said, Britain clearly was trying to revive in Poland the post–World War I anti-Russian *cordon sanitaire* of restraining nations on Soviet borders. In denying American sharing of the *cordon sanitaire* concept, Hopkins chose the same paradox that Byrnes was to use later: the United States genuinely wished to see only governments friendly to Russia on her borders, and wanted them to be the result of free elections. As Stalin knew and later candidly pointed out, free elections in countries hostile to Russia and occupied by Russian troops would not result in governments friendly to her. Presumably Stalin, therefore, chose to regard American assurances concerning friendly governments as having more emphasis than the unacceptable remainder of the statement. The two-man conference was candid enough and cordial enough to make Truman's approach to Potsdam one of optimism.

Chief matters that were to occupy the conferees were the occupation of Germany and her reparations, the procedures for writing the various peace treaties, and the implementation of the Yalta Declaration for the peoples of Central and Eastern Europe. These and lesser subjects were debated from July 17 through August 2 by the three heads of state. In the middle of the conference, Churchill's Conservative party was turned out of office by the Labor party, and his place was taken by a new Prime Minister, Clement Atlee. Truman's suggestion for the formation of a Council of Foreign Ministers, to be composed of the Big Three plus France and China, was accepted. The council was to begin work immediately on peace treaties for such nations as Italy, Hungary, Rumania, and Finland, and was instructed to find solutions to the many territorial questions remaining in the wake of the war. So that the other nations of the world might have a voice in the proceedings, the council's proposed peace treaties were subject to review by the United Nations.

A peace treaty for Germany also was on the agenda for subsequent meetings of the council, but it was agreed that first some suitable government must be established. Until that time, each of the four occupying powers was to control the zone allotted to it at Yalta. While it was realized and stated that each occupier would require some flexibility in administering its own zone, the conferees stated that a uniformity of treatment should be practiced whenever possible. To destroy forever Germany's potential for threatening her neighbors or the peace of the world, she was to be completely disarmed, her war capacity obliterated, and her political life denuded of Nazis and nazism and democratically reconstituted. To further this end, Germany's political and economic institutions were to be decentralized as far as possible. Reparations was far and away the thorniest problem. To the Russians, this meant more than it could possibly mean to the United States or Great Britain. The Soviets were bent upon smashing the nation that had twice sent its armies into destructive invasions of Russian soil within one generation. They were determined that the Germans must replace the factories and the equipment they had destroyed. They must pay for the enormous sufferings they had inflicted in their long years of occupying Soviet territory. The Russians worried not at all about the possibility of German revolt, since they knew very well what they would do in such a case. To the United States, Stalin's figure of $20 billion advanced at Yalta (of which half was to go to Russia) was merely the basis for further discussion, and it proved extremely difficult to shake Stalin loose from this figure. American diplomacy was chiefly directed towards reparations that would not crush the German people. They must still have the means to build workable economy; they must not be put in a state of such economic misery as to be potentially revolutionary; and above all, they must not become dependent on the United States for their very means of support. The British also considered that Germany should be permitted to regain at least enough economic power to furnish her people an adequate standard of living and to become a viable economic unit within a Western European structure. The French, oriented toward the punitive view of the Russians, were largely intent upon building up their economic strength at the expense of the contiguous German Ruhr and Rhineland areas.

The increasingly firmer front put up by the Anglo-Americans resulted finally in leaving a total reparations figure unfixed. Each of the four occupying powers was to stake out its claims within its own zone, and all were to share in external German assets. Since Russia was the most injured party of the four, she was also to receive 10 percent of German industrial assets that lay within the zones of the Western powers. In an even exchange, Russia also agreed to furnish Germany food and raw materials in return for the payment of 15 percent of such German equipment deemed nonessential for Germany's peace economy. In general, reparations were allotted more out of current resources of the German nation than out of future production. In the course of the reparations discussions, the Anglo-American partners became more resistant to Russian proposals as they became more upset over the Soviet indifference to the health and capacity to work of the Germans in zones other than their own. The Soviets, in turn, became more and more grimly positive that the Americans and British were more solicitous over the fate of Germans than they were cognizant of the greater and more sustained suffering the Russian people had undergone. Each attempt by the Anglo-Americans to sustain the German people's productivity was received by the wary and distrustful Russians as proof of pro-German and anti-Russian tendencies.

Stalin displayed the same angry incredulity when Truman and Churchill sought to avoid giving too large a chunk of eastern Germany to Poland. It had been agreed readily enough that Russia should have the Baltic port of Konigsberg, and that the balance of the East Prussia area should go to Poland. It had been tacitly agreed at Yalta that the new western boundary of Poland would once again be the Curzon line of post–World War I. This meant restoring to the Soviets lands that the Poles had seized by force of arms from the weakened Russian Bolshevik government in the 1920s. To make up for this, Stalin was determined that the new Poland should extend westward to the Oder River and its tributary, the Western Neisse River. Churchill argued stoutly for the upper reaches of the Oder and the Eastern Neisse River. The difference between the two positions included parts of German Silesia and Brandenburg, good farming area occupied largely by over 2 million Germans. The Polish heads of state put up convincing arguments themselves on the need for land to settle those millions of dispossessed Poles from east of the Curzon line. More privately, the London Pole elements now in the new government influenced the American delegation with explanations that the extreme western boundary line would aid the return of Poles from abroad and thus help to accelerate elections and stabilize Poland's economy. President Truman continued to insist that the question was one for the later peace conference to decide, much to Churchill's disgust at the postponement. Since the disputed area lay within the Soviet zone, its administration by Polish officials continued.

Although the three heads of state used Potsdam to give their respective foreign ministers far more responsibility than had been the case at either Teheran or Yalta, it did not serve to bring the three wartime allies to more amicable and trusting relations. Virtually the only group that did achieve closer harmony were the American and Soviet military staffs and their top military leaders. The forthcoming role of the Russians in the assault against Japan was thoroughly discussed, and Stalin told the American delegation that Soviet troops were expected to be in position for an attack upon Japan on or about August 8. An ultimatum delivered from Potsdam on July 26 calling upon Japan to surrender was officially rejected by the Japanese government as "absurd." The bomb which was to be used against the Japanese had just been successfully tested for the first time while the conferees were at Potsdam. Truman cautiously and in very general terms informed Stalin of the appearance of a deadly new weapon. To Truman's relief, Stalin seemed only mildly interested and expressed the hope that it would be put to good use against the Japanese.

The conferees were able to agree on the trial and prosecution of major war criminals. The London Agreement of August 1945 established an international judicial tribunal with representatives from the four nations occupying Germany. Indictments were brought against 24 major criminals and a host of secondary figures, as well as against criminal organizations such as the Gestapo and the Nazi party. The trials spread out the shocking Nazi activities in mass murders, tortures, and destruction over a ten-month period. Top figures of the Hitler regime such as Generals Goering, Jodl, and Keitel were among those sentenced to death. Many others were sentenced to life or long terms in prison. The war trials, held in Nuremberg, Germany, were not without criticism. Churchill considered that "the leaders of a nation defeated in war shall be put to death by the victors" had been established as a precedent. Others refused to consider that the judges of a victor nation were properly judicial, and many complained that the many small fry who were largely left for the German courts were getting off scot-free. The defense relied largely on the weak argument centered around the 1928 Kellogg-Briand Pact to outlaw war, and the unusual need to rebuke severely such enormous crimes against humanity. There was also the uncomfortable feeling that, if the defeated were left to judge themselves, there would be no judgment at all.

Potsdam thus continued to put off many decisions, some never to be decided except by time itself. This was true of a German peace treaty and the Western Polish border. A Council of Foreign Ministers was formed that would deal with peace treaties for the lesser defeated nations. Soviet aid in Japan's defeat was confirmed and proceeded on schedule, with its necessity being questioned only in the light of hindsight. But the questions of a divided Germany and her reparations were to be more and more acrimoniously disputed between the former allies, becoming finally two of the key points in the conflict barely short of armed hostilities between the United States and Soviet Russia that came to be labelled "The Cold War."

Cold War and Crumbling Alliance, 1945–1947

Many origins of the Cold War can be traced back to the early 20th century and into the 19th century. It could probably also be stated that one of a variety of soils that nourished such roots was a fundamental disparity in the political development of the United States and Russia. While the United States had pursued the ideals of an open society and developed democratic government and great personal freedom, Czarist Russia in both centuries continued to be a nation of vast distrustfulness, pervasive secrecy and censorship, and completely undemocratic political institutions. Soviet Russia changed nothing in these respects, and its success revived grave fears among Americans of domestic revolution. The occasion for the Bolshevik seizure of power in 1917 and the successes of the revolution led the Western allies to the extremely foolish move of sending American, British, French, and Japanese troops to aid the "white" counterrevolution against the Red Armies of Lenin and Stalin. Such intervention in a civil war was clear proof to Lenin of "inevitable capitalist hostility." The Allies feared that the social structure of Europe would suffer from Bolshevik ideology, but they helped account for an enduring hostility and suspicion from the leaders of the successful revolution because of such tactics. The Treaty of Versailles then sought to accomplish a similar sealing off of Western Europe from the Bolshevik virus by establishing a *cordon sanitaire* of Eastern European nations with satisfactorily anti-Soviet governments. As Walter Lippmann and others pointed out, it was not an arrangement that could be expected to endure.

The Red Scare of the 1920s reflected America's apprehension over its 19th century radical experiences and the existence of a new and

powerful force for international revolution. Following the ultimate establishment of the Soviet government, the United States reverted to the
moralistic tactic of refusing to recognize a government whose ideology
was displeasing, regardless of its obvious de facto status. Most nations
refused to follow this unrealistic course. The United States did, however,
dispatch millions of dollars of aid to the many Russians made homeless
and destitute by the revolution. In the middle and later 1920s, despite
the fact that the State Department did not recognize Russia's existence,
American industrialists did an increasing amount of business with the
Soviet Union. Such economic ties were largely instrumental in bringing
about official United States recognition by Roosevelt in 1933.

Russia looked upon the rise of Hitler with more accurate long-range
apprehension than did France and Great Britain. She sought, unsuccessfully, to gain the latter as allies against a resurgent Germany and bitterly
viewed their acceptance of Munich as another proof of Western attempts
to isolate her. The nations of the West, in turn, saw Russia's cynical
accord with Hitler in 1939 not as Soviet temporary protection against
an onslaught believed to be in preparation but as a betrayal of part
of Europe to the totalitarian aggressor of the times. The Nazi-Soviet
Nonaggression Pact knocked a majority out of the ranks of those Americans sympathetic to Russia. The Winter War against Finland, which
Russia brutally pursued to gain protection for Leningrad and nearby
Gulf of Finland waters, alienated most of the United States and permitted latent anti-Soviet feelings to surface. Such might be a skeletal
account of the U.S.-Soviet Cold War background prior to the Nazi attack
on Russia in June 1941.

While pre-1941 events properly describe the necessary historical antecedents and indicate the legitimate reasons for a mutual climate of distrust, the real Cold War only came about as a result of World War
II. That conflict brought to a chaotic close the two world military upheavals of the first half of the 20th century. The sum total of these
two wars, both of them brought about by the aggressive might of Germany, completely destroyed the traditional balance of power equilibrium. Much of the outcome of World War II derived not from politics
or diplomacy but from hurling back German armies throughout Central
and Eastern Europe by millions of Soviet troops, with the encouragement
of the Anglo-American allies. It should have been a surprise to no statesman or diplomat that the United States and Russia, the one superpower
and one near-great power left standing in the rubble of World War
II, would then be facing each other in what could readily become an
increasingly hostile situation. Only in land armies was Russia in any
way coequal with the United States as a world power in 1945. For
the truest basis and evaluation of world power—economic productivity
and resources—Russia was never close to the United States even before

the war's damages to the Soviet Union. By 1945, they had moved even further apart. The United States almost doubled its productivity during the war years, while devastation and millions of civilian deaths decreased Soviet productivity in the same period some 42 percent. Great Britain, Russia, and the United States had little else to hold them together beside their mutual need to defeat Germany, even though there undoubtedly were hopes shared by all for an era of postwar peace. It should also be noted that Americans were guilty of great self-deception in thinking that the defeat of nazism and fascism would automatically insure the establishment of democratic governments everywhere. Nor was there any recognition of Russia's historic attempts to blunt the many invasions directed at her by means of buffer states on her borders.

Activities proclaiming postwar tensions and hostilities were not absent even during the wartime struggles mutually undertaken. Early and late, Poland was a source of mutual distrust and friction between Russia and her Anglo-American allies. Poland had twice within one generation been the corridor for a German attack upon Russia, and Stalin had never made any secret of the fact that Russia intended to install a suitably friendly government and take back Russian-held areas of 1939. The Polish government in exile—the London Poles—was anti-Soviet, although they were not pro-Nazi, as Stalin insisted. But they were extraordinarily intransigent in their territorial demands to the point of exasperating Churchill and completely alienating Stalin. The London Poles could turn, in retaliation, to the thousands of Poles in Soviet labor camps and the alleged role of Russia in the slaying of Polish officers in the Katyn Forest. Allied, and particularly American, insistence on postponing all territorial questions to the end of the war thoroughly alarmed Stalin. He insisted that the tiny Baltic states and a piece of Finland already incorporated into the Soviet Union were not opened to discussion. And the eastern portion of Poland occupied by Russia in 1939 had also been a part of Russia before World War I and contained ethnic groups which made Stalin's claim to that area a reasonable one. The Poles would be compensated by territory on the west taken from German Silesia. Insistence upon postponement of such questions by Roosevelt and Hull were unrealistic attempts to preserve a vacuum. The decision was finally made by complete Soviet military occupation. The possibilities of compromise and conciliation quickly evaporated, leaving only the possibilities of acrimonious charge and countercharge. Attempting to put off the territorial questions even at Potsdam left no room for anything other than mutual distrust and increasingly harsher exchanges.

The question of launching a second front in the early war years led to exasperated communications among Stalin, Churchill, and Roosevelt. Both the Anglo-American leaders realized the importance of such a move, but Roosevelt was more breezily optimistic in his dates and assurances. The postponements from 1942 to 1943 to 1944 were to Stalin, whose deep suspiciousness came close to paranoia, sinister evidence that his allies intended to permit a massive Russian bloodletting to take place while Nazi armies similarly were being ground down. The postponement of the cross-Channel invasion from 1943 to 1944 brought on the bitterest statements yet from Stalin. While his remarks on the role of the Russian army were understandable enough even in their exaggeration, his allusions to the lack of integrity of his partners were insulting. The initial responses to Stalin had been patient, since the Russian people obviously had borne the chief brunt of the Nazi onslaught. On this occasion, however, Churchill lost his patience and responded in a recriminatory message of pent-up anger. Whether Stalin was able to understand the Anglo-American logistic difficulties more clearly in retrospect is dubious, but the Soviet resentment engendered helped to establish a foundation of ill will.

Soviet distrust of Anglo-American activities probably reached its peak over clandestine American attempts to bring about the surrender of the German armies fighting in northern Italy. A forerunner of trouble in this area came in 1943, when the Western allies were negotiating with a government to succeed Mussolini. Churchill and Roosevelt informed Stalin as to what was going on, but Stalin was not satisfied and his sharp message indicated that Russia was being excluded from a full knowledge of events. Even worse difficulties began in February 1945, when Allen Dulles and the OSS zealously initiated attempts to hold talks in Switzerland with German generals who might be able to arrange a separate surrender of the Nazi forces in Italy. In March, American and British generals in disguise continued the cloak-and-dagger operations. Although nothing actually came from the talks until near the end of all German resistance, the Western allies were worried about the possibility of an occupation presided over by Communist-led Italian Resistance forces. The British finally informed the Russians of the continuing talks in spite of American obstructions. The Soviets were asked to send only observers and not negotiators. In the ensuing exchange of messages, Stalin obviously did not believe Roosevelt's assurances of the lack of any political implications in the talks. Not only were Stalin's replies the high point of distrust during the war years, but the Soviet leader made amazing accusations of a scheme to accept German surrender in northern Italy and thus open the possibilities for moving such German troops to the Eastern front to bolster Nazi defenses against the Russian push. Roosevelt replied in his angriest of all communications to Stalin. While Stalin was wildly inaccurate and could readily have ascertained in time through his agents the lack of substance, at least where troop movement was concerned, Roosevelt was unfortunately less than candid regarding the political implications of the incident and the American initiative involved.

Italy was also the beginning of a series of discords between the Allies regarding surrender policies affecting all the nations that had sided with the European Axis. The first of the European nations to fall, its pro-Fascist and unpopular king was one of Churchill's monarchist postwar hopes. The United States did not care for either a monarchy or British postwar hegemony, but both Washington and London together found far more to be concerned about with the possibility of Kremlin postwar direction of the very large and very influential Communist-led Resistance. With the formation of an Allied Control Commission and the arrival of the Russian military representatives, Washington and London decided that the Soviet generals should have only an observer status and be completely excluded from actual operations or policy decisions. The Russians protested this treatment, pointing out that all three allies should arrange the surrender of each Axis nation. But they finally went along with this formula and even called for the Communist-led Resistance to unite with and support the interim Badoglio government. The United States and Great Britain made it very clear they intended to dominate Italian affairs. When the Russians attempted to extend diplomatic recognition, they were reminded that supreme authority resided in the Anglo-American military commander. The Soviets accepted these arrangements without further complaint, but they undoubtedly made note of the formula as a precedent that could work equally well in another surrendered country. When the second member of the Axis bloc surrendered—Rumania, in August 1944—the about-face in the positions of the Russians and the Western allies was quickly seen. When the United States and Britain made known to Molotov their expectations of full representation on an Allied Control Commission, the Soviet Foreign Minister stated very flatly that the functions of American and British military members "would be analogous to the position of the Soviet representative on the Allied Control Commission for Italy." The shoe clearly was on the other foot. Although the United States made vociferous representations along the same lines when Bulgaria and Hungary surrendered, the exclusion of the Soviets from the surrender of one Axis nation where they did not have primary interests was then used to exclude the Western allies in areas where Soviet interests were paramount. Only unheeded advisors of lesser diplomatic stature had pointed out the probable reaction to such a short-sighted Anglo-American approach.

Economic considerations during the war years also put heavy burdens and tensions on Russo-American relations. One of the Soviet's main hopes was to get American loans for postwar reconstruction. In January 1945 Molotov handed in a request for a $6 billion loan on a 30-year, 2.25 percent interest basis. Although loans to Russia had for some time been considered in the light of excellent leverage for Soviet political compliance on European questions, State Department sentiment was moving towards refusal to aid any postwar Soviet reconstruction efforts at all. Acting Secretary of State Grew warned the Soviets not to expect an early decision, even though news of the request had leaked out and received some favorable attention from the business press. By August the Soviets had turned in a new request, this one for only $1 billion. Nothing more was heard of the application. Six months after the second request the Russians finally made public the lack of any response to their applications, and the State Department, in circumstances that can only be described as incredible, announced that the August loan request had been misfiled and "lost." In subsequent months, Great Britain and France received loans of $4.4 billion and $1.4 billion respectively.

One day after Germany surrendered, the administrator of Lend-Lease, Leo T. Crowley, hastily put into effect an interpretation of the planned curtailment of that program. Not only were goods shipments at the piers returned to the manufacturers, but ships partially loaded were unloaded and vessels en route to Russian and English ports were summarily ordered to return. The latter part of the order particularly was evidently not part of the administration plan. The outcry from European nations was loud and immediate. The Soviet Union pointed out that it had obligated itself to continue as America's ally until Japan was defeated, and that necessary supplies for such cooperation were cut off. Secretary of State Stettinius, himself a previous Lend-Lease administrator, observed that the State Department had no notice of the action and considered such abrupt curtailment a shocking act. Truman, insisting that he had not read the order that he signed, reversed the cutoff order. Lend-Lease was finally stopped completely on August 12 with the defeat of Japan. Great Britain in particular had counted on such aid through the fall months of 1945 and complained fully as loudly as the Soviets. For Stalin, however, such "brutal" cessations of Lend-Lease merely corroborated further the Soviet suspicions of attempted American economic pressures in Eastern Europe. The United States fully intended to use all measures possible to bring about its plans and aspirations for a postwar open door economic world, and had required both Great Britain and Russia to sign Lend-Lease agreements that committed those nations to the acceptance of American free-trade policies. As William H. McNeill has observed, "The harsh fact of the matter was that while free trade promised to benefit American industry and agriculture, it seemed likely to damage both British and Russian national interests."[3]

In the closing months of the war, Anglo-American and Russian discussions and communications grew increasingly more divisive over the central issue of the Polish government. The Western allies' insistence on

---

[3] William H. McNeill, *America, Britain, and Russia: Their Co-operation and Conflict, 1941–1946*, (London, 1953), 445. [Arnold Toynbee, ed., *Survey of International Affairs, 1939–1946*, v. 3.]

a satisfactory inclusion of the London Poles in any provisional government was met by more than equal obduracy on the part of Stalin to form a government commensurate with Russian security. Stalin bitterly and with deadly logic told Churchill that he had made no remonstrance or even any inquiry as to the formation of governments in Belgium and Greece. He assumed, Stalin went on, that those governments were considered of importance to British security and would be based upon that fact. Why then could not his two allies recognize that Poland was even more vital to Russian security, with consequent Russian concern for a pro-Soviet government? Stalin grudgingly allotted four or five cabinet posts to the London Poles, but the majority remained in the hands of the Lublin pro-Soviet group. With this concession, the Western allies finally recognized with equal reluctance a Polish Provisional Government on June 29, 1945. To the United States and Great Britain, the Soviets were reneging on the Yalta agreements. Russian leaders were equally confident of proper interpretation of the ambiguous Yalta terms, but moreover were afraid their allies were trying to deprive them of their hard-earned victory and to set up another *cordon sanitaire*. The conference at Potsdam the following month, as already noted, failed to bring Polish and other problems much closer to solution.

Thus the Cold War moved through what might be considered its introductory phase, even as peace was supposedly reuniting the nations of the world. But with the cessation of hostilities, new crises or even more vexatious aspects of older problems presented themselves to drive the two great powers closer to the edge of still another clash. If the period ending World War II could be called an "introductory" stage of the Cold War, then the time span from middle or later 1945 to roughly later 1946 or early 1947 might be considered its "foundation" period. For in this short space of time were displayed a steadily mounting mutual anger, a rising tide of belligerency, and a matching whipped-up rhetoric that effectively combined to put down a solid base for the hardened structure soon to be erected. Hostility became more distressingly overt despite continuing contacts such as the London and Paris meetings of the Council of Foreign Ministers. Statesmen and heads of state were less and less willing to disguise, even diplomatically, their antagonistic feelings. Motives were impugned; threats were met by counter-threats. The problem of Germany's division and her reparations reached a hostile impasse. The introduction to the world of atomic weaponry raised not only frightful possibilities, but also bitter argument over its control. And in the Middle East the Soviets, denied a voice in management of the Dardenelles at Potsdam, sought to exploit a chaotic situation in Iran.

The semifeudal nation of Iran was used during the war years as one of several routes for shipping arms to the Soviets. To safeguard the route, Russian troops were stationed in the north on the Soviet borders. British troops had similar duties in the south, where they were also joined by small contingents of Americans. Under an agreement signed in January 1942 by Great Britain, Russia, and Iran all foreign troops were to leave six months after the cessation of hostilities. During the winter of 1945 the Soviets encouraged autonomous aspirations in the province of Azerbaijan, adjacent to Russia, under the direction of the local Communist (Tudeh) party. Stalin had also requested a Soviet-Iranian oil agreement similar to those being arranged by the Anglo-Americans, but was refused. When the province of Azerbaijan declared itself a separate republic, the government at Teheran sent troops northward, only to have Soviet forces intercept and stop them.

In January 1945 Iran complained to the UN Security Council, but nothing concrete had emerged from the resultant negotiations by March when all troops, under the Three-Power Agreement, were to leave. (British and American troops had already pulled out.) American indignation was aroused by the violation of the agreement, and a strong American protest followed several days after the British note of protest was delivered on March 4. Churchill's famous "Iron Curtain" speech on the next day at Fulton, Missouri, although not predicated upon the Iranian incident, perhaps also had some influence on the subsequent Soviet actions. Iranian Premier Qavam, after lengthy conferences in Moscow, concluded a satisfactory agreement with the Soviets. Russian forces left in May 1946, and a Russo-Iranian oil concession was to be signed if approved by the Iranian Parliament (Majlis). By the end of the year, Iranian troops had easily squashed the northern revolt, and the following year saw the Majlis decline to establish a joint-stock oil company with their Soviet neighbor.

The Russians, who had exercised a minor sphere of influence in the 19th century and sponsored a short-lived Communist separatist attempt after World War I on the northern Iranian-Soviet border, were evidently taken aback by the American and British protests. Although there were some vague historical antecedents for their behavior, the Soviets evidently considered that continued American and UN attention to such a situation might result in increased difficulties for them in much more important areas. The Iranian incident was not analogous with Poland, since Russian troops had never occupied all of the country. And only Northern Iran, adjacent to the vital Soviet Baku oil fields, was a problem relating to Russian security needs. The United States, at the same time she was experiencing persistent and contrary Soviet interpretations of terms affecting Poland and Germany, saw this as even clearer violation of a documentary agreement. At a lower level, American economic aspirations looked for a chance to rival Britain's oil concessions. The considerable British influence in Iran helped to bring the incident to a quiet conclusion. Although there was no actual confrontation, this early act of "containing" the Soviets contributed to stepped-up Russo-American animosities.

The great tug-of-war over Germany, one of the most important phases of the early struggle between the Anglo-American powers and the Soviet Union, revealed basic disparities in the victors' view of the defeated nation. To the United States, Germany was to become a unified whole, stripped of its war-making potential but entirely able to resume a useful role in a capitalistic Western European economy. Her Nazis must be tried and punished; her people needed reeducation; but her economy must be able to preclude any call upon the American taxpayer for basic sustenance. Reparations were considered appropriately punitive, but could never be carried to the point of endangering the basic economy, provoking serious disorders, or permitting Russia to grow strong at the expense of a weakened Western Europe. Where Great Britain was concerned, the advantages of a dismembered Germany were soon supplanted by the need to work for a unified continental power. British traditional balance-of-power approach to Europe, and her profound fears of having to feed starving Germans out of Britain's empty pocket, were deciding factors in working toward a single Germany. To the Soviets, Germany represented a nation that might be put under Communist control politically and was to be denuded in economic retribution for her wartime devastation of Russian productivity. The Soviets wavered considerably on the idea of unity, but intended to work toward a Germany unable ever again to invade Mother Russia. Thus the Big Three initially were agreed upon a theoretical goal of unity for Germany. However, each vastly preferred to integrate its zone into its own orbit if its political and economic conditions were not met. And, as Stalin sagely pointed out, each occupied area quickly took on the appearance and trappings of the occupier. France, which was chiefly brought into the position of an occupier by virtue of British realization that the United States was likely to remove its troops from Europe, did not seek German unity. For her security, she considered that the Rhineland, the Saar, and the Ruhr basin must be detached from any postwar Germany. Many early Anglo-American policies and decisions, therefore, were opposed more bitterly by France than by the Soviets.

The compromises reached at Potsdam (see above) virtually recognized a de facto economic division of Germany. France's nonparticipation at Potsdam and resultant obstruction of conference agreements, plus her initial desire to dismember Germany, brought an actual division closer. In the months following Potsdam, an American policy of moving beyond the prescribed reduced level of industrial production in their zone, and the beginning of a Russian policy of manufacturing goods in their zone for home consumption rather than shipping the plants themselves to Russian locations, proved additionally divisive. An important break occurred in May 1946. The Russians, dissatisfied with the trickle of reparations reaching them, refused to account for the amount and value of industrial equipment moved out of their zone, and in other ways had dragged their feet in the treatment of Germany as a single economic unit. Failing to receive the agreed accounting, General Lucius D. Clay, the High Commissioner of the American zone, thereupon ceased the movement of all promised reparations to the Soviets from his zone. This abrupt severance effectively ended a period of at least nominal collaboration. In July 1946 Secretary of State Byrnes' proposal of zone merger was accepted by the British, and in September he followed with a militant speech at Stuttgart on America's German policy. Byrnes insisted that Germany must be permitted increased industrial activity to make her self-sustaining and to aid European economic recovery. Alarming to both the French and the Russians were his suggestions that all Germans should now have the "primary responsibility for the running of their own affairs." He also dashed Russian hopes for an early withdrawal by announcing that United States troops would remain in Germany as long as those of other occupying powers. Bizonia, as the economic merger of the American and British zones was called, began its existence and operations January 1, 1947. Within the next few years this was to move rapidly into a separate West German government, to be met with a similar development in Russia's East Germany. Amicable agreement between the wartime allies over Germany would have been difficult enough even with common aims. But the Russians' desperate and justifiable need for reparations to replace Nazi destruction vied with Anglo-American fears of subsidizing the German economy and supporting starving Germans. British and American insistence on German reunion with Western Europe democratically and economically clashed with Russia's need for a Sovietized government to forestall any future German aggression eastward. As the foremost economic, political, and geographic prize in Europe—perhaps in the world—Germany's disruption became a focal point for Cold War beginnings.

Even with almost continuous diplomatic meetings from 1945 into 1947, relations between the Anglo-Americans and the Soviets deteriorated steadily and noticeably. These meetings moved from a quiet, semisecret basis to the blare of unlimited publicity. Acerbic and challenging debates in the UN and speeches by such leaders as Stalin and Churchill occupied the attention of the world between meetings and added to the jangling discord of international rhetoric. The first Council of Foreign Ministers met in London during September and October 1945. The completely inconclusive wrangling over the formation of peace treaties that resulted was only a forerunner of more discord to come. Molotov's insistence on recognition of the Rumanian pro-Soviet Groza government clashed with Byrnes' and Bevin's demands on free and immediate elections. Byrnes could not comprehend the paradox in expectations that any free elections in an Eastern Europe nation hostile to the Soviets could scarcely bring to power a government friendly to Russia, as Byrnes earnestly insisted the United States and Britain wished to do. Nor could Molotov understand their demands for "free" elections in an area that possessed no democratic traditions. Such democratic ideals were to him only masks for duplicity. Byrnes even went so far as tentatively, in a complete departure from American diplomatic tradition, to commit the United States to a four-power, long-term alliance to ensure continued German demilitarization. The council adjourned in October without results. In the following month, elections in Austria and Hungary, unopposed by the Russians, resulted in overwhelming defeats for the Communist parties. The United States and Britain had recognized their provisional governments in October and November 1945. In Bulgaria, where the party had always been strong, and in Yugoslavia, where Tito was completely dominant, the November election results were favorable to the Communists.

The Big Three repaired to Moscow in December 1945 hopefully to expedite their agreements, but accomplished only a mild warming-up of relations. Minor concessions were made on both sides. The Russians agreed to the American formula for a 21-nation peace conference to be held in Paris in the spring of 1946, and promised to broaden the representation of the governments of Rumania and Bulgaria. The United States, for its part, acceded to an expanded role for the Allied Council which was to "advise" Supreme Commander MacArthur in Japan's occupation. Before the official second session of the Council of Foreign Ministers convened in Paris during April and May 1946, two widely publicized talks helped to whip up the rhetorical aspects of the cold war. On February 9, 1946, Stalin made a political address in which he lauded the Soviet role in the defeat of Hitler's Germany as the acid test of the Soviet system. The Marxist view that the capitalist world held within itself its own destruction coming out of internal rivalries and eventual war was reiterated. But the Soviet Union must make itself strong. Three, maybe more, five-year plans would be needed, because there would be no peace in the world. And Molotov, three days earlier, had called upon Russians to overtake economically European nations and the United States. On March 5, in Fulton, Missouri, Winston Churchill's speech made famous the "Iron Curtain" phrase first used by Goebbels to describe the Soviet influence that stretched "from Stettin in the Baltic to Trieste in the Adriatic." Russia did not want war, Churchill said, but he sounded the tocsin of alarm and suggested a military and political alliance with Great Britain to guard against any further Soviet expansion.

Reaction to the ex–Prime Minister's speech was mixed in the United States, with many Rooseveltians criticizing it as "ganging up on the Russians" and "saving the British Empire." Stalin reacted far more angrily, accusing Churchill of warmongering on an English-speaking nation basis and reminding him obliquely of the defeated intervention of British and American troops in 1920. Thus, Stalin's February 9 speech had stated the possibilities of future world conflict; Churchill had suggested the new partnership that could properly prepare for one aspect of it. Neither aided the continuing diplomacy.

The second session of the council met in Paris in April and May 1946, recessed in exasperation for a month, and concluded its deliberations in June and July. The meeting was marked by full newspaper publicity, which reduced much of the oratory to addresses aimed more at home constituencies than at diplomatic progress. Disposal of Russian claims for trusteeship of Italian colonies, and the Italian-Yugoslavian border dispute were postponed and compromised respectively, but the peace treaties carried over until the council's third session, to be held in New York, November and December 1946. Agreements for the final peace treaties for Italy, Rumania, Bulgaria, Hungary, and Finland were eventually concluded at New York, with the formal signatures to be affixed in early 1947. However, the vitally important treaties for the countries of joint occupation—Germany and Austria—could not be satisfactorily compromised and were postponed for still a fourth session of the council. That session at Moscow in the spring of 1947 and the one beyond it in November remained locked in unsolvable wrangling. The de facto separation of Germany thus took place while the erstwhile war partners quarreled on and on. The Council of Foreign Ministers, established to work out the texts of all peace treaties, degenerated into bitter name calling and a forum for propagandistic harangues.

The larger forum of the newly created United Nations also added its share to the deterioration of United States-USSR relations. The UN, with 51 nations attending, opened its first session in London in January 1946. The Security Council immediately took up the charges of Iran against the Soviet Union and, as mentioned above, aligned the Western democracies against the Soviet Union. The embittered Soviets, complaining of being constantly outnumbered, moved to a heavy use of the veto power and the occasional dramatic device of stalking out of council sessions. During this first year of its existence, the Security Council heard a number of other charges that widened the United States-Russian breach, the most important of which were the Iranian incident and the nagging question of the new and awesome fact of nuclear weapons. The United States had released an early unofficial proposal on atomic management drawn up largely by the State Department in the spring of 1946. With the naming of Bernard Baruch by President Truman as the American delegate to the newly created United Nations Atomic Energy Commission, Baruch's more stringent proposal quickly gained favor with such military leaders as Admiral Leahy and Admiral Nimitz, and with the President himself. The Baruch Plan, offered in June 1946, called for the creation of an International Atomic Development Authority which would have control over all phases of atomic activity from raw material beginnings to finished end product. The treaty creating the Authority would set forth both the systems of inspection and the punishment for violators. When the United States was satisfied with the control, it would then relinquish its bombs as the treaty provided. Within the Authority, the United States would control a majority and could thus exercise the chief voice in the industrial development of nuclear power, even internally, where the Soviet Union was concerned. Although the Atomic Energy Commission was linked with the Security Council, the Baruch Plan forbade the use of the veto in that body. The Russians objected strongly to this possibility, and also to inspections on Russian soil and the retention of all nuclear knowledge in American hands. The Soviets retorted that all existing atomic weapons should be destroyed before a control system was discussed. After several months of disputatious arguments, the Russians gave way on the international inspections. They also agreed to forego the veto if and when punishment for violators was handed out. Baruch insisted that the entire American plan must be accepted without alteration. As a result of this impasse, no plan at all ever emerged. The Soviets obviously distrusted American motives, and refused to relinquish the veto as a necessary guardian of Soviet security. Equal American suspiciousness insisted upon inspections on Russian soil and some Authority voice in Soviet internal matters until complete control satisfaction was realized. An unbending approach was stiffened by advice from the military and politicians (but not from scientists) that Russia could not possibly develop her own A-bombs for at least seven to fifteen years.

By mid-1946 the United States was still groping uncertainly toward some new pattern, some conceptual structure, in which to frame and give direction to its postwar policies. A perceptive report from a Soviet expert, George F. Kennan, Deputy Chief of Mission in the American Embassy at Moscow, to the State Department played a very large role in defining the direction American policy toward Russia should take. Kennan's 16-page report attempted to analyze Soviet behavior and the Kremlin's probable future style of action. How American policy should be shaped to meet such behavior was couched in somewhat vague terms which would generally find Washington reacting to Moscow initiatives. The feeling in the State Department was that the analysis was so cogent as to form the basis of future American foreign policy toward the Soviet Union, although Kennan later disputed the interpretations Washington placed on some of his less specific suggestions. To Kennan, the Kremlin's absolute rulers had a "neurotic" view of world affairs based upon "the traditional and distinctive Russian sense of insecurity." (Unfortunately, the historic grounds for these attitudes were not stated.) Although the Soviet government should not be described as adventuristic, it would move steadily against what it considered to be the world of "capitalist encirclement." It might eventually face internal stresses which could provoke governmental crises, such as at the future death of Stalin. The United States, for its part, must "contain" Soviet aggressiveness by "adroit and vigilant application of counter-force at a series of constantly shifting geographical and political points," although "force" was never specifically described. The American public must be educated to the realities of Moscow's attitudes and their courses. And, Kennan warned, "the greatest danger that can befall us in coping with this problem of Soviet communism is that we shall allow ourselves to become like those with whom we are coping."

Kennan's report was published in *Foreign Affairs,* in the July 1947 issue, under the anonymous authorship of "X." Its publication brought opposition to its viewpoint from diverse sources such as journalist Walter Lippmann and Secretary of Commerce Henry A. Wallace. Lippmann, in an argument that most Russian historical specialists were later to accept, insisted that the Soviet push in Eastern Europe had little to do with communism, as such, but a great deal to do with traditional and Czarist attempts to create a protective belt around Russia. This traditional motivation towards national security could thus be reconciled by some neutralization of Central and Eastern European areas. Wallace, in a September 1946 speech that was allegedly read and approved by the Chief Executive, had already taken strong issue with the idea of "getting tough" with Russia. He insisted that America should have no more interest in Eastern Europe than should the Russians in Latin America, and that the United States should recognize Russia's need for security in what had been for her a traditional route of invasion. But neither Lippmann nor Wallace nor other spokesmen of their view could influence the Truman administration's course by this time. Secretary of State Byrnes, busily trying to get Soviet agreement to Anglo-American election policies in Eastern Europe, furiously demanded that Wallace be curbed. Ten days later, the President fired Wallace from his Cabinet post. By the end of 1946 the foundations of the Grand Alliance had completely crumbled, and new foundations for a cold war had been laid.

How then to answer the many-branched question on the great variety of causes that underlie the beginnings of the Cold War? Admittedly, what we think of as "The Cold War"—generally referring to the increasingly hostile confrontation between the United States and Soviet Russia—is easier to narrate than to explain. But a number of causes can be found in leaders and leadership of the times. They can be discovered in the postwar aspirations of Russia and America; in ideologies and in geography. They can be seen in new and vastly differing concepts of international affairs. And many events and developments in all these areas are laden with misunderstanding to the point of genuine tragedy.

In terms of leadership, the Russians were convinced that the change from Roosevelt to Truman in April 1945 was a change from near-white to black. This was not entirely correct, since Roosevelt and his administration in his last months found increasing need for angry remonstrations with the direction and implementation of Russian policy. Nevertheless, there was some justification for such sentiment. Senator Harry Truman, when Hitler attacked the Soviet Union in 1941, was widely quoted in the *New York Times* as advising with fine impartiality, "If we see that Germany is winning the war we ought to help Russia, and if Russia is winning we ought to help Germany and in that way kill as many as possible." Within two weeks of assuming the presidency, Truman was ready to take up the cudgels with Stalin in an attitude that could readily be described as "basically unfriendly." Both Truman and his Secretary of State, James F. Byrnes, were parochial and nationalistic politicians. Neither had any flair for or experience in internationalism. Where Roosevelt hoped, even with mounting evidence of differences with Stalin, to work within a framework of diplomacy and international understanding, Truman's essential man-in-the-street background led him quickly into belligerent and undiplomatic channels. Where Roosevelt was able to subdue or soft-pedal the anti-Sovietism among his advisers in behalf of long-range goals, Truman fully accepted their arguments and delivered them without regard for keeping diplomatic channels of communication open.

The Soviet leaders, Joseph Stalin and Vyacheslav Molotov, were, if anything, even more parochial and nationalistic. Their understanding of international affairs was severely limited in knowledge and perhaps even more restricted in both Russian and Soviet views of the world arrayed against them. Their grim xenophobia and their morbid mistrustfulness were firmly grounded in Russian culture and historical experience. Their abnormal suspiciousness was exacerbated by several incidents during the war years, such as the delay in a second front. In the postwar years Stalin's wary distrustfulness moved close to paranoia. He had additional handicaps in his position as Soviet leader. Perhaps foremost among these was an unusual duality which cast Stalin both in the role of a national leader intent upon uniquely Russian goals and in that of the chief spokesman for international communism. Paradoxical utterances and seemingly contradictory goals were confusing to American officials, since in no way could the Russian-Soviet duality be compared with the American duality that calls for the President to head both his country and his political party. Additionally, it may be suggested that Stalin had a genuine need to foster national hostility against the anti-Soviet world. No better method exists for the totalitarian or authoritarian government to rally its people to its cause, regardless of war weariness or low standards of living, than presenting a picture of unrelenting and implacable hostility as the attitude of other peoples and other nations. Finally, Stalin was charged with the terribly real needs of Russian security. In the face of Russian historical experience, such needs had considerably more legitimacy than their negotiation indicates.

In its postwar aspirations the United States reflected a policy of dynamic capitalist expansionism in its "open door" approach which sought to inhibit socialized or nationalized competition, whether British or Russian. As the most advanced and most powerful economic entity in the world, America strongly favored stability, even when it resembled an unrestorable ante bellum status quo. Politically, the United States aspired to a peaceful world. In part, this rested upon a successful UN, but it also pursued unrealistically a Wilsonian policy of democratic government and free elections in Eastern European nations that had no such traditions or experience whatever. The Soviet Union aspired to increased global Communist influence and prestige, but this was not permitted to take priority over Russian security. In this respect, the Soviet Union had well-developed expectations, and not merely aspirations, where Eastern Europe was concerned. Nations contiguous to Russia's borders must have neutralist and essentially friendly governments as in Finland and early Czechoslovakia, or have suitable governments arranged for them, as in untrustworthy Poland and Rumania. But Russia, the remaining great power in Europe, and the United States, the dominant world superpower, confronted each other's aspirations in Germany. To Russia, the Germans represented a dangerous and aggressive people who must either be suitably controlled or their potential power as an entity be satisfactorily thwarted. To the United States, although lip service was paid through much of 1946 to the ideal of an economic entity, it became more apparent that Germany must be economically restored and take her place with capitalistic Western Europe as an anti-Soviet bulwark. Only bitter enmity and a divided Germany could result.

Both nations were slow to see the geographic factor which, placing huge Russian armies throughout Eastern and Central Europe to defeat Germany, was itself one of the causes of the cold war. And geographically, the Anglo-Americans blew a chance for an allied say-so in Eastern Europe by a policy that deliberately excluded the Soviets from a voice in Italian surrender and occupation matters. It should have been no surprise when the Soviets effectively used this precedent to deny any great voice for the United States and Great Britain when Rumania surrendered. Nor was there an adequate understanding and recognition of the new balance of European power, particularly by the United States. The very expression continued to remain an anathema in American official circles even after its accompanying device, spheres of influence, was tacitly accepted for the nations on Russia's borders. When the United States attempted some penetration in areas where she previously had little or no activity by means of such economic arm twisting as loans, which were then withdrawn, the Soviets were understandably fearful and suspicious. The United States misunderstood the Russian need for border security, although it had incontrovertible historical evidence in support. Washington too readily assumed that such an obsession was merely an expression of Russian expansionism and perhaps a forerunner of aggressive designs on Western Europe as well as on the nations that lined her borders in Eastern Europe. It should be pointed out that Washington's fears of Soviet expansionism in 1945 and 1946 applied only to Eastern Europe. Such fears regarding Western Europe were largely a post-1946 phenomenon.

For their part, Stalin misunderstood and Molotov was utterly unable to comprehend the American combination of political idealism and economic self-interest in its approach to the nations of Eastern Europe. Americans failed to realize that the Soviets, even though accepted by nations of the world as a great power, would still have to depend on themselves for security measures rather than to submit them to a UN forum in which they were badly outnumbered. The Soviets failed to realize in turn that the new American concept of international affairs envisioned the United States as a world power that would no longer withdraw into isolationism of any variety. At home, American policy "to get tough" was supported by the unusual phenomenon of "Red fascism" and by Republican partisanship. Red fascism was the unhistorical and uncritical acceptance of a transfer of all the evils and motives of Hitler's Germany to Stalin's Russia. The Soviet Union was unthinkingly, but frequently enthusiastically, endowed with Hitlerian attributes in this misleading analogy, creating a kind of instant hostility and helping to support a belligerent confrontation with Russia. Many Republicans demanded, as a partisan device, that the Truman administration adopt a "get tough" or "get tougher" attitude toward the Soviets, without realizing that such rhetoric was of little avail and that moving beyond rhetoric generally could be accomplished only by the use of armed force. Bending to accommodate themselves to Republican demands, Senator Tom Connally complained bitterly, led Byrnes and the administration to favor the counsel of Republican Senator Arthur Vandenberg over his own at the London Foreign Ministers' meeting.

Possibilities for an accommodation between American and Russian needs and goals existed in 1945 and 1946. Failure to ameliorate in some way the tensions flowing from this early confrontation of interests must rest, in perhaps unmeasurable parts, upon Soviet intransigence and uncomprehending suspiciousness and upon the misunderstandings and errors of American foreign policy. By late 1946 or early 1947 the Cold War had witnessed the building of a foundation period and was ready to move into its frozen phase wherein attitudes and pattern of action became fully hardened, and implementations of those attitudes were to be put into motion. And once having been set in motion, they would acquire a momentum of their own that would prove tragically difficult to halt.

The Truman Doctrine and the Marshall Plan

Civil war in Greece and Soviet pressure on Turkey provided the vehicle for the first dramatic implementation of the rapidly changing official attitude toward the Soviets. The enunciation by President Truman on March 12, 1947, commonly known as the Truman Doctrine, marked a historically important change of direction in American foreign policy.

After German troops left Greece in 1944, Greek guerrilla armies attempted to seize the government and forestall the return of the despised monarchy. Although not predominantly Communist in makeup, they were Communist led, and the British army immediately sent in forces to crush the revolt of December 1944. As Churchill candidly stated, Stalin adhered to their earlier sphere-of-influence arrangement for the Balkans and stood aside while Communist-led resistance fighters (whom Great Britain aided and supplied during the war) were put down or driven over Greece's northern borders. During the civil war, both sides committed atrocities and slaughtered each other's supporters so mercilessly as to be described as the most barbarous struggle in Greek history since the Peloponnesian Wars of the 5th century B.C. Guerrilla armies, both Communist and non-Communist, accused the royalists of widespread political murder and terrorism after the British-arranged surrender of arms in February 1945. The United States was one of several nations (Russia refused to do so) whose observers certified the triumph of King George II's Populist party in the national elections of March 1946. The government's corruption and continued repressions encouraged the resurgence of guerrilla bands whose reprisals equaled those of the government. Aided by the three Communist regimes in Yugoslavia, Albania, and Bulgaria, they reached during 1946 a size and force that the royalist police and army could not control. Where Turkey was concerned, direct Soviet pressure was exerted instead of through other Communist regimes. The Soviets had been denied at Potsdam in their efforts to change the Montreux Convention that acknowledged control of the vital Dardenelle Straits in Turkish hands. Ever since Catherine the Great, the Czars had dreamed of breaking out of their landlocked seas and gaining a port on the Straits. The Soviets continued this traditional Russian policy by directing noisy propaganda at Turkey and massing troops on the Turkish border in 1946 and 1947.

The critical moment arose when Great Britain, which sponsored King George's government and had long exercised a dominant role in Greek affairs, admitted to the State Department in February 1947 that it could no longer furnish desperately needed financial aid to Greece and Turkey. Her own economic life was genuinely at stake in this lowest point in her entire industrial history, and such costly burdens must be assumed by some nation better able to bear them. Truman's advisers, at that time confident that the Greek situation was a manifestation of Soviet aggression, immediately drew up plans to stop the supposed Soviet move toward the Middle East through Greece and Turkey. Undersecretary of State Dean Acheson proved even more influential in congressional hearings than did Secretary of State Marshall by using an anti-Soviet approach and by equating internal Communist activities with Soviet military aggression. But the Republicans had just won control of Congress for the first time in 80 years, and were planning great budget slashes. The President, warned Republican Senator Vandenberg privately, must "scare hell" out of Americans if he wished bipartisan support for such expenditures. State Department officials thereupon talked to Congressmen or testified before congressional hearings in alarmist terms of the threat to "free" regimes from totalitarian nations. In an early and rather staggering version of the "domino" theory, Congressmen were told that if Greece and Turkey fell, not only all of the Middle East but all of Western Europe and all of North Africa would then topple.

On March 12, 1947 Truman appeared before a special session of Congress to request $400 million in aid for Greece and Turkey. By May it had received congressional approval and became official American policy. Truman's significant address asked Americans to extend their interests around the world. Without stating what comprised those interests, Americans must be

> . . . willing to help free peoples to maintain their national integrity against aggressive movements that seek to impose upon them totalitarian regimes. This is no more than a frank recognition that totalitarian regimes imposed upon free peoples, by direct or indirect aggression, undermine the foundations of international peace and hence the security of the United States.

The world was divided into "one way of life" that included free elections, representative government, and freedoms such as that from political oppression. "A second way of life" was defined as based upon the will of a minority, and relying upon terrorism, a controlled press, fixed elections, and the suppression of personal freedoms. With this launching of an ideological crusade marshalling the forces of anticommunism against those of world communism, the United States departed from its traditional role of noninterference in world affairs to a position of interventionist and counterrevolutionary activities through subsequent decades. Although to its critics the attempt to keep Greece and Turkey within the Western bloc was defensible and desirable, the Doctrine's sweeping declaration encompassing the entire world was attacked because it pledged American aid even in areas not essential to American interests or security. Others attacked its tone of a moral crusade, since this readily implied that no negotiated settlement of international affairs was possible. Its friends nevertheless deplored the complete circumvention of the UN. More stringent critics pointed to the fact that some of the nations that were lumped together under a "democratic way of life" were governments where little or no democracy existed. Greece and others, it was pointed out, had many of the political characteristics attributed to the totalitarian way of life. Before Truman's speech was delivered, George Kennan was one of those objecting within the State Department to both the hostile tone of the draft and its worldwide commitment. He also pointed out that military aid rather than economic aid to a nation on Russia's border was needlessly provocative. More militaristic policies prevailed, however, as the United States moved into the concept of containment. The Truman Doctrine proclaimed American willingness to intervene against communism and internal revolution susceptible to branding as communism anywhere in the world. And the "scaring hell" out of the American people suggested by Senator Vandenberg and fostered by Truman and Acheson was to become the basis of a feverish anti-Communist Cold War ideology that the United States would pursue long after "containment" became obsolescent.

It was quickly recognized by the administration that aid to Greece and Turkey shored up only two small economies, yet even the largest and most stable nations of Europe were in the most serious economic difficulties of their entire histories. The war had devastated them financially and economically; communications were shattered; unemployment rose to new highs. Churchill, in May 1947, described Europe as "a rubble heap . . . a breeding ground of pestilence and hate." American observers feared a wholesale economic and political collapse throughout Europe and a resultant rise to power of sundry Communist parties on a wave of economic chaos. Secretary of State Marshall came back from a European swing badly shaken. The Policy Planning Staff that he then established under George Kennan recommended policies of limited military aid, but extensive economic aid, throughout Europe, even including the Soviet Union and Eastern European nations in such a plan.

The first trial balloon went aloft with Undersecretary of State Acheson's speech May 8, 1947 at Cleveland, Mississippi, in which he stressed the fact that American goods exported were twice what Americans imported, and that credits and reconstruction for Europe were necessary to ensure this vital part of the American economy. Secretary Marshall followed the next month with a memorable address at Harvard in which European nations were urged to assess the extent of their recovery needs:

> Our policy is directed not against any country or doctrine but against hunger, poverty, desperation, and chaos. Its purpose should be revival of a working economy. . . . Any government that is willing to assist in the task of recovery will find full cooperation . . . on the part of the United States government. . . . The initiative, I think, must come from Europe. . . .

Although the invitation went to all European nations, the implementation of any such plan was carefully weighted against Russian acceptance, since it involved internal inspection of records by personnel sure to be American dominated. Great Britain and France enthusiastically called the nations of Europe together at Paris in June. Molotov showed up with an enormous retinue of economists, and the Soviets seemed keenly interested in the plan. Instructions from the Kremlin soon converted Russian interest to obstruction and finally complete withdrawal. By September, 16 other nations had drawn up a list of their basic needs, together with concessions such as tariff reduction in return for the American aid.

In the United States the economic reconstruction plan for Europe was largely received with approval. The chief reason for this was that the plan as envisioned would also provide insurance for the health of the American economy. Aid to Europe would not be cash but in the form of credits to be used primarily for the purchase of equipment, machine tools, and supplies in the United States and then shipped to the European nations. Pressure groups also ensured benefits by getting Congress to require, for example, that at least half such purchases be shipped in American vessels with American crews. Both industry and labor thus supported the idea. Congress, however, with a Republican majority intent upon budget slashing, took more persuasion. Administration arguments centered upon the containment of communism by stabilizing Europe's economy; the need to maintain American exports; curbing the threat of continued nationalization of industry and thus stimulating the investment of private capital; and creating a stable economy that could furnish the United States needed strategic goods and participate in future military cooperation. The program, usually known as the Marshall Plan but titled the European Recovery Program (ERP) moved readily through Congress against a background of urgency high-lighted by Russian announcement of a counterplan, the Molotov Plan of 1947, and the Czechoslovakian Communist's coup d'etat of 1948. Offi-cially known as the Economic Cooperation Act, Truman signed it into law on April 2, 1948. The act established an agency, the Economic Cooperation Administration (ECA), to direct the program. Truman named a Republican corporate executive, Paul G. Hoffman, president of the Studebaker Corporation, to head the agency. The Marshall Plan almost surely saved Europe from economic collapse. Within four years ERP aid had amounted to more than $12 billion. American exports were maintained at a satisfactory level, many of them financed through ECA funds. Strategic materials were purchased for stockpiling in the United States. European economics underwent an almost magical recovery, and the economy of West Germany was bound into international capitalism. The influence of the strong French and Italian Communist parties, with far less economic discontent to exploit, was considered to have been proportionately weakened.

The Marshall Plan evolved from and flowed naturally from the Truman Doctrine, although it avoided the sternly challenging tones of the former. The two were, as Truman expressed it, "halves of the same walnut." Combined within the Marshall Plan were traditional American humanitarianism, the postwar concept of an open door for American trade and American capital investments abroad, a need to bolster do-mestic industrial production, and a political weapon of containment di-rected against the Soviets and a supposed monolithic communism. The humanitarian and economic aspects of the plan must be adjudged a considerable success, with the political consequences less clear. Both American critics and Soviet propaganda asked why the plan had not been handled through the United Nations' Economic Commission for Europe (ECE) rather than unilaterally under American supervision. George Kennan had suggested the use of the ECE, since no possibility of Soviet veto existed in that body. The Truman administration had ignored this suggestion as well as an official invitation from the UN's Trygve Lie to use ECE. Soviet reaction to the ERP was seen in varied ways. It was linked in denunciatory terms with the anti-Russian pro-nouncements of Undersecretary of State Dean Acheson. The Soviet grip on the border states of Eastern Europe in 1947 was evidently not a secure one, and the Kremlin moved to tighten its grasp in response to the threat of economic penetration by forcing Poland and Czechoslo-vakia to abandon their interest in ERP participation. The internal coup in the latter country resulted, at least in part, from Marshall Plan poten-tial. More immediate and direct responses in 1947 were the formation of the Molotov Plan and the establishment of a propaganda agency, the International Communist Information Bureau (Cominform). The

Marshall Plan, insofar as its use for containment was concerned, thus had the effect of polarizing further the cold war divisions in the world and reemphasizing American abandonment of neutrality and nonintervention.

The Beginning of the Fair Deal

Domestically, Truman faced stiffer partisan politics and a rockier road with Congress than in the early postwar years of foreign policy. On September 6, 1945, shortly after Japan's surrender, Truman presented the "Twenty-One-Point" message to a special session of Congress. Many of the items included, such as the need for expanded social security and an extensive slum clearance and public housing program, could be traced back to Roosevelt's Economic Bill of Rights of the 1944 campaign. Others, such as continuation of war controls, reorganization legislation, increased unemployment compensation, and a permanent Fair Employment Practices Commission, were measures already being supported by the Truman administration. Several of the points, like veterans' benefits and congressional salaries, were largely noncontroversial in nature. Most of the domestic policies were later to become known as the Fair Deal. Although conservatives found in the Twenty-One-Point Message an irritating revival of the New Deal, liberals glimpsed in it a possible lack of commitment and a faulty organization, based upon its lack of specific details, its failure to mention bills already in Congress, and a complete lack of priorities. To some it appeared that an overly cautious Truman actually expected a balky Congress to carry out some of the functions of presidential leadership.

One of the bills already in Congress and of high priority was a full-employment act. It looked to the principles of John Maynard Keynes in fixing the responsibility for maintaining full employment upon government, and it drew on fears of massive unemployment and a sharp depression such as followed World War I. "Full employment" after the war had also been a Democratic party pledge of 1944. The great record of coordinating labor's and industry's resources during the war by means of government planning and national cooperation suggested that the means were readily at hand for every citizen to have an opportunity to contribute to and benefit from full, national employment and productivity. Although most Congressmen were agreed as to the principle of maximum employment, the more conservative harked back to laissez faire concepts in their insistence that private enterprise rather than government should have primary responsibility for any such implementation. The Senate version of the bill was acceptable to the Truman administration, but in the more conservative House of Representatives its many rural-oriented members refused to accept, among other items, the term "full employment." In the joint committee considering the final version of the bill, "full" was stricken from the title and "maximum employment" replaced it. Provisions for government spending in times of recession, in order to underwrite employment, were taken out of the act, and in their place appeared a more vague directive that the government would "utilize all . . . its resources . . ." to reach the desired ends. The Employment Act, as finally signed by the President in February 1946, also included a provision for a three-member Council of Economic Advisers who were to assist and advise the President in preparing an annual economic report to Congress. Although weakened to a considerable extent, the act contained a significant innovation in fixing the responsibility for promoting goals of maximum employment, productivity, and purchasing power squarely upon the federal government. Even though it contained no guarantee that the government would take action, its new acknowledgement of responsibility meant that both Democratic and Republican administrations would thereafter use governmental powers any time a recession appeared imminent.

Another act that Truman had requested before the war's end was one to establish policy for the domestic control and development of atomic energy. The atom, Truman warned, was "too important to be made the subject of profit seeking," and a government agency should be created to supervise its development and future usages. The military, which exercised authority over atomic research during wartime, insisted that they must continue to do so. Admiral Leahy, as a spokesman for Navy and Army leaders, objected violently to turning "over the making of one of the most effective weapons of war to a civil commission which would dole out its product, if it decided to make any, as it saw fit." But congressional suggestions for military control ran into a hail of objection from atomic scientists, educators, and liberals who considered that the end of war should also bring about an end to military dominance. Congressional debate stretched through the spring and summer of 1946 before Republican Senator Vandenberg suggested a compromise "military liaison board" that would advise and consult a civilian commission without actually posing a challenge to civilian control. Truman was then able by August to sign into law the Atomic Energy Act of 1946. The act created the Atomic Energy Commission (AEC) with complete control over all fissionable material. To head the four-man commission Truman appointed David E. Lilienthal, former director of TVA.

By the time for congressional elections in November 1946, New Dealers were considerably disenchanted with the Truman performance and the resignation or discharge of many Rooseveltians indicated to many that the New Deal organization was falling apart. Foreign policy disagreements, as previously noted, moved Truman to ask for the resignation of Henry A. Wallace as Secretary of Commerce. His place was taken by W. Averell Harriman, former Ambassador to Great Britain. Truman cared neither for Secretary of the Treasury Henry Morgenthau's plan to reduce Germany to a "pastoral" nation, nor for Morgenthau's insistence that he accompany the President to Potsdam. Following the latter's resignation, Truman appointed Fred M. Vinson, former Senator from Kentucky and director of OWMR, to the post of Secretary of the Treasury in July 1945. About a year later Truman named Vinson to be Chief Justice of the Supreme Court, and brought in a Missouri banker, John W. Snyder, to head the Treasury. Attorney General Francis Biddle was another dissatisfied New Deal member of Truman's Cabinet to resign, his place being filled in June 1945 by Thomas C. Clark of Texas. Lewis B. Schwellenbach of Washington replaced the first female Cabinet member, Frances Perkins, as Secretary of Labor; and Clinton P. Anderson of New Mexico became Claude R. Wickard's successor as Secretary of Agriculture. By far the most publicized departure from Truman's Cabinet was that of New Dealer Harold Ickes, Secretary of the Interior. President Truman had proposed a California businessman, Edwin W. Pauley, for the post of Undersecretary of the Navy. What seemed to be a routine appointment of a heavy contributor to party coffers was transformed by Secretary Ickes' testimony before the Senate Naval Affairs Committee. Ickes fiercely challenged Pauley's competence on the basis of alleged improper requests that the government take a negative attitude toward its title to tidelands oil properties. Truman continued to support the nomination of Pauley, although he did veto in August 1945 a bill that would have given tidelands oil control to the states. Ickes resigned in February 1946 with a parting blast at the administration, and Truman appointed Julius W. Krug, Wisconsin head of the War Production Board, to be Secretary of the Interior. Truman understandably wanted advisers well known to him. The replacement of Rooseveltian aides in White House positions with the group that came to be called the "Missouri Gang," nevertheless sadly suggested to many a further dismantling of the New Deal structure.

At election time Truman also faced wide hostility for what seemed to be wishy-washy and inexplicable decisions regarding high prices and wartime controls. When Congress passed a weak bill extending OPA controls for a year, Truman's veto thereupon ended all price controls. Scarce goods (particularly beef) flowed back into the market, but at prices that enraged housewives. Another OPA bill, Truman apologies, and administration wavering on price controls followed. By October Truman had ended meat controls, and he quickly removed all other controls but rent and sugar. Consumer resentment, farm bitterness at long being denied higher prices for their products, and the divisive Wallace fracas all united in unfortunate array against the Democrats at election time. Added to these party drawbacks were the disenchantment of the liberals and labor, and the dissatisfaction among conservative southern Democrats over Truman's attempts to get a permanent FEPC. In what was clearly the low point of Truman's presidential career, the Republicans slaughtered their ancient political enemies in the congressional and gubernatorial elections of 1946. In the Senate, Republicans dominated with a 51 to 45 majority. In the House, the GOP had a 246 to 188 margin in what was the first national victory for the Republicans since 1928. They also were victorious in 25 gubernatorial contests around the nation. So overwhelming was the Republican surge that Democratic Senator William J. Fulbright of Arkansas bitterly suggested that Truman resign after appointing a GOP Secretary of State so that the line of succession would thus also give the Republicans the White House as well. Truman retorted sarcastically, and his fight upward in 1947 and 1948 in both national and party regard was a thoroughgoing rebuttal of his many critics. It marked a political comeback without rival in American presidential history.

The Republican-dominated 80th Congress that convened on January 3, 1947, was anxious to put into practice that party's campaign pledge to curb the power of the nation's unions and their leaders. In this aim they had the support in particular of conservative Southern Democrats and in general of many legislators who reflected their constituents' distaste for the rash of strikes in the first postwar years. A two-day national railway strike in May 1946 brought the restrictive Case bill safely through Congress, with provisions for a sixty-day "cooling-off" period after unions had notified management of intent to strike, union liability in civil action damage suits, and prohibition of secondary boycotts. Truman had advanced legislation of his own to Congress which included such measures as "cooling-off" periods, but considered the Case act too "punitive." His veto on June 11 was narrowly upheld in the House by five votes. But shortly after the November elections of 1946 fuel was added to the public indignation over strikes by the high-handed actions of John L. Lewis of the United Mineworkers' Union. Lewis and the UMW defied a federal restraining order and struck the coal mines, forcing railroads to curtail schedules and many cities to revive wartime lighting restrictions. Haled into court, the defiant Lewis was saddled with a $10,000 personal fine and the UMW a whopping $3.5 million citation, both for contempt of court. The public temper was further keyed up to an antilabor stand by the generally one-sided press, which used sensationalism to convey to the man in the street the image of the very atypical John L. Lewis and a few others as being more representative of labor than its more numerous responsible union leaders. Labor's abuses of its power and the public climate readily forecast congressional antilabor legislation.

Within two months of the 80th Congress' first meeting, its two Labor Committee chairmen were faced with more than 50 bills to restrict labor in a variety of ways. Two omnibus bills finally emerged from the Senate Labor Committee, chaired by Senator Robert A. Taft (Republican of Ohio), and the House Committee on Education and Labor headed by Representative Fred L. Hartley, Jr. (Republican of New Jersey). These were then reconciled into a jointly accepted bill. The Labor-Management Relations Act of 1947, or as it was better known, the Taft-Hartley Act, was passed by large margins in Congress and sent to the President. It called for a number of important changes which labor fought bitterly but without being able to overcome the superior weight of lobbying and propaganda used by the NAM, the U.S. Chamber of Commerce, and interested industrial groups. The new law forbade the closed shop, although it permitted the union shop where a majority of employees voted for it.[4] It did away with the "checkoff" or deduction of union dues from the worker's paycheck, unless he agreed to it voluntarily in writing. It prohibited the jurisdictional strike and the secondary boycott, and forbade federal government employees from striking. Unions were made liable for damage suits arising from abrogation of contracts and would have to publish annual statements detailing their organization and finances. The cooling-off period appeared in somewhat more extended form than in previous unsuccessful legislation. Unions must give notice of an impending strike and wait 60 days before doing so. However, if it was an industry-wide strike or one proclaimed as affecting the national interest, the cooling-off period became 80 days and the National Labor Relations Board would poll the workers to ensure their acceptance of the strike call. Unions were forbidden to make contributions to national primary or general elections, and their leaders were required to submit annual affidavits stating that they were not members of the Communist party.

After Congress sent the bill to President Truman on June 9, 1947, the greatest volume of mail ever reported arriving at the White House on a legislative issue declared itself in favor of a presidential veto. Labor redoubled its efforts against the bill with petitions, meetings, advertisements, and parades. Most Democratic party officials, excluding the South, urged veto of the bill. Truman's Cabinet was reported divided in its sentiments, but the newly established Council of Economic Advisors recommended disapproval of the act after close analysis. A number of the council's reasons were included in the vigorous and denunciatory veto that Truman presented to Congress on June 20. He found that

---

[4] The closed shop required union membership as a precondition of employment; the union shop permitted employment without being a union member but with the proviso that the individual join the union after a certain length of time on the job.

the bill would be more likely to increase strikes than the opposite, particularly if a no-strike clause was requested in a labor-management contract. Voluntary agreement between union and employer, since "cooperation cannot be achieved by law," would deteriorate, and such agreement would become even less possible by provisions of the act that broke down many of labor's security and welfare arrangements. Truman deplored the increased need for governmental intervention, and castigated discriminatory provisions permitting refusal of certification for an entire national union if even one union official refused to sign an already discriminatory non-Communist affidavit. The House, however, quickly overrode the veto by a vote of 331 to 83. The Senate considered the veto message until June 23 but then also voted against the President, 68 to 25. In the House 106 Democrats and in the Senate 20 Democrats joined the Republicans in overriding the veto—virtually all of them from the South.

The Taft-Hartley Act turned out to be neither the "Slave Labor" Act that labor designated it nor did it place the chains upon unions that much of management had envisioned. It could better be described as a control act that led to more publicized information on union funds and organization, although one which still left union leaders with considerable power over the rank and file. There was no increase in strikes, although the number of cases before the NLRB and in the courts increased. The NLRB defeated the few union attempts to circumvent the closed shop provision, but the courts knocked out as clearly unconstitutional the act's ban on union expenditures in support of political candidates. What the Taft-Hartley Act particularly accomplished was to make evident to the friends of labor the perils of abstention from the polling place. Labor fought back strenuously in the election of 1948, and Truman's veto must have carried with it some recognition that antilabor actions by a Republican-dominated body could properly be exploited politically against this partisan viewpoint.

The 80th Congress had few pieces of domestic legislation to its credit, but it did pass a National Security Act in 1947 and made a start on needed executive reform with a Presidential Succession Act. World War II had brought home to Truman the antiquated defense arrangements of the nation's military, and the need for prevention of costly duplication and the continual interservice pulling and hauling had long pointed to the need for reform. Despite intense opposition from many officers, and particularly those concerned with the Navy's "independence," Truman had set military and civilian officials to the establishment of a unified armed service goal. After more than a year and a half of conferences and meetings under Secretary of the Navy Forrestal's leadership and Truman's prodding, a plan for unification was passed by Congress in July 1947 as the National Security Act. The act created a separate

Air Force and kept the Marine Corps intact. The former Secretaries of War and Navy were abolished. In their place, as subsecretaries, were three lesser Cabinet posts representing the Army, Navy, and Air Force. All were subordinated to a new Cabinet post, the Secretary of Defense, and James V. Forrestal became, in September 1947, the first to assume that office. A Joint Chiefs of Staff with a rotating chairmanship was set up to provide additional coordination among the services. The act also established three agencies soon to become the object of serious controversy because of their secrecy and the assumption of powers not granted them in the legislation. These were the National Security Resources Board (NSRB), the National Security Council (NSC), and the Central Intelligence Agency (CIA). The NSRB and the CIA were to furnish information on national resources and the collection and analysis of information to the NSC for the President's use. Observers soon objected to the policy making of the CIA and the great powers secretly exercised by the NSC as further abandonment of democratic processes. President Truman admitted his own misgivings after leaving the presidency. Although the necessity for additional reform was soon evident, the unification of the armed services consummated many years of work toward such a goal. Squabbles between services still were carried into the public arena and to Air Force or Navy supporters in Congress, but the national defenses were far more coordinated than before World War II.

Truman's sudden accession to the presidency also brought into sharp focus the provisions for presidential succession and the vacating of the office of Vice President. Under the terms of the 1886 act then in effect, Truman could appoint his successor. He did not consider that this was in accord with democratic practice, and, therefore, asked Congress to adopt his proposal. (The office of Vice President remained vacant for the balance of Truman's first administration.) Truman's suggestion would have placed the Speaker of the House of Representatives and the President of the Senate at the head of the line for presidential succession since, as publicly elected officials, they were in sharp contrast to the purely appointive status of the Secretary of State and other members of the President's Cabinet. He did not expect that such a succession would be more than temporary and suggested that a special election be held or that the regular off-year congressional elections be used if they should occur at an earlier date. After several defeats the Presidential Succession Act became law in June 1947. It contained Truman's suggestion of moving the succession away from the Secretary of State and Cabinet officers to the presiding officers of the House and Senate respectively, but failed to embody the idea of an election to choose a new President and Vice President. The act provided for some of the reform needed in the executive structure, but left unsolved the ticklish question of how to decide that a President was too ill or disabled to carry out properly the functions of his office. The cases of Garfield and Wilson remained to haunt students of American government, and a third case was soon to arise with Eisenhower.

Allied to this act, although with different motivations and from a different quarter, was the Republican-sponsored move to amend the Constitution so as to preclude another Rooseveltian four-term grasp upon the office of President. Joined by conservative and anti-FDR Democrats, Congress in March 1947 adopted a proposal to amend the Constitution limiting the presidency to two terms. With the explicit exception of the current officeholder, it barred any individual who succeeded to that office and served in it for more than two years from being reelected to it more than once. In effect, this limited an elected President to eight years in office and restricted one who succeeded to the office to a maximum of ten years as President. The proposal was ratified by the necessary 36 state legislatures to become the 22d Amendment to the Constitution as of February 25, 1951.

Truman's actions in other legislative quarters earned as much political credit for him as had his stout veto of the Taft-Hartley bill in labor's behalf. In 1946 Republicans introduced a bill incorporating large cuts in the federal income tax. Although Truman was sympathetic to the principle of reducing wartime taxes, he vetoed the bill on the basis that it would not only promote the inflation eroding citizens' purchasing power, but that the proposed cuts would chiefly benefit the rich. The veto was narrowly upheld, and a second such effort the following year was also vetoed and upheld. Early in 1948 Congress presented Truman with still a third attempt, this time with reductions on all tax brackets. Again the President sent the bill back to Congress with the tart retort that the bill still suffered from inequities that saw nearly 40 percent of the reductions go to less than 5 percent of all taxpayers. This time the Republicans were able to muster enough Democratic strength to override the veto.

Truman also profited from Republican demands that farm price supports be cut back from their flat 90 percent of parity to a sliding scale of 65 to 90 percent of parity. With strong farm support and pressure, the administration was able to secure a bill calling for the continuance of the 90 percent basis for another 18 months. Truman's record in 1947 and 1948 also helped to win him the support of black voters. Although Truman's voting as a Senator on civil rights issues was a liberal one, it was not widely known. By 1947, however, Truman was cautiously indicating that he approved of full equality in practice as well as principle where blacks were concerned. He added social integration to his previous supports of political and economic integration, although this remained more a rhetorical postition than one of staunch political support. He emphasized the need in 1947 for the United States to practice the values that it preached, since not only the United States but the cause of democracy itself suffered around the world because of American race problems. As President, Truman had appointed a Committee on Civil Rights which issued a smashing indictment of segregation practices. His advisers were acutely aware in 1948 that Truman must have the support of the black vote as well as many other groups. His appointment in earlier years and his cautious, although continued, advocacy of civil rights were sufficient in the eyes of most black voters to establish his superiority over his political opponents.

The latent strife in the Democratic ranks of the later New Deal, although considerably sublimated in wartime, erupted to hit Truman with force in the postwar years. But from a low in popularity in 1945 and 1946, much of it brought about by attempts to please all groups at once, Truman made a spirited comeback in 1947 and 1948. His efforts in foreign policy such as the Truman Doctrine and the Marshall Plan were well accepted, but his efforts on behalf of labor, the farmer, blacks, and the consumer and low- and middle-income taxpayers were to become the basis for the most astounding upset in the history of American presidential elections. The Republican-dominated 80th Congress helped Truman considerably by its intransigency and inaction in the face of the national problems with which the President continually confronted it. It was scarcely a political accident that led to Truman's decision to call the 80th Congress back into special session in the critical summer of 1948.

Suggestions for Reading

A list of suggested readings has been arranged for each chapter of this book. The student should realize they are selective, and that the bases for that selectivity are works which are significant, stimulating, and of continuing use. Many of the titles shown are available in paperback and this is indicated by an asterisk. Interested students of American history, however, should be aware of the most complete and most fascinating bibliography source of all, *Harvard Guide To American History*. This magnificent volume, found in the reference room of any college library, not only has complete citations by topic in endless variety, but even describes for the student the novels bearing upon each period in American history.

Two general works tell the entire Truman story in Cabell Phillips, *The Truman Presidency* (1966), and Alfred Steinberg, *The Man from Missouri* (1962). Truman tells it himself in his *Memoirs*, 2 vols., (1955). See also B. J. Bernstein and A. J. Matusow, eds., *The Truman Administration: A Documentary History* (1966), and B. J. Bernstein, ed., *Politics and Policies of the Truman Administration** (1970).

On the atomic bomb, see R. C. Batchelder, *The Irreversible Decision, 1939–1959* (1962), and J. I. Lieberman, *The Scorpion and the Tarantula: The Struggle to Control Atomic Weapons, 1945–1949* (1970). The possibility that the United States may have dropped the bomb for secondary reasons of diplomatic pressure on Russia is barely mentioned in Herbert Feis, *The Atomic Bomb and the End of World War II* (1966) and in Len Giovanetti and Fred Freed, *The Decision to Drop the Bomb* (1964). This becomes an emphatic theme in Gar Alperovitz, *Atomic Diplomacy: Hiroshima and Potsdam* (1965). On the Potsdam Conference see Herbert Feis, *Between War and Peace* (1960). On the postwar trials, see Eugene Davidson, *The Trial of the Germans: Nuremberg 1945–1946* (1966), and the very relevant Telford Taylor, *Nuremberg and Vietnam: An American Tragedy* (1970).

The literature on the Cold War grows steadily larger. The older writings, for the most part, took the view that the difficulties could virtually all be laid at the Soviet door. Such are W. H. McNeill, *America, Britain, and Russia* (1953); John Spanier, *American Foreign Policy Since 1945* (rev. ed. 1965); Norman Graebner, *Cold War Diplomacy: American Foreign Policy, 1945–1960* (1962), and Herbert Feis, *Churchill, Roosevelt, and Stalin** (1953). The more recent works have tended to put more of the blame on American foreign policy for its lack of understanding of Russian background and needs, and for its insistence on the status quo in the world order. Perhaps the most scholarly is Walter LaFeber, *America, Russia, and the Cold War** (rev. ed. 1972). LaFeber also edited two useful collections, *The Origins of the Cold War, 1941–1947** (1971), *and America in the Cold War: Twenty Years of Revolution and Response, 1947–1967** (1969). A powerful revisionist scholar is Gabriel Kolko, whose works include *The Politics of War: The World and United States Foreign Policy, 1943–1945* (1965); *The Roots of American Foreign Policy: An Analysis of Power and Purpose** (1969), and *The Limits of Power** (1971). See also David Horovitz, *The Free World Colossus: A Critique of American Foreign Policy in the Cold War** (rev. ed. 1971); the same author's *Empire and Revolution* (1969); Ronald Steel, *Pax Americana** (1967); T. H. Paterson, ed., *The Cold War Critics** (1971); D. F. Fleming, *The Cold War and its Origins*, 2 vols. (1951); and L. C. Gardner, *Architects of Illusion* (1972). Still another group has attempted to see the Cold War rivalry chiefly in terms of the imbalance following the upset of Europe's balance of power by World War II, such as Lewis Halle, *The Cold War as History* (1967). A detailed and detached European view is in André Fontaine, *History of the Cold War*, 2 vols. (1970). See also John Lukacs, *A New History of the Cold War** (1966). Herbert Feis has continued his traditional view in *From Trust to Terror: The Onset of the Cold War, 1945–1950* (1970). J. L. Gaddis, *The United States and the Origins of the Cold War 1941–1947** (1972) rejects many of the revisionist arguments. A fine essay by a contemporary of the early postwar events is Walter Lippmann, *The Cold War** (new ed. 1972). A scholarly survey of the changes involved for the United States is W. G. Carleton, *The Revolution in American Foreign Policy** (1967). The dispute between cold war points of view can be seen readily in L. C. Gardner, A. M. Schlesinger, Jr., and Hans Morgenthau, *The Origins of the Cold War** (1970).

For the Far East, see Herbert Feis, *China Tangle*° (1967); J. K. Fairbank, *The United States and China*° (rev. ed. 1971); Tang Tsou, *America's Failure in China, 1941–1950*° (1963); and K. S. Latourette, *The American Record in the Far East, 1945–1951* (1952). For documents consult the United States Department of State, *United States Relations with China, 1944–1949* (1949).

For Russian-American relations, see A. B. Ulam, *Expansion and Coexistence: The History of Soviet Foreign Policy, 1917–1967* (1968), and the same author's *The Rivals: America and Russia Since World War II*° (1972).

2

President in His Own Right

Truman and the Election of 1948

IN JUNE of 1948 the Republicans moved jubilantly toward Philadelphia to nominate "the next President" in that rare combination of honky-tonk carnival, flamboyant rhetoric, and hard-headed political vote swapping that is the American presidential party convention. Their reasons for celebration were understandable. With a resounding victory for the GOP behind them in 1946, the smug assurance that they had defeated administration proposals in Congress, and with excellent public opinion polls in the background, Republicans had ample cause for premature rejoicing. Leading contender for the first prize was New York's Governor Thomas E. Dewey, the darling of the eastern international wing of the party, and whose awesome organization was leaving no possibility of adding delegates unexplored. His chief threat was Senator Robert A. Taft of Ohio, a man of integrity and congressional leadership, but seriously hampered by isolationism, antilabor conservatism, and a severe lack of voter appeal. Close behind the acknowledged front-runners were Harold E. Stassen of Minnesota, a liberal internationalist attractive to the younger voter, and a clutch of favorite-son entries.

Early presidential state primaries had established the favorites and virtually eliminated other hopefuls. General Eisenhower, then president of Columbia University, had flatly declared his refusal to be a candidate. General Douglas MacArthur, then military administrator of Japan, coyly announced in March that he would accept any public duty to which he might be "called." An organization underwritten by several men of wealth and supported by the Hearst papers then began a search for

delegates. Early primaries in Wisconsin and Nebraska quickly disillusioned the General's supporters, since he finished a remote second to
Stassen in the former state and far down in a long list of also-rans
in Nebraska. Stassen's showing, however, caused the Dewey organization
to move in force into Oregon to curb this potential danger. Several
weeks' intensive campaigning served to bring home a smashing victory
for the Dewey candidacy. As the candidates moved toward Philadelphia,
Dewey and Taft were clearly the leaders, with Stassen in the wings
if the two should deadlock. Favorite son Earl Warren, popular and
liberal Governor of California, and Senator Vandenberg of Michigan
both had a handful of delegates but were not considered to be serious
contenders.

The GOP 1948 convention was noteworthy in several respects of
widely varying importance. From a popular viewpoint it was unusual
since it was the first presidential convention to be carried on the new
medium of television. Several million set-owners on the Eastern seaboard
were able to view the spectacle. Of considerably more significance was
the fact that, although the Republicans denounced the men, the methods,
and the philosophy of the New Deal, they made no attempt whatever
to condemn or repeal any of its legislative enactments. No better indication of the enduring place of the reforms of the New Deal could have
been made. The domestic planks of the Republican platform generally
followed the Taft leadership in Congress. Credit was claimed for tax
reduction and the Taft-Harley Act in the labor-management field. For
the future, a cautious promise to take action in the field of federal
low-cost housing and urban slum clearance was made, since here Senator
Taft (variously styled as "Mr. Republican" and "Mr. Conservative")
was several steps ahead of his very conservative Southern Democratic
allies. A relatively strong civil rights plank was offered that called for
legislation to end lynching and poll taxes and demanded "equal opportunity to work." In the field of foreign policy the leadership of Senator
Vandenberg and the international wing, aided by a concurrent crisis
in Allied occupation of Berlin, won over the isolationists and Colonel
Robert McCormick's *Chicago Tribune* following. President Truman's
Marshall Plan was obliquely supported by the approval accorded to
the principle of American aid to friendly and peaceful nations.

Although a potential joint effort against Dewey was begun between
Taft supporters and more ardent isolationists, the effective and well-
organized Dewey machine showed an impressive 434 votes out of a
needed 548 on the first roll call. Taft followed with 224 votes and Stassen
was third with 157. Favorite sons Vanderberg with 62 and Warren with
59 headed a long list of those obviously out of contention. Dewey
workers swayed additional delegates their way after the first ballot.
The second round moved Dewey up to 515, only 33 short of a majority,

while Taft made only imperceptible progress. A recess disclosed the impossibility of a combined anti-Dewey effort and all candidates thereupon withdrew so that Dewey's nomination could be unanimous. The nominee's choice for Vice President was Governor Warren of California, much to the dismay of the Midwestern elements of the party so accustomed to an important place on every national ticket since the days of Abraham Lincoln. A promise to Warren that the vice presidency would be liberated from its unimportant role brought the reluctant Governor around, and the convention accepted their presidential nominee's choice by acclamation.

In stark contrast to the joyous Republicans, the Democrats made their way to Philadelphia several weeks later in an atmosphere of pessimism and gloom. Truman's chances were considered remote by virtually all but Truman himself. His opposition sought out General Eisenhower as a popular contender, but the General not only refused the offer but discovered, in any case, that he was a Republican. A known favorite of the late President Roosevelt's for high office, Supreme Court Justice William O. Douglas, was also approached, but Douglas refused to consider any such offer. With these two possibilities disposed of, the convention settled down to give Truman the delegate votes he had known he possessed all the time. The refusal of some Southern delegates to vote kept the nomination from being unanimous. Truman's acceptance speech disclosed his intent to call the balky 80th Congress back for a special summer session, and simultaneously revealed a fiery, scrapping candidate who would never admit defeat until the votes were counted. Only the choice of vice presidential nominee and a plank on civil rights offered the delegates any opportunity for controversy. Truman preferred Justice Douglas, but he refused again. The issue of a running mate was resolved by the keynote speech of the temporary chairman of the convention, Senator Alben W. Barkley of Kentucky. That 70-year old made such a rousing, fighting speech as to provoke a 30-minute demonstration from a previously lethargic body and ensure his nomination for the vice presidency.[1]

The Democratic platform reviewed and heartily approved all of the administration's efforts in the field of foreign policy. The Republicans were heatedly blamed for inflation and for failure to take action in many of the nation's problems as set before them by President Truman. The platform went on in specific terms to commit the Democrats to legislative action for expansion of Social Security, repeal of Taft-Hartley, a raise in the minimum wage, slum clearance and federal low-cost housing, a national health program, and federal aid to education. The real

---

[1] As Vice President, the amiable Barkley's most memorable contribution was his coining of the appellation "Veep" to describe the position he occupied.

fireworks came about with a civil rights plank. Here the Southern delegates favored the usual weak and ambiguous statement. In the end, however, this policy and several Southern amendments were decisively defeated in favor of a strong and forthright commitment from Northern and urban forces led by Hubert H. Humphrey, Jr., the Mayor of Minneapolis and a candidate for Senator. The position of the Democratic party thereby became a strong dedication to such principles as the right to full and equal political participation; the right to equal opportunity of employment; the right to security of person; and the right of equal treatment in the armed services. By so doing, the Democrats were, for the first time, repudiating and rebuking those many Southern conservatives who consistently allied themselves with Republicans in opposition to liberal or civil libertarian legislation. This new "bill of rights" was too much for some Southern delegates, and the Mississippi delegation and part of Alabama's marched out of the convention defiantly waving the Confederate flag. Although Senator Richard Russell of Georgia reaped some of this dissidence in polling 263 votes on the first presidential ballot, Truman's total of nearly one thousand votes ended what was a formality in any case.

Two new political parties advanced presidential candidates in the summer of 1948 to further add to Truman's political headaches. Anti–Truman and anti–civil rights groups from among the more reactionary elements of the deep South gathered in Birmingham to create the States' Rights Democratic party (popularly known as Dixiecrats) and nominate for President and Vice President respectively Governors J. Strom Thurmond of South Carolina and Fielding L. Wright of Mississippi. The hold that these state officials had on the electoral machinery of their states was of far more importance than their leadership in the rest of the South, but the loss of any electoral votes at this point was a potential blow to Democratic strength. Countering this threat from the right was the impending loss of votes from the left occasioned by the naming of Henry A. Wallace as the presidential candidate of the newly formed Progressive party. The Progressives, with Senator Glen Taylor of Idaho as vice presidential nominee, were a mixture of independents, radicals and idealistic young voters who were drawn to Wallace through his speeches attacking America's belligerent part in the Cold War. The platform also called forthrightly for equal rights for all minority groups, but reserved its emphasis for a denunciation of the Truman Doctrine and the Marshall Plan and in demands for disarmament and destruction of all atomic bomb stockpiles. Wallace was clearly not a Communist, but many of his young supporters failed to see the strong influence of a small group of Communists who were successful in guiding the platform and the convention along desired lines.

The 80th Congress, called into special session by Truman on July

26, readily furnished the President with the ammunition he had expected. After denouncing the President's move as a political one—which it obviously was—the Republican majority faced the dilemma of going along with Truman in passing the demanded legislation and letting him take political credit, or defying him and risk being tagged and labeled by the failure to enact even those measures that were a part of their own platform. Secure in the predicted victory of a Republican to the presidency, the Republican-dominated 80th Congress chose the latter course and delivered themselves over to Truman as a whipping boy for the campaign. But Truman faced enormous odds. With the Republican victories of 1946 still evidently part of the political climate, the President was additionally burdened with vote losses in the South to the Dixiecrats and similar defections to the Progressives in New York and other key Eastern states.

Truman's campaign was largely of the "whistle-stop" variety, with a total estimated audience of 6 million, most of them in relatively small groups. Truman's speeches were unsophisticated but pugnaciously confident, and he was frequently at his best in extemporaneous talks and bantering repartee from the rear platform of a special presidential train. He went out of his way to remind labor of the perils they faced from the Republican party, and what the Democrats had done to assure labor of its right to organize and bargain collectively. The farmers were another target for Truman's homey and occasional bitter comments. During one of his most violent moments Truman accused the Republicans before a huge farm audience in Iowa of "sticking a pitchfork in the farmer's back." Republican efforts to curtail farm price supports were recited, and a Republican-dominated Congress effectively pinpointed as the cause for the current shortage in storage bins that farmers were then experiencing. The consumer in general was reminded of Republican opposition to rent controls and action against inflation. Urban groups received strong civil rights talks, and Truman's earlier hasty recognition in May 1948 of the first provisional government of the new nation of Israel was undoubtedly influential with the Jewish urban vote. Crowds greeting Truman grew larger and friendlier. Truman responded readily to approving shouts of "Lay it on 'em, Harry!" and "Give 'em hell, Harry!" by lambasting the 80th Congress as the "Do-Nothing Congress" and the "worst Congress in American history." Observers were still not convinced that the turnouts and the reaction were anything more than the American admiration for a spunky, fighting underdog.

The campaign by Dewey was in sharp contrast with Truman's. He traveled about half as far, but with twice the entourage and number of reporters. The speeches were far fewer, prepared well in advance for press use, and lacking in spontaneity. Truman's invective was matched by a sweet reasonableness in Dewey's talks, so that the general

President Harry Truman begins his scrappy cross-country campaign for reelection in 1948 in front of the nation's capitol. (National Archives)

effect was Dewey as incumbent and Truman as a fierce challenger. Truman's homey earthiness and occasional "corn" was met by Dewey's ringing platitudes and a variety of clichés. Governor Dewey acknowledged that many problems beset the United States, but had "no trick answers and no easy solutions." Americans would soon "begin to move forward again shoulder to shoulder," and the Republican candidate would undertake a great "unsnarling, untangling operation" in Washington. As the acknowledged front-runner, Dewey was chiefly determined not to alienate a single vote with excessive discussion of issues or concrete promises on courses of action.

Truman's victory—the most amazing upset in American presidential history—was predicted only by Truman himself and a few of his aides. Newspapers, pollsters, and columnists were caught with their print down, describing a Dewey victory that never occurred. One of the more blatant of these was preserved in a memorable photograph which shows a grinning Truman the day after the election holding aloft the *Chicago Tribune* with its banner headline, "Dewey Defeats Truman." The surprise of the victory was further accentuated by the decisive margin of its accomplishment. In popular votes, Truman had 24,179,345 to Dewey's 21,991,291 for a plurality of 2,188,054. Thurmond and the Dixiecrats polled 1,176,125, with Wallace and the Progressives virtually the same at 1,157,326. The entire vote was low, with a poor 51.2 percent of the electorate represented. The votes going to the variety of third parties left Truman with only 49.6 percent of the turnout, with Dewey commanding 45.1 percent. In electoral votes, Truman accumulated 303 to Dewey's 189 and Thurmond's 39. The Dixiecrats were able to deny to Truman the electoral votes of Alabama, Mississippi, Louisiana, and South Carolina, but these were of little consequence. Truman was hurt more by the votes going to Wallace in populous states such as New York and Michigan, where Dewey's narrow margin of victory was clearly brought about by voters who chose the Progressive candidate at the expense of the Democratic nominee. On the other hand, Truman's victory was not decided until the following morning because of extremely close races in Ohio, California, and Illinois. A Dewey win in these states would have given him the presidency despite the fact that he lost three states to Truman in the Midwest—Ohio, Wisconsin, and Iowa—that he had previously held against Roosevelt in 1944. The congressional elections followed the same trend, giving the Democrats a 54 to 42 edge in the Senate and a 263 to 171 majority in the House of Representatives.

The lack of accurate information on the 1948 election could in large part be blamed upon various polls such as Gallup, Roper, and Crossley. Chiefly, they failed to carry their inquiries into the last weeks of the campaign, when the issue was evidently decided. They failed to make an accurate assessment of those first listed as "undecided," and their persistent claims and arrogant tone of scientific infallibility led even journalists and politicians to forsake their own findings. More important, however, was accounting for the winning number of voters. The labor vote and the energetic turning out of eligible voters by labor organization workers was a prime factor. A significant item was Truman's appeal to the farmer with his warnings of Republican efforts at undermining price supports. The black vote moved more solidly toward Truman, partly because of the inheritance of the New Deal and his cautious moves in civil rights, but partly also because the rebellion of the Dixiecrats clearly marked the Democrat party as the most logical refuge for the black voter. Truman picked up votes from ethnic and nationality groups for continuing American aid to European countries and for defending immigration statutes against Republican restrictions. In heavily Catholic areas, Truman's belligerent anticommunism evidently served to attract a high vote. Among middle-income and fixed-income groups, Truman was able to point to the Republicans' poor record against inflation and to label successfully their taxation bill as a "rich man's" blessing. In short, Truman had exploited Republican policies that affected a wide range of voters. He had deliberately abandoned the reactionary right wing of the Dixiecrats and the tainted left wing of the Progressives and had achieved his plurality in the huge center that commonly produces a victor in the American presidency race. His fighting spirit and passionate conviction in his cause provided the final clincher.

The presidential election of 1948 was noteworthy for several reasons. It gave fresh evidence that the Democratic party was genuinely the majority party of American politics. Truman's victory and the congressional results effectively put aside Republican claims that previous Roosevelt triumphs had been aberrations explainable by unusual depression circumstances. Voter performance also had further consequences. It warned of dependence on bandwagon psychology of polls and the press, and it successfully moved the professional pollsters from arrogant claims of infallibility to needed changes of technique. Additionally, the closeness of the electoral vote and a possible perversion of the popular will by a House of Representatives' choice for President spurred on attempts to reform the antiquated electoral college.

The Fair Deal, 1949–1952

On January 5, 1949, President Truman's Inaugural Address contained the domestic program which he hoped the new 81st Congress would carry out, labeled specifically for the first time as the "Fair Deal." After referring to the great progress that the country had made in production, prosperity, and new opportunities, Truman went on to point out many areas where additional action was vitally needed. He called attention to the housing plight of many, to the inequities in national health, and to the inadequacy of schools in many localities. The President found acute shortages in electric power, minimum wages far too low, and small business "losing ground to growing monopoly." Labor, Truman said, was unfairly discriminated against by the Taft-Hartley Act, and the nation's farmers faced "an uncertain future." But the 81st Congress, although now with a Democratic majority, showed itself to be just as unresponsive or outrightly hostile to Truman's program as the castigated "Do-Nothing" 80th Congress had been. (The 81st soon came to be referred to in Washington as the "Ho-hum" Congress for its general apathy and sluggishness.) Southern Congressmen used the familiar filibuster tactics to defeat Truman's civil rights efforts, and the Republican-southern Democrat coalition successfully opposed nearly all of the Fair Deal proposals. The 82d Congress of 1951–1952 was no different, and the

Fair Deal was significant more for what it was able to accomplish in the face of opposition than for any path-breaking new efforts in economic measures or social welfare enactments.

One of the significant accomplishments of the Truman administration was the Housing Act of 1949. Ever since the close of the war a serious housing shortage, swollen by demands of returned veterans, had existed. Truman had requested various emergency measures, but inadequate provisions were further weakened by interagency rivalries and the ineptness of the construction industry. Another proponent of federal housing action was "Mr. Republican," Senator Robert A. Taft of Ohio. Taft had tried earlier with the unsuccessful Taft-Ellender-Wagner bill of 1947, admitting that private enterprise had failed in this area and that many communities could approach a solution only with federal help. Taft lent his powerful support to a new bipartisan effort in 1949 which found him joined with Republican Senator Tobey of New Hampshire in urging its passage. Opposition to the bill came from the real estate lobby, conservative Republicans such as Senator John Bricker of Ohio and Harry Cain of Washington, and Southern conservative Democrats Harry Byrd and Willis Robertson of Virginia and John McClellan of Arkansas. The National Housing Act, as finally passed, provided for 810,000 low-cost housing units to be built over the next six years. Provisions for loans and grants for slum clearance and rural housing were also included. The number of units was far below the national need, but passage of the bill marked a recognition of decent housing as an important factor in a democratic society. More importantly, it marked the first move toward the urban renewal programs of the future by its emphasis on a renovation of the inner-core black ghetto areas.

The Truman administration managed to get a few of its recommendations passed. In 1949 Congress amended the Fair Labor Standards Act of 1938 by raising the minimum hourly wage to $0.75 per hour, although at the same time adding to the number of jobs to be exempted from the act's provisions. The Social Security Act of 1935 was expanded in 1950 to bring an additional 10 million within the coverage of the Old-age and Survivors' Insurance plan. Benefits were raised more than 75 percent, and another amendment to the Act in 1952 increased benefits by a further 12.5 percent. Truman reluctantly signed, in 1948, a restricted measure permitting 205,000 persons displaced by the march of nazism and communism to enter the United States. He criticized the bill's discrimination against Jews and Catholics, asking that Congress act more generously. The Displaced Persons Act of 1950 then raised quotas to 415,000 and without discrimination, but still fell far short of the number of refugee applicants. Truman was also successful in opposing legislation sponsored by oil interests to transfer title of offshore, undersea lands to several states. Three states—Texas, Louisiana, and California—were anxious to work with oil companies planning to sink exploratory oil wells in continental shelf areas far outside the tideland limit. The Supreme Court had repeatedly held that the federal government had "dominant rights" over such territory, and Truman insisted that, like any other federal lands, they were the property of the nation's 48 states and not just 3 of the coastal states. He also noted the value of potential oil resources to the needs of national defense. In his successful veto of the proposal Truman tartly stated that "it would be the height of folly for the United States to give away the vast quantities of oil contained in the continental shelf and then buy back this same oil at stiff prices for use by the Army, Navy, and Air Force in the defense of the nation."[2]

Truman's efforts to simplify and make more efficient the executive branch of government met with considerable approval from Congress. The Hoover Commission, a bipartisan group appointed for the task in 1947, had presented its two years of effort in a series of reports that found a variety of duplication, inefficiency, and unclear lines of responsibility and authority in the executive branch. With a warning from the commission that such defects severely inhibited the nation's Chief Executive in the performance of his duties and in his response to national crises, Congress passed the Reorganization Act of 1949. Under the terms of the act, Truman was to present his solutions to Congress for its approval. More than two dozen such plans affecting various agencies under the President were sent to Congress. Only one, the Truman proposal to create a department of public welfare, was turned down. Most of the changes accepted enabled Truman to coordinate scattered programs, eliminate duplicative agencies and governmental departments, and generally improve and control administrative bureaucracy in the executive branch.

In general, the program of the Truman administration for 1949–1952 was more thwarted than rewarded. Notable among the legislative proposals that were defeated was the Brannan Plan, named after Truman's Secretary of Agriculture appointed in 1948, Charles F. Brannan. The plan was an innovative look at the frustration of national farm policies. It proposed a completely new approach through perishable farm commodities, leaving the nonperishable products largely unchanged.[3] Under the Brannan Plan, both the farmer and the consumer would have benefited. Instead of paying once through taxes for government subsidies to farmers and twice through high retail prices for farm products, the

---

[2] Harry S. Truman, *Memoirs: Years of Trial and Hope*, Vol. 2 (Garden City, N.Y.: 1956), p. 487.

[3] Chiefly meat animals, milk, butter, poultry, eggs, fruits, and vegetables, which Brannan said accounted for "roughly 75 percent of cash farm receipts."

consumer would pay only the price that the normal market might demand for perishable products. Assuming that this would be lower than a supported price, the Brannan Plan would have assured the farmer any difference between a low market price and an estimated fair price. The latter would be arrived at by means of an "Income Support Standard" instead of the old parity method, meaning a continuously adjusted average of gross farm income for the latest ten years. Since the ten years prior to 1949 were generally good farm years, the Income Support Standard would have assured the farmer a fair price for his products over a foreseeable length of time while also giving the consumer lower prices. The joker in the Brannan Plan was directed against Big Agriculture, with a provision that no farmer could receive government price supports in excess of $26,100 worth of his crop. This brought the instant opposition of the organization representing the largest agricultural interests, the American Farm Bureau Federation. Although the Farm Bureau and the Grange sought to publicize the idea that the Brannan Plan would provide more government "interference" than previous government supports, their lobbying against the $26,100 limit in payments was in sharp contrast to the favorable arguments for its acceptance by the small farmers' organization, the National Farmers' Union. Conservative Republicans and Southern Democrats, many citing as their reason "more" government control of the economy, defeated the plan. In its stead was enacted an Agricultural Act that provided for the 90 percent of parity supports to continue for another year. After 12 months, it could drop 10 percent, and by 1951 was to become a "flexible" support ranging between 75 and 90 percent of parity.

Administration efforts at extending federal aid to education also ran into several cross fires and consequent defeat. The initial proposal immediately drew militant amendments from black Congressmen assuring that no federal aid would go to segregated schools, and public insistence from Roman Catholic clergy that their parochial schools share equally in any such federal benefits. Controversy within the Democratic party itself over black and Catholic demands was so convulsive that the measure quickly died. Another notable failure was the Truman national health insurance program. The 1949 proposal differed slightly from Truman's previous plans for such service, but in general the plan followed suggested combinations of costs born by employers, employees, and government subsidies. It was opposed by the American Medical Association with even more intensity than the organization had brought against Social Security and all other public health proposals. The association levied a special assessment on each member and fought the legislation through newspaper and radio means as well as with heavily increased lobbying in Congress. Its use of the media was constant enough to retain in the public mind the stigma of "socialized medicine" with which the AMA successfully labeled the idea. Although the slogan was of dubious political reference, and although Truman vehemently pointed out that the proposal did not even bring the nation's doctors into the program, as did the English version of nationalized medicine, it was not sufficient to overcome public apathy and congressional distaste. The administration bill never even reached a vote in Congress. Truman was equally unsuccessful in bringing about a Missouri Valley Authority patterned after TVA, or in initiating consideration of similar treatment for the Columbia and Colorado River valleys. Truman's efforts to bring about repeal of the Taft-Hartley law were to no avail. Large groups in Congress, including Senator Taft himself, were willing to modify some of the bill's original provisions; but Truman, with labor's urging, held out for total repeal. Only a very minor amendment was finally voted in 1951 providing for some opportunities for union-shop clauses in labor contracts.

The 1948 resurrection of New Deal strength that brought Truman in as a surprise presidential winner was never reflected in congressional approval of his Fair Deal program, and his popularity slowly slid downhill again from that high point. The conservative Republican-Southern Democrat alliance was the chief factor responsible, although another strong influence was the focus of national attention on foreign affairs. The corruption exposed among Truman aides and appointees, although obviously not attributable to Truman, was scarcely advantageous to the administration image. Truman's friend of National Guard days, Harry H. Vaughan, who was promoted to Brigadier General in that body as a White House aide, was found to be guilty of dispensing governmental favoritism to a friendly businessman and receiving a gift of several deep-freeze units. Two of Vaughan's friends, commonly referred to as "5 percenters" because of the commissions extracted for influence peddling, were sent to jail after Senate investigations. George Schoeneman, a Truman appointment as Commissioner of Internal Revenue, resigned amid tax scandals that caused the discharge of dozens of BIR personnel and the jailing of nine. Seen in retrospect, the Fair Deal's chief claim to historical fame was that it actually accomplished as much as it did, considering the times and the adverse Congresses. In attempting to stem the tide of inequitable tax bills, xenophobic immigration acts, and antilabor legislation, Truman probably vetoed more major enactments than any President since Grover Cleveland. It is perhaps significant in itself that, although it did not open up any innovative domestic measures, it was nevertheless able to preserve the social legislation of the New Deal and even expand it in some directions. Truman's Fair Deal was influential in reducing and tempering the hostility of business toward labor, and of advancing a great public awareness of national social needs that was to be of value a decade later.

Civil Rights, the Hiss Case, and McCarthyism

Harry Truman's early approach to civil rights for blacks was cautious and sometimes ambiguous. He was at first more concerned with equality of rights than with the moral imperatives of desegregation, and invariably kept his support for civil rights measures within the bounds of public sentiment and congressional priorities. When the southern Senators filibustered his Fair Employment Practices Committee legislation in 1946, Truman refused to take any action in Congress or publicly against such tactics. The same group effectively blocked subsequent attempts in 1950 and 1952, and the Republican-Southern Democrat coalition scuttled virtually all of the President's civil rights program. His Committee on Civil Rights published its report, *To Secure These Rights,* in October 1947, and this formed the basis for his ten recommendations to Congress. Other presidential committees had stoutly recommended an end to segregation in the armed forces and in higher education. Truman endorsed the results, although without supplying any active leadership from the White House, and Congress ignored both reports and recommendations. With the advent of the 1948 campaign, Truman became much more forthright in the cause of civil rights. His willingness to cease Southern appeasement was indicated by his strong appeals to urban blacks and various ethnic groups. Truman was the first President of the United States to campaign in New York City's Harlem. Under persistent pressure from black and liberal groups and with the threat of Henry Wallace cutting into Democratic voting strongholds in the great industrial sites, Truman barred discrimination in federal jobs and named a committee to consider means for desegregating the armed forces. By executive pressure and directives and by aiding the committee's quiet investigation, the armed services were persuaded to end most of the practices of segregation and provide equality of opportunity to white and black alike. Although a huge and important beginning was made, there were still some segregated units in the Korean War. Integration in European units did not get under way until 1952, Truman's last year in office. The Department of Justice in Truman's administration also was active in breaking down the bars of segregation in interstate transportation and higher education. Following a Supreme Court decision outlawing restrictive real estate covenants, federal housing agencies moved slowly to implement the decision.

By the time the Korean War bagan in 1950, Congress and the nation were exhibiting rising hostility toward civil rights efforts. Those who sought an end to segregation were frequently denounced as Communists, and the nation moved into another of its historical periods of irrational intolerance and hysterical attempts to ensure the loyalty of its citizens.

In this area of civil rights Truman was too deeply committed to Cold War anticommunism to weigh very heavily the possibility of demanding individual rights against the menacing factor of subversion possibilities. He was also fearful that the Republicans would exploit the issue politically. As early as March 1947, he instituted by executive order a Loyalty Review Board through which the federal government could discharge employees on "reasonable grounds for belief in disloyalty." He came to this reluctantly after heavy pressure from the FBI, the Attorney General's office, and their congressional allies, and after the Republican congressional victories of 1946. Congressional witnesses such as J. Edgar Hoover and Attorney General Thomas Clark insisted that the nation was gravely threatened by subversion and, although supposedly directed against actual sabotage or overt acts, it became evident that such government officials considered any political radicalism or individuals with whom the employee associated sufficient to establish a "proclivity" for subversion. By 1950 Loyalty Review Board standards had deteriorated to the point that mere suspicion or doubt had replaced tangible evidence in bringing about discharge or necessary lack of security clearance for federal employees. The administration used the clause in the Smith Act of 1940 making it illegal to "advocate the overthrow and destruction of the government" to seize 11 of the Communist party's hierarchy for prosecution. In a much publicized trial running for the first nine months of 1949 before a federal grand jury, they were found guilty and sentenced to prison by Judge Harold R. Medina. The verdict was finallly upheld by the Supreme Court in *Eugene Dennis et al.* v. *the United States,* although the dissenting Justice William O. Douglas warned that the road to the police state was reached by judging free speech on the shaky grounds of intent rather than on actual substance.

In 1950 a number of security proposals before Congress were tied together under the designation of the McCarran Internal Security Act, named after its chief sponsor, Democratic Senator Pat McCarran of Nevada. This highly involved and severely restrictive bill set up a Subversive Activities Control Board, which, after hearings, could pronounce an organizaton subversive. The organization was then required to register with the board and submit its membership lists and an account of its financial resources. The act barred Communists from employment in defense industries; made them ineligible, even though citizens, to receive an American passport; provided for the arrest of Communists in wartime; and forbade Communists or any other foreigner who had belonged to a "totalitarian organization" from migrating to the United States. Truman vetoed the bill for two reasons. The Justice, State, and Defense Departments and the CIA all advised Truman that the bill would seriously damage their intelligence and security operations rather than aid them. Secondly, Truman felt that it was legalistically vague and unduly discriminatory, and that its provisions were completely un-workable. He used the homey analogy of being as practical as "requiring thieves to register with the sheriff" to describe its registration provisions. Congress, in an atmosphere of semihysteria, quickly overrode his veto. Senator McCarran was also the cosponsor of the McCarran-Walter Immigration and Nationality Act of June, 1952. The first major overhaul of the immigration laws since 1924, the act nevertheless retained the sorely outdated national origins quota system. It also sought to battle communism by permitting deportation of immigrants, even though citizens, once they were accused of subversion. They could also be subject to denaturalization proceedings. Despite the evidence offered of the vital contribution of immigrant genius and industry in American growth, patriotic and veterans' organizations were able to offer Congress more acceptable arguments on prohibiting the admission of aliens. The act's only generous feature was a provision setting up for the first time an admission quota for Orientals (2,000 per year) and permitting them to become citizens. Truman's protesting veto based upon its discriminatory and undemocratic restrictions was shouted down by margins as substantial as its companion bill of two years before.

The basis for the social and political climate that supported the Truman administration's Loyalty Board procedures and restrictive legislation, such as the McCarran Acts, was readily apparent. Anti-Soviet feelings emerged even before the war's ending, and the crises of the postwar period accentuated the fears expressed regarding Soviet communism. The House Un-American Activities Committee, permanently established as of 1945, was quickly engaged in seeking information on alleged Communist infiltrations and in revealing attempts at Communist propaganda. The committee's irresponsible and wildly aimed charges at every sector from the Chief Executive to Hollywood's movie makers and the predeliction of its members for publicity at any cost helped to discount the committee's accusations. Nor were the Communists as an organization an appreciable threat to American government. Claiming a probably exaggerated membership of 75,000 in 1946, it shrank during the early 1950s to less than 25,000 and, according to FBI Director J. Edgar Hoover, was in a continuing decline. The thorough purging of Communist influence in CIO unions in 1949 and 1950 by an aroused membership added to the diminution of Communist importance. Nevertheless, continuing espionage and spy-scare cases were far better known to the general public than the FBI statistics and were responsible for mounting fears and apprehensions.

In the immediate postwar years, espionage seemed disturbingly close when a Canadian investigatory commission exposed more than 20 Canadians who were sending classified information, some of it referring to atomic matters, to the Soviet Union. In February of 1950, however, the arrest for espionage in England of Dr. Klaus Fuchs, a well-known atomic scientist, provided alarming consequences in the United States. Dr. Fuchs, a German citizen, had fled to Britain in 1933 in the face of Nazi seizure of power. As a part of the British atomic research effort, Fuchs was one of many English scientists and those of other countries who came to the United States to assist on the Los Alamos atomic project. He had subsequently returned to the British atomic research center at Harwell, where he supervised the section on theoretical physics. Fuchs' confession revealed that he had handed over information to Soviet agents on British and American nuclear developments. But Fuchs' confession implicated his American confederates. The first arrest was that of Harry Gold, a research chemist in a Philadelphia hospital clinic. Gold also confessed, and the espionage ring was found to include David Greenglass, an Army sergeant and machinist at Los Alamos; his sister and her husband, Ethel and Julius Rosenberg; and Morton Sobell. Dr. Fuchs received a 14-year prison sentence in England. Gold, Greenglass, and Sobell received varying prison terms. The Rosenbergs, convicted of passing atomic data to Soviet consulate officials in New York City, were given the death sentence. Despite appeals to the Supreme Court, the sentence was upheld and carried out in June 1953.

The most celebrated and publicized case of all these unhappy times came about from the House Un-American Activities Committee's sifting through the charges made by repentant ex-Communists. One Whittaker Chambers, who testified that he had been a Communist party member from 1924 to 1936 and had already turned over this information to federal authorities in 1939, revealed in testimony given before the committee a number of names active as cell leaders in underground communism. One of these he alleged to be Alger Hiss, then head of the Carnegie Endowment for International Peace. The scion of a noted Baltimore family, Hiss was a Johns Hopkins and Harvard Law School graduate who had started in his government career as a secretary to Supreme Court Justice Oliver Wendell Holmes. He had been on the legal staff of AAA in the Department of Agriculture and had moved to the State Department in 1936. Here he advanced to a deputy directorship in Special Political Affairs, and became a specialist in the organization of the embryo United Nations. In this capacity he was part of the American delegation to the Dumbarton Oaks, Yalta, and San Francisco conferences and the first UN meeting at London. Secretaries of State Hull and Stettinius considered him of exceptional ability, and Republican Senator Vandenberg, James Byrnes, and Dean Acheson all thought highly of him.

Hiss immediately requested a hearing, during the course of which he denied under oath that he had ever been a member of the Communist party or that he knew Chambers. In a subsequent confrontation, Hiss hesitantly identified Chambers by another name, but continued to insist that he had not been a Communist. When Chambers repeated the latter charge in public, Hiss sued for libel. Chambers introduced evidence purporting to show that Hiss had given him photographs of secret government documents, and Hiss was indicted for perjury by a federal grand jury. After a trial of six weeks the jury was unable to reach a verdict. A second trial began in November 1949 and a second jury found Hiss guilty of perjury in January 1950. Sentenced to five years in prison, Hiss entered the penitentiary in 1951 insisting upon his innocence. He emerged less than four years later after having been refused another trial. Still denying Chambers' charges, Alger Hiss faded into obscurity as a bookstore proprietor.

The significance of the Hiss trial was widespread, but in symbolical terms. To those who originally held all New Deal and Fair Deal adherents to be the epitome of evil, Hiss was living, breathing evidence of their previously unheeded protests. Repudiated ultraconservatives and Roosevelt haters of varying degrees combined to find in Alger Hiss the embodiment of the despised intellectual Brain Truster who had come to positions of influence in government and had been so instrumental in turning around and turning out the traditional 19th century values. All that had gone wrong in the world or that offered a threat to America, from the growing challenge of Soviet strength in Europe to Communist victories over Chiang in China, could conceivably be pinpointed in this ex–government official. Furthermore, if Hiss were guilty, who could say how many more similar ex–New Dealers might be entrenched in the upper reaches of government? On the other hand, liberals angrily rejected such scapegoatism and guilt by association. New Deal and Fair Deal supporters saw in Hiss not alleged treason but a convenient target for the frustrations of the opposition and the uninformed. Additionally, both American and English students of jurisprudence found the trials and the evidence shockingly lacking in the substance needed for a verdict of guilty. They pointed to the dependence upon a chief witness who was a confessed perjurer and whose testimony was subsequently found to be shot through with elaborate misstatements, and to the role of a committee noted for the sensationalism of its charges rather than for the accuracy of its evidence. To many it seemed as English analyst Alistair Cooke described it, a generation on trial, and against a backdrop of near hysteria induced by the fears and crises of the times.[4] Subsequent technical challenges such as were raised in conjunction with the photographic evidence, and the puzzling, unresolved aspects of the case continued to cast a dubious aura around the verdict. But the clamor surrounding the trial was of considerable

---

[4] Alistair Cooke, *A Generation on Trial* (New York: 1952).

value to publicity-hungry demagogues who could readily exploit such public fears and apprehensions under the guise of rooting out "disloyalty" and protecting the nation from "treasonable" activity. No one was less scrupulous and more successful than the senatorial demagogue who left behind the term "McCarthyism" to describe the essence of his activities.

The Joseph R. McCarthy who was later to become the Junior Senator from Wisconsin began, constructed, and ended his political career on an amazing succession of lies. When he first ran for a state judgeship at age 30 against an incumbent who was 66 years old, he not only represented his opponent as age 73 (or occasionally 89) but sliced a year off his own age for added effect. Both their ages were a matter of public record, but Joe McCarthy discarded recorded fact for the big lie and never looked back when he found that he got away with it. Campaigning for a senatorial seat after the war, he claimed to have been wounded, which was completely false; to have enlisted in the Marines as a buck private when he had actually written for a commission; and to have been a tail gunner with many combat missions to his credit when neither assertion had an ounce of truth in it. After four obscure years in Congress, McCarthy hit upon the issue of communism to promote his sagging political fortunes. In a speech delivered to the Republican Women's Club of Wheeling, West Virginia, McCarthy waved a piece of paper at his audience which he said contained the names of 205 Communists infesting the State Department. (The number was reduced in subsequent speeches to 81 and 57.) There was not a word of truth in the accusation, and McCarthy was never able to document his charges, nor was the FBI ever able to find any substance in any one of his reckless slanders. He found, however, that the big lie technique served to keep one's name in the headlines, and that both press and public were too preoccupied by ever newer and more sensational charges to worry about checking on last week's accusations. McCarthy also found that a large element of the electorate—confused, tense, and embittered over world crises they were too uninformed to assess—was all too willing to believe that victories in the Far East and Europe by those defined as enemies of the United States could have been brought about by possible "treasonous" behavior in their own government.

With the outbreak of the Korean War in 1950, this attitude intensified and McCarthy's power grew. Politicians were afraid of crossing the Senator from Wisconsin for fear of being branded "Red" or "pro-Communist," and even men of integrity such as Senator Taft of Ohio were willing to endorse McCarthy's vicious demagogery for partisan advantage. McCarthy trampled roughshod over constitutional rights, severely damaged the United States' reputation and the American image abroad, and subjected respected public figures ranging from General Marshall and Dean Acheson to his colleagues in the Senate to guttersnipe abuse. McCarthyism employed guilt by association, incredible innuendo, and outright massive and multiple lie techniques to ruin the reputation of hundreds in his headlong rush to publicity. Not a single charge was ever proven, but a climate was created that provoked and sustained suspicion of many with backgrounds of liberalism or of those who insisted too strongly on the constitutionality of rights for all Americans. McCarthyism stifled dissent and promoted ideological conformity; it undermined the faith of democratic people in their own government without any rational basis for such a loss. Republicans found McCarthy's irresponsible charges to be of benefit to them as attacks upon a Democratic administration and the congressional majority. But they were to find that McCarthyism could backfire, and that the reputations of Republicans could be blackened with its excesses as readily as could the Democrats.

The Truman administration had moved to a position of restrictiveness in individual civil rights even though it moved at the same time to widen civil rights for blacks. Beginning with federal employee loyalty oaths in 1947, it advanced increasingly into the area of "loyalty checks" and security hearings for its employees or those engaged in defense activities. Many, as Truman later admitted, were discharged on the thinnest kind of evidence. The wild speeches of Attorney General Howard McGrath and other administration figures warning that Communists were likely to be found on any street corner or in any classroom were tactics that aided and abetted the spread of McCarthyism. In attempting to achieve absolutes in security and in efforts to preempt the Republicans where disloyalty and internal security issues were concerned, the Truman administration helped to foster a climate of repression and irrational emotionalism. Although President Truman and his associates initially and sincerely sought to erect the necessary safeguards for the protection of individual liberties, the swelling wave of federal measures and partisan pressures soon pushed aside or submerged constitutional rights that would have been unquestioned a decade before.

Continued Containment

The United States, having pronounced itself in 1947 wedded to the policy of containment of what was considered to be Soviet Communist expansionism, proceeded to implement that policy in a variety of ways. It sought to achieve containment through foreign economic aid and increasingly after 1949 through military aid. American military strength was improved, and work begun and completed on the development of a hydrogen bomb. Containment was sought through achieving these considerations within the UN and, when this yielded relatively small results, by unilateral action bypassing the UN. Regional organizations were established and promoted, and regional alliances that abandoned all the traditional warnings of American foreign policy were adopted and fostered.

Foreign economic aid, one of the earliest of postwar considerations because of the crushed economies of Europe, was also one of the prime factors in bringing about in Berlin the first major crisis to confront the second Truman administration. Perhaps if Germany had not been split into zones, her conquerors might have had to face her problems in some degree of unity. But as Walter Lippmann had commented, even if all four powers had been veritable angels they could not have agreed on policies for Germany. Divided into four zones with varying economic bases and resources, whose occupiers acted from differing philosophies and domestic pressures, the "German problem" was impossible of ready solution. France, not having been invited to Potsdam, was an occupying power which did not feel constrained to obey the Potsdam agreements. She was evidently the first to seek to achieve some measure of reparations out of current production, although both the United States and Russia later evaded this regulation. The French continued to obstruct the idea of zonal merger, particularly since they feared that the American commander, General Lucius Clay, would build up the giant German industries of the Ruhr and include pro-Nazi or ex-Nazi administrators in control. By 1948, however, the control possible in a unified West Germany outweighed the French difficulties in trying to make a separate entity out of the Ruhr. France joined her allies and the Benelux nations (Belgium, the Netherlands, and Luxembourg) in a London conference out of which came an agreement on the formation of a West German government. German productive capacity, with aid from the Marshall Plan which would become possible under such a plan, could play an important role in European recovery. To assure the success of such a venture, a new, uniform, and stable currency was needed to replace the old German mark that was so badly inflated that workmen lacked incentive even to pursue their normal job loads. At the announcement regarding the new currency made in March 1948, the Russians began a variety of harassing actions directed against Allied traffic moving through their sector to Berlin. When on June 23 the new currency was actually introduced (the Russians also introduced a new Soviet mark into East Germany and East Berlin) the Russians completely blockaded all rail and automotive access to Berlin. The Allies' agreement with the Soviets unfortunately did not include any documented right of land access. There was, however, a written agreement which specified definite air corridors across the hundred miles of Soviet-held territory between

Berlin and the area held by the Western powers. General Clay had first suggested that the blockade be smashed by armored troops, but Truman refused. Instead, an enormous airlift was established with every available American and British plane pressed into service to supply Berliners not only with food and coal, but even raw materials to keep factories producing. The airlift was steadily expanded and presented an amazingly efficient and psychologically successful operation. At the same time, the three Western powers instituted their own blockade, cutting off East-West trade and traffic. Negotiations dragged on for nearly a year, with neither four-level talks nor UN compromise proposals making any great progress. In May 1949, the Soviets proposed that both sides end their blockades and convoke a meeting of the Council of Foreign Ministers to consider both the Berlin and the Germany questions. The Western powers were glad to accept such conditions and the blockade came to an end on May 23, 1949.

The Berlin blockade was clearly a Soviet blunder. Not only had it not achieved its aims, but during the interim the Communist candidates had been badly defeated in the Berlin city elections and the Western zones of occupation had become unified. Moving through successive phases as "Bizonia" and "Trizonia," the 11 German states forming the American, British, and French sectors adopted a democratic constitution establishing the Federal Republic of Germany. It chose Bonn as the capital of its new federal system and on September 15, 1949 organized its own government with Konrad Adenauer of the Christian Democratic party as the first chancellor. The Soviets quickly followed suit by denominating their East German zone as the new German Democratic Republic. The United States refused to recognize East Germany's government, but officially signed a peace treaty with the Adenauer government on August 2, 1952.

The Western powers' reasons for not moving out of a position militarily indefensible and lacking in European security reasons were nevertheless understandable enough. Prestige was a powerful factor which could be protected without full-scale warfare, and the new American commitment to maintain forces in Europe could be readily demonstrated. Additionally, an obligation to Berliners and the wish to keep open this window on the Soviet zone were considerations. For the Soviets, the blockade evidently was triggered by the fear of a unified Germany and the hope that such pressures could prevent it. The Soviets were both fearful and suspicious of the American presence in Europe: fearful that the United States would bring about the resurgence of their late mortal enemy, and suspicious because they had been led to believe, by American traditions as much as by Roosevelt's acknowledgment of them, that the Americans would soon withdraw their troops from European soil. Probably the idea of a blockade was conceived as a probing operation to test the truths of these suppositions. Its application only served to expedite efforts directed at European mutual security that were already in progress.

The United States, in addition to its economic efforts to bring the European nations back to production and stability, also sought to bring about their unity for purposes of self-defense. A first step was the Anglo-French Treaty of Dunkirk, a mutual defense arrangement signed in March 1947. Just one year later, with State Department encouragement, all five of the English Channel nations (Great Britain, France, and the three Benelux countries) signed the Brussels Pact. This was a 50-year alliance that bound its signatories to mutual aid in the event of military aggression. While the Dunkirk pact of 1947 was influenced by the still fresh thoughts of German aggression, the larger Brussels Pact of 1948 was clearly bolstered by fears of a Russian military threat to continental Europe. Without American military help, however, the pact was of little strength. A few days after it was signed, Truman told a joint session of Congress of his confidence that the United States would extend to the pact nations "the support which the situation requires." He also asked for legislation on universal military training and a new Selective Service act.

The obvious need for American military support in order to keep the Brussels Pact alive ran head-on into long-standing traditions holding the United States aloof from permanent and entangling alliances as well as into necessary legalistic considerations. The latter were readily resolved under the sponsorship of Senator Vandenberg and the State Department by the use of the Treaty of Rio de Janeiro of 1947 as precedent. The Rio treaty in turn contained the sanctions found in Article 51 of the United Nations Charter. Formally designated as the Inter-American Treaty of Reciprocal Assistance, the treaty was signed by 19 American nations in September 1947. Aimed at strengthening the 1945 Act of Chapultepec and previous pacts that sought closer ties among the nations of the Americas, it established a regional defense alliance recognized as appropriate in Article 51 of the UN Charter. On this basis the Vandenberg Resolution (Senate Resolution 239) was drawn up permitting American participation in regional security alliances anywhere in the world and passed by a 64 to 4 vote in the Senate, June 11, 1948. The way was thereby cleared for the expansion of the Brussels Pact into a 12-member North Atlantic Treaty Organization (NATO). This alliance was signed in Washington on April 4, 1949, and ratified by the Senate by a 82 to 13 vote on July 21, 1949. Its other signatories were Belgium, Canada, Denmark, France, Great Britain, Ireland, Italy, Luxembourg, the Netherlands, Norway, and Portugal. (Greece and Turkey were admitted in 1952 and West Germany in 1955.)

The NATO treaty had its troubles both before and after its establishment. A small band of senators led by Senator Robert Taft of Ohio leveled three potent objections against it: It violated the spirit of the UN even though it derived some legalistic sustenance from Article 51 of the charter; it brought to an abrupt end a long, American tradition of avoiding entangling alliances; and it might seriously impede Congress' right to declare war. Other objections pointed up the fact that "defensive" alliances had often developed aggressive concepts in the course of history; some were alarmed at the potential of an American land war policy in Europe. Truman characterized it as "an offensive-defensive alliance to maintain the peace in the North Atlantic area but without automatic provision for war," and the Senate majority readily accepted this version. At Truman's request, Congress then approved in September 1949 the Mutual Defense Assistance Act, which supplied $1.3 billion for military assistance to the NATO countries and to Turkey, Greece, Iran, Korea, and China. This marked the beginning of the shift in emphasis from economic to military aid. Subsequent NATO developments saw both West Germany and West Berlin brought under the protection of the organization, with approval for rearming the Bonn government gradually overcoming the reluctance of France. Headquarters for NATO were set up near Paris, and in a December 1950 meeting at Brussels the foreign ministers of the NATO nations agreed upon General Dwight D. Eisenhower as the Supreme Commander of the Allied Powers in Europe. On top of the complex NATO structure more cumbersome machinery appeared two years later, designed to solve the difficulties of integrating armed forces for NATO's use. This organization was designated as the European Defense Community (EDC), and consisted of Great Britain, West Germany, Italy, and the Benelux nations. (Although France was a NATO signatory, her parliament finally rejected the EDC in 1954 after two years of bickering and delay.)

The NATO treaty contained articles dealing with the economic and political unity of Europe. These issues, organized within an American-oriented Western block, were initially more important to Dean Acheson and the Truman outlook than the military aspects of the alliance. The Russians made the expected denunciations of NATO as "aggressive," yet no military leader, Russian or American, could realistically describe the motley collection of NATO's hoped-for divisions as capable of aggression or even defending Europe against the huge Soviet forces that crushed Germany. Much European opinion held that Russian bluster was deliberately used to conceal severe internal stresses and shortenings. There was never any indication that the Soviets contemplated marching to the Atlantic, and most Europeans felt that the Soviets were fully occupied in rebuilding the productive capacities of their country and consolidating their control in the satellite nations. Nevertheless, that consolidation itself, coupled with Soviet belligerent statements, created a psychological climate of apprehension over future Soviet intentions. European nations also welcomed the large American contribution to their expensive defense desires.

Explosion by the Russians of their first atomic bomb in the same year that NATO was formed further reduced the need for conventional land forces in any defense of Europe. The Soviets, despite their propaganda against NATO, evidently did not consider it a threat. Only after their feared enemy in West Germany was admitted to NATO in 1955 did the Soviets hastily set up a counterorganization, the Warsaw Pact. NATO as a military alliance may not have been necessary except temporarily as a "trip-wire" type of deterrent for the dubious possibility of Russian land warfare. By 1950, however, economic and political objectives of an "Atlantic Community" were completely subordinated to military aid programs. President Truman and many Americans, given the Cold War climate of the times, considered a variety of containment activities necessary. And judged by its own criteria, containment displayed some success in Europe. The Soviet Union had added Czechoslovakia to its Eastern Europe satellite border states, but a stoutly nationalistic Yugoslavia, while retaining its own internal brand of communism, had thrown off Kremlin control. The Russians had intensified their control in the states on their borders, but the noncommunist nations of Western Europe made miraculous gains in prosperity and political independence. Only a divided Germany remained as a symbol of a continued uneasy confrontation in Europe.

In 1949 the Truman administration also stepped up its program of economic aid to include the underdeveloped nations of Latin America, Africa, and Asia. In his inaugural address of January 20, 1949, Truman outlined a four-point program on which American foreign policy should be based. The first point was the United Nations, the second was the Marshall Plan, the third was a North Atlantic Alliance (NATO), and the fourth was his "bold new plan" for American technical assistance and perhaps private investment to improve the living standards of backward nations. A hastily written part of the address, the new plan lacked even a name. The press immediately dubbed it "Point Four," and both the designation and the dramatic hopefulness of the plan seized the imagination of the world. Truman's program sought to use American technical knowledge and industrial and scientific techniques to help the industrially backward peoples help themselves. The so-called "underdeveloped" nations were primarily producers of raw materials, which furnished only a low standard of living. With the aid of technical skills and capital, they could establish the beginning of an industrialized economy that would lead to a higher standard of living. To reassure nations regarding possible future American investments, Truman insisted that they would have to be devised to benefit the peoples of the investment area and under suitable control.

Congress acted more than a year later, in June 1950, by passing the Act for International Development (AID) with a beginning grant of $35 million to get Point Four under way. Administration of the program was placed under the State Department, which already had some experience in Latin American projects of this nature. The program was an instant success. After six months Truman could report applications from more than 30 nations, and more than a thousand technical cooperation projects begun in 27 Latin American, African, and Asian countries. Impressed by the results both in the recipient nations and in benefits to the United States, Congress voted to increase its appropriations fourfold. Like the other three points in the Truman inaugural address and the Truman Doctrine, Point Four was a part of United States containment policy. Hopefully, sending U.S. technical knowledge abroad and bringing representatives of the underdeveloped nations to this country for technical training would help to eliminate the poverty and backward conditions so often exploited by communism.

Latin American nations were very much a part of the Point Four program, but they nevertheless considered that their relations with the United States under the Truman administration suffered by comparison with the Good Neighbor policy under Roosevelt. For one thing, the obsession of the United States with the European developments of the early Cold War period effectively precluded directing much attention to South America. For another, the wartime benefits that allegiance to the American and Allied cause was supposed to produce after the victory was won were nonexistent in Latin American eyes. The war virtually closed off Latin American trade, except with Great Britain and the United States. Dependence upon these more restricted areas for sale of her raw materials and purchase of her manufactured goods left South America even more economically dependent than before the war, and profits from foreign-owned Latin American enterprises continued to flow out of the area and back to American and British owners. At the Bogota Conference of 1948 Secretary of State Marshall made it very clear that the United States expected Latin America to rely largely on private investment rather than government loans and that the North American half of the hemisphere looked very coldly on any nationalization of enterprises or their expropriation. This Economic Agreement of Bogota had its political counterpart in the establishment of the Organization of American States (OAS). The OAS charter contained articles that prohibited political, military, or economic intervention in the affairs of a state by another state or group of states. This much desired Latin American request was weakened by a subsequently approved U.S. resolution (Resolution 32) that implemented the American containment concept by providing means to protect the hemisphere against "international communism or any other totalitarian doctrine." Although Resolution 32 was viewed at the time as a vague and relatively innocuous addition, less than two decades later it became evident in the American intervention in the Dominican Republic that the resolution could override many of the articles in the OAS charter. The Truman administration was much more willing than its predecessor to help establish and to join a regional alliance of American nations. Not only did the arrangement counter some of the feelings of neglect in Latin America, but OAS also provided the means for exclusive military arrangements between the United States and its southern neighbors and aided thereby the expansion of the containment concept.

Failure in the Far East

With the surrender of Japan in August 1945, Japanese-American relationships took on a totally new direction. As the emotions and misapprehensions of the Cold War moved the United States to a confrontation with her former ally, Soviet Russia—but with the former enemy, Germany, now at the American side—in the Far East, Japan was destined to shift quickly from enemy to allied status where the United States was concerned. For the occupation which followed Japanese surrender, Russia requested a large portion of the northernmost main island, but Truman rejected outright any idea of such Soviet participation. General Douglas MacArthur was named Supreme Commander of the Allied Powers, and the occupation was quickly and firmly organized without resistance from the Japanese people or army. A small number of Japanese war criminals were brought to trial and executed, but occupation authorities were far more absorbed in a wholesale restructuring of Japanese society. Her land system was reformed in a program admired by colonial and semicolonial nations in Latin America and Africa. The powerful elitist industrial lords were severely restricted in the exercise of future monopolistic powers, and the growth and independence of labor unions was encouraged. By the end of the Truman administration a Republican Wall Street lawyer who frequently advised his party on foreign affairs, John Foster Dulles, was preparing a peace treaty at the President's direction. With the introduction of women's suffrage and democratic reforms in Japanese politics and with similar reforms in national education, Japan was discernibly moving toward closer and very peaceable terms with the United States.

In Southeast Asia, however, the seeds of future trouble were being sown. Roosevelt had stated firmly and at length his convictions that

France, because of her poor record of colonial government, should not be permitted to return to her imperial possessions in Indochina after the war. Both Chiang Kai-shek and Marshal Stalin supported his suggestion for an international trusteeship for the area over the remonstrances of Winston Churchill. However, the Churchill-Roosevelt agreement on the disposition of Allied troops in Indochina was interpreted by the English leader and his area commander, Lord Mountbatten, as supporting the return to control of French troops. Although Generals Hurley and Wedemeyer complained to Washington in the days just after Roosevelt's death, there existed no documented or formal policy to implement Roosevelt's strongly anticolonial hopes. Virtually by default from the Truman administration and through British fears that "trusteeship" meant eventual independence for their own colonies, the French armed forces moved back into Indochina. Nationalist Chinese troops turned over the northern part of Vietnam to the American OSS-supported Ho Chi Minh, nationalist leader against the Japanese invaders. Ho and his Vietminh[5] proclaimed the independent Democratic Republic of Vietnam (North Vietnam) in 1946. But the fragile agreement with the French satisfied neither the Vietnamese who took very literally the Anglo-American promise to the world of the Four Freedoms nor the expectations of the French in returning to their accustomed role. Fighting soon broke out in a war that was to rage on for eight years. France claimed that her costs for prosecuting the war amounted to double the $2.2 billion she received in Marshall Plan aid. With the arrival of weapons from the Communist Chinese to help the Vietminh, the Truman administration began large-scale military aid to the French in 1950. The ultimate defeat of the French in 1954 was to have enormous repercussions in future American foreign policy.

The Americans traditionally held high hopes for the Chinese. In the 19th century the United States worked hard at Christianizing and Westernizing the Chinese, and many Americans came to a particular, if somewhat paternalistic, fondness for the Chinese people. American diplomacy worked at least relatively unselfishly for Chinese interests at the turn of the century and into the 20th century. The United States recognized the weak Chiang Kai-shek government in 1928, and Roosevelt and his advisers had excessively optimistic visions of lifting China up to great-power status and a role filling the vacuum of defeated Japan as a Far East stabilizer. Despite Churchill's audible snorts, Roosevelt insisted that China was a major power and thus entitled to a permanent seat on

---

[5] Viet Minh was short for Viet Nam Doc Lap Dong Minh Hoi, or League for the Independence of Vietnam. Ho Chi Minh, meaning "He Who Enlightens," was the name taken by the Vietnamese patriot, Nguyen Ai Quoc, who joined the French Communist party in 1920 and worked steadily for Vietnamese independence.

the Security Council of the new United Nations. With U.S. influence, the Sino-Soviet pact of 1945 was also initiated, under the terms of which Stalin recognized the Nationalist government and dispatched the military aid to Chiang that he had pledged. But neither rhetoric nor American pressure could make Chiang's government a respected or unified one, much less a great power.

Long before the war Chiang had broken with the Communists in the Kuomintang (Nationalist) government and did his best to wipe them out. But their famous 6,000-mile Great March (1934–36) into the remote rural and mountainous northern China had preserved the military cadres of the Communist Chinese, and their guerrilla assaults on Kuomintang strongholds were generally more successful than were Chiang's attempts at their destruction. In the rural areas under· their control the Communists carried out profound and far-reaching reforms of the land system and other social reforms. Practices such as foot binding and concubinage were eradicated along with the fearful usury levied on the peasantry by landlords and merchants. The Communists gained the increasing support of the masses of peasantry and even that of small merchants and some of the intelligentsia. Although such items as reform of the feudal landlord system had been entrusted by the late Sun Yat-sen, leader of the Chinese Revolution, to his brother-in-law and political heir, Chiang Kai-shek, the latter's regime ignored such reforms and carried on instead an administration containing such political reactionaries and corrupt practices as to alienate increasing numbers of Chinese. Chiang's counterpart was Mao Tse-tung, son of a rich peasant from Hunan, onetime student and one of the founders of the Chinese Communist party. Mao was chiefly responsible for turning the Communists' drive away from the unsatisfactory proletariat of Chinese cities to the masses of peasantry as the base for a successful Communist movement. Harnessing the traditional peasant dissent that was a major factor in the mid-19th century Taiping Rebellion and many other such outbreaks, Mao's reform tactics attracted millions of northern Chinese peasants to the CCP and the Chinese Red Army. When the Japanese invaded China in 1937, the willingness of the Red Army to attack the invaders drew to its ranks many more nationalistic Chinese. The war and its inflation was infinitely more damaging to Chiang's Kuomintang than to the Communist mobile guerrilla armies. The United States continued to send aid to Chiang after Pearl Harbor and urged him to form a coalition with the Communists and present a united Chinese front against the Japanese. Chiang refused, and observers received the impression that while the Red Army was more interested in fighting the Japanese, Chiang was more intent on attacking his Communist rivals. Both armies, however, and the Chinese people as well, suffered greatly at the hands of the invader and from severe inflation.

With the sudden advent of V-J Day, the United States airlifted or transported by water nearly 500,000 Nationalist troops to seize possession of China's great port cities and parts of North China before the Chinese Red Armies could seize them. More than 50,000 American Marines were also rushed to key cities, mines, and railroad points in the north for the same purpose. The United States also ordered the Japanese to hold their arms and their areas of occupation and turn over both to Chiang's troops. But despite these advantages and stepped-up amounts of American military aid, Chiang's cause suffered from severe handicaps. In the first place, large areas of North China and China had been held by the Red Army against both Chiang and the Japanese, and these continued firmly under Communist control. Second, the Russians delayed their departure from Manchuria. When they departed they removed considerable capital equipment as war booty and left behind large supplies of captured Japanese arms which the Red Army quickly seized. Third, Chiang's face-saving insistence on pushing far into North China and Manchuria left his forces fearfully overextended and readily vulnerable to Red Army attack. Finally, not only did Chiang and his government stonily ignore American advice to bring about needed social and political reforms, but also the returning Nationalist officials who flowed back into Chinese cities thoroughly alienated (by their corruption and carpetbagging practices) those same Chinese who had first welcomed them.

Washington was well aware of the weakness and unpopularity of the Kuomintang government. It was particularly fearful of a renewed outbreak of civil war between Chiang's forces and the Communists. Although heavily committed to the Nationalists, it was realized that they could not win an all-out conflict with the Red Army. Even more, the United States feared an intervention by the Russians in any civil war. With American support tied in so strongly with the Nationalists, this could lead to a full-scale confrontation that public opinion would never support. To forestall such a possibility, President Truman sent General George C. Marshall to China in December 1945 to arrange a cessation of hostilities and a unification of China by a coalition government that would include all shades of political opinion, whether Kuomintang, anti-Kuomintang, or Communist. Marshall also informed Chiang that once peace and unity had been realized the United States stood ready to furnish extensive aid to rehabilitate the country and renovate its industries and its agriculture. A coalition government had been proposed before by General Patrick J. Hurley, and General Marshall's efforts to implement this policy showed some hopeful progress at first. A cease-fire agreement was signed in January 1946 by the Nationalists and the Communists. But extremists on both sides continued their objections. Groups and individuals in many cities who publicly opted for peace were beaten and even assassinated by the Kuomintang government. The Red Army would not permit Nationalist troops to enter its territories and set up their own administration, and the Kuomintang insisted that such control must be realized before any coalition could be affected. Both sides violated the cease-fire agreement in April and the Nationalists, with American logistic aid, mounted a major offensive against the Communists. The United States, represented by General Marshall, was in the uncomfortable position of trying to end a civil war with its left hand while its right hand actively aided one of the antagonists. With a final blast at the irreconcilables on both sides, Marshall gave up and left for good in January 1947.

The Truman administration soon announced that it could do no more to reconcile the warring groups but would continue to support Chiang's government financially and militarily. It was realized that only full-scale intervention by the American Army and Air Force could save Chiang, and there were many who doubted that even such an unprecedented move would suffice to save a regime so lacking in popular support. American public opinion, in any case, would not have supported such a continuation of intensive war efforts. Truman announced in January 1947 the withdrawal of American troops throughout China.[6] He gave as his reasons for not committing the United States more fully to the Asian continent, the several European crises and growing Soviet intransigence in Eastern Europe. Like Roosevelt, Truman had to decide that Europe had priority over Asia when it became obvious that America, even with its vast resources, could not extend itself to support both continents simultaneously. Although Truman's decision was attacked in the short-sighted retrospection of the McCarthyite period, the Chinese people themselves had already decided Chiang's destiny, as the next two years clearly showed. Against the advice of the American military, Chiang left large garrisons in Manchurian cities only to lose them after terrible hunger sieges in the northern winter. Tales of the land reforms and the honest administrations in the years of Communist-controlled territories brought peasants, small merchants, and hordes of defecting Nationalist troops to the side of Mao Tse-tung and his followers. Chiang's strategic attempt to rechannel the Yellow River did not stop the Red Army advance, but it further alienated hundreds of thousands of homeless Chinese. Superior Kuomintang forces were unable to defend key cities from the Communist attack. Whole armies of Chiang's conscripts fled to join the Communist armies, taking their American arms and equipment with them. After a series of humiliating defeats for the Nationalists, Mao Tse-tung proclaimed the People's Republic of China in

---

[6] Even in the cities that U.S. Marines had turned over to the Kuomintang, Chinese resentment ran high at the presence of American troops. Marines guarding Chinese ports and railroads were fully as eager to leave China behind them.

September 1949. In October, the government was formally organized in Peiping and quickly received Russian recognition.

Dean G. Acheson had succeeded the now ill General George C. Marshall as Secretary of State in January 1949. Accurately foreseeing the causes of Chiang's incipient defeat, Acheson warned Americans of the folly in hanging on to a government that was repudiated by overwhelming numbers of its own people. Although Acheson also calmly pointed out after the formation of the People's Republic of China that embassies are established not to indicate approval of a regime but because of diplomatic necessities and benefits, American moralism and partisan politics blocked recognition of the same government that Britain and others soon acknowledged. Widespread American belief held the Chinese Communists to be tools of the Kremlin. Mao Tse-tung and his followers and some observers were painfully aware that this was not the case. They knew from bitter experience that Stalin had suggested in 1927 and again in 1945 that they subordinate themselves to the Nationalist government. They had complained bitterly of Russia's shipments of arms to Chiang prior to 1941. They had no further doubts that their future was consistently subordinated to the Kremlin's needs of the moment, and Moscow's disavowals of Mao for his unorthodox use of peasants in place of the proletariat made this increasingly clear. The genuine nationalistic rifts between the two contiguous powers of northern Asia was to become clear enough in later decades, but in the turbulent early years of the Cold War Americans saw communism as a monolithic Kremlin horde. Although the State Department and witnesses such as General Wedemeyer and Chief of Staff General Omar N. Bradley explained that no amount of American arms could have upheld a government whose citizens would not support it and whose soldiers refused to fight for it, partisan critics utilized the public trauma over "losing" a friendly China to mount bitter attacks on the Truman administration. Those isolationists who considered Asia of more importance than Europe insisted that Chiang could not have fallen if Truman had only supplied more aid. Senators such as William F. Knowland of California (known by his colleagues as "the Senator from Formosa"), Styles Bridges of New Hampshire, and Robert Taft of Ohio raised the question of pro-Communists in the State Department who in some way were to blame for Chiang's debacle. In the divided America of the McCarthyist climate of 1949, no recognition of the People's Republic of China was possible. That government's virulent anti-Americanism did not improve matters, but Chiang as a symbol of anticommunism made the essential difference. Chiang's 2 million soldiers, flown to Formosa (Taiwan) and taking over the ruling of 12 million resentful Formosans, became the official "China" of the State Department. American refusal to recognize the de facto government of 600 million Chinese occupying all of mainland China was a probable factor in the war in neighboring Korea that soon followed.

The nation of Korea, conquered and annexed by the Japanese in 1910, was one of the many areas discussed during wartime summit conferences. In 1943 at Cairo, Roosevelt, Churchill, and Chiang agreed that once the Japanese were defeated Korea should "in due course," regain her independence. At Potsdam in 1945 the United States, Great Britain, and Soviet Russia agreed that, with Russian troops in northern China and American troops in Japan and the neighboring waters, Soviet forces should occupy the former Japanese conquest north of the 38th parallel and American forces south of that line. Agreement over a unified country and what form its government would take was no more successful than had been the case with Germany, with angry complaints from the resistance movement in the South over the American military government's use of Japanse police and of Japanese collaborators as administrators. In September the Korean dispute was referred to the United Nations. That body recommended a national election and named a United Nations Temporary Commission on Korea. But visiting Korea in early 1948 the commission was denied permission by the Soviets to move north of the dividing line. Elections were nevertheless held in the American sector of southern Korea. The assembly elected in May 1948 adopted a constitution in June, picked a President in July, and established itself as the Republic of Korea (ROK) in August. They chose as their leader the conservative Nationalist, Dr. Syngman Rhee, who had headed the Korean Provisional Government in exile for several years. The United States began training South Korean troops and supplied them with limited arms. When American occupation forces were all withdrawn by June 1949, only the military advisers remained.

North of the 38th parallel the Soviet Union began molding the less numerous population of North Korea politically and militarily just as the United States was attempting in its own area, although the North Korean forces received more armaments than their counterparts in the South. A People's Democratic Government was set up at Pyongyang in September 1948, and the Russian military, with the exception of military advisers, left at the same time that American troops were pulled out. Kim Il-sung, the head of the northern state, was fully as belligerent in his demands for unification as was Syngman Rhee in the South.

Evaluating the American position in the Far East after the fleeing of Chiang and his followers to Formosa, Truman and Dean Acheson, who had succeeded General Marshall as Secretary of State, carried forward their reluctant assessment of the badly defeated Chiang. The United States could no longer regard with any seriousness the idea that the remnants of the Nationalist Chinese could play a vital role in containment. In addition, there was considerable speculation (or hope) that the now visible nationalism of Mao's China would bring about a full-scale clash with Russia, and thereby serve American interests. The idea of some sort of limited war in which the United States might become involved was evidently not considered. Thus in January 1950 Dean Acheson spelled out publicly what the United States would have to consider in the protection of its national security as a "defense perimeter." Such a line would have to run through the Aleutians, Japan, the Ryukyus (mainly Okinawa), and the Philippines. Neither Formosa nor Korea were mentioned by name, but were included under a generalization that stated if any areas outside the perimeter were attacked, they would have to furnish much of their own defense and also call upon "the commitments of the entire civilized world." The decision not to involve American forces in any attempt by the Communist Chinese to retake Formosa from Chiang invoked a storm of partisan abuse from Republican Senators led by William Knowland of California. At a time when the McCarthyite crusade had influenced many political opponents of the Truman administration and had persuaded many American citizens with the simplistic explanation that Chiang's defeat could be readily ascribed to dim figures within the State Department rather than to the Chinese people themselves, it then followed logically enough for many that Chiang's last bastion must be protected against the Communist Chinese.[7]

The forces of South Korea had been lined up facing the more heavily armed troops of North Korea at the 38th parallel for more than a year. Both sides had sent skirmishing groups against each other in a continual series of border clashes. Both the Soviet choice in the North, Kim Il-sung, and his American-controlled counterpart in the South, Syngman Rhee, bitterly assailed each other's regime and both repeatedly warned of invasion to accomplish their purpose. Both obviously hoped that their respective sponsors would back their individual ideas as to how unification should be accomplished. President Rhee was so belligerent that he was refused tanks and planes and equipped with "defensive" arms and artillery for fear that he might gamble on involving the United States by beginning an offensive. General MacArthur, however, had comforted Rhee and his troops with many statements of personal support on his own. In early 1950 the State Department, disturbed over the beatings and prison sentences meted out by Rhee's administration to his political opponents, insisted that he hold elections. The resultant balloting in May 1950 completely repudiated the Rhee government. One month later, on June 25, in the midst of stepped-up border clashes, heavy forces and tanks of North Korea moved in attack south of the

---

[7] One thing both Chiang and Mao agreed upon without reservation: Formosa (Taiwan) was an integral part of the Chinese nation and must be treated as such.

38th parallel. Whether Kim Il-sung thought he could successfully embroil his Soviet partners, or whether he thought Rhee's strong statements presaged an attack northward, is not known. Secretary of State Acheson's statement regarding American defense perimeters may possibly have persuaded Kim that the resultant clash would be regarded solely as a civil war. Although Russia was widely believed at the time to have ordered the move, the fact that she had stripped herself of any preventive action veto in the UN has raised serious doubts on this question and suggests the possibility of a bold stroke by Kim Il-sung at the tottering Rhee government.

President Truman's reaction to the attack was quick and decisive. The invasion was brought before the Security Council of the UN. That body voted nine to nothing to request that North Korea immediately withdraw her forces north of the dividing line. (The Russian delegate, who could have stopped this and subsequent action by a veto, was busily boycotting the Security Council because that body had refused to give China's seat to Mao's People's Republic.) This was followed by another vote of seven to one (Yugoslavia opposed; India and Egypt abstained) to ask that UN members contribute forces under a UN command to repel the attack. Truman, after conferring with leaders of both parties in Congress, ordered General MacArthur to send two divisions of American occupation troops to Korea and authorized American bombers to hit North Korean targets. Fearing that either Chiang might exploit the opportunity by attacking the mainland, or that the Communist Chinese might complicate matters still further with an assault upon Formosa, Truman ordered the American Seventh Fleet to interpose itself between the two Chinese enemies. Republican opposition agreed wholeheartedly with the anti-Communist tactic of resisting the North Korean attack, but strongly criticized the Formosa decision as not carrying anticommunism far enough, regardless of all-out war with China. On July 9, at Security Council request, Truman named General MacArthur as commander of United Nations forces.

The initial push of some ten North Korean divisions rolled up the South Koreans and those American troops hastily thrown across their path. The North Koreans were better armed than Rhee's forces, more numerous, and with evidently much higher morale. They took Seoul quickly, and in two and a half months of steady southward pressure and swift flanking maneuvers had pushed back American and South Korean units to a small 140-mile perimeter around the southeastern port city of Pusan, MacArthur's principal supply base. Here the U.S. Eighth Army of General Walton H. Walker dug in and held against repeated North Korean attacks. With full command of the sea by combined American and British naval units, MacArthur launched an extremely hazardous but brilliantly executed amphibious landing on the Inchon peninsula near Seoul. A Marine division made the landing on September 15 and fought its way into the occupied capital of Seoul by September 27. Combined with an Eighth Army offensive, the North Koreans were soon streaming back across the 38th parallel.

Although the United Nations had undertaken its action to repel aggression, it now had to consider whether aggressive action should be taken into North Korea territory. On October 1 General MacArthur issued a manifesto demanding that all North Korean soldiers surrender and place themselves "under such military supervision as I may direct." At the same time, the People's Republic Premier, Chou En-lai, warned that China would not stand idly by and see her neighbor invaded. In Washington, MacArthur's supporters insisted that his advice as field commander should be followed, and complained that his hands "were being tied" by the United Nations. Truman and Acheson, with support from Great Britain, then put a resolution before the UN General Assembly which recommended that MacArthur take all "appropriate steps . . . to insure conditions of stability throughout Korea." This was passed by a vote of forty-seven to five, with eight abstentions, on October 7, 1950. Red China again sent warnings, this time through Indian diplomats, that UN troop movements across the parallel would bring counteraction. On October 15 General MacArthur met with President Truman on Wake Island in the Pacific for an accounting on the war's progress. MacArthur told the President that there was "very little" chance of Chinese intervention. He estimated that the Chinese could get no more than 50,000 or 60,000 of their 300,000 or 400,000 men in the area across the Yalu River which formed the border between North Korea and Chinese Manchuria. If they did, MacArthur stated, those forces would be annihilated. All resistance, he went on, would be ended by Thanksgiving.

Before the UN sanction to move into North Korea had been passed, ROK troops aided by American planes had already begun the pursuit. On October 7, the same day of the UN resolution, American forces joined in the northward movement. But by late October Chinese troops were reported as having attacked South Korean units near the sensitive Yalu River border. They came into conflict with American forces in early November, but their contacts were cautious and not in heavy numbers. In late October the Red Chinese had surprised many by stating that they would send a delegation to the UN for the November hearings scheduled before the Security Council on Formosa. Many hoped that it might mean the beginning of negotiations. But three days before the Chinese arrived, heavy bombing attacks were launched against bridges across the Yalu. Simultaneously with the arrival of the Chinese delegates on November 24 came the headlines announcing MacArthur's all-out offensive to the Yalu. The troops probably would be home by

Christmas, was the word from MacArthur. Seldom in history has military intelligence been more sadly in error. Chinese forces were not only present in large numbers at the border, but with the move toward the Yalu they struck with tremendous power in the gap left between the two widespread wings of the MacArthur offensive. The U.S. Eighth Army, now under the command of General Matthew B. Ridgway, was pushed back in confusion. In the far northeast, Marines, Army divisions, and ROK troops fought rearguard actions in snow and bitter cold to get to the port of Hungnam, where the Navy rescued them to rejoin other UN elements in the South. Chinese forces now plunged south across the parallel, taking Seoul. Finally, in January 1951, UN forces rallied and counterattacked. The battered city of Seoul was again finally recaptured and the Chinese and North Koreans were eventually pushed back slightly north of the dividing line at the 38th parallel. There the fighting stabilized, although truce talks did not begin until July 1951, and these were to drag on for another two years.

The Truman-MacArthur Controversy

In the wake of the November disaster, with UN forces reeling backward before the Chinese, President Truman made a belligerent statement regarding world communism before his press conference of November 30. What provoked a furious storm of worldwide reaction were his remarks indicating that if United Nations approval was forthcoming for action against Red China, then MacArthur would have the authority to use all military weapons—including the atomic bomb. All of the fears of European and UN nations regarding atomic warfare, combined with their accumulated distaste for MacArthur's repeated ignoring of UN suggestions and proposals, produced the most profound revulsion against American policy that her friends and allies had yet manifested. Ambassadors of NATO countries asked by cable and by personal visit what MacArthur was trying to do with UN forces. Prime Minister Attlee of Great Britain came to Washington as the unofficial spokesman for all of Western Europe, with amazingly complete unity of support. While Truman would not give specific assurance to Attlee on the use of the atomic bomb, it was clear that the unprecedented world reaction had severely inhibited the possibility of its employment.

MacArthur insisted that the failure of his November offensive and the Chinese intervention were the fault of his superiors. He blamed everything on the "inhibitions" that Washington placed upon him, plus the fact that both Washington and the United Nations refused to let him bomb or blockade China, and denied him permission to employ Chinese Nationalist troops and let Chiang harass the Chinese mainland.

MacArthur and his "China Lobby" Republican supporters clearly desired war with Red China, even though she had been an ally of Russia since the February 1950 signing of the Sino-Soviet Pact, and notwithstanding the fact that her Russian ally had had atomic weapons since 1949. Criticism as to the provocative dash to the Yalu became more widespread and conservative editorials inquired why MacArthur publicly described the building of a trap for UN forces and then walked into it several weeks later. The Truman administration, while fully as anti-Communist as MacArthur, was infinitely more concerned with containing Soviet power in Europe. This policy had been at odds with "Asia First" politicians and some military since the beginning of World War II. Truman and his advisers also felt far more keenly the need to prevent World War III and were compelled thereby to contain MacArthur's unilateral decisions.

But General MacArthur had made so many decisions contrary to the explicit orders he received from his military superiors, the Joint Chiefs of Staff, and his civilian superiors, including the President of the United States, that in retrospect it is amazing that he was not removed from his command long before the decision was finally made. Many of MacArthur's actions seemed motivated out of a willingness or a desire to bring on a war with Red China. His early orders not to bomb along the sensitive Yalu River border were frequently disobeyed. Military instructions to use ROK troops near the border instead of American forces, when the Joint Chiefs of Staff were still hoping to keep the Chinese from entering the conflict, were ignored on grounds of "military necessity." MacArthur's fatal November offensive jumped off on the same day that Red Chinese delegates voluntarily came to the UN hearings, and hopes were high for the beginning of negotiations. When notice was received from the Joint Chiefs of Staff in March 1951, at a time that the fighting was stabilized, that the United Nations was ready to discuss settlement, MacArthur delivered his own unauthorized invitation to the Chinese to admit their military failure and surrender to him, a shocking assumption of national sovereignty. The Chinese angrily refused, and the fighting continued.

MacArthur also undertook a variety of actions that were either forbidden, unauthorized, or obviously in political and public conflict with his constitutional superiors. His July 1950 trip to Formosa, and Chiang's gratified talk of "Sino-American military cooperation" which he did not in fact have, drew immediate presidential disavowal. General MacArthur then sent a message to the Veterans of Foreign Wars insisting that the United States defend Formosa and describing Truman's position as "appeasement and defeatism." On this occasion Truman ordered MacArthur to withdraw the speech, but although it was not made its contents were deliberately leaked to the press. At the Wake Island conference of October 1950, Truman ordered his field commander to refrain from any more provocative public statements. On December 6 Truman issued another order forbidding all civil and military officials from making statements on foreign policy without first clearing the substance with the State Department. Yet MacArthur continued to criticize American policy and to suggest that the Joint Chiefs of Staff furnish support for a Nationalist invasion of the mainland and begin a war of bombardment against Red China. The Joint Chiefs of Staff promptly turned down these suggestions. MacArthur's impromptu request for a Chinese surrender brought still another presidential warning.

General MacArthur not only paid no attention to these warnings, but he also chose to challenge American foreign policy favoring a limit to the conflict and an early peace. Bypassing all regulation channels and ignoring the traditional position of the American military, MacArthur jumped directly into the field of politics to achieve his aims. In a letter to Republican Representative Joseph W. Martin, Jr. of Massachusetts, minority leader of the House, MacArthur sharply criticized administration policy and called for all-out war against communism in Asia. He denounced the idea of limiting the war and insisted "there is no substitute for victory." Several days later, Representative Martin read MacArthur's letter to the House of Representatives. Truman could not overlook this final and flagrant challenge to constitutional authority. His proposal to relieve MacArthur was endorsed by the Joint Chiefs of Staff, and President Truman on April 11 issued the necessary order relieving MacArthur of all his commands and replacing him with General Matthew B. Ridgway.

The dismissal brought about an immediate clamor, much of it disapproving. But as Truman was to note later, "MacArthur left me no choice—I could no longer tolerate his insubordination." Representative Martin and other Republican supporters of MacArthur called for congressional hearings on the incident. MacArthur returned to the United States for the first time in 16 years (he had been in Asiatic and Pacific commands since the mid-1930s) and received a hero's ticker-tape welcome. On April 19, 1951 MacArthur appeared before a joint session of Congress and delivered an emotional account of his relations with the administration, ending with the dramatic notation that "Old soldiers never die; they just fade away." The Senate Armed Services Committee and the Senate Foreign Relations Committee held joint hearings on the incident beginning May 3 and carrying through until June 25, presided over by Senator Richard B. Russell of Georgia. MacArthur, as the first witness, insisted that he had not disobeyed any order. He refused to find any distinctions between political and military situations, and blandly denied that blockading the Russian base at Port Arthur or bombing the Sino-Russian railways leading to it could possibly have led to Russian intervention. However, the weight of military testimony against MacArthur's actions and proposals was overwhelming. General Omar

War Zone in Korea

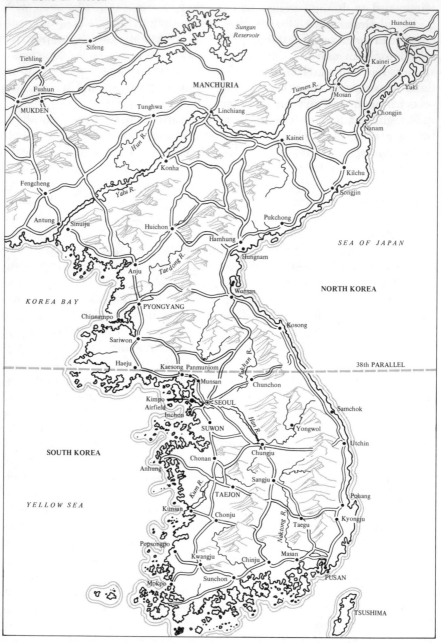

Bradley neatly summed up MacArthur's strategy by pointing out that it "would involve us in the wrong war, at the wrong place, at the wrong time, and with the wrong enemy." As Army and Air Force generals, Navy admirals, and civilian authorities testified in similar vein, the great American emotional outburst in behalf of MacArthur dissipated, and public opinion moved away from his views, never to return. MacArthur clearly had violated the constitutional and traditional authority of the civil government over the military, and had accumulated many dis obeyals of his military superiors as well. Regardless of his strong agreement with his Republican supporters on the need for an anti-Communist crusade in Asia, as a field commander he should not have used his authority to promote ideological convictions at odds with the nation's foreign and military policy. The nation gave him its momentary ovation as a tribute to his military service and as a symbol of its frustration over the unfamiliar and unwelcome concept of limited war. But it refused to accept his recommendations for expanding the war against Red China or risking nuclear conflict with Russia. The General was a passing figure at the Republican presidential convention of 1952. Only one part of the MacArthur predictions came true: The old soldier did, indeed, fade away into the background.

On July 10, 1951 General Ridgway began armistice negotiations with Chinese and North Korean officers. The talks were held in the town of Panmunjom, but dragged on for two years with occasional fighting continuing and with the lines relatively stabilized just north of the 38th parallel. Approximately 18 months of these talks, with continuing casualties, were brought about by the wrangle over the return of prisoners of war. The United States inaugurated a policy of "reeducation" of its Chinese and North Korean prisoners designed to prove the authoritarian nature of those regimes, while the Chinese carried on similar aims with UN captives. Some 100,000 out of 170,000 prisoners preferred not to return to their respective countries, U.S. negotiators told their Chinese and North Korean counterparts. The latter insisted that the usual principles of the Geneva Convention must apply, wherein all prisoners are repatriated without delay after hostilities cease. The large number of Chinese and North Koreans refusing repatriation resulted in a propaganda victory for the United States, Chiang, and Rhee, but it meant additional confinement and varieties of brainwashing for the prisoners on both sides, as well as continued United Nations casualties. The war finally ended on July 10, 1953. South Korea received about 1,500 additional square miles of territory when the new boundaries were drawn. A two-and-one-half-mile deep demilitarized zone was established along the border between North and South Korea, and the job of overseeing the peace and repatriating the prisoners turned over to commissions of neutral nations. The belligerent Synghman Rhee did his best to scuttle the armistice talks by withdrawing ROK troops from the UN command and threatening to invade North Korea, but the United States managed finally to bribe him into acquiescence to the war's end with offers of economic aid and rehabilitation.

The Korean War was technically a UN command. In actuality, the United States bore the largest share of the war's financial costs and suffered casualties of 23,000 killed and 103,000 wounded. Of the UN forces, nearly half were American. Somewhat more than 40 percent were those of the Republic of Korea, leaving approximately 10 percent to be divided among a variety of nations. Of these, the chief contributors to the fighting forces were Great Britain, Australia, Turkey, and the Philippines, with small contingents of French, Thais, Greeks, Abyssinians and others. Within the American forces the Korean conflict was noteworthy for dealing a deathblow to policies of unit segregation on racial grounds. In the moves toward the Yalu or away from it, in the bitter hill warfare of the truce period, GI blacks fought alongside of GI whites in terms of mutual respect. For Americans generally, the Korean conflict was a traumatic experience. On the one hand, no longer could the Western nations think to put down every Asiatic conflict by superior force of arms. Large numbers of Orientals armed with all the modern weapons from automatic rifles to jet planes, and motivated fully as strongly as their Western opponents, if not more so, could at least gain a stalemate short of resorting to nuclear weapons. And on the other hand, the possible use of such cataclysmic weapons and the potential of reprisal meant that the only kind of war possible was a strictly limited war that had to stop short of MacArthur's absolutes of "complete victory" lest universal disaster befall. During the war the United States sought to promote a security system with nations of the Pacific and Far East areas. A mutual defense treaty was concluded with the Philippines as of August 1951. In September the United States, Australia, and New Zealand signed a Tripartite Security Treaty (ANZUS). At the same time, the United States and Japan signed a peace treaty as well as a security treaty, and in 1954 the Senate ratified a Korean Mutual Defense Treaty guaranteeing South Korea's security. The war undoubtedly established the Peoples' Republic of China as the great power in Asia, and reaffirmed to mainland China that the United States was its chief enemy. For the United States, the war also helped to bring to an end two decades of Democratic administration.

Decline of the Democratic Party

The impact of the Korean War on the home front had a variety of impacts, none of them advantageous to the incumbent Democratic administration. The rearmament program was greatly stepped up, and although this meant a bonanza for airplane producers and military suppliers, it also meant higher taxes to pay for the increased appropriations. Pumping up the country's economy with war expenditures soon brought inflation and rising prices. Labor asked for wage adjustments to meet inflationary costs, and sought a renewal of World War II price controls. To lessen the dangers of inflation, and at the same time to assure defense industries the necessary priorities, Congress passed the Defense Production Act in the fall of 1950. Although it gave the President broad powers to bring about wage and price stabilization while maintaining uninterrupted production, the act did not go far to meet pressing wage and inflation problems. When their demands for wage increases to meet the rising cost of living were turned down, workers turned to the strike with greater frequency. The presidential election year of 1952 saw a considerable increase over labor stoppages in the two preceding years of the Korean War, although virtually all were settled without important production delays. What promised to be the most serious strike came after the Wage Stabilization Board's recommendations for a $0.15 per hour increase for steelworkers was flatly rejected by the entire steel industry. Philip Murray, president of the United Steel Workers, issued a strike call on April 3, 1952, and President Truman promptly seized the steel mills of the nation as a defense emergency, denouncing the steel companies for their refusal to accept a proposal "fair to both parties and the public interest." But several weeks later Judge David A. Pine of the United States District Court denied that the President had inherent constitutional powers sufficient for such a seizure. Two months later the Supreme Court, in *Youngstown Sheet and Tube Company* v. *Charles Sawyer,* upheld Judge Pine's decision of government illegality by a six to three vote. Although the court did not deny that the President constitutionally possessed powers inherent in his office for the solving of national crises, it ruled that Congress had not authorized such seizure.

Manpower needs of the war resulted in the acceleration of Selective Service calls as the armed services were more than doubled from 1.5 million to 3.5 million men. Many Army and Air Force Reserve units were called up with little notice, with strong blasts at the administration from reservists who had neither expectation nor premonition of such demands. The Republican leaders had unanimously agreed with Truman's initial decision in Korea and had publicly complimented him upon his quickness and courage. Yet the course of the war and its limitations and frustrations soon brought about that simplistic personalization that Americans had been guilty of ever since the days of "King George's War" and "Mr. Madison's War." The Korean conflict became "Truman's War."

To add to Democratic dismay, evidence of collusion and corruption among government officials mounted and became alarmingly publicized. Although none of the many incidents in any way compromised President Truman's unquestionable integrity, some of the individuals involved were cronies of his, and Truman was never one to back away from old acquaintances. One such disclosure involved Major General Harry Vaughan, the President's military aide. Vaughan had used his newfound nearness to the seats of the mighty to aid businessmen in the consummation of government-approved contracts. A Senate committee hearing established the fact that one company's gratitude was expressed in terms of a deep-freeze unit valued at $500. A White House stenographer, whose husbands's position in RFC enabled him to expedite loans, received a $8,500 mink coat when the loan application was granted. Two of General Vaughan's friends, Colonel J. V. Hunt and John Maragon, used the General's White House office to promote their "5 percent" activities, in which they used their influence to swing lucrative government transactions for businessmen for a 5 percent commission. George Schoeneman, the Commissioner of Internal Revenue and a charter member of the Missouri Gang, resigned in 1952 in the midst of tax scandals that turned out scores of Internal Revenue and Justice Department people and sent others to prison. Truman enlisted the services of Newbold Morris, a prominent New York City Republican attorney noted for his reform efforts, to mount an intensive effort to weed out corruption and influence-peddling among federal employees. Morris was to be under the direction of Attorney General J. Howard McGrath, but when McGrath saw the questionnaire to be filled out by members of Congress and began receiving complaints, he immediately sacked Mr. Morris. McGrath, who evidently had been losing the presidential confidence for some time past, was quickly discharged in turn, probably as an act of election year political appeasement. In the following week Truman sent to Congress for their approval a plan to reorganize the Bureau of Internal Revenue. Designed to place all positions except the Commissioner's under civil service, it was readily legislated by Congress. As far as influencing the coming presidential elections, it was obviously a matter of too little and too late. The deep freeze and the mink coat became readily accepted symbols of misfeasance in office, and the Republicans triumphantly added corruption to their list of election campaign complaints against the Democratic administration.

According to Truman's memoirs, he decided very early in his second administration that he would not run again. He had been in public office at a variety of levels for 30 years, but principally he thought that no one should be President for more than 8 years. This secret memo was read to his alarmed staff in 1951, and his decision not to run was made public in March 1952. His administration, as it turned out, was not to differ fundamentally (except for rhetoric) from the administration which ousted him. Even the persistent and pervasive anticommunism of Truman and Acheson was not sufficient for the semi-hysteria of the 1950s induced by McCarthyism, the defeat of Nationalist China, and the frustrations of a limited war concept in Korea. An era of Democratic party rule had come to an end.

Suggestions for Reading

On Truman, see the biographical works mentioned for Chapter 1. R. E. Neustadt, *Presidential Power: The Politics of Leadership** (1960), has excellent material on the Truman presidency. For the great upset presidential race of 1948 see Irwin Ross, *The Loneliest Campaign* (1968), and K. M. Schmidt, *Henry A. Wallace: Quixotic Crusade, 1948* (1960).

An important piece of the Fair Deal is discussed in S. K. Bailey, *Congress Makes a Law: The Story Behind the Employment Act of 1946** (1950). Labor and labor legislation is covered in H. A. Millis and E. C. Brown, *From the Wagner Act to Taft-Hartley* (1950). See also A. J. Matusow, *Farm Policies and Politics in the Truman Years* (1967), and R. O. Davies, *Housing Reform during the Truman Administration* (1966).

Richard Rovere does an excellent job on McCarthy as national demagogue in *Senator Joe McCarthy** (1959). W. F. Buckley, *McCarthy and his Enemies* (1954) is adulatory and uncritical. See also M. P. Rogin, *The Intellectuals and McCarthy** (1967); Robert Griffith, *The Politics of Fear* (1970) on the Senate; and Earl Latham, *The Communist Conspiracy in Washington** (1966). Best on the Hiss case is Alistair Cooke, *A Generation on Trial* (1950). See also Alger Hiss, *In the Court of Public Opinion* (1957), and Whittaker Chambers, *Witness* (1952). The domestic scene is drawn in Eric Goldman, *The Crucial Decade and After: America, 1945–1960** (1960); and Fred Cook, *The Nightmare Decade* (1972).

The works cited under Chapter 1 for the Cold War are all applicable. See also M. F. Herz, *Beginnings of the Cold War* (1966). Memoirs by the participants in events include Dean Acheson, *Present at the Creation** (1969); James F. Byrnes, *Speaking Frankly* (1947); and G. F. Kennan, *Memoirs, 1925–1950* (1967). See also R. H. Ferrell, *George C. Marshall* (1966); Gaddis Smith, *Dean Acheson* (1972), and McGeorge Bundy, ed., *The Pattern of Responsibility* (1952) on Acheson's speeches.

On Berlin, see the memoirs of the commanding general in L. D. Clay, *Decision in Germany* (1950). A scholarly account is W. P. Davison, *The Berlin Blockade: A Study in Cold War Politics* (1958).

On the Far East, see the works mentioned in the preceding chapter. A summary of the Korean War may be found in David Rees, *Korea: The Limited War** (1964). Why China entered the war is carefully explicated and analyzed in A. S. Whiting, *China Crosses the Yalu: The Decision to Enter the Korean War** (1960). The partisan use of the war as a domestic issue is explained in R. J. Caridi, *The Korean War and American Politics; The Republican Party as a Case Study* (1968). On the controversial dismissal of MacArthur by Truman, see the careful account by J. W. Spanier, *The Truman-MacArthur Controversy** (1959). Other good coverage is in Trumbull Higgins, *Korea and the Fall of MacArthur* (1960), and R. H. Rovere and A. M. Schlesinger, Jr., *The MacArthur Controversy and American Foreign Policy** (1965).

New and comprehensive works on the whole Truman administration are daughter Margaret Truman's *Harry S. Truman* (1973), and a highly critical account representing the latest trend of historical judgment on Truman, Bert Cochran, *Harry Truman and the Crisis Presidency* (1973).

For the earliest American involvement in Indochina, see J. T. McAlister, *Vietnam: The Origins of Revolution** (1969), and Marvin Kalb and Elie Abel, *Roots of Involvement* (1971). The best one-volume work on the entire American history of involvement in Indochina is G. M. Kahin and J. W. Lewis, *The United States in Vietnam** (rev. ed. 1969). Essays of revisionist criticism on American Far Eastern policies are in Edward Friedman and Mark Selden, eds., *America's Asia: Dissenting Essays on Asian-American Relations** (1971). Invaluable for both narrative and source material covering the United States in Vietnam from Truman through Johnson are *The Pentagon Papers*, either in the five-volume Senator Gravel Edition (1972) or the one-volume paperback New York Times Edition (1972).

3

The First Eisenhower Years

The Election of 1952

FROM the comfortable perch of hindsight, no important differences in basic American policies distinguished the Eisenhower administration from the Truman administration. There was a great deal of rhetoric and partisan clamor that made very minor fundamental differences appear to be giant sized at the time. Truman was frequently forced from a mildly liberal position to the middle of the road by circumstances, public opinion, and partisan opposition. Eisenhower early staked out a claim to a moderate conservatism through natural preference, although a strong wing of his party often sought to move the nation to the extreme right fringes of American national politics. Eisenhower sought to broaden his possible base of support by describing his political stand, with dubious linguistic logic, as "liberal conservatism" or "dynamic conservatism."

The legacy of the New Deal period in the American experience was used by both and rejected by neither. Where economic crises appeared, both utilized government powers as an intervening force in the national economy, albeit Eisenhower less readily than Truman. The Truman administration could probably point to somewhat more legislative accomplishment, but both were able to extend several of the institutional New Deal social innovations. Both were strongly anti-Communist. Both took the position that America's chief reason for being was to halt the spread of a supposed Kremlin-directed international communism, real or suspected, internal or external, at home or around the globe. Both were frequently belligerent, yet both rejected extremists who would readily

97

have risked nuclear warfare for passionately held ideological convictions. The era spanning both presidencies, therefore, had a continuity in generally prosperous complacency, a lack of innovations or social solutions, and a shared negative credo of anticommunism in lieu of a broadly positive American example for the world.

Hopes were understandably high in Republican circles in 1951. Public opinion tides, whether moved by revelations of corruption in the Democratic administration or by the frustrations of the Korean War, clearly flowed toward the opposition party. People were tired of high prices and high taxes, and an uncomfortably large proportion of Americans thought that McCarthy's character assassinations might conceivably produce some good effects. One of the leading Republican figures of the day, Senator Robert A. Taft of Ohio, thus declared as early as September 1951 his bid for the Republican presidential nomination. Taft had lost the 1948 nomination to the Eastern, internationalist, and more progressive wing of the Republican party in the person of Thomas E. Dewey, Governor of New York. Taft's support came from virtually the same groups and areas that were loyal to his candidacy in the past. They included the very conservative wing of the party, the isolationists strongly based in the Midwest and the West, the McCarthyites, the Old Guard pros, the "Asia Firsters," and the statehouse and courthouse representatives. The Ohio Senator had never been one to hide his strong convictions, however, and this tactic also made him an extremely doubtful winner to those politically sharp Republicans who realized that a presidential winner must be able to attract considerable numbers of Democratic and independent voters. Taft had alienated many with his strong support of McCarthy's irresponsible onslaughts. His equally strong support for General MacArthur's views cost him potential votes even in his own party after a Senate committee, through the measured statements of Secretary of State Marshall and Generals Omar N. Bradley and Hoyt Vandenberg, had revealed the dangerous nature of MacArthur's provocation and insubordination. His propensity to give the Far East more attention than Europe worried many within his own party, and his early 20th-century republicanism was more attractive to the small town and rural American than to the more numerous urban voter.

An outstanding figure was lacking to represent the more progressive and internationalist wing of the party, particularly where a broad base of popular support was concerned. Governor Earl Warren of California and Governor Harold Stassen of Minnesota were able and acceptable standard-bearers, but neither possessed the requisite national exposure. A growing possibility was General Dwight D. Eisenhower, in 1951 the commander of NATO. Soon after his defeat in 1948 Dewey had pushed the General's name into consideration, and in announcing his refusal to be considered a candidate for 1952, Dewey had given Eisenhower another strong push. Aid for the General's candidacy came from such liberal Republican Senators as Henry Cabot Lodge, Jr., of Massachusetts and James H. Duff of Pennsylvania, and Eastern Governors such as Sherman Adams of New Hampshire. The latter warmly recommended putting Eisenhower's name on the ballot in New Hampshire's Republican primary, the first in the nation. In January 1952, the Green Mountain state gave Eisenhower a clear majority over Taft and Stassen. Although other early primaries were indicative more of sectional preferences than anything else, an intensive campaign was launched to line up financial support among Big Business circles and to put pressure on the General to accept. More than passive acceptance was necessary to edge out the strong Taft push for delegates and, at the insistence of his campaign managers and friends, Eisenhower resigned his NATO command and returned to the United States to begin direct appeals to the voters in June 1952. Despite his first few fumbling speeches, "Ike," as he soon came to be called, was a popular favorite. Voters had no idea as to his political or economic philosophy or where he stood on many important issues of the day, but his engaging friendliness, together with his reputation as a war hero, seemed sufficient in public opinion polls.

Taft's hard-working supporters had more delegates already pledged to their candidate than did Eisenhower's when the Republican convention met in Chicago in July 1952. The Taft forces also had control of the convention machinery, but the votes over many contested delegations went to Eisenhower supporters. It indicated a movement of unpledged groups toward Eisenhower, and the first ballot confirmed this. The General received 595 votes, only 9 short of victory. Although Taft had received 500 votes, with Warren 81, Stassen 20, and MacArthur 10, the fact that Eisenhower was within a hair's breadth from winning brought about an immediate transfer of votes. Eisenhower reached 845 to Taft's 280, and a second ballot was not even necessary.

For Vice President the convention, with the blessing of Eisenhower's advisers, chose the junior Senator from California, Richard M. Nixon. Nixon, at 39, was already a veteran of the Republican anti-Communist crusade. As a member of the House subcommittee that interrogated Alger Hiss he had achieved favorable publicity, and had used this plus some bitterly criticized tactics of improperly associating Democratic Senator Helen Gahagan Douglas with "pro-Communist" stands to defeat her. Nixon's congressional voting record could in no way offend the Taft wing, and he came from a politically important Pacific state.

The party platform adopted a condemnatory stand against Democratic proposals and the Democratic record, although it called for extension of social security and the promotion of slum clearance and urban renewal projects. Wary of the defeats of 1948 in farm states, it promised to carry on a support of farm prices at 90 percent of parity. It took strong stands against federal aid to education and Truman's efforts at a mandatory federal health insurance program as matters best left up to the states. The Republican platform also took more cognizance of the Southern states by backing off somewhat from its 1948 civil rights pronouncements. It sought states right's positions, where states in the South and West were concerned, by advocating that offshore resources (such as tidelands oil) be controlled by the states rather than by the federal government. The foreign policy plank was largely the work of John Foster Dulles. It embraced collective security and rejected isolationism, yet it accepted foreign commitments only with the qualification that they not endanger the economic well-being of the United States. To appease the "Asia Firsters," it promised not to neglect the Far East at the expense of the West. The Truman program was described as a "negative, futile and immoral policy of containment." Instead, the platform promised "liberation," and spoke of making the nation a "dynamic, moral and spiritual force" in the world. In the usual fashion of partisan platforms, it left many areas suitably vague and subject to the widest variety of interpretations.

The Democrats faced a problem that the Republicans had been dealing with unsuccessfully for 20 years—that of fielding a candidate to struggle against the White House and its extensive base of support. Truman's early announced refusal to run again, even though eligible, left the field wide open. Several years earlier, Truman had attempted to recruit Supreme Court Chief Justice Fred M. Vinson as his successor. But Vinson had firmly declined on reasons of health, and eventually Truman settled on Governor Adlai E. Stevenson of Illinois as the candidate whose political, administrative, and campaigning abilities he most admired.

In spite of the large number of those who were glad to be considered available, there were serious obstacles facing most of them. The earliest front-runner was Senator Estes Kefauver of Tennessee, who had compiled a television following through heading a special Senate committee investigating crime. But his liberalism and civil rights were offensive to the conservative South, and his early scramble for delegates before the President had even announced his intentions was regarded by many party regulars with the same disfavor that might have befallen a boy who has seized too many of the goodies on the family table without asking permission. Kefauver also had created animosities among some city politicians by exposing tie-ups between local politicos and criminal elements.

Truman had kind words to say about Secretary of Commerce W. Averell Harriman of New York and Vice President Alben W. Barkley of Kentucky. But Harriman had little experience in politics and lacked any base of support outside his own state. Barkley might have been in the running except for his age, which was 74. For this reason, labor leaders refused to give him their support. Although Truman urged him to put his obvious popularity to the test with the convention, Barkley decided to withdraw. Senator Robert S. Kerr of Oklahoma was an announced candidate, but his close association with the oil interests of the Southwest was damaging. Kefauver finally eliminated him from the race by a primary defeat in Nebraska. Another favorite son was Senator Richard Russell, a conservative anti-Truman candidate. But Russell, although highly respected in the Senate, had little other support outside of Southern conservatives and Dixiecrats.

With the memory of the disruption of the party in 1948 still hanging over them, the convention rejected an attempt of Northern liberals to insist that all delegates must pledge their support to whomever the party nominated. Party unity won out instead, and several objecting Southern states were quietly seated without pressing the issue. The initial ballot reflected the hard work and primary victories of Kefauver, with Stevenson in second place and Russell leading several also-rans. But as the various favorite sons dropped out, Stevenson moved steadily ahead to a victory on the third ballot. For Vice President the Democrats chose a Southerner, Senator John J. Sparkman of Alabama, liberal except where civil rights were concerned and a staunch supporter of the Truman administration.

Although the worst cracks in the Democratic party facade were lightly plastered over, a considerable seam developed in the unity of the Republicans. This was occasioned by the tactics of Taft and his supporters, many of whom gave promise of "going fishing" at election time. Eisenhower therefore sought out Taft and, after an extended talk which took place at Eisenhower's New York residence, announced that the two were largely in accord. The harmony was actually achieved by Eisenhower agreeing to many of Taft's orthodox Republican positions, much to the distress of Eisenhower's liberal friends. It took the General several steps to the right but it brought the Taftites back into the fold and preserved party unity. It also meant that the uncomfortable "Ike" found himself on the platform with such candidates as Republican Senator Jenner of Indiana, while listening to denunciations of his old friend, General George C. Marshall, as "a front for traitors." Eisenhower was not well informed on domestic issues, nor did he actually have any articulate philosophy of government or economics. But his fumbling delivery improved with coaching, and the voters appreciated his undoubted friendliness and warmth. They reacted strongly in favor of his impromptu remarks, even though they were banal generalities, because his sincerity, informality, and integrity were considered more important. The shriller wing of the Republican party vilified the Democrats in terms of "Korea, communism, and corruption" (sometimes expressed in pseudochemical formula as "K1C2"), but Eisenhower spoke against the administration in more measured tones. His running mate almost suffered a disaster when it was disclosed that a group of wealthy California businessmen had furnished Senator Nixon an $18,000 secret slush fund. Since this seemingly paralleled the corruption the Republicans were committed to eradicate, there was considerable worried discussion as to whether Nixon should be dropped from the ticket. But the young Californian made a perfectly executed television appearance with his attractive wife and the family dog. Instead of dealing with the obvious questions posed by such contributions, he concentrated on his past as an American log-cabin example of the rise of a poor but honest man in politics. He pointed to his wife's "respectable Republican cloth coat" (not the expensive mink coat recently in ill repute) and asked that his listeners make their decision known to the Republican National Committee. The response was heavily in Nixon's favor, and Eisenhower welcomed him into the fold. A subsequent Republican effort to find something of similar dubiety in Governor Stevenson's background had little success. The financial exposure wound up with both candidates voluntarily baring their income tax returns for the last ten years.

Adlai Stevenson's campaign presented to the voters one of the finest speakers in American political history. He had a wicked wit, a fine intelligence, and a talent for the appropriate phrase. He was undoubtedly a man of high principles, integrity, and idealism. Richmond, Virginia, audiences, hearing from the candidate a refusal to discuss his attitude on civil rights in anything but candid and painfully honest terms, were impressed by his integrity but not willing to vote for it. Stevenson had obvious obstacles in attempting to disassociate himself from those portions of the Democratic record under attack, and chose to emphasize instead the rise in the standard of living under Democratic administrations. But ultraconservative elements of the Democratic South in South Carolina, Florida, Virginia, and elsewhere announced themselves as "Eisenhower Democrats" and attempted separate electoral slates with some success. Senator Joe McCarthy vilified Stevenson and his election aids on the radio, and vice presidential nominee Nixon echoed the McCarthy line. The climate of McCarthyism nourished the growth of anti-intellectualism, and the slang term "egghead" became the derisive label for the intellectual.

The Democrat slogan, "You never had it so good," to remind voters of American prosperity was effectively countered by Eisenhower's promise that nothing would be taken away. (The farmers were even promised 100 percent of parity instead of the Democrats' 90 percent.) A last-minute promise by Eisenhower that, if elected, he would personally go to Korea to try to wind up the war, was a telling stroke. But Eisenhower's overwhelming appeal was an unstated reassurance to the average voter that under his benign guidance nothing could possibly go wrong. Stevenson's appeal to the rational intelligence was readily topped by Eisenhower's appeal to the emotions. Coupled with his undoubted status as a genuine national hero, it meant a landslide victory. The General captured the entire North and West, and Virginia, Tennessee, Florida, and Texas in the South. His electoral count was a huge 442 to Stevenson's 89, and accounted for 55 percent (33.8 million) of the popular vote to Stevenson's 44 percent (27.3 million). It was an Eisenhower vote rather than a Republican vote, however, for the Republicans narrowly retained control of the Senate by one vote, 48 to 47, and by a 221 to 213 margin in the House. Several extreme isolationist Republicans were defeated, and candidates like Senator McCarthy in Wisconsin, Jenner in Indiana, Bricker in Ohio, and many others ran far behind the Eisenhower totals in their states and regions.

Dwight D. Eisenhower

The incoming President was born on a farm in Denison, Texas, in 1890, but when less than a year old the family moved to Abilene, Kansas. Here he grew up and acquired the lifelong nickname of "Ike." He graduated from high school in 1909 and two years later, despite his mother's strongly pacifistic religious background and consequent disapproval, he entered the United States Army Academy at West Point. Young "Ike" graduated in 1915 in the upper 40 percent of his class, and while stationed in San Antonio, Texas, in 1919 he met and married Mamie Doud of Colorado. During the First World War he served as a tank instructor near the Gettysburg, Pennsylvania, area he came to love. After the war he held various assignments and was selected for further study at the General Staff School and the Army War College. In the 1930s he held an executive position in the office of the Assistant Secretary of War, and spent the years from 1933 to 1939 as General MacArthur's assistant in the Philippines. Eisenhower made an impressive record in the 1941 Louisiana war games. His rise became accelerated, and he filled a variety of high-level planning positions. Eisenhower moved from Army Chief of Operations to Commander of American Forces in the European theatre, and in November 1942 became Commander in Chief of Allied Forces in North Africa.

Eisenhower's performance in North Africa and in the Sicilian and Italian campaigns made him a figure of repute, and he was chosen to be Supreme Commander of the Allied Expeditionary Force which invaded France and moved successfully into Germany. His decision to move on a broad front to the Elbe River instead of attempting a reckless push toward Berlin, although criticized politically by the British, was upheld militarily and historically. It was, in any case, Eisenhower's own decision, as he made abundantly clear. When he returned to the States in 1945 to become Army Chief of Staff, he was undoubtedly America's most popular military figure. When he retired in 1948 he accepted the presidency of Columbia University and in 1950, at President Truman's request, he assumed leadership of the newly organized NATO.

Modern warfare called for tremendous organization, and a large military bureaucracy emerged to provide the necessary consideration of a highly complex series of varied operations, many of them in partnership with allies. Eisenhower's greatness was in creating the necessary organization to carry on the war's operations, and in his combination of crisp command and adroit reconciliation in running a large and nationally varied team in smooth cooperation. Although there was never any doubt as to who was boss, Eisenhower possessed personal talents of patience and flexibility plus firm convictions on subduing nationalistic rivalries to achieve unity of command. Eisenhower had to deal with strong-willed political figures such as Roosevelt, Churchill, and de Gaulle. He also had to contend with military prima donnas like Montgomery and Patton, and his qualities of patience and tact combined with his professional characteristic of decisive and forceful action to place him in an unquestioned position of military and administrative supremacy.

Eisenhower had little or no knowledge of the machinery of government or of the history of American politics. His view of the presidency was essentially a negative and passive one in which the Chief Executive did not so much lead as referee, and then only when needed. The only area staked out for prime government responsibility was in budgetary and credit policy. Eisenhower's administrative style was the military chain of command and delegation of authority which he was so used to in the Army. The role of strong executive leadership practiced by the nation's great and near-great Presidents was put by in favor of greater authority and initiative from Cabinet members and advisers. The President, as Eisenhower saw his office, did not initiate policy even where Congress was concerned. Cabinet officers and department heads were to run their operations without presidential directive or participation, and advisers and Cabinet officers were to recommend policy as well as implement it. The President wanted to participate only when all the staff work was completed and a final decision was necessary, rather than suggest policy direction or listen to suggestions as to how it could be shaped. Material requiring executive decision was to be presented orally or boiled down to less than a page, although the latter course assumed that every matter shared equal importance with every other matter. The entire process therefore meant the assumption of far more authority and importance by Cabinet and department heads and the presidential advisers. It also meant the screening out of dissenting opinion or importuning Congressmen. Without direct presidential involvement, agency function could readily become divorced from policy and presidential knowledge, as in the frightening example of the U-2 case. (See Chapter 4.)

The President's economic philosophy was apparent in his Cabinet appointments. Both Eisenhower and his advisers paid tribute to the world of business in terms that did not differ widely from Coolidge's famous dictum that "The business of America is business." Where business was concerned, Presidential Aide Gabriel Hauge told the San Francisco Commonwealth Club, "The Eisenhower conservative deplores its reckless denunciation, either directly, as when its moral basis is attacked, or indirectly, as when attempts are made to drive out or keep out of government service those who have risen in its ranks." The Cabinet which Eisenhower formed was almost completely chosen from the front ranks of corporate affairs. Secretary of State was John Foster Dulles, an attorney associated with the prominent Wall Street international law firm of Sullivan and Cromwell. Dulles had acted in a foreign policy advisory position on a variety of occasions. He had attended the San Francisco Conference of 1945, and was Truman's representative in negotiating the peace treaty with Japan. A man of rigid moralism and stern Presbyterianism, Dulles was also a man of intelligence and knowledge-ability in foreign affairs who had assiduously groomed himself for his post. The fact that his maternal grandfather and his uncle had both been Secretaries of State (John W. Foster under Benjamin Harrison; Robert Lansing under Wilson) seemed to give him additional assurance that a providential design had ordained that he be Secretary of State. Dulles was supremely confident, self-assertive, and easily the strong man of the Cabinet. Eisenhower had complete confidence in him, and Dulles supplied content as well as implementation in the area of American foreign policy.

Strongest Cabinet voice in domestic policy and probably the second most influential of all was George M. Humphrey as Secretary of the Treasury. An accurate reflection of Eisenhower's basically conservative views, Humphrey was president of the giant Cleveland holding company and steel manufacturer, M. A. Hanna and Company. A successful industrialist, Humphrey came to Washington to balance the budget, eliminate waste, and curtail government operations. Another strong voice was the president of General Motors, Charles E. Wilson. Wilson quickly provoked congressional and public opinion when he opposed divesting himself of $2.5 million in General Motors stock. His remark at this point that, after all, "what was good for the country was good for General Motors, and vice versa," was widely publicized (although frequently in the "vice versa" aspect) and drew amazed and bitter comment. Wilson finally agreed to let go of his holdings and was confirmed for the post of Secretary of Defense, where his announced policy was to rechannel government purchases away from a variety of small and middle producers to a relatively few and allegedly more efficient major producers. Of the two ultraconservative Cabinet appointments, Secretary of Commerce Sinclair Weeks of Boston and Secretary of the Interior Douglas McKay of Oregon, the former also caused immediate furor. He fired the head of the Bureau of Standards because that agency produced a report damaging to the manufacturer of a battery additive, and Weeks considered this a lack of awareness of "the business point of view." The subsequent public and congressional furor caused Weeks to back off and to reemploy the discharged bureau director.

Secretary of Agriculture Ezra Taft Benson was a Taftite by conviction as well as by family ties. A Utahan and one of the powerful ruling Twelve Apostles of the Mormon Church, Benson believed that government farm subsidies should be stringently reduced. His subsequent efforts, although not entirely successful, made him the most cordially detested Eisenhower Republican in all the farm states. The new Attorney General was Herbert Brownell of New York, a close Dewey adviser in the realm of national politics who assumed a similar position with the President. The chairman of the Republican National Committee, Arthur E. Summerfield, a Michigan used-car dealer, received the traditional political appointment to Postmaster General. Congress approved the establishment of a new Cabinet position, the Department of Health, Education, and Welfare, several months after Eisenhower's inauguration, and to that post the President appointed Mrs. Oveta Culp Hobby of Texas. Mrs. Hobby had been the commander of the new Women's Auxiliary Corp (WAC) during World War II, and was the politically influential wife of a Texas newspaper publisher. The only nonwealthy, noncorporate, non-Protestant member of the Cabinet was the Secretary of Labor, Martin P. Durkin of Maryland. Durkin was head of the AFL Plumbers' Union, and a Catholic liberal Democrat. His incongruous presence in the Cabinet provoked the Washington wisecrack description of the Cabinet makeup as "nine millionaires and a plumber." Although the description was close rather than precise, it did convey accurately the general tone and outlook of Eisenhower's appointments. Durkin's complete lack of shared viewpoint with his fellow Cabinet members brought about his resignation after only ten months. He was replaced by James P. Mitchell of New Jersey, whose previous post as a New York City department store executive made him a more compatible member of the new team.

Eisenhower contributed several innovations to the organization of the White House staff. Two new positions were added to aid with the volume of paper work flowing between the White House and the Cabinet: a Staff Secretary and a Secretary to the Cabinet. Additionally, posts which had functioned without title, recognition, or organizational form were given new status. These were the Special Assistants to the President, which Eisenhower used to bring in specialists in various fields; and the Assistant to the President, which formalized the closest advisory position to the President. The latter post was filled by one of the most influential members of the Eisenhower administration. This was Sherman Adams, former Governor of New Hampshire, whose ready access to the President's ear was second only to that of Dulles. Appointed soon after Eisenhower's election, Adams was considered by Eisenhower as his Chief of Staff. His exact duties and responsibilities were never specifically defined, but Eisenhower sought to free himself from many of the burdens of state by giving Adams unprecedented authority over domestic and administrative affairs, including political decisions. No other presidential aide or adviser in American history was ever given such powers. Because of his sweeping responsibilities and Eisenhower's confidence, and because he assiduously channeled so many policy and decision-making functions through his own office, Adams was properly regarded as the Number Two man in the government.

Press Secretary for the White House was James C. Hagerty, also an important confidant of Ike's. Eisenhower had less to do with the press than any president since Coolidge, and Hagerty frequently functioned as a public relations man in turning up material for news stories and soothing the generally hostile Washington press corps. Most noteworthy among the many Special Assistants to the President who moved rather quickly in and out of the administration were Nelson A. Rockefeller and Emmet Hughes. The multimillionaire Rockefeller, soon afterward to become Governor of New York, was supposed to function in the areas of peace and disarmament proposals. Before being elbowed out of the picture by the displeased Secretary of State, Rockefeller had a large share in drawing up the President's Atoms for Peace project and developed the "Open Skies" proposal that he presented to the Soviets at the Geneva Conference of 1955. Emmet Hughes, a writer for Time and Life magazines and later a columnist for Newsweek, wrote some of Ike's campaign speeches and acted as an assistant and adviser. He was largely credited with the idea of having Eisenhower go to Korea if elected, and his voluminous notes of the many inside meetings he attended became the basis for a judiciously critical account of the Eisenhower presidency, The Ordeal of Power (1963).

As President, Eisenhower was principally an administrator and an efficient organizer. He left many of the routine affairs of state, even major ones, to assistants, and reserved himself for the top decisions. For guidance in these Ike relied upon staff briefings, and he had a high regard for visual presentations accompanied by charts. Eisenhower's administrative innovations helped to maintain a smooth flow of paper work; his use of the National Security Council reflected a new integration of diplomatic and military decisions of state; and his Cabinet members were expected to run their departments without any aid from the White House. Eisenhower did not exert strong leadership where Congress was concerned, and Capitol Hill found this an unusual change from his Democratic predecessors.

Modern Republicanism

Domestically, "modern republicanism" turned out to be a disappointment to the ultraconservative wing of the GOP which had hoped for a dismantling of New Deal and Fair Deal enactments. The administration stand was rather that the structure of social welfare legislation was generally satisfactory but that expenditures might be curtailed and a more businesslike management would be established. There was a strong conviction that more government should be left to the states where possible; that free enterprise receive all possible advantage; and that government regulations of industry would be eased through favorable appointments to the regulatory agencies. Both Eisenhower and his Secretary of Agriculture Benson believed that farmers would be better off without government subsidies or government marketing restraints, but Congress (and the farmers themselves) would accept very little change in support policies. The new administration believed that a balanced budget was both necessary and possible; that the establishment of a "stable dollar" was essential to the nation's well-being; and that individual and corporate income taxes should be cut. Defense expenditures were not to be an excessive burden on the nation. It was not so much an active program as a vow to carry out government operations more efficiently and more cheaply.

The new administration immediately set about the inauguration of its new fiscal policies. The Federal Reserve Board withdrew its support of government bond prices, but the free market price immediately slumped. Rather than sell their bonds on a falling market, bankers raised their loan requests from the Federal Reserve in order to accommodate their customers' credit needs. The "Fed" thereupon upped the interest rate which it charged member banks—the rediscount rate—and made credit more difficult and costlier. Member banks then had no choice other than to raise their own interest rates on loans. The administration's attempts to balance the budget only helped further to tighten the supply of money and credit available. Civil Service vacancies were left unfilled, reducing the federal payroll by 100,000 individuals or so. Government departments were ordered to cut back spending wherever possible. With the approach of an armistice in Korea, military spending was cut back sharply.

The result of such cutbacks and a tight money policy was, however, not merely antiinflationary but a movement toward a dangerous deflation in the economy. The business cycle in the fall of 1953 took a severe drop, and the nation clearly was on the threshold of a sharp recession. The Eisenhower administration bravely and euphemistically referred to the downswing as a "rolling readjustment," but nevertheless quietly undertook Keynesian measures to restore economic equilibrium. The Federal Reserve reversed its tight money policy, the federal budget was permitted to display a $3 billion deficit, and taxes were reduced by a similar amount. Although budget cuts had been made, the large items for military expenditures and foreign aid prevented any major slashes. Much to the audible dismay and anger of the GOP ultraconservatives, the first Eisenhower budget called for a deficit, as did four others during the Eisenhower years. The campaign promise to reduce taxes culminated in the disputed Internal Revenue Act of 1954. Under the terms of this legislation, wartime excise taxes on luxury items such as jewelry, luggage, furs, and theatre tickets were reduced as much as 50 percent. Federal taxes on transportation and telephones were also reduced, but levies on tobacco and alcohol were unchanged. Despite the protests of Democrats that the working man was being neglected, the new income tax law provided little relief for the lower-income brackets. Some additional consideration was given to retired persons and pensioners; but stockholders were singled out for $50 tax-free exemptions on dividends, and business received more generous depreciation allowances. All in all, the new tax law was best described by the opposition as one which furnished most tax relief to those who needed it least.

The oil, public utilities, and natural gas industries all received special privilege at the hands of the Eisenhower administration. Although Truman had successfully vetoed a bill to hand over the government's off shore resources of oil to the states and had ordered the tidelands set aside as a naval petroleum reserve, President Eisenhower and a Republican Congress set out to maintain their campaign pledge of reversal. The principle that such federal tidelands belonged to all the people of the nation was upheld by the courts, but Congress, with enthusiastic support from the Southern Gulf states, moved to override it. The Submerged Lands Act of 1953 declared that the undersea resources belonged to the several states in such measure as their boundaries proclaimed when they entered the Union. Generally this was three leagues (10.3 land miles), but this confusion gave rise to a number of court cases that were not finally decided until 1960. When the legal dust had settled,

Louisiana, Mississippi, and Alabama received title only to a point three nautical miles offshore (3.45 land miles). Texas and Florida, which originally had made staunch claim to three leagues, received the greater undersea boundary. The states, under the new legislation, permitted oil companies to work such deposits with far less control and supervision, and with greater returns in royalties, than would have been possible under the federal government. No return was provided for the nation.

A fight of some years duration carried on by public power advocates and conservationists against the Idaho Power Company over Hell's Canyon, a deep gorge in the Snake River between Oregon and Idaho, was resolved in favor of the private utility company. Numerous reports pointed out that the single large dam called for by public power and conservation groups would provide far more power than the three smaller dams the Idaho Power wanted, and would also furnish irrigational and recreational services for the public. Both Eisenhower and Interior Secretary McKay of Oregon let it be known that they favored private business solutions over federally sponsored projects. Their proposal was referred to as a "partnership" between government and private enterprise. Under the terms of this arrangement, the federal government paid for such portions of the dam as the floodgates and navigation locks. The private utilities financed the powerhouse and maintained the generation equipment. As their share in the "partnership" concept, the utilities companies then received a monopoly over the dam's power production and its profits. Although congressional opposition publicized such a curious "partnership" arrangement and showed that a single high dam would produce far more power at lower costs than the Idaho Power Company admittedly preferred by constructing three smaller dams, the high dam was denied by the Federal Power Commission and Hell's Canyon handed over to the area's private utilities. Efforts to reverse the commission's decision in Congress were narrowly defeated. The Eisenhower administration later approved a $750 million federal project for irrigation and water supply dams on the Upper Colorado River, in an area of extreme construction difficulties and without proposals from private power companies.

A far more satisfactory outcome to proponents of public power was the decision to undertake jointly with Canada the Saint Lawrence Seaway project. Private interests had sought for several decades to exploit the hydroelectric potential of the Saint Lawrence River, particularly from the New York boundary of the river. But the river was as much, if not more, Canadian than American, and the Ottawa government had been steadfast in its refusal to permit private industry to exploit the river's resources. The growing national need for electric power resulted in a series of investigations and reports on development of the Saint

Lawrence River, all of which recommended joint Canadian-American development of ship locks, navigation aids, and power plants.

In the United States, strong political pressures operated to prevent any progress. After World War I much of the successful opposition to Saint Lawrence development came from powerful private utilities, effectively blocking public power proposals. In the 1930s the private utilities were no longer so powerful, but railroad interests and East Coast ports, fearing substantial economic losses through rerouting of shipping, blocked all attempts to develop the seaway. After World War II the economic picture changed. The great steel companies of the East and Middle West became increasingly dependent upon Canadian iron ore, particularly the deposits in northern Quebec. Political pressures increased with the knowledge that the exasperated Canadians were planning to undertake the ambitious project by themselves if the United States continued to procrastinate. These pressures, plus a more enlightened attitude from eastern Congressmen persuaded Congress to pass the Wiley-Dondero Act in 1954 establishing the Saint Lawrence Seaway Development Corporation, which would construct and operate the American share. Dredging the river and constructing the locks was undertaken jointly by the two nations, but the power plants were to be operated by the New York State Power Authority and its Canadian provincial counterpart, the Hydro-Electric Power Commission of Ontario. The completed project was opened in 1959, making it possible for ocean liners and freighters to dock at the inland ports of the Great Lakes by using the Saint Lawrence River passage and its access locks.

Although Eisenhower as a presidential candidate in 1952 had stated that he would not "impair the effective working out of TVA," it quickly became evident that his views on private enterprise were to curtail government participation in the power industry wherever it existed. TVA had had a steady growth, and the defense needs of the Atomic Energy Commission preempted a growing portion of the booming electric power demands of the area's population and industries. To meet the combined needs, TVA directors had requested funds for an additional steam plant at Fulton, Tennessee. Such an addition would not only help supply the AEC, but would also satisfy the swelling demands of the Memphis area. President Truman had seconded the request, and budget funds were made available for the construction. Eisenhower's budget director had, however, demonstrated to the president that TVA consistently attracted industry by its cheap power rates, and that such attractiveness multiplied as the incoming industry helped to snowball new power demands. Faced with the continued expansion of TVA, Eisenhower acted to cut back the agency. The budgeted funds were refused, and the administration turned to private utility companies for aid. A group of utilities, headed by Edgar H. Dixon of Middle South Utilities, Inc., and Eugene A. Yates of the Southern Company, offered to build a plant in Arkansas across the river from Memphis to supply both the city and AEC. Their original offer of $200 per kilowatt was rejected, and a new offer of $149 was submitted, although the government would have to furnish more than $6 million for transmission lines for the proposed plant.

In the ensuing thicket of negotiation and argument, which involved governmental agencies ranging from the Security and Exchange Commission to the Corps of Engineers, the administration arranged for the AEC to sign the Dixon-Yates contract for $107.25 million in October 1954. Public power advocates and friends of TVA, led by Republican Senator William L. Langer of North Dakota and Democratic Senator Estes Kefauver of Tennessee, opposed the contract in Congress. Kefauver denounced it as a "no-risk" monopoly handed over to private business by the government. Others criticized the increased governmental and taxpayer costs of a $4 or $5 million raise in power rates, and the undermining of the TVA "yardstick" principle which effectively kept consumer power prices down. The administration forces had the upper hand, however, until a conflict of interest brought the breath of scandal to the new administration. It was ascertained that Adolphe H. Wenzell, who acted for the Budget Bureau in accepting the allegedly higher Dixon-Yates bid, was also an official of the First Boston Corporation which was the investment house underwriting the bonds supporting the contract. The embarrassment of an administration which avowedly had come to office to eradicate just such scandals was only avoided by a timely statement from the city of Memphis. That municipality would have nothing to do with the Dixon-Yates plant, city officials said, and it would be far cheaper for the city to construct its own plant. Since this effectively destroyed a large part of the Dixon-Yates potential market, President Eisenhower used this announcement to cancel the Dixon-Yates contract in July 1955. The Dixon-Yates utility group had already spent some $3.5 million on the project, so they sued to recover these expenditures from AEC. After half a dozen years in the courts, the Supreme Court finally held that the AEC could not be held liable for the contract because of the conflict of interests.

The public power-private power political conflict continued throughout the Eisenhower years, with TVA actually increasing its generating facilities by more than 50 percent from the era of the Dixon-Yates conflict to the end of the Republican administration. A compromise legislative bill was the TVA Revenue Bond Act of 1959, under the terms of which TVA as a public corporation was permitted to issue its own revenue bonds to provide for expansion, instead of requesting appropriations from Congress. In the year following the act, the agency successfully floated a $50 million bond issue for construction. Others followed in subsequent years. The power controversy also took on new life when President Eisenhower recommended that private enterprise be permitted a hand in atomic development. The ensuing congressional struggle produced a compromise, the Atomic Energy Act of 1954, which made atomic information, material, and production facilities available to private industry under AEC safeguards. The act could be regarded as a victory for the President, although in 1957 a Democratic majority voted for the government to build and operate three steam atomic reactors which would sell steam to private utilities for the generation of electricity.

Natural gas received a favorable hand from the administration similar to its stand on private utilities. Interstate gas pipelines came under the jurisdiction of the Federal Power Commission's authority to oversee "rates, charges, and services" in such interstate commerce. President Eisenhower hoped that by exempting the gasoline companies from FPC's price control, the industry would be encouraged to expand production and thus eventually bring about a lower price for natural gas consumers. A 1956 congressional proposal for such exemption had the support of Southern conservative and Southwestern oil Democrats together with most Republicans. The measure was headed for routine passage when a bribery revelation temporarily halted its progress. Republican Senator Francis P. Case of South Dakota dramatically exposed the offer of $2500 from an oil company for his campaign. He had not solicited the funds, Senator Case said, and the company clearly expected his vote on the natural gas bill. Instead, he sent the money back and voted against the measure. It still passed, but President Eisenhower vetoed the act. He favored the legislation, the President announced, but he could not permit the passage of a measure with such support.

The Eisenhower administration's outlook on agriculture contained the same basic elements stated for other fields: more control to be centered away from the federal government; reduce government costs; and move, wherever possible, toward a "free" market. In none of these respects was Republican farm policy very successful. Farmers were understandably concerned at their standing in shares of the national income. Whereas the rest of the country had seen a steady rise in income, farm income had declined noticeably. Thousands of farmers had been driven off the land, but the remaining units still turned out huge surpluses When Eisenhower was campaigning in 1952, his famous farm speech delivered in Kesson-Minnesota promised the farmer ". . . not merely 90 percent of parity," but "full parity." In the face of the importunities of Secretary of Agriculture Ezra Taft Benson, however, Eisenhower changed his mind and supported a cut in the parity figure rather than a raise to 100 percent parity. Benson was convinced that if the government reduced its parity payments, the farmers would turn away from the overproduction of already surplus crops and grow more profitable commodities. Also, it would save expenses for the government.

After a stiff fight in Congress, the administration's Agricultural Act of 1954 was passed. It called for authority vested in the Secretary of Agriculture to cut supports on basic commodities—wheat, corn, rice, peanuts, and cotton—to 82.5 percent in 1955 and to 75 percent in 1956. The act also permitted the secretary to sell the government's purchased surpluses abroad at low prices ("dumping"), and provided for some of the surplus to go into the public school lunch program. But farm prices fell, Benson's name was anathema, and the farm debacle was one reason why the voters returned a narrow Democratic majority to Congress in 1954 to displace Republican domination. Two years later Eisenhower and Benson again attempted to reduce farm surpluses by paying farmers not to grow the five overproduced staple commodities. The resultant Agriculture Act of 1956 contained an idea from Democratic farm proponents, the so-called soil bank. This provided for leaving the land fallow or planting only soil-building cover crops for a period of five years, during which time the government compensated the farmer for the lost crop income. The program was very similar to New Deal concepts, but it was equally unsuccessful in reducing farm surpluses or the mounting costs of government farm supports. Far from reducing the budget in farm expenditures, the Eisenhower and Benson program increased from less than $3 billion in 1953 and 1954 to more than $5.5 billion in 1960. Commodity inventories on hand grew proportionately. In good part, technology was more to blame than Eisenhower and Benson, since newly developed nitrogen fertilizers and disease-resisting new varieties of wheat and corn permitted the farmer to put half of his acres in the soil bank and collect a check for doing so, while growing the same or more than before on the remaining half of his acres. The basic problem of simply too many Americans engaged in farming remained untouched as before. Although the Benson farm policies were more damaging to small farmers than large and reduced the number of agricultural units in the nation, the remaining large ones continued to produce surpluses of farm products.

Prolabor forces who had taken heart from Eisenhower's appointment of Martin Durkin as Secretary of Labor or from the President's message suggesting that the Taft-Hartley Act needed amendment were quickly disillusioned. Eisenhower soon handed the issue of Taft-Hartley amendments over to strongly antiunion Congressmen and appointed antilabor individuals to such agencies as the National Labor Relations Board. An administration-favored bill was introduced in the Senate with antilabor provisions, such as a government-supervised vote before strikes could be called, and was only defeated when even the antilabor Senators became resentful over Republican "steamroller" tactics. Labor's suggestions regarding unemployment in the recession of 1953–54 were ignored, and the administration viewpoint overlooked reliance upon job training or retraining and placed heavy reliance on the communities' responsibility. On this topic, Defense Secretary Wilson again put his foot in his mouth by his analogy on the plight of the unemployed: "I've always liked bird dogs better than kennel-fed dogs myself—you know, one who will get out and hunt for food rather than sit on his fanny and yell." This remark, with its origins in 19th century Social Darwinism, pained the administration and provided more ammunition for Wilson's many critics. Organized labor nevertheless benefited from expansions in the unemployment insurance system and continued its steady growth. The CIO had improved its public image by expelling its Communist-dominated unions in 1949 and 1950. After several years of negotiations, labor moved to present a united front against its political enemies by its re-union as the AFL-CIO in 1955. With the passing away of its old craft union-industrial union disputes and its older leaders, the two bodies merged under a new constitution with George Meany of the AFL as president and Walter A. Reuther of the Automobile Workers Union as head of the strong industrial union department.

Some aspects of social welfare received legislative treatment in the first Eisenhower administration, and many more remained in abeyance. In 1954, the Social Security Act was extended to cover self-employed persons such as proprietors of small businesses, farmers, and professional men, and to cover occupations such as the domestic servant. Two years later a larger variety of self-employed were admitted, and the age limit for receiving benefits was reduced for women to 62 and for disabled persons to age 50. Further expansions in the second Eisenhower administration raised the benefit payments and relaxed the retirement age for men to 62 years also. Congress acted to increase the benefits to railroad workers under the Railroad Retirement and Railroad Unemployment Insurance Acts. Eisenhower had requested Congress to raise the minimum wage from $0.75 per hour to $0.90, but Congress chose to put the figure at $1.00 instead.

Where the issue impinged upon a sector of the private economy, little or nothing was done by the federal government. The Housing Act of 1954 provided for only 35,000 units to be constructed in the nation, while the Housing Act of 1955 added only 45,000 units of public housing to the total. (Eisenhower had originally requested 140,000 such units.) Subsequent acts within the next five years provided for additional units, plus allocation of funds for slum clearance and easing mortgage restrictions. In no case were the measures adequate as an approach to this grave national problem. In the field of medical care and national health insurance, the issue brought out great controversy but no solution. The lack of medical care for large numbers of Americans, and statistics that showed the United States eighth in the world in infant deaths, behind such poorer nations as Holland and Sweden, were facets of the national medical care scene that had long enlisted the attention of many. The steadily rising costs of hospitalization or private health insurance coverage also exacerbated the problem. The opposition, frequently led by the American Medical Association with charges of "socialized medicine," insisted that the federal government need not be responsible for subsidizing the health of its citizens and objected to the cost of such a project. The administration, following its principle of favoring free enterprise, sought a compromise which would have given the subsidies to private insurance companies to lower the costs of medical care for those in income brackets preventing their normal participation. Both sides attacked the proposal, however, as either too much or too little government attention to the problem. The proposal never saw the light of legislative day.

Another national problem that came no closer to solution was the need for federal aid to education. The shortage of teachers and classrooms was acute throughout the nation, and many states were financially unable to meet any further costs. Proponents of federal support in the area of education argued that, as an activity utterly vital to the economic health of the nation and the productivity of its citizens, the federal government had a basic responsibility of support, even from this restricted viewpoint. Supporters of federal aid also pointed out grimly that its opponents must face the reality that state and local government were literally at the end of their financial tether and that no other source of support existed outside the federal government. Opposition to the idea came from those who fought any expenditure of federal funds other than for military purposes; from conservative Republicans who insisted that it transgressed constitutional limitations; and from conservative Southern Democrats who feared a break in the wall of segregation through such legislation. The administration, unwilling to take a strong stand on the issue, presented a feeble proposal to aid only the neediest states. But the several states were no more willing to take a demeaning educational pauper's oath than were individuals in the field of welfare, and a combination of partisan politics and conflicting selfish interests was able to stifle any congressional approach to this national problem.

One area in which the Eisenhower administration was willing to expend federal funds was in pursuit of road building, where it had the active support of Democrats. The description of such expenditures as both a defense measure and as one enjoying wide public approval brought out bipartisan support. The Federal Highway Act, passed in 1956, provided more than $33 billion to be spread over a period of years to construct some 41,000 miles of interstate roads and superhighways throughout the nation. The federal government was to bear approximately 90 percent of the cost, with the balance coming from the states. A concurrent raise in the federal tax on gasoline and allied road-use products was to defray a large part of the cost. The act provided a stimulant for the construction and roadbuilding industries, and a subsequent act in 1958 added more funds for the project.

The Waning of McCarthyism

Although many anti-McCarthy Republicans argued that the return to the White House of a Republican administration would be the best way to bring the demagogic Joe McCarthy to heel, this turned out to be a completely fruitless and illogical argument. It did not take into account that whatever "deal" may have been made between McCarthy and the aspiring administration during the campaign would be swiftly junked by the junior Senator from Wisconsin when it was to his advantage to do so. Nor did it consider that the demagogue must always attack to retain his status and his public stature. Further, McCarthy had made headlines on his own so far, so he owed nothing to Eisenhower or anyone else.

Senator Taft and other powers in the Senate considered that they had successfully pocketed McCarthy by giving the Communist-investigating chores to the bumbling Senator William F. Jenner of Indiana as Chairman of the Senate Internal Security Committee and to Representative Harold R. Velde of Illinois as Chairman of the House Un-American Affairs Committee. McCarthy was given the Chairmanship of the Senate Government Operations Committee, which was given over to nothing more thrilling than reading reports from the General Accounting Office. But McCarthy soon found that one of his subcommittees could be utilized to investigate virtually anything an aggressive chairman wished, and in this capacity in the 83d Congress McCarthy was soon lambasting any target in sight, Republican administration or no. The State Department, McCarthy's earliest target, furnished the first occasion for a clash with the administration. President Eisenhower had appointed a long-time career diplomat, Charles E. Bohlen, as Ambassador to the Soviet Union. Because Bohlen was identified with the hated Roosevelt and Truman presidencies which had been vilified in the 1952 campaign as "20 years of treason," and because Bohlen (as Roosevelt's State Department interpreter) had defended the despised McCarthyite symbol of the Yalta Conference, McCarthy denounced Bohlen as a "security risk." Senator Taft, who regarded McCarthy as a useful partisan tool but of dubious senatorial value, now intervened. Assuring his colleagues that there was absolutely no suggestion by anyone reflecting on Bohlen's honesty, the appointment was confirmed, 74 to 13.

But McCarthy was not through with the State Department. Two of his assistants set off on a bizarre and thoroughly buffoonish "investigation" of the State Department's Information Centers in European nations. Roy M. Cohn, a young New York attorney, and G. David Schine, the 26-year-old scion of the Schine hotel chain, were McCarthys' committee counsel and "chief consultant." Schine's credentials as "an expert on communism" rested upon a six-page pamphlet of amazingly inaccurate information titled "Definition of Communism," evidently printed by his father's hotel chain. The pair made a lightning trip through European capitals and American embassies (4 hours in Paris, 16 in Bonn, 19 in Frankfurt, 20 in Rome, 6 in London, etc.) checking library catalogues for suspect volumes or embassy operations for "efficiency." Their frequent press conferences en route were the shame and embarrassment of American diplomatic officials, as the ignorance of the pair was delightedly exhibited by the press for the amusement of Europe. Other than some belated "book burning," neither this "investigation" nor one of the Voice of America produced anything other than the usual brand of McCarthy publicity. President Eisenhower indicated his contempt for the book burners in a public address, and was obviously upset by the genuine morale problem in the ranks of Foreign Service Officers and State Department personnel, a number of whom had resigned in protest over the attacks by McCarthy and his aides. Although he had categorized McCarthy as a gutter fighter by his refusal to "get in the gutter with that guy," Eisenhower refused to discipline McCarthy publicly or officially. Eisenhower had an almost negative concept of the role of presidential leadership, and he feared an open break with the right wing of the GOP. The Senator also had friends in high places, including FBI Director J. Edgar Hoover, who publicly avowed his friendship with and admiration for McCarthy while his agency was presumably investigating the Senator from Wisconsin at the direction of the Senate.

Senate reports, whether setting forth his unexplained expenditures of funds collected for anti-Communists drives, his support of the German SS troops who slaughtered unarmed U.S. soldiers at Malmedy, or his improper accusations in the election defeat of Senator Tydings of Maryland, had no effect upon McCarthy. His colleagues, and particularly his Democratic opponents, were amazingly silent. Only Senator Ellender of Louisiana fought to limit McCarthy's committee to the actual duties assigned to it, and only Senator Fulbright of Arkansas voted against the absurd $214,000 appropriation McCarthy requested for its new operations. It was not until McCarthy attacked a venerable and more cohesive institution than the State Department—the United States Army—that he started down the path to his ultimate downfall. He had been investigating alleged espionage in a secret radar center at Fort

Monmouth, New Jersey, and from there got on the track in January 1954 of an Army dentist who may have been a Communist. Dr. Irving Peress, who had been routinely promoted to major at nearby Camp Kilmer, had refused to answer portions of the "loyalty" questionnaire and had enraged McCarthy by taking the Fifth Amendment when subpoenaed to appear before his committee. Peress applied for an honorable discharge, and the Army took the easy way out by granting it. Snuffling angrily at the suddenly vacant trail, McCarthy bloodhounded Brigadier General Ralph Zwicker to the stand to explain the potential victim's escape. He demanded to know the identity of the faceless individuals who might be "responsible" for the promotion of "a Communist." (McCarthy did not trifle with such legal niceties as using "alleged" before an actual verdict was arrived at, partly because his senatorial status exempted him from any libel or slander suit.) When General Zwicker, who was testifying under Army orders, was unable to pinpoint such individuals or seize the now-discharged dentist for a court-martial, McCarthy vented his distemper on Zwicker. The General, a decorated war hero, had to listen in angry silence to McCarthy telling him he "wasn't fit to wear the uniform of his country" and other personal insults.

At first the administration, through Secretary Robert T. Stevens, sought to iron out differences in an "inter-family" meeting with McCarthy, but the Senator represented the quiet conference as an appeasement of his activities despite Stevens' later agitated refutations. The Army found a way to strike back in the person of McCarthy's brash young assistant, G. David Schine. The influential scion of a hotel chain had been inducted as a private, and the other half of the McCarthy investigating duo, Roy M. Cohn, badgered officialdom from the Secretary of the Army on down to exempt Schine in some way or get him a commission and put him in some Washington sinecure. These activities of Cohn were detailed by the Army and leaked to the press. McCarthy leaped to the fray, roaring that the Army was holding Schine as a "hostage." The ensuing official hearings by McCarthy's committee of the Army-McCarthy charges and counter-charges became one of the most bizarre and dramatic episodes of the decade. Carried live on television for 35 days during daytime hours, it attracted an audience estimated at 20 million during the spring of 1954. Not only was it a unique political circus unrivaled in American history, but McCarthy in action caused a tremendous public revulsion. Most viewers found it difficult to watch the vulgarity and crudity of the man, the viciousness and lack of decency and fair play which characterized his every move, without registering a strongly negative reaction to the McCarthy spectacle, regardless of previous sympathies.

Soon after the Army-McCarthy Hearings ended, Republican Senator Ralph Flanders of Vermont introduced a resolution of censure against

McCarthy based upon the latter's contempt for the truth and contempt for the Senate. A select committee of three Republicans and three Democrats headed by a stern Mormon and ex-federal judge, Republican Senator Arthur V. Watkins of Utah, was named to hear the charges. In September the committee asked for McCarthy's censure for "conduct . . . unbecoming a member of the United States Senate." Since McCarthy was in the hospital, the vote on the recommendation was not taken until December 2, 1954, when McCarthy's colleagues voted 67 to 22 in condemnation of his behavior. With two thirds of the Senate boldly voting against him and even the White House belatedly complimenting the committee, and with his public image considerably tarnished, McCarthy's demagoguery lost its power to threaten or impress. His influence dissipated, his feeble efforts to reassert himself ignored equally in politics and in the media, McCarthy drifted into a frustrated backwater of Washington activities. In May 1957 he died of obscure causes, evidently aggravated by the heavy drinking of his latter years. McCarthy's demagogic and mendacious attacks upon individuals and institutions was a pathology that afflicted most of the United States. It contained elements of the isolationism, the antiintellectualism, and the antilibertarianism that were frequently found just beneath the surface of American life. Its persistence in the 1950s and 1960s reflected the more extremist hysteria of Cold War fears, and resulted in additional erosion of American civil liberties.

The climate of the times that had supported McCarthyism was also responsible for the Eisenhower administration's expansion and tightening of the government internal security system and the loyalty regulations bequeathed them by Truman. A massive rechecking and recombing operation of government employee files was carried out by the FBI, and in early 1954 Eisenhower was able to announce that more than 2,200 "security risks" were no longer in government employ. Neither the names of the ex-employees nor their alleged offenses were made public, but the press was able to find out that the charges more often than not had little to do with communism, and that many of the 2,200 were resignations which were a normal part of employee attrition. Much of the press belabored the administration for this "numbers game" which lumped a variety of causes from drunkenness to homosexuality together and implied subversion to all. It not only defamed all individuals leaving government employ in that period, but gave a false picture of the subversion supposedly a part of previous government operations. But the administration was bent upon impressing the public with its vigor in eradicating subversion from government circles, in sharp contrast to the alleged "softness" of the preceding presidency.

One of the more unusual victims of this compulsion and the crippling Cold War mentality of the times was the outstanding American scientist,

J. Robert Oppenheimer. A distinguished and influential physicist, Oppenheimer was the head of the World War II Los Alamos atomic bomb project. Subsequently, he had been chairman of the Atomic Energy Commission's General Advisory Board, and was under contract as a consultant with that agency. A crank letter brought Oppenheimer's file up for rechecking. Although it was well known that he had had friends in the 1930s who were or had been Communists, and had admitted to spending the night with a young lady who was a Communist, these associations were considered to take on added seriousness in the climate of the early 1950s. The President ordered Lewis L. Strauss, Chairman of the AEC, to place a "blank wall" between Oppenheimer and any AEC material and to request his resignation. Since much of the formation of the atom bomb had come originally from Oppenheimer's mind, the "blank wall" seemed superfluous. Without actual charges, Oppenheimer refused to resign and preferred to submit to a hearing. During 1954 a special commission listened to government charges that Oppenheimer had associated with Communists in the past, had told conflicting tales of the associations, and had not been "enthusiastic" about promoting the development of the hydrogen bomb as a newer and more potent superweapon. Oppenheimer reiterated his lack of any attachment to the Communist cause—which was granted—but in an evident conflict between public and private loyalties the conflicting stories he had told in the past proved damaging. He had, for example, warned authorities of an attempt by a Communist to gain information from a friend of his, but had tried with a variety of stories in suspicious fashion to keep his friend's name out of the account. Behind the scenes, but evidently damaging to Oppenheimer's case, were his differences with the Strategic Air Command in continental defense policies, with Edward Teller in the development of the hydrogen bomb, and with Admiral Lewis L. Strauss of the AEC over atomic energy policies. No one ever questioned Oppenheimer's loyalty, nor did the commission weigh his enormous contribution against his imprudent, if undamaging, acts of the past. The commission pronounced him "loyal," but considered him tangled tales and his past associations to be evidence of "fundamental defects of character" that precluded his security clearance with the AEC. Both the arbitrary nature of the hearings and the commission's findings against a man of Oppenheimer's admitted stature and contributions served to alienate a number of the nation's scientists. Oppenheimer did not suffer socially or academically from the verdict, as many other victims of the era of McCarthyism did; but his tribulations and the oddities of a hearing which proclaimed no lack of loyalty, while denying a further role in atomic energy to one of its founding fathers, reflected the obsessions of the times.

McCarthyism slowly subsided, leaving victimized individuals and a somewhat eroded support of civil liberties in its wake. The climate of the times was born of the emotional disappointments of World War II and the postwar years. The grand alliance against Hitler soon became another conflict, but against the previous ally, Russia. Both Russia's aggressiveness and hostility and the successes of world communism brought American society to an agony of apprehension. The new and terrible atomic horror hanging over mankind was compounded by the successful Soviet atomic breakthrough in 1949, and the incidents of espionage and the defection of scientists heightened the atmosphere of fear and suspicion. In 1949 a new and powerful nation of communism, the People's Republic of China, ousted America's client, Chiang Kai-shek, from the mainland; in 1950 another American client government in South Korea became the focal point of a war which not only included Chinese Communist troops inflicting casualties upon American soldiers, but frustrated the United States with its exasperating duration and its new concept of the limited war. These many, terrible, and disturbing events and setbacks were responsible for a "Red Scare" mood and accompanying witch-hunts that far outdid the 1920s in size, effect, and intensity. A miasma of suspicion that set citizen to investigating citizen was slow to dissipate. A nation floundering without goals was being forced to acknowledge its fallibility, and many of its average citizens felt betrayed when the verities and platitudes of their youth no longer seemed to hold true. Countless intellectuals and professional people, particularly in such spheres as journalism and advertising and among the writers of Hollywood, were blacklisted and denied a livelihood because of associations of two decades before. Perhaps an even more important aftereffect of the suspicions and countless investigations of the 1950s was the driving away of many Chinese scientists who thereupon put their newly developed talents to the production a few years later of China's first atomic explosion. Aeronautical engineer Tsien Hsue-shen, a brilliant professor of aeronautics at Caltech and a rocket specialist, and Chao Chao Chungyao, a Caltech nuclear physicist, were to have an important part in the People's Republic atomic growth. They were typical of the other top 80 or so Chinese nuclear scientists who were trained at such institutions as M.I.T., Chicago, Caltech, Michigan, and California, and who were harassed out of their aeronautical and teaching jobs by investigations or because of the treatment that others had received, and chose instead to return to the honors that mainland China was eager to bestow on them.

The Democrats of Congress, intent upon asserting their staunch anticommunism, were instrumental in passing the seldom-used Communist Control Act of 1954 outlawing the Communist party. But politicians were no longer so eager to run on a platform composed largely of anticommunism, and the Supreme Court in 1957 (*Watkins* v. *the United States*) warned Congress that the right to investigate did not include exposure for its own sake or as a political publicity vehicle. The American Communist party, weak, publicly discredited, honeycombed with disguised FBI agents, was never in any case a threat to the security of the United States.

The Brinkmanship of John Foster Dulles

Eisenhower's trust in John Foster Dulles and the latter's prideful awareness of his personal and family background contributed to a continuing self-confidence in his diplomatic decisions. Dulles' knowledge of international affairs plus his tenaciously held convictions and dominating personality were sufficient to put down any other Cabinet member unwary enough to venture an opinion in the area Dulles regarded as his particular domain. A cultured and somewhat cold individual, Dulles' complex personality was dominated by both a tough, corporate legalism and the stern self-righteousness of a Presbyterian elder. Although of subtle mind and possessing great energy, Dulles' consideration of compromise as essentially a sign of weakness was evidence to his critics of severe flaws as a diplomat.

Dulles was profoundly aware of how the high winds of anticommunism—particularly from the extremists in his own party—had buffeted his predecessor, Dean Acheson. He was determined that both Congress and the public must be convinced that the Eisenhower administration's policies toward the Communist world were tougher, more dynamic, and more positive. The McCarthyite wing of the GOP was appeased by more stringent security regulations throughout government ranks and by allowing McCarthy and the right wing to dominate and run the State Department's Bureau of Security. Dulles also sought rhetorically to convince all that the Eisenhower administration was distinguished from its predecessor by the much sterner face and more positive policies it presented to the Communist world. Thus, words or phrases associated with Truman and Acheson such as "containment" must be replaced. Dulles' subsequent efforts blessed the new administration with a far greater variety of slogans but with little actual change in basic policy. The generic term that was loosely applied to the entire Dulles approach derived from a quoted interview:

> The ability to get to the verge without getting into war is the necessary art. . . . If you try to run away from it, if you are scared to go to the brink, you are lost. We've had to look it square in the face—on the question of enlarging the Korean War, on the question of getting into the Indochina

War, on the question of Formosa. We walked to the brink and we looked it in the face. We took strong action.[1]

Both press and public took considerable alarm over approaching so boldly the very imprecise and never clearly seen "brink" of war, but the media's apt description of "brinkmanship" took hold.

Dulles' choice of a policy to substitute for containment, which he had denounced as negative and immoral, was "liberation." This was a position, according to Dulles, based upon American moral principles and aimed at the oppressed peoples behind the Iron Curtain. Like most of Dulles' pronouncements, it unrealistically divorced ends from possible means. Nevertheless, it was ideologically satisfying to the ultranationalistic wing of Dulles' party, and seemed to presage further American activity. The first of several opportunities to test the new policy came in June of 1953, when spontaneous demonstrations by East Berlin workers over increased work loads expanded into rioting through a sizeable part of Soviet-occupied East Germany. Soviet tanks were finally necessary to put down the riots, and Germans fought the Russian tanks with no other weapons than stones. A number of people were killed. The hollowness of the "liberation" policy, encouraged by the tone of American broadcasts in Europe, was sadly evident by the absence of any possibility for United States reaction. Neither the Eisenhower administration nor the American people were willing to go to war with Russia for the East Germans or any other "unliberated" peoples, and American reaction was limited to ignored protests and a supply of free food to those East Berliners who surged into West Berlin to accept it.

Dulles' first year in office saw still another of his increasingly famous slogans aborted. The occasion was the European Defense Community, a project originally dreamed up by France's Pleven to avert the proposed American-British decision to rearm West Germany. Wary of a newly armed nationalistic Germany, the French plan would instead have used German troops only in an integrated European army. But both the French and the British were reluctant to implement the plan or even present any actual detail. The Eisenhower administration was annoyed over such foot dragging, and Dulles finally threatened an "agonizing reappraisal" of the American policy of leaving its troops in Europe if France and Great Britain did not get on with the business of European unification. Six months later the French Assembly flatly rejected EDC entirely. No "agonizing reappraisal" came about, since both France and Great Britain fully recognized that the United States could not afford and did not really intend to pull out of Europe.

Another threat which fell upon stony ground was incorporated in Dulles' speech of January 12, 1954, to the Council on Foreign Relations.

---

[1] James Shepley, "How Dulles Averted War," *Life* (January 16, 1956), p. 78.

Divided Germany and Austria (top). Berlin's Channels to the West (bottom).

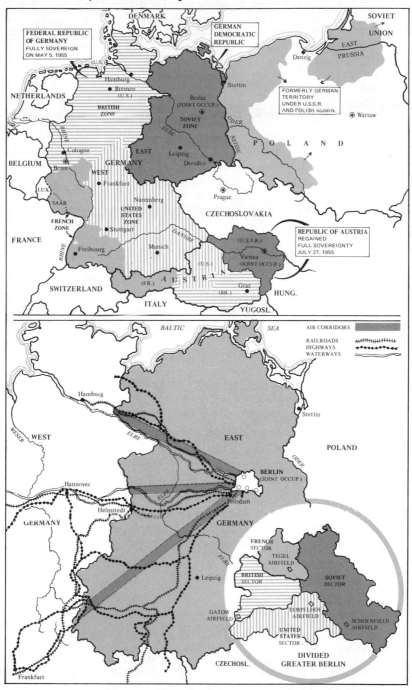

This was the "new look" concept of "massive retaliation," which warned that the traditional policy of meeting aggression by local resistance was too costly to be continued indefinitely. Thus it might be necessary, Dulles warned, that whether Soviet aggression was noted in Korea or elsewhere, the response might have to be a "massive retaliation" of nuclear proportions by the Strategic Air Command at a point not necessarily confined to the actual area of aggression. In other words, Moscow itself might be considered hostage to Communist aggression around the globe. Since Russia had added the hydrogen bomb to her atomic arsenal the year before, "massive retaliation" was a militarily obsolescent statement that badly frightened American allies in Europe. These nations and Dulles' domestic critics insisted that a bombing of Moscow and its retaliatory reaction could scarcely be equated with some Communist success in an area not vital to Amerian security. Whether such an ultimate threat, even given American nuclear superiority, deterred the Soviet Union cannot be known.

Nineteen fifty-four was a year of even greater crises for the Eisenhower administration, particularly in the Far East. In Indochina, aid for the French military campaign against the Vietminh had leaped up precipitately from the amounts furnished in the last years of the Truman administration. By 1954, more than $1 billion flowed out of Washington to the French effort, underwriting 80 percent of their costs and comprising the largest single element in all of American foreign aid. The scares of the Korean War and the fact that the leadership of the Vietminh (Independence League) forces was Communist contributed to increased Washington apprehension over the Indochinese outcome. Unfortunately, the Eisenhower administration continued to communicate to the American public the fiction that Emperor Bao Dai was a popular Nationalist figure heading an independent government instead of the unpleasant fact that his was a completely French-dominated government with very limited popular support. American efforts to bolster Bao Dai's independence by funneling Vietnamese aid funds through his government officials had been resolutely prevented by French authorities. Also communicated to the American public—and largely accepted by Washington[2]—were frequently inaccurate French military reports which persistently represented the Vietminh as being on the verge of defeat. In late 1953 the French Commander in Chief, General Henri Navarre, with

---

[2] Although Senator John F. Kennedy as early as November 1951 had correctly pointed out that: "In Indochina we have allied ourselves to the desperate effort of the French regime to hang on to the remnants of empire. There is no broad, general support of the native (Bao Dai) Vietnam Government among the people of that area." In 1953 he also commented ironically on the continued assurances of imminent victory, but without result. John F. Kennedy, *The Strategy of Peace* (New York: 1960), p. 60.

American encouragement undertook an offensive campaign in a final, desperate hope of gaining a bargaining position with the grimly resolute Vietminh.[3] The last and most disastrous episode of the inglorious "Navarre Plan" was a fortress complex deep in the heart of enemy territory, Dienbienphu. Located in the far north, on the border of Laos northwest of Hanoi, a French army of some 20,000 was completely overrun despite a heroic defense. It marked the final defeat of French forces in Indochina.

In March 1954, the precarious condition of the Dienbienphu garrison was reported to the United States in terms of "large-scale American intervention or we are lost." Admiral Radford, Chairman of the Joint Chiefs of Staff, (although admittedly speaking only for himself) called for immediate intervention by air forces from carriers off the Indochinese coast. Vice President Richard Nixon declared that the United States must send troops if necessary. Dulles also pushed for military intervention, and atomic bombs reputedly were considered. But Eisenhower insisted on such stipulations as virtually to preclude any such American military involvement. Britain must be willing to join militarily in such a venture, preferably with Australian and New Zealand approval and aid, and with hopes of participation from some Southeast Asian nation such as Thailand or the Philippines. Congress must also give its assent. But the British flatly refused, and without allies congressional leaders were equally adamant, even though Eisenhower had enunciated the so-called "domino theory" in an April speech.

Even as the French defenders of Dienbienphu were undergoing their last futile agonies, a conference was meeting at Geneva in hopes of bringing Asian conflict to a peaceful halt. The Geneva Conference of 1954, which covered the period from April 26 to July 21 (including several lengthy adjournments), gave the French the opportunity for a graceful withdrawal and seemed to give the Vietminh many of the fruits of their military successes. It was agreed that a line drawn at the 17th parallel would temporarily divide Vietnam, with the Vietminh being given administrative control over the Northern half. Civilians were given 300 days to move freely from one half to the other as they wished and without hindrance. Two years from the date of the signing of the declaration, July 20, 1956, a national election would be held under international supervision with a view to uniting peacefully the North and South portions of Vietnam. The armistice agreement stated that no troop

---

[3] In the fall of 1953, six months before the Dienbienphu disaster, General Navarre was the cover subject of *Time Magazine*. Here was enunciated the "light at the end of the tunnel" analogy foretelling the imminent defeat of the Vietnamese nationalist rebels. Eighteen years of warfare later, the United States military and the Nixon administration were still using the same analogy against the same, very much undefeated opponents.

reinforcements or additional military personnel could be brought in and forbade any new military bases. The final declaration endorsing the agreements was supported by the United Kingdom, the USSR, the People's Republic of China, France, Laos, Cambodia, and the Vietminh. Secretary of State Dulles refused official United States assent to the declaration, as did the officially unrecognized Bao Dai faction of the divided southern half of Vietnam. However, the United States made clear it supported the election arrangement by an official statement from Undersecretary of State Walter Bedell Smith:

> In connection with the statement in the declaration concerning free elections in Vietnam, my government wishes to make clear its position which it has expressed in a declaration made in Washington on June 29, 1954, as follows: "In the case of nations now divided against their will, we shall continue to seek to achieve unity through free elections, supervised by the United Nations to ensure that they are conducted fairly."

Although in the declaration Smith referred to the United States as having "declared" that it would "refrain from the threat or the use of force" to disturb the armistice agreements and "would view any renewal of the aggression in violation of the aforesaid agreements with grave concern and as seriously threatening international peace and security," the refusal by Dulles to make the United States a signatory revealed the only unwillingness among the major powers to resolve the Indochinese conflict. France, faced with major domestic upheavals over the endless and futile casualties, was most anxious to sign the peace. She still hoped to retrieve some economic benefits from the debris of Vietnam. Great Britain was strongly opposed to any return to colonial involvement, and considered that the possibilities of widening the Indochinese conflict into a great power confrontation were far too dangerous. Both the Russians and the Chinese, with domestic considerations and other more important problems, were glad to sign the Geneva Conference agreements. Reportedly, they also pressured the Vietminh to take much less than the Ho Chi Minh forces' vast successes and their future potential would have warranted. The Vietminh were also mindful of the costs of further military campaigns and had no doubt that any unhindered election throughout Vietnam would bring them to a victorious unification of the nation under their own leaders. When the United States also declared its willingness for a UN-supervised national election, and made no reference to a "North" or "South" Vietnam, the Vietminh had no reason to fear the results of any popular election.

For Dulles, however, it was a matter of principle not to sign any agreement that might indicate Communist successes, whether they were by the bullet or the ballot. He had made this position painfully clear in a New York City speech one month before the Geneva Conference on Far Eastern Affairs began. Dulles was also inhibited from any nego-tiations involving Communist China because of the fury of the primitive wing of his own party toward any diplomatic exchanges whatsoever with Communists, whether Russian, Chinese, Korean, or Vietnamese. This group, frequently known as "Asia Firsters" or the "China Lobby," was headed by Senator Knowland of California, and included a small but very vocal group of Senators such as Jenner of Indiana, Bricker of Ohio, and Bridges of New Hampshire. This Old Guard of the Repub-lican party feared that any peaceful settlement in Indochina would result in an eventual victory for the Communists and perhaps be an opening wedge for Communist China's admission to the UN. This group also felt that any agreement leaving Korea divided meant that the United States had abandoned an unfinished war. Partly because of these domes-tic pressures, partly because of Dulles' own reluctance to be a party to any diplomatic agreement with Communists, Dulles left the Geneva Conference after the first week, leaving Undersecretary of State Walter Bedell Smith behind virtually as an observer.

The Geneva Conference not only did not bring peace to Indochina but the hostility displayed solely by the United States to any peaceful agreement contributed greatly to the resurrection of what was soon to become the Second Indochinese War. During the conference the Em-peror Bao Dai, who was sojourning on the French Riviera, appointed an old political opponent, Ngo Dinh Diem, to be his Prime Minister. Diem was a doctrinaire Catholic of North Vietnam and Mandarin, French-educated background, who had spent the previous four years largely in the United States, where he had worked for and received considerable support among religious and political leaders. The ambi-tious Diem gained some support from an October 1954 public letter from President Eisenhower addressed to him as Prime Minister regarding American aid ". . . to assist the Government of Vietnam in developing and maintaining a strong, viable state, capable of resisting attempted subversion or aggression through military means." When American pres-sure on Bao Dai resulted in Diem's chief rival being removed from command of the military forces, Diem then asserted his control over the army. American support grew behind Diem as the most likely figure to rally Nationalist forces, and the idealization of Diem as popular na-tional leader, very much as Chiang had been officially idealized for many years, began its steady growth in Washington news releases. In 1955 Diem held a thoroughly rigged referendum that chose himself over the still-absent Emperor Bao Dai by 98.2 percent of the vote. (He probably would have won even in an honest election, but Diem chose to ignore his American advisers on this as on many subsequent ques-tions.) Three days after the election, on October 26, 1955, Diem pro-claimed the Republic of Vietnam with himself as President. In the period allotted for mutual movement north and south of those who wished to change their domicile, U.S. propaganda and naval transport played a major role in the resettlement of some 900,000 North Vietnamese, most of them Catholic, in the area below the 17th parallel.[4] A number of the French-educated Catholics replaced other Vietnamese in the bureaucracy of the Saigon capitol. This heavy influx of Catholics raised the number of their faith in the South to slightly over a million, or about 7 percent of the largely Buddhist new nation. They gave Diem his major base of political power, but they also were a latent disruptive factor precariously balanced at the apex of a pyramid based largely upon non-Catholic, anti-French nationalism.

During 1956, when the national election for unification was to be held, the Hanoi regime repeatedly reminded the French of their commitment to this end as part of the Geneva Accords. French political leaders blamed their unwillingness on American pressure, and in April France served official notice to the Cochairmen of the Geneva Conference that she was completely disengaging herself from South Vietnam and her obligations therein. Invitations from the Cochairmen to both North and South Vietnam for consultation on the organization of the national election brought response only from the North. Diem repeatedly ignored efforts to plan for any election, and finally announced that, since South Vietnam was not a signatory to the Geneva Accords, he did not intend to be a party to such an election. Diem had the full support of the United States in refusing to hold a UN-supervised unification election since, as President Eisenhower later candidly admitted, American and other foreign observers had already concluded that Diem could not possibly win a majority in any unrigged nationwide vote. American aid and American military advisers mounted steadily throughout the 1950s and were directed almost wholly to strengthening the Diem government. Virtually all of the economic benefits flowing into South Vietnam aided the small urban middle class, who thus became most intent on preserving the status quo. It was the numerically preponderant rural Vietnamese, both Communist and non-Communist, whose resentment over the Saigon government's repressive measures and failures to inaugurate American-suggested reforms formed the basis of the civil war that was to bring about future American military involvement. The Eisenhower administration, with strong pressures from Secretary of State Dulles, from some of the military, and with warnings that the "national interest" was involved from the President himself, stepped up to formidable proportions the financial aid and official support of Diem that marked a still larger step in the march toward American military participation.

---

[4] Some 150,000 Vietminh, mostly military, were transported to the North on Polish and Russian ships. Nonmilitary Vietminh were urged to remain in the South and work towards the anticipated general election turnout.

Dulles had attempted, even before Geneva, to establish a containment pact for Southeast Asia similar to NATO, but the British in particular were unwilling to prejudice the planned negotiations. After the Geneva Accords were concluded, Dulles pressed for a treaty which would prevent the expected Communist moves into Southeast Asia. After several months of preparation, the United States met at Manila with seven acceptants from among the Pacific nations or those with Pacific interests. On September 8, 1954, Great Britain, France, Australia, New Zealand, Pakistan, the Philippines, Thailand, and the United States signed the Southeast Asia Treaty Organization (SEATO). Although intended to be patterned after NATO, there were substantial differences. The signatories, with the exception of the United States, were far more cautious regarding military commitments. The pact thus called only for consultative measures rather than for binding and automatic military agreements. In the event of an attack upon one of the members or "against any state or territory which . . . (they) may hereafter designate," Article IV stated that signatories "will . . . act to meet the common danger in accordance with its constitutional processes." Dulles wished the pact to be very specific about a Communist threat, but the proposal was defeated. At Dulles' insistence the United States then added its own special appendix to the treaty, stating that its adherence was based upon an attack or other aggression by Communist powers.

The treaty was of dubious value, not merely because of its consultative nature, but because the nations of Southeast Asia and East Asia were largely absent. Most of the signatories objected to the inclusion of doubtful entities such as Chiang's Formosa or Rhee's South Korea. The largest and most powerful nations of the area refused to join—Japan, India, and Indonesia. Smaller and neutralist nations such as Burma and Ceylon, deploring continued Western ties with the area, also preferred not to join. South Vietnam, Laos, and Cambodia, although named as under the protection of Article IV, were not members of the Manila agreement, and invocation of the article was on a permissive rather than a mandatory basis. The continuing containment of SEATO was perhaps more rhetorical than anything else. Widely attacked in the nontreaty nations of Asia, it received relatively little attention in the United States. Nevertheless, SEATO was not without significance, since Dulles acknowledged to the Senate that it also committed the United States to preventing and countering "subversive activities directed from without."

Frictions between Chiang Kai-shek's Formosa-based government and the Chinese mainland furnished several crises for the new administration. Although Eisenhower had no more intention of getting into a war with the Chinese Communists than did Truman, it was important that the Eisenhower-Dulles foreign policy be made to look more militantly anti-

Communist than the previous Democratic administration. At Dulles' suggestion, Eisenhower, early in 1953, revoked Truman's order which interposed the Seventh Fleet between the two adversaries. Instead, the President said, "the Seventh Fleet (would) no longer be employed to shield Communist China." This was referred to as the "unleashing" of Chiang. In actuality, Chiang was in this analogy a toothless old Pekingese whose debilitated forces were completely incapable of taking the smallest nip at the rump of the Chinese mainland. However, Eisenhower's statement was widely interpreted as a new China policy for the United States. It elated the American "China Lobby," which group actually thought the announcement was the forerunner of a Nationalist surge back to Peking. It alarmed American allies in Europe, who saw in the threat a new source of instability in the Far East, and a possible road to war with the People's Republic of China or a nuclear confrontation with Soviet Russia.

Peking said nothing regarding this policy until after the Korean War was brought to a conclusion in July 1953. The following summer a belligerent series of statements emanated from Peking to the effect that Formosa (Taiwan) was to be reunited with the mainland China government. Eisenhower immediately served notice that the Seventh Fleet would resist such an attempt. When the Communist Chinese began bombarding Quemoy, a small island several miles off the Chinese coast near Amoy several weeks later, the executive branch began an internal debate as to whether the tiny offshore islands of Quemoy and Matsu should be included in the defense-of-Formosa commitment. Congressional friends of Chiang were all in favor of United States armed intervention, but General Matthew Ridgway, the Army Chief of Staff, considered the islands as virtually valueless to Chiang and difficult to defend. Eisenhower was determined that Formosa alone was the only proper and reasonable commitment for the United States, and confirmed this view with a bilateral treaty dated December 2, 1954, between Nationalist China and the United States. The treaty included the defense of the Pescadores Islands, much closer to Formosa and inhabited by Nationalist Chinese, but did not include the islands of Quemoy and Matsu. Chiang also agreed not to take any offensive action against the mainland without first consulting Washington. The Seventh Fleet again interposed itself between the Chinese rivals, thereby snapping the "leash" back on Chiang and resuming the Truman-Acheson approach.

The Communist Chinese continued their bombardment, however, and the implied threat was enough to get Congress to agree to the presidential request for armed forces to defend Formosa. By a one-sided vote Congress quickly reported out on January 28, 1955, a Formosa Resolution, which gave the President wide latitude to use whatever means he saw fit for the defense of Formosa and the Pescadores and

Formosa, The Offshore Islands, and Adjacent Area

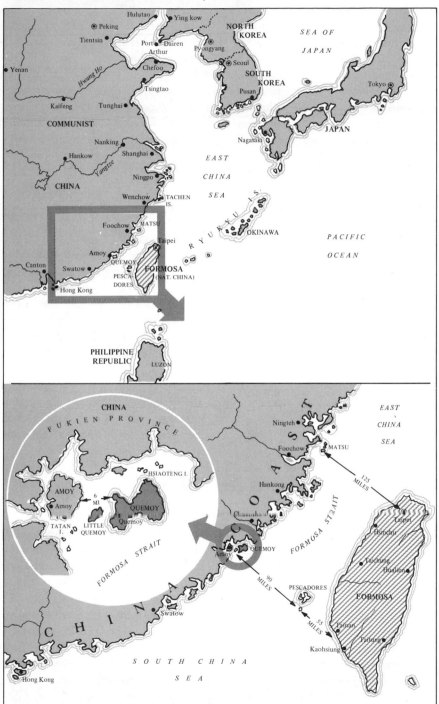

". . . such related positions and territories . . . now in friendly hands as he judges to be required and appropriate. . . ." Eisenhower continued to view the Formosa Resolution as a margin of safety in judging whether a future attack on Quemoy or Matsu could be ignored or responded to if it proved to be the first stage of an assault on Formosa. Dulles preferred to think that, since the Red Chinese leaders spoke of conquering all islands, the commitment should be spread over Quemoy and Matsu as well. This was the occasion for the coining of the term "brinkmanship," when Dulles threatened China with war. Mao Tse-tung denied that the threat had actually deterred him, and the bombardment of the islands gradually subsided, not to resume until three years later. The Formosa Resolution, although it was specific in its limitations of purpose and place, was significant as an early grant of congressional war-making authority to the President and served as a basis for later expansions. The Chinese turned to expanding their political and diplomatic influence in Southeast Asia and Africa, using as a jumping-off point the Bandung Conference held in April 1955 in Indonesia, where Afro-Asians met without a single Western nation and declared their unending opposition to colonialism.

Fearing the withdrawal of British troops from the Middle East would create a gap in the fence he was intent upon constructing around Russia as well as China, Dulles began negotiating in 1954–1955 another treaty based upon the NATO-SEATO concept. Intended to include Egypt, it was tentatively scheduled as METO (Middle East Treaty Organization). Egypt, however, refused to participate, and a treaty known as the Baghdad Pact set up an alliance in November 1955 among the four pro-Western states of the so-called Northern tier—Iran, Iraq, Pakistan, and Turkey—plus Great Britain. Although Dulles promoted the pact, in a series that his critics were describing as "pactomania," the United States preferred to let Great Britain act as its proxy, since it might thereby avoid involvement in any Arab-Israeli war. In any case, the United States already had bilateral military treaties with all the signatories except Turkey. The treaty gave the United States and Great Britain military bases adjacent to the USSR to continue the containment policy, but it had many disadvantages. It drew down the wrath of much of the Arab world, led by Nasser of Egypt, and promoted a tug-of-war for Arab leadership between Iraq and Egypt, wasting efforts and resources which each could have used to better domestic advantage. The Baghdad Pact, with new United States bases close to Soviet borders, was also cause for additional alarm in Russia. The pro-Western King Feisal of Iraq was assassinated in 1958, and a military clique overthrew his government and set up a new, pro-Nasser republic. It then withdrew from the Baghdad Pact in 1959, and the shortened alliance became known as CENTO (Central Treaty Organization) with its new head-quarters in Turkey's capital of Ankara.

Egyptian and Arab resentment toward the Western world helped to bring about a far more serious crisis in the Middle East. Some of the more recent origins of Arab dislike of American and British policies in that area went back to the November day in 1947 when the United Nations voted in favor of a resolution providing for both Arab and Jewish sovereign states in Palestine, even though the Arabs sought to claim all of it. In May 1948, the new Zionist government proclaimed itself the nation of Israel. President Truman extended United States recognition some 15 minutes later, to be followed by all of Western Europe at a more sedate diplomatic pace. Border clashes and guerrilla raids continually violated the truce terms, with the Arab nations rallying behind Egypt's new leader, Gamel Abder Nasser, who called persistently for the destruction of the new state and who insisted that the Israelis must be "driven into the sea." The continuing conflict created a dilemma for the United States, which had continually supported the wish of the Jews to achieve an independent national state in their homeland of Palestine, and whose struggles had drawn political support in the United States over and above their Zionist support. Washington also looked to Israel for aid in rejecting a Soviet foothold in the Middle East. At the same time, the United States and Western Europe desired the friendship of the Arab world not only for reasons of world stability and Soviet containment—which concerned the Arabs not at all—but for powerful oil reasons. These conflicting policies were further complicated by the fierce and strident nationalism and anticolonialism of the Arabs, their own internecine squabbling, and the gradual withdrawal of the British military forces from the Suez Canal area.

Both the United States and Great Britain refused to send arms to either the Jews or the Arabs, but by promising economic and technical aid to Egypt they hoped not only to block Soviet penetration in that strategic nation but also to divert Nasser's militant fanaticism away from Israel's destruction and into constructive internal programs for Egypt. In 1955, the erroneous rumor that the United States was planning to dump surplus cotton stocks on Europe at giveaway prices was one of the factors in a severe drop in world cotton prices. For Egypt, with cotton as some 85 percent of her exports, this was a serious matter. Some of her world customers cautiously held off on their purchases. The Soviets exploited the opportunity by arranging a number of barter deals between Egypt and their client states such as Rumania, Hungary, and Czechoslovakia, in which arms were exchanged for cotton. To the Egyptians, rebuffed by the Western nations on arms purchases but with unquenchable military designs on Israel, it was an arrangement to be desired. To the Russians, it was an opportunity to bypass the supposed fences of the Baghdad Pact. The Egyptians subsequently stepped up their commando raids on Israel and also transshipped arms to the Algerian rebels, much to the anger and irritation of France.

The United States and Great Britain sought to divert Nasser from his militant activities by offering financial aid to help build the greatly desired new Aswan Dam on the lower Nile. Planned as the largest dam in the world, Aswan would provide a gigantic 30 percent increase in irrigated acres for the Egyptian economy, and furnish needed hydroelectric power for its industrialization. The World Bank, headed by Eugene Black, agreed to join the United States and Great Britain in providing the finances for the initial stage of the dam. Thereafter, Egypt was to absorb the largest cost of the $1.3 billion project. The United States avoided consummation of the loan arrangements for the early months of 1956 because of distaste for the growing Egyptian-Soviet arms accord and inability to get Nasser to curb the Egyptian commando raids. In May, Nasser compounded American distrust by recognizing the Peoples' Republic of China, and hinting that there might be other financial sources besides the United States and Great Britain. In July 1956, while Nasser's ambassador had arrived in Washington to ask that the loan be officially committed, Dulles suddenly announced that it would be refused. The Secretary of State's blunt and abrupt announcement shocked even World Bank President Eugene Black, who had no expectation of such a development. Although Dulles was advised by the American ambassador to Cairo that such a denial of the loan would push Nasser irretrievably into the arms of the Russians, he was pressured in the other direction domestically. The China Lobby insisted Nasser should be punished for recognizing Mao Tse-tung's government, and Secretary of the Treasury Humphrey complained that the loan would unbalance the budget. Dulles himself had perhaps more compelling reasons. He was sure that Khrushchev, as a source of financial and technical aid, was an unreal and propagandistic image, the public shattering of which would be a crushing blow to Soviet world prestige. Further, the refusal of the loan based partly on hints regarding the instability of the Egyptian economy would bring Nasser to a crashing political defeat.

Dulles was tragically mistaken on both counts. Since the British and the World Bank loan were tied into the American portion, the entire underwriting fell through. There was a wild and angry reaction in Egypt, and a few days later Nasser announced the seizure of the British and French-owned Universal Suez Canal Company. Its revenues, he said, would now be diverted to Egypt and would be used to finance the Aswan Dam. It was now Britain and France's turn for angry reactions. Dulles, in great consternation, urged American Western allies not to use force and to set about establishing, through a series of meetings, some accommodation for all parties concerned. He attempted internationalization of the canal through a "users association," which neither Nasser nor the British and French were willing to accept. Dulles' mediations were exasperatingly wavering and unclear to friend and foe alike. Although one day he would insist that force was not the answer, the next day's mediations were likely to contain warnings to Nasser which Britain and France might readily interpret as American compliance with military pressure. The two Western allies, with their exasperation over Dulles' zigzag tactics further irritated by the personal hostility between Dulles and Prime Minister Anthony Eden, made plans for military interference. Dulles was notified and refused to take them seriously, but the French despised Nasser for his arms aid to the Algerian rebels, and both France and England refused to have Nasser's stranglehold on their vital oil supplies. The Israelis were readily enlisted in a joint enterprise, since the combining of the military staffs of Egypt, Syria, and Jordan, and the increasing commando raids made it clear to Israel that she must strike first or go under.

On October 29, 1956, Israeli forces struck the Sinai peninsula and rolled up Egyptian men and tanks in a complete rout. France and Britain promptly presented an ultimatum for a cease-fire—withdrawal of both Israeli and Egyptian troops ten miles back from the canal, and Anglo-French occupation of strategic areas. Accompanied by a threat of intervention, the demand was quickly accepted by Israel, but rejected by Nasser. British and French planes then began bombing of Egyptian airfields, and on November 5 their troops began to land at Port Said. The United States scolded Israel for resorting to force and insisted that Washington had no knowledge of the tri-national invasion. The Soviet Union took a strongly admonitory tone, threatening to send "volunteers" and armed forces sufficient to bring peace to the area. The United Nations called for a cease-fire, and the United States, sternly admonishing its allies for the "error" of their ways, also sought—through limiting the flow of Latin American oil replacements—to forestall Anglo-French seizure of the canal. The UN cease-fire and withdrawal was accepted by all parties on November 7, and preparations got under way for United Nations troops to move into the disputed areas.

Although the entire crisis and operation was over within one week, its consequences were of long duration. For the British and the French, it was particularly damaging. Both were weakened in the Middle East; both brought down on the Western world revived apprehensions of colonialism from the Third World nations. Their bitterness toward Dulles' vague diplomacy seriously divided the NATO powers. In England, an electorate split over the propriety of such a move brought about Eden's political downfall. France directed bitter comment on the willingness of the United States to abandon its European allies for Mid-

The Middle East, 1961, and the Suez Crisis, 1956

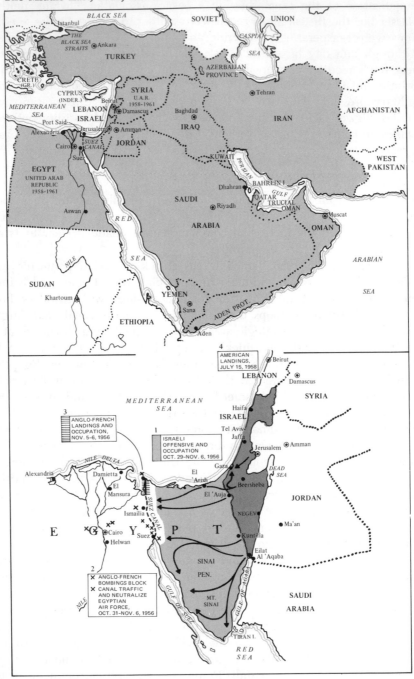

dle East advantages. General De Gaulle's coming to power two years later only increased France's anti-American feelings, and the two nations were never to reach the same level of accord of former years. Additionally, France's recognition that she could not depend on her transatlantic partner gave a major impetus to French development of an independent nuclear deterrent. Israel achieved her immediate objectives of ending the border raids and causing the Arab nations to think twice before entertaining any plans for her destruction. Nasser also profited from the Suez crisis. By his nationalistic coup of seizing the British-controlled canal, and by his refusal to accede to the Anglo-French demands, Nasser readily reinstated himself as an Egyptian hero. Even the Egyptian military defeat, by laying the blame on "superior" British and French forces with little mention of the Israeli contribution, could not effect Nasser's new position.

To the Russians, who lived up to their promise of Aswan Dam[5] aid and who offered to replace Egyptian military equipment losses, it was the beginning of major influence in the Middle East. The governments of that area were also inclined to give the Soviets the full credit for the UN cease-fire on the basis of their threat to intervene. Suez may also have been a beneficial distraction for a crisis in Soviet-satellite affairs. Poland's Nationalist Communist premier Wladyslaw Gomulka, perhaps stimulated by Khrushchev's own de-Stalinization speeches and policies, began making what were too rapid changes for the Soviets. Although Khrushchev made several threatening moves, Gomulka's warning that he would call out the entire Polish nation evidently proved a greater challenge than the Poles' program of de-Stalinization, and Gomulka won the round. Gomulka's domestic and national brand of communism and his increased freedom to maneuver politically evidently triggered a similar, but more extreme, reaction in Hungary. Students swarmed into Budapest streets demanding that Ernö Gerö, the Russian-appointed head of government, be replaced with the very popular Nationalist Communist figure, Imre Nagy. The efforts of the secret police only brought workers into the streets to aid the students, with the highly publicized result of the toppling of Stalin's huge statue in the middle of Budapest. The Soviets agreed to the popular demand for Nagy, and even acquiesced to the request that Soviet troops leave Hungarian soil.

---

[5] In 1958 the Soviets agreed to a loan covering the first stage of construction, and a loan agreement for the second stage was signed in 1960. Work began that year and, although it had been estimated by American and British sources as a 15 to 20 year project, work was completed in just over 10 years. It required some 2,000 Russian technical advisers and more than 35,000 Egyptian workers. Its statistics are massive: the largest dam in the world, it is 17 times larger than the huge Cheops' Pyramid at Giza. It rises 364 feet above the Nile, has a base 1,072 yards wide, with roads on its 130-ft wide top. Behind it, Lake Nasser will extend upstream for 344 miles, well into the Sudan. Built under Soviet supervision aid financing, it is a monument to Soviet-Egyptian cooperation.

On October 28, 1956, the day before the Israelis struck at Egypt, the withdrawal of Soviet tanks began. But three days later Imre Nagy went much farther than his Polish colleagues by announcing that Hungary was leaving the Warsaw Pact. At the same time that British and French troops were landing at Port Said and advancing on the Suez Canal, Russian tanks moved back to Budapest and crushed the rebellion in two days of bloody fighting. Nagy was seized on a pretense of negotiations and secretly executed in Russia some months later, to be succeeded by a more trustworthy Soviet puppet.

To the United States, Suez was an unqualified diplomatic disaster. The Eisenhower administration had been far more concerned with Soviet penetration of the Middle East than with the equity of the British and French positions. Neither view triumphed. The USSR, with both Aswan Dam aid and military aid precipitated by the crisis over the loan and the subsequent canal seizure, had readily leaped over the Baghdad Pact (CENTO) that supposedly reinforced the fence of containment. And the State Department could only look on helplessly as Hungarians died before Soviet tanks during the thick of the Suez crisis, while critics scored the overly passionate tones of American radio propaganda which gave many Hungarians an exaggerated idea of the aid that might be expected from the United States.[6] Dulles defenders insisted that, since the Egyptians were probably going to nationalize the canal 12 years later when the current lease expired, his "calculated risk" policies did no great harm. Yet its immediate seizure on July 26, 1956, resulted from Dulles' handling of the Aswan loan, and brought about a war several months later which completely changed major power influences in the Middle East.

The Search for Peace

Perhaps the most passionate concerns of President Eisenhower were the cause of universal peace and the diversion of the fearfully mounting costs of armament into humanitarian channels. An event occurred some six weeks after the new administration took office which provided the impetus for a fresh look at world atomic and disarmament policies. This was the death of Joseph Stalin on March 5, 1953. Eisenhower considered that the time had come for firm offers for world peace instead of continued indictment of the Soviet Union, coupled with a challenge to Moscow to make similar concrete offers. Using the occasion of a

---

[6] Eisenhower was reelected on the day after the Hungarian revolt was crushed (November 6) and hastened to say that the concept of "liberation" had nothing to do with the use or contemplation of use of American armed forces. Hungarians who had managed to escape across the border were offered sanctuary in the United States.

scheduled talk to the American Society of Newspaper Editors on April 16, the President delivered an address titled "The Chance for Peace." On the terrible costs of modern arms Eisenhower said:

> Every gun that is fired, every warship launched, every rocket fired signifies, in the final sense, a *theft* from those who hunger and are not fed, those who are cold and are not clothed. . . .
> We pay for a single fighter plane with a half million bushels of wheat. We pay for a single destroyer with new homes that could have housed more than 8,000 people. . . .

Although cautiously opposed by Dulles, who favored neither a conclusion to the Korean stalemate nor an admitted end to China's civil war, the President asked for "the conclusion of an honorable armistice in Korea" and "throughout Asia as throughout the world, a peace that is true and total. . . ." The Soviet Union was invited to show its sincerity of purpose toward such ends by some specific act such as signing the Austrian peace treaty[7] or releasing the last of the World War II prisoners. Eisenhower put the United States concretely behind

> . . . a declared, total war, not upon any human enemy, but upon the brute forces of poverty and need. . . .
> This government is ready to ask its people to join in devoting a substantial percentage of the savings achieved in disarmament to a fund for world aid and reconstruction. . . .

Eisenhower's dramatic speech was hailed as a major step toward peace in both domestic and foreign media. Many observers, in retrospect, considered "A Chance for Peace" the finest address of his career. Churchill, in the following month, surprised many by a speech to Commons which virtually abandoned the Cold War. Churchill insisted that security of Russia and the freedom and safety of Western Europe were by no means insoluble problems. The Russians were entitled to their own security, Churchill said, and to that end he proposed a "new Locarno"[8] and later called for a meeting of the four powers "at the summit."

The summit meeting was to take two more years becoming a fact. With the final truce of July 1953 settling the Korean War, despite Syngman Rhee's brash efforts to thwart it by releasing thousands of North Korean prisoners, Eisenhower sought to move ahead on atomic policy. The news that the USSR had tested its first hydrogen bomb in August 1953 lent added gravity to the situation. (The United States had com-

---

[7] On May 15, 1955, the four powers finally signed a peace treaty with Austria, including withdrawal of occupation troops, leaving that country a sovereign and evidently neutralized nation.

[8] The Locarno Pact of 1925 gave a British guarantee to France against German invasion and vice versa.

pleted its own H-bomb several days before Eisenhower's election in November 1952.) The President used a long-standing invitation from the United Nations as a vehicle for a carefully planned talk on "Atoms for Peace," on December 8, 1953, before the UN General Assembly. In this speech, Eisenhower called attention to the idea of developing the peaceful atom as a means of diminishing "the potential destructiveness of the world's atomic stockpiles." He suggested that both the United States and Russia put aside in an atomic bank some of their fissionable material for the use of peaceful atomic knowledge for less-developed nations. The Russians refused, but this idea was incorporated in the Atomic Energy Act of 1954 by authorizing the AEC to provide atomic technical knowledge to friendly nations for peaceful pursuits.

Nuclear policy in Russia was very much a part of the struggle for power going on in the wake of Stalin's death, and the first two years after that event found Soviet policy to be wavering and unclear. The new premier, Georgi Malenkov, warned early in 1954 that a third world war would clearly mean the end of world civilization. But after his fall from grace in 1955, Foreign Minister Molotov repudiated the Malenkov awareness that all nations would suffer from any nuclear conflict, and insisted that any new war would far more likely destroy the "rotten social systems" of the capitalist nations. The new Prime Minister was Nikolai Bulganin, but the real power soon became visible in the First Secretary of the party, Nikita Khrushchev. Russian governance became stable and more assured. A willingness to relax international tension and seek peaceful coexistence became the policy of the new ruling group. This new attitude was manifested in 1955 by Soviet renunciation of naval-military bases in Finland, by a friendly accord with the independent Tito and Yugoslavia, and by signing the treaty which gave Austria her sovereignty as a nation.

In 1954 and 1955 the brinkmanship of Secretary of State Dulles and the crises in Indochina and over Quemoy and Formosa kept American allies in Europe in a state of escalating alarms. The threat of the new hydrogen bomb and several years of unrelieved fears brought about a wide response to the Churchill suggestions for a meeting "at the summit." The British Labor party had strongly supported Churchill's idea, and it seemed probable that after his resignation in April 1955, his successor, Anthony Eden, might even be defeated if Great Britain did not lend her every effort to such a summit meeting. Public feeling in the United States ran strongly in favor of such a conference, reinforced by Republican desires to balance the budget. Eisenhower had successfully overruled the demands and threats from China Lobby senators and military heads in the wake of the Genevan Indochina Conference, but he was still concerned over the atomic stalemate. The four-power meeting was, therefore, arranged for July 1955, at Geneva in the hope that problems dealing with world atomic policy as well as those bearing on German reunification could approach solution.

In view of the fact that the peoples of Great Britain, France, and the United States definitely yearned for some relief from an impending nuclear holocaust, this first meeting of heads of state since Potsdam ten years before was opened on a worldwide wave of hopeful publicity. To meet with President Eisenhower, Britain sent the new Prime Minister, Sir Anthony Eden. The French representative was Premier Edgar Fauré. Although Marshall Nikolai Bulganin was Prime Minister, the real head of the Soviet delegation was evidently Nikita Khrushchev. Although the atmosphere was exceedingly friendly on all sides, the summit conference at Geneva proved almost barren of results. Eisenhower's notable solution was the so-called "Open Skies" proposal, which would permit both the United States and Russia to carry out aerial photography of each others' atomic facilities, and would include an exchange of blueprints of military establishments. From the American point of view, this was assurance against a nuclear Pearl Harbor, which was first in American minds. What was not realized, however, was that in America's open society almost any busy newspaper and journal reader could get a fairly accurate notion of the location of American bases. The Russians would not be getting a great deal from such an offer. Secrecy was to them not merely a helpful aid, but rather an integral and vital part of a national defense which occupied a secondary position in world armaments. Their counterproposal was equally unlikely of acceptance, since the essence of it called for a complete ban on nuclear weapons, after which they would then be willing to talk about inspection plans. Several years later, Khrushchev admitted to President Kennedy that Russians could only consider the open-skies proposal as another method of espionage. The question of German reunification was just as unyielding of results. The only basis on which the Soviet Union would consider reunification through popular election was an agreement which, in effect, would commit the United States to withdraw its forces from Europe.

Although the Summit Meeting was intended to be exploratory and to be followed by a meeting of Foreign Ministers, neither was able to bring about any important agreement. So alarmed was the United States over the Pearl Harbor possibilities in nuclear warfare, that secret reconnaisance flights over Soviet territory were begun shortly afterward. In 1960 this was to result in an international incident which was judged by Eisenhower's successor to yield more in undesirable tensions than in technically beneficial results. Eisenhower's "Open Skies" proposal contained many impracticalities, and probably indicated some of the President's naiveté in diplomacy. Moreover, the Geneva Summit of 1955 had a pessimistic backdrop of numerous Cold War years which, coupled with an unreasoning and emotional public demand for the impossible instantaneously accomplished, helped to accentuate its unproductiveness. Yet Eisenhower's warmth and sincerity were evident to all, and this earnestness perhaps here induced the Soviets to begin their turn away from shrill insistence that the West was actively planning their military destruction. Six months later, Khrushchev advanced the new phrase of "peaceful coexistence" before the 20th Congress of the Communist party. No longer was war inevitable between capitalist and Communist nations, but a peaceful struggle would ensue, according to Khrushchev, which would result in various peoples choosing communism because it had more to offer than did the capitalistic way. At the same time, he made it clear that there was no third alternative to peaceful coexistence or "the most devastating war in history." He also went further in demonstrating Russia's new direction of "de-Stalinization" by a startling speech which confirmed all the cruelties, excessive measures, and pathological suspicions that were a part of the dead Stalin in the mind of the West. Although Eisenhower could not point to Geneva as a diplomatic triumph, it demonstrated that the United States was aware of the need for disarmament and revealed the President's great wish to suggest to the world hopeful paths to peace and his own attempt to meet new Russian attitudes with American ones.

Suggestions for Reading

President Eisenhower has written his memoirs on the presidency in *The White House Years*, 2 vols. (1963–1965). Also favorable is Arthur Larson, *Eisenhower: The President Nobody Knew* (1968). More critical and more representative of the historical consensus is E. J. Hughes, *The Ordeal of Power* (1963), and Marquis Childs, *Eisenhower: Captive Hero* (1958). A recent historical survey is Herbert Parmet, *Eisenhower: The Necessary President* (1972). Accounts by insiders include R. J. Donovan, *Eisenhower: The Inside Story* (1956); E. T. Benson, *Cross Fire* (1962); R. M. Nixon, *Six Crises* (1962); and Sherman Adams, *Firsthand Report** (1961). See also D. A. Frier, *Conflict of Interest in the Eisenhower Administration* (1971), a scholarly examination.

On the policies of the Eisenhower Administration, E. J. Dale, Jr., is critical of economic tactics in *Conservatives in Power: A Study in Frustration* (1960). Both the Eisenhower and Kennedy administrations are dissected and compared in S. E. Harris, *The Economics of the Political Parties* (1962). See also the penetrating and well-written explanation of John Kenneth Galbraith, *The Affluent Society** (1958).

For the politics of the period an excellent overview is Samuel Lubell, *The Revolt of the Moderates** (1956). Eisenhower's Democratic rival is seen in Bert Cochran, *Adlai Stevenson: Patrician Among Politicians* (1969). David S. Broder's *The Party's Over: The Failure of Politics in America* (1971), takes the story from Eisenhower to Nixon. For the waning of McCarthyism, see the references in the preceding chapter. Add D. T. Bazelon, ed., *Point of Order!** (1964), the Army-McCarthy hearings which exposed the Senator's tactics to public view. See also the Oppenheimer case, covered in P. M. Stern, *The Oppenheimer Case* (1969); N. P. Davis, *Lawrence and Oppenheimer* (1968); and Peter Michelmore, *The Swift Years: The Robert Oppenheimer Story* (1969). The demise of the Communist party receives scholarly treatment in D. A. Shannon, *The Decline of American Communism* (1959), and in Nathan Glazer, *The Social Basis of American Communism* (1961).

Additional works on the foreign relations of the period include the incisive W. A. Williams, *The Tragedy of American Diplomacy** (1959); Edmund Stillman and William Pfaff, *The New Politics: America and the End of the Postwar World* (1961), and H. A. Kissinger, *Nuclear Weapons and Foreign Policy* (1957). Important for its background is N. A. Graebner, *The New Isolationism* (1961).

Secretary of State Dulles is objectively treated in Richard Goold-Adams, *The Time of Power* (1962); warmly described by a former subordinate in A. H. Berding, *Dulles on Diplomacy* (1965); and critically dealt with in Herman Finer, *Dulles Over Suez: The Theory and Practice of His Diplomacy* (1964). See also Hugh Thomas, *Suez** (1967).

For works on the early phases of Vietnam, see in addition to the works mentioned in Chapter 2 the two fine works by the noted French authority, B. B. Fall, *The Two Viet-Nams: A Political and Military Analysis** (1964), and *Street Without Joy: Indochina at War, 1946–1954** (1961). Informative are Robert Shaplen's *The Lost Revolution* (1965), and *Time out of Hand: Revolution and Reaction in Southeast Asia* (1969). A scholarly study of the French episode is Ellen Hammer, *The Struggle for Indochina, 1940–1955* (1966). See also Victor Bator, *Vietnam: A Diplomatic Tragedy* (1965); Melvin Gurtov, *The First Vietnam Crisis** (1967); and Jean Lacouture, *Vietnam: Between Two Truces** (1966).

4

The Second Eisenhower Administration

We Still Like Ike

THOUGH the Geneva Summit of July 1955, did not accomplish much of substance, Eisenhower's great popularity moved to even greater heights at its completion. But while he took a vacation in September in Denver, his party's hopes for the reelection of America's favorite in the coming year received a serious jolt. On the morning of September 24, the President complained of severe chest pains which were quickly diagnosed as a coronary thrombosis. Ike was taken to Fitzsimons General Hospital, and the nation was informed that the President's heart attack was a "moderate" one. During the next two months of recuperation, the nation's business was in the hands of an informal group consisting of close adviser Sherman Adams; the Vice President, who chaired the Cabinet; Secretaries Dulles and Humphrey; and Attorney General Brownell. Sherman Adams acted as the liaison between the ill President and both the executive branch and the public, while Press Secretary James C. Hagerty released daily reports of the President's recovery to an anxious world.

By November Eisenhower was able to move to his farm in Gettysburg, Pennsylvania, and to attend a Cabinet meeting on November 22. In February 1956 the nationally known heart specialist, Dr. Paul Dudley White of Boston, was able to pronounce his noted patient fit to carry on his presidential duties. On February 29 Eisenhower told the American people he felt in top shape and had agreed to be his party's nominee for another four years. This disparity between Republican gloom of September and the dancing-in-the-streets exuberance of February would be difficult to exaggerate. Preparations for the August nomination convention quickly got under way, although the only question mark was a momentary one regarding the vice presidency. Eisenhower had offered Nixon a Cabinet position, but Nixon had declined and announced in April his intent to seek the renomination. A month before the convention was to meet, Harold Stassen, the presidential adviser on disarmament, announced to the press that Nixon as a running mate to Eisenhower would reduce the President's vote by 6 percent, according to private polls. Although not made explicit, the alleged discrepancy was brought about by Nixon's strong base in right-wing republicanism and the possibility of his replacing a President suffering from cardiac trouble. Eisenhower maintained a neutral attitude. He had not specifically endorsed Nixon, but he had said he would be "delighted" with Nixon or with several other possibilities as a running mate. But Nixon had great strength among the Republican party regulars, who were additionally in favor of keeping the 1952 ticket intact. Stassen had proposed Governor Christian A. Herter of Massachusetts as an alternate to Nixon, but the movement quickly fizzled out.

The Republican camp suffered another temporary setback when President Eisenhower had to undergo an emergency operation for ileitis, an intestinal disorder, on June 8. But Ikes' recovery was rapid. In July he took off for a Panama gathering of the Organization of American States looking perfectly fit. Both party nominating conventions were scheduled for August, the latest such since Civil War days, with the Republicans gathering at San Francisco's Cow Palace on August 20. The Republican convention was sedate and dull, with such controversial figures as General MacArthur and Senator Joseph McCarthy carefully screened out of the proceedings. Both the press and television viewers found little sustenance in the convention, since the essential business of the gathering was fully decided in advance, and both Eisenhower and Nixon were quickly nominated by unanimous acclamation. The party platform carried forward administration policies of the partnership principle in developing natural resources, flexible farm supports, and a federal aid program for schools. In the area of civil rights, the platform emphasized the Supreme Court's own phraseology of "all deliberate speed." In foreign policy, the themes of collective security and United Nations support were continued. So were the alliance system and aid to underdeveloped nations, but the hope of peaceful coexistence tempered the Eisenhower presentation considerably in contrast to 1950's belligerence. The entire platform was of less than secondary importance to the very popular figure of Eisenhower himself.

The Democratic convention, meeting in Chicago a week earlier, had provided little more opposition or excitement. Adlai Stevenson, the party's titular leader, had long before declared his intentions of running again. His only challenge in the primaries had come from Senator Estes Kefauver, who had officially withdrawn in his favor a week before the convention began. Stevenson's only other threat was from Governor Averell Harriman of New York, who had achieved some support by a forthright statement of backing from former President Truman. But the Stevenson organization readily maintained its lead, and was finally joined by the delegates of favorite-son Governors Williams of Michigan and Meyner of New Jersey. On the first convention ballot, Stevenson easily went over the top with 905.5 votes to Harriman's 210.

The surprise of the convention was Stevenson's politically shrewd tactic of throwing the nomination for Vice President open to the delegates' decision. This produced a wild political scramble, but it also gave the embattled Democrats a campaign point where the prepackaged choice of Republican Richard Nixon was concerned. Front-running favorites for second place on the ticket were Stevenson's erstwhile opponent, Estes Kefauver; the latter's fellow-Tennessean, Albert Gore; the young Senator from Massachusetts, John Kennedy; followed by Mayor Robert Wagner of New York City and Senator Hubert Humphrey of Minnesota. On the first ballot Kefauver, with strong support from labor and with regional help from the Midwest, led Kennedy, whose votes came from the East and, surprisingly, from the South. Although Kennedy's lead on the second ballot reflected the distaste felt for Kefauver's liberalism in the South and in many party organization circles, transfers of votes from Midwesterner Humphrey and Tennessean Gore put Kefauver's winning vote to 755.5 over Kennedy's 589. One of the more significant results of the contest was the great reservoir of goodwill accumulated by young Senator Kennedy through his good-natured acceptance of the vote and his sincerity in asking that Kefauver's nomination be made unanimously.

The Democratic platform viewed with traditional alarm the Republican efforts in every field from agriculture to foreign policy. It pledged 90 percent of rigid price support to the farmers instead of Benson's flexible supports, called for repeal of the Taft-Hartley Act and for more tax reduction for those with small incomes. In place of the Republican partnership principle in utilities it called for public power development, plus requests for government plants for the production of atomic power. Civil rights, which was expected to produce the worst intraparty difficulties, was a gingerly handled topic. It brought forth a carefully compromised plank which recognized the importance of recent Supreme Court decisions as the law of the land but made no pledge to implement the ideal of desegregation. In foreign policy, the Democratic platform differed little if at all from its partisan rival, supporting the United Nations and implying that stronger defenses for national security would be carried out under a Democratic administration.

The campaign reflected the great handicap Stevenson was under in challenging a popular idol. He took to the trail early and covered even more territory than in 1952. His talks were also directed more at the man in the street, with consequent decline in their wit and intellectual content. Stevenson and Kefauver tried vainly to answer Republican assertions regarding the ending of the Korean War and current prosperity by pointing out that Stalin's death probably had more to do with ending the war than did Eisenhower's election promises, and that Democrats had aided the President in domestic legislation more than had his own party. Stevenson attempted to draw his Republican opponent into a discussion of issues by proposing a cutting back of the draft and by suggesting that the United States offer to Russia a mutual cessation of hydrogen bomb tests. Although a relatively vulnerable issue such as Dulles' "massive retaliation" concept might have suffered from Democratic attack, the draft curtailment proved to be easily defensible in Eisenhower's hands. He labelled it as a weakening of national defense and quickly put it aside. The President did not consider the nuclear testing an appropriate issue, and dismissed it on the same grounds. (Although Eisenhower was to make the same proposal before his term was completed in 1960.)

The Democrats had little more success in criticising the failures of leadership under Eisenhower and alluding to the health factor and its effect upon future leadership. This inevitably led to more potshots at Nixon, whose previous "hatchet man" tactics in partisan warfare made him the favorite target for all Democrats. The Vice President countered with the sale of a "new Nixon" and a withering barrage of favorable economic statistics illustrating the national prosperity. The Democratic campaign continually seemed without planned direction and poorly coordinated, while the Republican machine moved smoothly through larger and more appreciative audiences. President Eisenhower was displayed only enough to reassure audiences of his good health, although unexpected Democratic victories in Maine for Governor Edmund S. Muskie and beseeching calls for aid from second-place Republican senatorial candidates briefly shook administration strategies. In the last weeks of the campaign, the crisis in the Middle East and the use of Soviet tanks in Hungary were before the electorate.

Either the voters had already made up their minds, or the crises redounded to Eisenhower's favor, because on November 6, 1956, an avalanche of ballots swept Eisenhower back into office. He polled 457 electoral and 35.5 million popular votes to Stevenson's 73 and 26 million. The Democratic candidate was able to take only Arkansas and Missouri outside of the Deep South states of North Carolina, South Carolina. Georgia, and Alabama. In rolling up majorities larger than in 1952 (with the exception of the Midwest farm belt) Eisenhower had surpassed all records since the Roosevelt 1936 mark. But like the results of 1952, the President's popularity did not help his party. The Republicans, nudged out of congressional control in the off-year election of 1954, remained a minority party in the new 85th Congress by 49 to 47 in the Senate and 232 to 199 in the House. The loss of both houses while winning the presidency was unprecedented, probably reflecting a switch of Democratic votes brought about by Eisenhower's personal popularity.

Domestic Policy and Developments, 1957–1960

Early in January 1957, President Eisenhower presented to Congress a proposed budget of nearly $72 billion. Although it was the largest peacetime budget on record, it embodied the minimal commitments set forth by Eisenhower in his Inaugural Address for foreign aid and national defense, plus such items as school construction and the conservation of national resources. But on the same day that the budget message went to Congress, Secretary of the Treasury Humphrey publicly criticized the President's figures, stating that there were many places where it might be cut. In a press conference, he deplored ". . . the day we thought we couldn't ever reduce expenditures of this terrific amount, the terrific tax take we are taking out of this country. If we don't, over a long period of time, I will predict that you will have a depression that will curl your hair." The irresolute Eisenhower then confused the issue further by supporting his Secretary's criticism of his chief's budget. Under the circumstances, a resolution adopted by House Republicans for deep slashes in the budget was understandable, and the resultant total cut in the President's budget by about $4 billion was less than might have been expected. The cutback in mutual security funds from $3.86 billion to $2.8 billion, however, was regarded as a defeat both for Eisenhower and the progressive Republicans who wished to support his original budget figures.

Not a hair-curling depression of the Humphrey[1]-prophesied type but a serious enough recession greeted the public as the national economy moved into the latter half of 1957. A number of factors contributed, but most critics singled out the administration's tight money policy and its accompanying rising level of interest rates. A severe decline in business investment programs was noted, and a decrease in consumer purchase of durable goods caused producers to cut their expenditures and plant capacity. An additional factor was a shift in government spending

---

[1] Humphrey resigned as Secretary of the Treasury in late 1957 and was replaced by Robert B. Anderson of Texas, whose personal conservative philosophy paralleled that of Humphrey. Anderson had stated publicly, however, that he would not hesitate to use deficit tactics if faced with a major depression.

which moved funds out of military aircraft purchases and created a severe unemployment crisis in Southern California. The largest of several postwar economic slumps, the 1957–1958 recession was inhibited from more disastrous levels by the various stabilizing legislative acts of the Roosevelt-Truman era which incorporated checks on economic downturns. Eisenhower moved in cautious fashion to ameliorate the unemployment and the drops in industrial production. Although the recessions of 1952–1953 and 1946–1947 were successfully treated by tax cuts, Eisenhower and Humphrey refused this suggestion. The administration acted to stimulate industry by reducing down-payment requirements for FHA housing and by encouraging urban renewal projects and other construction. It also pumped several billions of dollars into the highway program. The Federal Reserve acted to make more funds available by reducing the discount rate and lowering bank reserve requirements. Congress passed legislation permitting the federal government to provide hard-pressed states with additional unemployment compensation funds. The recession apparently bottomed out by September 1958, but a low point of unemployment showed some 5.3 million unemployed (7.5 percent) in August. Industrial production dropped off 13 percent from August of 1957 to April of 1958. Partly because of the reduced tax receipts and partly because of additional emergency government expenditures, the fiscal year 1958 showed a $2.8 billion deficit. For 1959, with increased defense expenditures, this had moved to a deficit of more than $12 billion. The 1957–1958 recession was unusual in that the gross national product continued steadily upward, showing an increase from $419.2 billion in 1956 to $444.2 billion in 1958. The cost of living also moved slowly upward during the second Eisenhower administration. Economic national experience for the period reflected a retarded economic growth and a general prosperity, although the persistent minimal figure of four million unemployed cast a shadow on the national statistics.

An event of 1957 produced the most traumatic reaction among Americans since Pearl Harbor. This was the launching on October 4 of the world's first man-made earth satellite, "Sputnik," by the Soviet Union. Weighing 184 pounds, it circled the globe once every hour and 35 minutes, with its radio transmitters relaying scientific information during its earth orbit. The announcement was met by unruffled calm at the White House, coupled with agency explanations that the United States had moved in the direction of military missiles rather than space projects. But scientists pointed out that the United States' most optimistic planning was with a space missile only one seventh as large as Sputnik. Scientific estimates were largely of awe and admiration, and many pointed out that this meant a Russian capacity to put much larger missiles into space. As if to bear them out, the Soviet Union launched Sputnik II on November 3. This satellite weighed an impressive 1,120 pounds, orbited the earth at a distance of 1,056 miles, and contained —in an obvious forerunner of more significant developments to come—a live dog in a pressure-sealed, air-conditioned compartment. The new launching substantiated previous Soviet claims of their ability to project an intercontinental ballistic missile, and effectively destroyed the comfortable American assurance in the superiority of United States technical know-how.

Public exasperation and confusion pressured the Defense Department into two completely disastrous launching failures in December. The world press had a field day with such sarcastic names as "Flopnik" and "Sputternik." Finally, on January 31, 1958, the United States was able to announce the successful orbiting of "Explorer," although its weight of only 30 pounds severely limited its "pay-load" capacity of scientific instruments. The Soviet accomplishment had far-ranging consequences. Around the world it not only boosted Soviet prestige to new heights but tended to displace the United States from its previously undisputed top ranking in science and technology. In Washington, there was general agreement that most of the discrepancies between the two nations could be explained by the fact that the Soviets had concentrated their efforts and resources far more in this particular area than had the United States, but also that the American effort suffered badly from overlapping, duplicating, poorly directed efforts and some lack of financing. In November 1957, President Eisenhower appointed the president of M.I.T., Dr. James R. Killian, Jr., to a newly created post as Special Assistant to the President for Science and Technology to coordinate and supervise the nation's missile and space research. In April 1958, the President introduced in Congress a bill for the reorganization of the Defense Department. Despite the opposition of Rep. Carl Vinson of Georgia, the long-time head of the Armed Services Committee, the Defense Reorganization Bill became law in August. Although Eisenhower did not receive all that he asked for, the new bill cut back on the ability of the various services to lobby before Congress for their own appropriations. It enlarged the Joint Chiefs, took authority for combat operations out of any hands except the Secretary of Defense, and permitted him to consolidate or abolish functions to increase efficiency. A new office of Director of Defense Research and Engineering provided for the supervision of all such work within the Department. Congress also passed in July 1958, a bill creating the National Aeronautics and Space Administration (NASA), an independent agency charged with the promotion of the nonmilitary projects in the American space program.

The United States, smarting under Soviet propaganda and world taunts, pushed rapidly ahead in space and missile development. Both nations orbited a variety of vehicles and satellites which provided valuable scientific data, although the Soviets were able to claim firsts for orbiting the sun and for landing an unmanned vehicle on the moon. On April 12, 1961, the Soviets established another prestigious first by launching the first manned space craft, Vostok I, which carried Major Yuri Gagarin in the 10,460-pound satellite on a 25,000-mile trip in space around the earth. American efforts to send a man into space were intensified with President Kennedy's occupation of the White House in 1961. On May 5, 1961, only three weeks after Major Gagarin's trip, the United States launched Freedom VII carrying Commander Alan B. Shepard, Jr. Shepard's flight, however, was only a short suborbital flight which acted as a preliminary to the more ambitious type of flight made by Gagarin and his colleague, Major Gherman S. Titov, who circled the globe 17 times on August 6, 1971. Not until February 20, 1962, was Colonel John H. Glenn, Jr. successfully orbited three times around the earth, and only after years of crash programs and the expenditure of enormous sums. Psychologically, however, it gave the nation an enormous lift and put the United States into the forefront of the space race. Although it was considered that the Russians enjoyed a temporary lead in rocketry, it was generally agreed that the United States had demonstrated its superiority in scientific space instrumentation.

Space programs and new agencies were not the only consequences of the Sputnik scare. The public apprehension over Soviet advances carried into the realm of education, where many viewers could glimpse the origins of Russian space superiority. Soviet schools, many pointed out, were far tougher than the permissive, nobody-flunks-out secondary school system of the United States. Soviet schools started to emphasize science and languages in the fourth grade, ruthlessly weeded out the incompetents, and conversely pushed ahead and heavily subsidized the outstanding students in higher education. American education, its critics abundantly demonstrated, was too devoted to caring for the mediocre student to be able to reward or even train the brilliant student, and too fearful of political and parent reprisal to introduce difficult science or language courses at the elementary level. Efforts of the Eisenhower administration to aid education were gingerly put forward, with Eisenhower reluctantly agreeing to federal aid for schools. Weak administration efforts were additionally pushed and pulled in several directions by Congress. Many Republicans could not come even to the President's reluctant proposal of using federal funds. Southern Democrats joined in the opposition through fears that any aid to education would contain desegregation processes, and liberal Democrats thought the administration efforts were unrealistically timid.

The American public had already been alerted to the deficiencies of its public education system. Works such as Arthur Bestor's *Educational Wastelands* (1953) and the very popular Flesch's *Why Johnny*

Can't Read (1955) had excited fierce debate over the shortcomings of American mass education. The alarm over Sputnik brought renewed public pressure on Congressmen. Only with links to and emphasis upon "defense" and "national security," however, was Congress able to pass the National Defense Education Act in September 1958. Based both on grants and loans, the NDEA provided for more than 5,500 graduate fellowships for future university teachers, and nearly $3 million in long-term loans which were forgiven by 50 percent if the college graduate agreed to teach in the elementary or secondary school systems for five years. The bill authorized an appropriation of $280 million for grants to state schools on a matching basis for improvement programs in science, mathematics, and modern foreign languages. Although NDEA clearly was of aid in the areas it chose to emphasize, it was only a relatively small step in any attack upon the problem of American education.

Opposition to Republican dominance blossomed in 1958 as at no time since Eisenhower's initial election. The recession of 1957–1958 had given political ammunition to the Democrats, but they also got the chance to pin the corruption label on Republican shirtfronts instead of Democratic. Charges of using their office to promote their own finances brought about a number of resignations at high levels in the Eisenhower administration. Both Richard Mack and John C. Doerfer, Eisenhower appointees to the Federal Communications Commission, were forced to resign for accepting costly gifts or "fees" from the very industry they were supposed to regulate in the public's interest. C. Wesley Roberts of Kansas, the Republican National Chairman, and Robert T. Ross, the Assistant Secretary of Defense, both were pressured out of office through congressional investigations of their conflict of interest cases. The presidential candidate who had promised to "roar clear across the country" for a "decent operation" in government had little or nothing to say as the revelations mounted. Secretary of the Air Force Harold Talbott, Jr., in the face of flagrant conflict of interest testimony, left his sub-Cabinet position with Air Force bands playing and in receipt of the Air Force Distinguished Public Service medal and a presidential commendation.

The gravest test of Eisenhower's campaign promises to "substitute good government for bad government" came with the disclosure by a House subcommittee that Sherman Adams, the President's closest aide and "Mr. Assistant President," as many called him, had intervened with federal agencies for a business friend and received costly gifts and services in return. The friend was Bernard Goldfine, a textile manufacturer who was in violation of the Wool Labeling Act, for whom Adams interceded with the Securities and Exchange Commission and the Federal Trade Commission. Adams and his wife had received a $700 vicuna coat, a $2,400 oriental rug, and several thousand dollars of hotel bills. Although Adams admitted "errors of judgment," Eisenhower continued stubbornly to defend his top assistant, saying "I need him." By the summer of 1958 enough Republicans had pressured the White House over the political damage being done to bring about Adams' resignation in September. (Goldfine subsequently was imprisoned for income tax irregularities.)

The off-year elections of November 1958, were influenced to some degree by the growing evidences that corruption was not confined to one party or the other, and by the recession of 1957–1958. Perhaps a more potent factor in the Democratic victory that followed was the decision in a number of states to put so-called "right-to-work" laws on the statute books. Right-to-work laws were nothing more than a euphemistic slogan to disguise antilabor legislation which, in this case, would have prohibited the open shop. Republicans identified themselves with such attempts and drew in opposition the most intense efforts of labor on behalf of Democratic candidates. Union members, considering they were fighting for something close to survival, rang doorbells and mounted "get-out-the-vote" campaigns in unprecedented fashion. This turnout was considered instrumental in the many resounding Democratic victories that followed. The right-to-work laws were defeated in all the industrialized states (although they won out in several agricultural states such as Kansas), and Democratic governors were elected in such Republican strongholds as Iowa and Ohio. Even in the Republican party itself, voters showed a clear preference for the more progressive candidate. Several upsets occurred, such as the defeat of the venerable Senator Bricker in Ohio, in the course of a Democratic capture of the House and Senate by wide margins. The Democrats moved their lead in the Senate from 49 to 64; in the House, from 235 to 283.

In the wake of such election results, it would have seemed that the 86th Congress, assembled in January 1969, would have pushed ahead on progressive legislation. But very little legislation of any importance passed through Congress in the 1959–1960 session. Where the majority Democrats were concerned, they had to a large extent permitted themselves to become prisoners of Eisenhower's own "spending" issue. Others pointed to the fact that the leadership of Senator Lyndon Baines Johnson of Texas in the upper house and Sam Rayburn of Texas in the House of Representatives was a conservative and cautious arrangement which frequently supported the Republican President. To a large extent, the President's veto power had also been restored to him by the alliance of conservative wings in both parties, and its frequent threat served to inhibit Congress. The small quantity and quality of legislation that was produced came only after the most workable compromises had produced the predictable lowest common denominator of enactment. Washington was becalmed, one commentator observed, "in the collision of planned drift and masterly inactivity." Bills to bring about increased public housing and medical care for the aged were both defeated. A weak civil rights act was enacted in 1960. Congress finally brought the number of states in the union up to 50 in 1959 by admitting both Alaska (January) and Hawaii (August).

Perhaps the issue that most stimulated Congress into action was labor. Much of the actual stimulus had been supplied by the investigations of a special Senate committee headed by John L. McClellan of Arkansas, beginning in 1957. The committee's energetic chief counsel, Robert F. Kennedy, brother of Senator John Kennedy, played a large role in unearthing the racketeering practices in several national unions, particularly the Teamster's Union. His subsequent book, *The Enemy Within* (1959), became a best seller which publicized the committee's findings. The Senate investigations turned the spotlight on David Beck of Seattle, head of one of the least democratic unions in the country, the powerful Teamsters' Union. Although it was alleged that Beck had used union funds for his own use, his actual indictment and conviction came on income tax evasions. The Teamsters promptly elected James Hoffa of Detroit, whose reputation even surpassed Beck's for shady union dealings. Counsel Kennedy and a Senate committee continued their pursuit of new Teamster president Hoffa into a subsequent congressional term, but in 1959 friends of labor attempted its defense without much success. They were able to show that the AFL-CIO had begun to take action against its own corrupt leaders before the Senate committee investigation had ever started and was continuing to do so. Beck and Hoffa were also being presented to the public, they complained, as typical of union leaders so as to bring all of organized labor into disrepute.

Public and congressional opinion ran strongly against organized labor, accordingly, in 1959. In August Congress passed the Labor Pension Reporting Act, which required an accounting by union officials of all pension and welfare funds in their custody. Labor could object to the fact that it was the only segment of the economy so discriminated against, but could scarcely disapprove the genuine protection it offered to the union rank and file. A far more complex and resented piece of legislation was the Landrum-Griffin Labor-Management Reporting and Disclosure Act, passed in September by overwhelming margins in both House and Senate. The act carried further the curbing of possibilities of improper practices by requiring union officials to report regularly to the Secretary of Labor all union financial policies and practices. The bill also contained "bill of rights" provisions to assure union members fuller democratic representation and voice in union affairs without pressures from officials. Labor objected again to the discriminatory nature of the Landrum-Griffin Act, but was most perturbed by what it considered its antilabor provisions. These were expansions of the Taft-Hartley restrictions on secondary boycotts and further curtailment of permissible union activities in labor jurisdictional disputes. Neither the White House nor a majority in Congress were in any mood to respond even to the most valid portion of labor's complaints.

America the Affluent

The population of the United States increased from more than 136 million in 1940 to about 180 million by the end of the 1950s. During that time the gross national product (GNP), or the sum total of all goods and services produced, increased from $228 billion to $502 billion. Total national wealth, in other words, increased 120 percent in the same period that the national population was increasing only 32 percent, meaning that theoretically each individual received a far larger share of the nation's productivity by 1960 than he had at the beginning of the two decades. Statistics and information indicated that the family of average income supported this theory, but the families in the bottom economic bracket made no appreciable increase whatever.

In an era characterized as one of "high mass consumption," the average American family was, in 1950, composed of husband, wife, and two children. The national birth rate was slowly climbing upward. The average parents were in their early 40s, with the wife usually several years younger than her husband. The 1950 census statistics revealed that the average family lived in a house of four rooms and bath, probably self-owned but definitely mortgaged. The house probably contained complete kitchen and bathroom facilities, a radio and a telephone, with occasionally a television set. The husband most likely was employed in an urban area, and the median family income, according to the Census Bureau, was $3,300, although the purchasing power of the 1950 dollar was considerably more than in 1960 or in 1970. Prosperity was the most common impression the average observer received, and the average consumer was able to buy a seemingly generous portion of the nation's varied goods. Yet an improved standard of living which was far more evident to the average consumer in the 1950s than it had been in the 1930s was nevertheless still denied to approximately the same percentage of the population that had suffered from sadly inadequate income for more than a generation.

The United States, although its GNP climbed steadily upwards, was still plagued by the persistent problem of maldistribution of income. In the early 1930s, the Bureau of Labor Statistics revealed that the income of the lowest one-fifth of American families was only $607, moving up to $1,080 by 1950. The second lowest one-fifth moved from $1,349

Population Change, 1940–1960

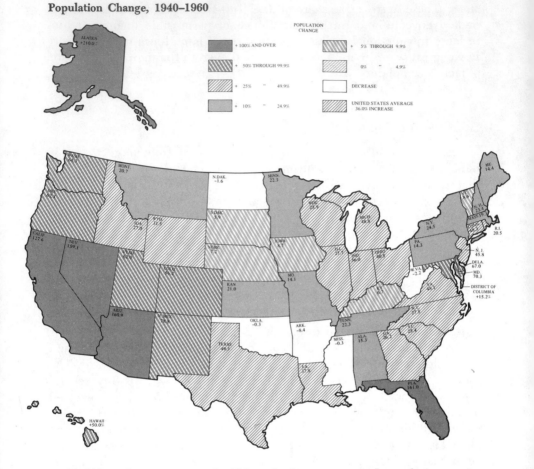

POPULATION
CHANGE

+ 100% AND OVER

+ 50% THROUGH 99.9%

+ 25%   "   49.9%

+ 10%   "   24.9%

+ 5% THROUGH 9.9%

0%   "   4.9%

DECREASE

UNITED STATES AVERAGE
36.0% INCREASE

to $2,444 in the same period. Although this represented an obvious gain, BLS figures for 1950 showed that an income of $3,717 was still necessary to maintain a family of four on a "modest" budget. More revealing figures are those which show what share of the national wealth went to these groups. In the early 1930s, the lowest 20 percent of American families received only 4.1 percent of the national family income, while the highest 20 percent were receiving 51.7 percent. By 1950, with some tax changes in the New Deal and World War II, the richest 20 percent had moved down to 45.7 while the poorest one-fifth had improved slightly to 4.8 percent. At the end of the 1950s, the figures had stabilized at 45.5 and 4.7 percent respectively. In other words, the poorest one-fifth could show some absolute improvement because the entire society realized an increased income, but the significant figures that revealed the built-in maldistribution of national income were those which showed that the poorest one-fifth of American families received relatively the same infinitesimal portion of the nation's income whether the date was 1930, 1950, or 1960.

In a rich land, the poor were yet to be found in all regions. They were black dirt farmers in Mississippi, Mexican-Americans in New Mexico, whites throughout the coal-mining towns of Appalachia. They were unskilled or semiskilled blacks in ghettoes throughout the larger cities, farm migrants in California and the Western states, underemployed whites and school dropouts in the industrial cities of the North and Midwest. There were more such families in urban areas than in rural ones, and more white families than nonwhites. They lived in a hopeless culture of their own which provided little or no opportunity to break out of a vicious circle of impossible economical and social circumstances, effectively denied the "choice" which their critics insisted was their only barrier to a more productive life. They were no longer so physically visible in the 1950s, since interstate roads rarely ran through rural backwaters and the suburban commuter's route usually bypassed the urban ghetto. But their number was variously estimated by 1960 at 15, or 20, or even 25 percent of the number of American families, and their continued marginal existence was a blight on American resources and American affluence.

During the early 1950s many concerned individuals were sure that welfare and tax legislation of the previous two decades had made sizeable inroads in the large numbers of those in the poverty brackets of American society. They considered that such legislation would bring about some genuine redistribution of income, and that government spending would aid this trend. But by the end of the 1950s, the evidence was obviously shattering these myths. Statistics showed an increase in average income only for the middle groups, and taxes were having no income redistribution effect. While income tax was "progressive" only in slight degree, even this distinction was offset by well-known loopholes such as the deductibility of mortgage interest for the middle income brackets. State and local taxes were roughly proportionate for everyone *except* the very poor; sales taxes and growing social security taxes were equally regressive for those of inadequate income. Nor had government spending accomplished what its proponents had expected. National housing insurance had been defeated and public housing emasculated. The few public programs of the 1950s aided the middle class with road building and education and the rich with airports, but the poor were more apt to be bulldozed out of the way to make room for interstate highways.

By the end of the decade, statistical studies graphically portrayed the unchanging status of the nation's poor. In 1962 Leon Keyserling, Truman's economic adviser, reported in *Poverty and Deprivation in the United States* that 40 percent of American families were in this category.

In the same year Michael Harrington's *The Other America,* a poignant exposé of the poor, found 40 to 50 million people in this bracket, using Bureau of Labor Statistics figures. Official AFL-CIO reports arrived at similar conclusions. From Jacob Riis' passionate cry of the late 19th century for "the other half" to Franklin Roosevelt's "one third of a nation" and the statistics of the late 1950s, the presence of millions of persons in abysmal poverty in the midst of the nation's plenty was a virtually unchanging picture.

The world of the giant corporation was a relatively healthy one in the decade of the 1950s. Multimillion-dollar corporations gave way to billion-dollar conglomerates, with 27 such noted in contrast to the handful in earlier periods. Giants even among such companies were organizations such as General Motors and American Telephone and Telegraph, with the latter joining the auto manufacturer in the 1950s as the first two corporations to post profits of over $1 billion. The simpler problems of the monopoly in the early 20th century gave way to the more complex difficulties posed by the oligopoly of the 1950s; domination by a few rather than by one. In every field, a relatively small number of corporate giants accounted for the vast majority of sales in that field. In combined sales for the nation for 1955, for example, more than 25 percent of the entire gross national product was accounted for by the 50 largest corporations, all of them of at least demi-billionaire size. In insurance, 90 percent of all such assets in the U.S. were held by some 50 insurance companies. Although there were almost 14,000 banks in the country, the 24 banks with assets of over $1 billion made the feared "Money Trust" of the Progressive period look like a collection of piggy banks. Among these, the dynamic Bank of America, an outgrowth of California institutions and mergers, had assets of $9 billion and growing power and influence.

The growth, by merger, of the Bank of America was illustrative of an outstanding characteristic of the decade: The large, corporate fish swallowed the small or medium, corporate fish. In the first five years of the decade, the relatively small number of banking firms in California (149) was reduced to 86, or a disappearance rate, through merger and consolidation, of 60 percent. According to the Federal Trade Commission, the year 1959 saw 812 companies swallowing up 1,116 other corporate entities. That one year's statistics revealed that 42 percent of all the corporation with assets over $100 million had assimilated at least one other corporation. Yet if a company could resist merger, its survival chances in the climate of the 1950s was excellent. Of the 1,001 largest manufacturers in existence at the beginning of the decade, 854 were still thriving at the end of that period. Of the 147 disappearances, 138 were accounted for by mergers, strong evidence that manufacturing enterprises enjoyed a degree of security that accounted for a 99 percent survival rate. Another characteristic of the Great Merger Movement was the fact that most mergers were not carried out for the traditional adding of new capacity and output, but rather for the expansion of corporate assets through product diversification.

The public did not seem to evince any great interest in the possible results to the economy of such oligopolistic tactics, unless it presented a well-publicized and dramatic threat. The Celler-Kefauver Antimerger Act of 1950 did, however, produce some federal prosecution of trusts in paper, steel, and sugar. Senator Estes Kefauver of Kentucky, chairman of a subcommittee on antitrust and monopoly, was able to stimulate public interest to some degree by his findings. Hearings and testimony produced vast evidence to indicate that price competition, the heart and essence of capitalism, was no longer observed among the new oligopolies. The automotive industry furnished evidence to show that its bellwether, General Motors, set prices based upon a desired rate of return and its "competitors" moved their prices up or down in conformity to the General Motors scale. In steel, Kefauver was able to demonstrate that an annual increase in productivity of from 3 to 4 percent was divided fairly amicably between labor and management, although the consumer, who in traditional capitalism would buy more of the produce because of price decreases brought about by increased efficiency, was totally ignored. It was not until Kefauver presented dramatic evidence that the drug industry sometimes made as much as 1,000 percent on some items that the public was stirred from its apathy. Legislation designed to protect the consumer was noticeably absent in the 1950s, however. The Eisenhower administration was noted more for its actions to stimulate business, and legislation of the period provided corporate tax laws which favored the absorption of less fortunate companies by those with accumulated tax credits.

Antitrust actions were not notably more successful in the world of corporate giantism than were the Kefauver subcommittee revelations, although there were several outstanding decisions in the decade. In 1957 it took the Supreme Court to pull apart two closely linked U.S. giants, General Motors and DuPont Company. In a suit begun by the Justice Department of the Truman administration, the Court ruled that the ownership by DuPont of 23 million shares of General Motors (some 23 percent of the total) could act "substantially to lessen competition or to tend to create a monopoly," and was therefore in violation of the Clayton Act. But just how the two corporate bodies were to be pried apart made still another case which the Supreme Court finally resolved in 1961 by ordering DuPont to divest itself of its General Motors stock within 90 days and dissolve all other connections over a period of 10 years. In 1960 a Philadelphia grand jury returned a criminal indictment against General Electric, Westinghouse, and several smaller manufacturers of electrical equipment, charging conspiracy in constraint of trade. The Justice Department's indictment accused company executives of meeting secretly to arrange for divisions of the market and to determine periodically whose turn it was to submit a winning "low" bid on large contracts. The Court sent several company executives to jail for short sentences, although they were generally regarded by the business community as honored martyrs. However, sentences against the offending corporations included severe fines as well as full liability to additional suits from the buyers who suffered financially from the conspiracy. An additional insight into the pricing activities of the electric equipment manufacturers, although not litigated, was the high bids of American companies over British manufacturers on turbines for the Atomic Energy Commission. The insistence by the American manufacturers that the difference was accounted for by lower labor costs in England was effectively rebuked by a demonstration that, with labor costs removed from both bids, the continuing higher cost of the American bids could then only be explained by the insistence on a far greater rate of profit.

Of increasing importance to Big Business in the postwar years and the 1950s were Department of Defense contracts for armaments. By the end of the decade, Defense was accounting for some 58 percent of all government expenditures. The great bulk of military hardware and research contracts went to a relative handful of corporations. The manner in which these were handled provoked cries of resentment by less-favored companies and from Congress and the public over waste and inefficiency. The instrument commonly used by the Pentagon was the "negotiated" contract, which omitted the usual capitalistic essence of competition. Such contracts were let on an agreed upon amount, or on the basis of the cost of a product plus a reasonable profit percentage added on. The Pentagon defended the practice as permitting a closer supervision by the military over the requested product, but critics focused upon numerous drawbacks. The lack of multiple bids frequently meant higher costs than in the negotiated contract, and the "cost-plus" feature permitted the corporation to throw every variety of "cost" into the guaranteed basis before its profit figure was tacked on. Increasingly, since the Pentagon was a hugely complex and baffling institution, corporations snapped up those retiring admirals and generals who had been a part of the Pentagon's contract and decision processes in order to maintain and influence defense contacts. Such arrangements served further to concentrate the same few companies within the main stream of Department of Defense orders. Some corporations, such as General Dynamics Corporation, were relatively new entities which were almost completely dependent upon Pentagon armament orders for their business livelihood. Dozens of others counted defense business as their major source of revenue. Closer and closer ties, therefore, were forged between a large segment of industrial society and the military, based upon mutual desires and accommodations. In an era of continually rising military expenditures and federal budgets, this "military-industrial" linkage became a matter of increasing concern. President Eisenhower's Farewell Address contained words of warning on this development in the portion of the speech that he designated as "the most challenging message I could leave with the people of this country:"

> This conjunction of an immense military establishment and a large arms industry is new in the American experience. The total influence—economic, political, even spiritual—is felt in every city, every statehouse, every office of the federal government. . . .
>
> In the councils of government we must guard against the acquisition of unwarranted influence, whether sought or unsought, by the military-industrial complex. The potential for the disastrous rise of misplaced power exists and will persist.
>
> We must never let the weight of this combination endanger our liberties or democratic processes. . . .

Both organized labor and the farmer shared generally in the affluence of the 1950s, although both were affected structurally by technological developments of the decade. Labor unions, which had come of age in the 1930s and moved further ahead in the war years, stagnated in terms of membership in the 1950s. Labor's earlier militancy was replaced by stodginess, its enthusiasm with complacency. The issue of skilled versus unskilled labor was long since settled. In a period of two weeks in 1952 both Philip Murray and William Green died, and with them died the personality clash that had helped to keep the CIO and the AFL apart. The new heads, Walter Reuther of the United Auto Workers for the CIO and George Meany of the Plumbers' Union in the AFL, soon brought the two organizations together. By an overwhelming vote of the membership, the two allied themselves in 1955 as the AFL-CIO, with George Meany assuming the presidency.

Organized labor was faced with many difficulties in the 1950s. Perhaps foremost among these was automation and the concomitant reduction of workers in manufacturing. The societal stage of industrial maturity in which manual labor is increasingly replaced by automation[2] became reality during the decade. The growing national work force now revealed its largest numbers to be among service and trade industries and various levels of government. While economists would consider such a category

---

[2] Automation might be defined as the use of self-regulating devices in the industrial sequence through a feedback principle so that electronic sensing mechanisms automatically pass information back to earlier parts of the processing machine, correcting for tool wear or other control devices without human aid.

the maturest stage of a national economy, it meant a stagnation or even retrogression in numbers for organized labor. Generally, those involved in service pursuits or government employ, whether professors or physicians, bank tellers or civil servants, considered themselves as white-collar workers and were traditionally unorganized, although strong beginnings in such unions were visible in the 1960s. Historically, technological improvements have meant more jobs in the long run, but the painful short-run aspects prompted such struggles as occupied the Brotherhood of Locomotive Firemen from 1959 to 1963 to insist on the retention of firemen on diesel engines. Without coal to shovel, the position of a fireman in such a case was about as scientifically useful as teats on a bull. It finally took an act of Congress to reconcile the issue, but government aid and management cooperation in arranging for transitional periods and retraining programs helped to bridge a difficult gap.

Another difficulty which hampered the growth of organized labor was the antilabor opinion shared by Congress and the public based on Communist associations and corruption. The CIO had actually removed Communists from its ranks as the decade began, but the image persisted. A more potent and fresher image of labor was that of corrupt labor bosses, which derived from congressional investigations such as Senator John L. McClellan's special committee, with the diligent Robert F. Kennedy as counsel. These probings revealed the Teamsters' Union as an owner of whorehouses and gambling institutions, and its president, David Beck, as an exploiter of union funds for his private benefit. Domination by gangsters and racketeers was also demonstrated in the case of the International Longshoremen's Union by a New York State Crime Commission. Such revelations as these were responsible for the Landrum-Griffin Act of 1959, which was restrictive of many union administration activities but attempted also to protect the rank and file of union membership from dictatorship and exploitation. The new AFL-CIO soon expelled the ILA and the Teamsters, but both continued to thrive. The Teamsters actually gained in membership between 1957 and 1960 (from 1.4 million to 1.7 million) while the AFL-CIO slipped from 15 million to 12.5 million.

The nation's farmers made a considerable contribution to its affluence, but they too felt the winds of change. Agriculture was a thoroughly minor component in the sophisticated economy of the 1950s, yet an increasingly productive one. Technological innovations meant more mechanical pickers and sprayers. New chemicals killed more weeds and insects, speeded up growth of chickens, doubled the yield of wheat and corn. Farm units more and more became highly organized factories in the fields, moving produce from the earth to canning operations or into refrigerator trains with assembly-line speed and efficiency. The agricultural change was particularly felt in numbers and in small farm occupancy. Farms in the United States declined from 6.8 million in 1937 to 3.7 million in 1961, and the downward trend showed no signs of stopping there.

But perhaps a more revealing statistic was one which showed that 1.4 million farms accounted for 87 percent of all agricultural production. The balance of 2.5 million farms were those owned by the sharecroppers of the South and the marginal farmers of the Midwest and Appalachia. Their production was of little or no significance in the national economy, and most of them subsisted poorly even when they held second jobs in nearby towns. They were largely the group who formed the movement from farm to city, and were all too often part of the permanent poor in the United States. The direct subsidies of the 1930s were no longer relevant in American agriculture of the 1950s due to the amazing growth in technology and the phasing out of one-family farms into huge agricultural corporations. Federal farm subsidies were lush and unneeded bonuses to the latter, and inadequate for most of the former category. Yet despite the Eisenhower administration's efforts to eliminate or reduce the subsidies, little progress was made because of the social difficulties of destroying family farm units under the label of inefficiency, and the political difficulties of a Democratic party enmeshed in idealized Jeffersonian concepts of the small, one-family farm. Huge agricultural enterprises continued to flourish. Adequately sized farms shared satisfactorily in the American affluence. Both categories continued a stepped-up productivity which gave the American consumer outstanding food values, but at the same time continued to fill warehouses—at federal expense—with farm surpluses. In 1960, the government had 1.38 billion bushels of wheat in storage in everything from grain elevators to mothballed ships, for which it paid enterprising capitalists approximately $1.5 million daily in storage costs. At the bottom of the agricultural list, the small, inefficient one-family farms provided an infinitesimal portion of the nation's production and inadequate livelihoods for their owners. Their number declined steadily as the young, in particular, deserted traditional farm life and moved to the city. By the end of the decade less than 8 percent of the American population lived on farms and the annual percentage went down steadily.

Unemployment proved to be a nagging factor in an otherwise affluent society. The two recessions of 1953–1954 and 1957–1958 contributed heavy unemployment figures, but the significant item was the fact that recovery rarely brought the percentages back down to previous lows. Thus, in July 1958, when recovery was conceded to be well under way in most areas, there were still 5.3 million jobless. In mid-1959, it had dropped to 3.7 million, but by the time that President Kennedy was inaugurated in January 1961, the figure was back up to nearly 5.4 million. Labor leaders and some Congressmen called for public work projects

Population Density, 1960

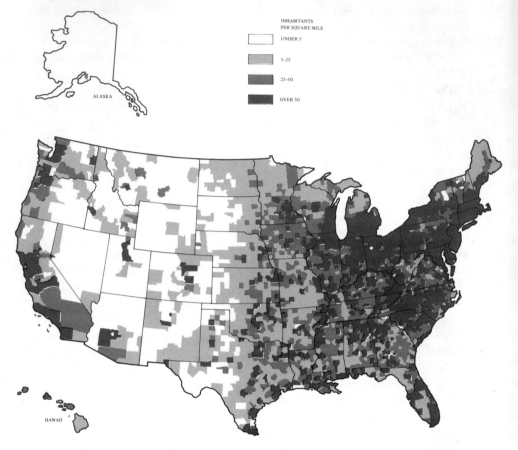

to furnish jobs, but Eisenhower and Secretary of the Treasury Humphrey put their greatest emphasis upon balancing the budget. The President's approach to the budget was couched more in 19th-century moralistic exhortations regarding the virtues of thrift than in an understanding of the economy's status and needs in the 1950s. The federal budget, nevertheless, generally grew larger throughout the decade and showed no signs of retrogression.

The 1950s would have to be accounted a period of general affluence, and an advancing economy, even though continued maldistribution adversely affected a sizeable disadvantaged element. Such factors as population growth, technological and scientific advancement, growing consumer demands, and the powerful stimulus of government purchases and government participation in the economy all helped to account for an expanding and productive economy, and a higher standard of living. The economy of the 1950s had a number of distinguishing characteristics. It was an era of unprecedented merger into the superrealm of oligopoly. It was a decade that marked, not the actual beginning of automation, but such widespread and penetrating use of automation as to be of serious influence in labor, business, and social affairs. The economy was more stable than in prewar years. True, there were sharp recessions in 1953–1954 and 1957–1958, but the various floors provided by New Deal legislation and the government intervention provided by the Employment Act of 1946 prevented the repetition of a severe depression. A continuing force of unemployed, with the advantage of only minimal efforts at training for new skills, remained as a nagging doubt about the stability of the economy.

An additional significant feature of the decade was the greatest growth in history of American investment abroad. It jumped from about $10 billion as the decade began to some $30 billion by 1960, and the trend was sharply upward. Canada still received the largest American industrial investment with $10.2 billion in 1960, followed by Latin America with $8.2 billion. But Western Europe, with $5.3 billion, was increasing rapidly. One of the factors responsible was the penetration of the European market by American automotive manufacturers, with Ford Motor Company active in the Simca of France and General Motors acquiring interests in the German-built Opel. Other manufacturers made a variety of American products from soft drinks to toothpaste fairly ubiquitous in Europe. Government policies helped American industrial investment abroad in various ways. Federal tax policies took no levy on such profits unless they were brought back into the United States. Corporations thus could use them for expansion into another country or area. Although some nations levied high taxes on corporate profits, others welcomed such funds with little or no taxes. Corporate profits abroad were protected through the International Cooperation Administration (1948) by insurance against expropriation or the freezing of assets. Many Latin American industrial investors and oil corporations doing business in the Middle East took advantage of this extremely low-cost protection to expand their overseas activities. The Export-Import Bank, the operations of which were greatly expanded by the Eisenhower administration, also aided American business by lending foreign nations the funds to purchase American products. Another unusual feature of the economy of the 1950s was also related to the world scene. With the movement of the economy into one of high mass consumption, Americans demanded more and more foreign goods. This caused a reversal of the historic trend of a relatively small volume of imports, which had been a characteristic of the American economy since the late 19th century. In the 1950s the United States moved ahead of Great Britain to become the nation with the largest amount of imported industrial and consumer goods in the world.

The Eisenhower administration's role in the economy was a frequently criticized one. The regulatory agencies were staffed with appointments reflecting the view of the business group to be regulated rather than the interests of the consuming public they were supposed to uphold. It sought stringently to hold the line on expenditures, to balance the budget, and to reduce the national debt. Its critics pointed out that, while these were worthy objectives, such tactics during the recessions of 1953–1954 and 1957–1958 were at the expense of the unemployed and of national economic growth. President Eisenhower consistently vetoed bills providing for job-relief programs, although he sanctioned increases in hospital construction and health research. Both the federal budget and the national debt continued to rise. Government expenditures were reduced from $74 billion in 1953 to $64.5 billion in 1955, but by the end of the decade were back up to $82 billion. Nevertheless, in relation to a growing population and its service demands and to a productive national economy, this was not unusual. Both the nation's productivity[3] and the GNP increased. The steel and automotive industries, once the fastest growing of American industries, faced increasing difficulties. Steel had stronger foreign competition. The automotive industry did not reveal any major technological innovations, but gave its customers larger engines with more horsepower, power steering and brakes, and chrome trim. Its efforts to build a "compact" car to meet the competition of imports such as the German Volkswagen were not of great avail. In terms of fast growth, steel and auto making were surpassed during the 1950s by electronics, chemicals, and aircraft, all of which spent large sums on research and development.

Thus, many changes were to be seen in the affluent decade of the 1950s. Many of the traditionally distinctive characteristics of capitalism were either negated or severely diminished, yet the nation's economy could scarcely be described as socialistic. An additional complicating factor was the very considerable presence of the government in the economy, including its role as virtually the sole and noncompetitive customer of new aircraft and defense manufacturers. The resultant institution was frequently described, for lack of a more pungent term, as a "mixed" economy. Although criticism was directed at the slow national growth rate, economists were generally optimistic about the decade's performance and the future of the economy. Most of society shared in a larger portion of national income and in a higher standard of living. Basic problems such as the continuing percentage in the poverty bracket and the steadily increasing funds and influence flowing into the mili-

---

[3] A representative example of increased productivity largely through mechanization was the coal industry. In 1937, 422,000 coal miners produced 445 million tons, whereas in 1960 only 197,000 miners were producing 410 million tons, or a daily output per miner of nearly 13 tons as contrasted with 4.7 tons in 1937.

tary-industrial complex persistently carried over into the following decade.

Eisenhower, Blacks, and Civil Rights

Demands of blacks for equal rights had made minor but steady progress in the postwar years. It was most favorable in the armed services, where Truman ordered the implementation of a recommendation by an armed force committee on racial matters in 1948. Although complete desegregation was to be achieved by 1954, the Korean War speeded up the process. The task of training thousands of men quickly was complicated enough without attempting segregation methods, and many area and camp commanders disregarded race entirely. White recruits frequently found themselves taking orders from black drill sergeants and eating at the same mess table with black soldiers. Army discipline made it all seem reasonably natural. When black replacements were put into white combat units, army officers found that black soldiers fought fully as well as the man next to him. This experience, repeated many times, thoroughly demolished the stereotype of the black soldier solely as labor battalion material. By the end of the Korean War, desegregation was virtually complete in the armed services.

Areas such as education were a totally different story, however. The Supreme Court had made some decisions which seemed to foreshadow a doctrine contrary to the 1896 *Plessy* v. *Ferguson* ruling on "separate but equal" facilities. A ruling in 1938 required Missouri to provide appropriate graduate facilities for blacks. Oklahoma was similarly warned. In 1950, *Sweatt* v. *Painter* ordered Texas to admit a black applicant to the state law school at the University of Texas, because the state's law school for blacks was manifestly unequal in quality. Many Southern states rapidly increased the amount of capital outlay expended on their schools for black students. For many areas, however, particularly the rural ones of the South, only negligible amounts were spent on education for blacks.

A historic decision of the United States Supreme Court on May 17, 1954, projected the most difficult and most emotional domestic issue on the American scene during Eisenhower's second administration. This was *Brown* v. *Board of Education of Topeka,* which completely repudiated the *Plessy* v. *Ferguson* concept. The Court had considered several such suits simultaneously so as to cover all aspects of desegregation. Earl Warren, former Republican Governor of California, whom Eisenhower had appointed Chief Justice the year before, spoke for a unanimous court: "We conclude that in the field of public education the doctrine of 'separate but equal' has no place. Separate educational

facilities are inherently unequal. Therefore, we hold that the plain-
tiffs . . . are, by reason of the segregation complained of, deprived of
the equal protection of the laws guaranteed by the 14th Amendment."
The Court decided that, given the great importance of education in
the mid-20th-century world, minority groups were being deprived
through segregation of equal educational opportunities, even where
physical facilities might be equal. The separation of black children
"from others of similar age and qualifications solely because of their
race generates a feeling of inferiority as to their status in the community that may affect their hearts and minds in a way unlikely ever to
be undone." The Court further ruled on May 31, 1955, (also unanimously) that federal courts would "require that the defendants make
a prompt and reasonable start toward full compliance with our May
17, 1954 ruling," and gave the responsibility to local school boards.

Resistance to the Court's rulings was considerable and took various
forms. The border states began a graduated desegregation, and Delaware
and the District of Columbia undertook a rapid compliance. A journalistic rule of thumb quickly showed the most resistance to be in those
rural areas of the Deep South where slavery had concentrated the largest
number of blacks. Thus, six years after the momentous decision, Virginia showed 170 out of 211,000 black pupils in integrated schools;
North Carolina 50 out of 319,000; Florida with 755 out of 201,100; and
Texas had 3,500 out of 288,900. But in all of Georgia, South Carolina,
Alabama, Mississippi, and Louisiana (with the exception of a few schools
in New Orleans) no school district showed any intent to abide by the
law. Forms of resistance varied. White supremacists revived the Ku
Klux Klan to some extent, but more attention was given in 1955 and
1956 to the formation of White Citizens' Councils. These ostensibly
sought legal methods to combat desegregation, but were all too frequently the source for extralegal intimidation. Threats and sometimes
violence were used by the more fanatical among the white supremacists.
Some Southern legislatures went to amazing lengths, some even passing
resolutions declaring themselves the only constituted authority and denouncing the Court's decision as "unconstitutional." The Virginia state
legislature went back to the early 19th century days of John C. Calhoun
and "interposed" itself between the federal government and the state
of Virginia. In Congress, 19 Senators and 81 Representatives issued a
"Southern Manifesto" in 1956 declaring their intent to reverse the
Court's decision. Most Southerners opposed integration in principle and
hoped it could be postponed at least in their own times. Others recognized the inevitability of integration, not simply through a Court decision, but because it was an obvious affront to professed American
ideals and because of the damage done to the American image throughout the world by segregation. Extremely few, however, were willing

to work towards implementation of the *Brown* v. *Board of Education* ideal.

The fallacious argument consistently advanced by southern whites that blacks were content with the status quo was rudely assaulted by militant strivings among the black communities of the South. In December 1955, black citizens of Montgomery, Alabama, refused to recognize the regulation requiring them to sit in the back of Montgomery's busses. When the bus company refused to change the ruling Mont gomery's 50,000 blacks, in an unusual display of solidarity, boycotted all bus service. Efforts of blacks to transport each other through car pools were harassed by the police. Ninety-two black leaders, many of them ministers, were arrested under a variety of 19th-century laws. Nevertheless, the protest continued. The principal leader of the boycott organization, and soon to become the nationwide symbol of black protest over inequalities in American life, was the Reverend Martin Luther King, Jr. King held the Ph.D. from Boston University, and had just come to Montgomery from his Atlanta home to accept his first church. Although militant in his determination to right the many wrongs visited upon blacks, King advocated love instead of hatred for the enemies of blacks and followed the Ghandi principle of nonviolence. NAACP attorneys were able to obtain a favorable court decision against bus segregation and the Supreme Court dealt another blow to segregation efforts by upholding the lower court's decision in 1956.

The bus boycott captured the imagination of the black community and led directly to other uses of direct action. Bus boycotts were undertaken in 1956 in Tallahassee, Florida, and Birmingham, Alabama. In 1957 blacks in Tuskegee, Alabama, site of a famed black university, formed the Tuskegee Civic Association. This group boycotted local merchants for their part in the state legislature's gerrymandering most of the city's black voters outside its limits. It was carried on for three years before the Supreme Court ruled the gerrymander unconstitutional. In 1957 Martin Luther King moved to the forefront of coordinated, direct-action activities in the South by forming the Southern Christian Leadership Conference (SCLC).

The voting rights of blacks became increasingly of concern to the Republican party. The party platforms of 1952 and 1956 contained civil rights planks, and when Eisenhower came into office he appointed a number of blacks to important positions.[4] His administration carried on the desegregation of the armed forces and ended segregation in veterans' hospitals. Presidentially appointed committees also succeeded in persuading firms working on government contracts to eliminate much job discrimination. Blacks were impressed and, coupled with their re-

---

[4] Perhaps the most outstanding was the appointment of J. Ernest Wilkins as Assistant Secretary of Labor.

sentment over the dominance of the Democratic party by conservative southern Congressmen, demonstrated their feelings by switching over to the Republicans.

Politicians from the Northern wing of that party were supremely aware of black voting rights as an issue, and were further aware how Truman in 1948 and Eisenhower in 1952 had demonstrated that support from large industrial states was vital, whereas Southern support was not. Urban Republicans began pressuring Eisenhower's sympathetic Attorney-General, Herbert Brownell of New York, for a more forceful administration position on civil rights. Eisenhower's own position on civil rights was somewhat less than lukewarm when it came to leadership on the national level, and his great popularity made this position virtually unassailable. However, with the heart attack of 1955 and the possibility of a new Republican nominee, the administration became more responsive to civil rights pressures. The Cabinet agreed to let Brownell prepare a voting rights bill but, since it was known that the President had no enthusiasm for such a measure, thought that the bill should bear Brownell's name. Although both Eisenhower and the Cabinet held back administration support from the voting rights portion of the bills Brownell's Justice Department had prepared, the Attorney General quietly sent the entire package to Congress. After lengthy debate, the House passed a bill permitting the Attorney General to seek injunctions in federal courts to protect citizens' rights to vote. It also provided for an additional Assistant Attorney General specializing in civil rights, and created a special commission to study civil rights. Although the bill passed the House, the nearness of the election of 1956 stopped its passage in the Senate. In 1957, a diluted bill passed the Senate after Majority Leader Lyndon Johnson talked his Southern colleagues out of their usual civil rights filibuster. Instead of permitting the Justice Department to take action on behalf of any citizen deprived of any of his rights, the bill empowered the department to seek an injunction only when a citizen had exhausted all other legal remedies and only on the issue of voting rights. A variety of loopholes inserted at Southern insistence made the Civil Rights Act of 1957 a weak and unsatisfactory piece of legislation. It did provide more obstacles for state and local election boards which might try to interfere with the blacks' right to vote. More importantly, it was the first civil rights act to pass since Senator Charles Sumner's bill enacted in 1875, and thus marked a small, but significant, step.

At the same time that the Civil Rights Act of 1957 was nearing passage in the Senate one of the more disgraceful episodes in American civil rights history occurred. In Little Rock, Arkansas, the school board had planned for a beginning of desegregation in the city's public schools by September. Nine black students had been carefully chosen to begin the gradual plan in the city's Central High School. A group of white supremacists obtained an injunction several days before school was due to open, and Governor Orval M. Faubus had testified that the desegregation move would incite mob violence. The state court promptly overruled it, holding that the threat of mob violence could not be used to nullify the laws. Governor Faubus nevertheless ordered the Arkansas National Guard to surround Central High School. Although he insisted that this was only "to prevent racial violence," it was obvious that the troops were also barring the entry of the nine black schoolchildren. Faubus' guardsmen were thus violating the federal court's injunction and provoking a direct confrontation between the authority of a state government and the national government.

President Eisenhower, who was vacationing at Newport, Rhode Island, was not publicly committed to the idea of desegregation. He was deeply reluctant to intervene, and persistently throughout his full term of office refused to comment on the morality of the issue or the role of the nation's leader in the face of such a momentous crisis. Nor was the President's lukewarm participation in the administration civil rights bill calculated to inhibit the stubborn Faubus. However, Faubus met with the President at Newport on September 14, and evidently received little satisfaction. Eisenhower told the Arkansas Governor that as President he was sworn to uphold the constitution and would do so "with all legal means" at his command. Faubus did not remove the guardsmen until the federal court's injunction was served on him a week later. The day after the troops were removed, the nine black students were slipped into the school under police protection. But the news provoked an angry mob which surged around the school and was barely contained by the police. Photographs of the mob, which appeared around the world, were revealing. No well-dressed men or women participated. Interviews indicated house painters, truck drivers, and unemployed filling station attendants to be representative of the educational and economic level of the mob, with strong contingents of leather-jacketed rowdies who evidently welcomed the temporary social acceptance of violence and mob action.

In the face of the mob, school authorities sent the black children home. On the following day the crowd refused a presidential order to leave the enjoined grounds. Regardless of his refusals to commit himself on desegregation or the Supreme Court's decision, Eisenhower was quite clear regarding the supremacy of the federal government and could not ignore Faubus' demagogic defiance of a federal court. The President acted immediately to put the Arkansas National Guard under national army command and thus under the Commander-in-Chief's order, and on the next day dispatched 1,000 paratroopers from the 101st Airborne Division to the scene. On September 25, the nine black children went to Central High School surrounded by the bayonets of para-troopers and the mob was kept in check. As tempers subsided, the soldiers were gradually withdrawn. Their armed escort for the black students ended in December, but a small National Guard contingent re-mained on hand until May 1958. Two years later, four other senior high schools in Little Rock were desegregated without incident. The newspaper photos of nine black students protected by fixed bayonets of paratroopers from a ragtag mob was a humiliating spectacle to most Americans and a shocking one for the rest of the world. Not only had racism raised serious threats to the professed democratic ideals of equal-ity, but it had also brought state officials to a defiance of United States authority for the first time since the Civil War.

Yet the immediate effect of the Little Rock crisis was to provoke state legislatures to further resistance to desegregation. Virginia and Arkansas passed what were described in the former state as "massive resistance" laws which ordered local officials to close down the schools if commanded by the courts to integrate. Some went beyond this to a clearly unconstitutional extent by requiring local school officials to use public funds for establishing private segregated schools. Schools in Arkansas and in three Virginia cities, including the largest city, Nor-folk, were closed in 1958 under the new state provision. But such tactics provoked a differing reaction. No matter how much some deplored de-segregation, they would not permit the schools to be closed and their children to be deprived of an education. Nor were businessmen pleased by continued turmoil and mob appearances. Citizens who sincerely be-lieved in law and order realized this meant obeying unpleasant laws as well as those they approved of, and further recognized the futility and the dangers inherent in resisting federal court injunctions. In January 1959, both Virginia state courts and federal courts pronounced the "mas-sive resistance" laws a violation of state and federal constitutions. Vir-ginia schools were reopened in February 1959 and integrated in the fall, although schools in Prince Edward County in southern Virginia closed down completely and finally rather than integrate. Arkansas held out until August, when a federal court finally knocked out Faubus' school-closing law.

The commission on civil rights established under the Civil Rights Act of 1957 turned in a lengthy report in 1959. Among its strong recom-mendations was the need for special presidentially appointed registrars to register qualified blacks as voters in all areas where significant electoral racial discrimination appeared. This was to get around the practice of registrars in the deep South of denying voting registration to qualified blacks by a variety of devices, some under dubious state laws, some of personal whim. No action was taken until 1960, when the election of a Republican successor to Eisenhower again pressured events. The administration bill was a weak one, since it did not even include the suggested voter registration plan. It was nevertheless greeted with the usual filibuster by southern Senators and further weakened to permit its eventual passage May 6, 1960. The Civil Rights Act of 1960 contained a complicated system of referees to supervise discriminatory practices for registering of black voters. If the Department of Justice were required to bring suit to get local registrars to register qualified blacks, it could then also request a federal judge to find that a "pattern" of discrimination accounted for the registrar's actions. If a federal judge so agreed, he would then appoint referees who would be authorized to register qualified black citizens for voting. The act also provided that it would be a federal offense to transport dynamite for illegal purposes, which meant that the Federal Bureau of Investigation could be called into future church and school bombings. As even the opposing Senators cheerfully pointed out, the Civil Rights Act of 1960 was a futile piece of legislation with negligible effects. In the month following its enactment the new Attorney General, William P. Rogers, warned the officials of four Southern counties that unless their discrimination against black voters ceased they would be prosecuted under the new law. But the strongest wave of the coming Negro Revolution and its greatest involvement of the presidency was to come about under the following administration.

The Cold War, 1957–1961

Foreign policy matters of the second Eisenhower administration were largely concerned with the problems of disarmament and the ticklish Berlin question, accompanied by alarms and excursions in the Middle East and growing involvement in Southeast Asia. The campaign of 1956 had brought the dangers of nuclear testing into public debate, based upon the deadly radiation visited upon Japanese tuna fishermen by the American Bikini atoll test of the hydrogen bomb in March 1954 and on subsequent revelations of the fallout menace. Adlai Stevenson's call for a ban on nuclear testing was defensively repudiated by Eisenhower. His successful reelection and the continuing public outcry moved the President to a consideration of such a ban, but Dulles' intervention in favor of a test ban tightly bound to all other arms control measures put the proposal in an untenable position. As Hugh Gaitskell, the leader of the British Labor Party, remarked, "If everything has to be dependent on everything else, there is endless scope for obstruction, delay, and confusion." With both American and Soviet tests continuing to pollute the atmosphere with radioactive matter during 1958, public and international pressure mounted for a test ban agreement separate from all other issues.

In March, Russia, after completing a series of test explosions, announced unilaterally that she was suspending further testing of nuclear weapons. Although Dulles denounced the plan as a "gimmick," it clearly put the United States on the defensive. On April 28 Eisenhower extended a proposal to the new Soviet Premier, Nikita S. Khrushchev, for a ten-nation conference of scientists and technical experts at Geneva on such practical matters as the supervision and control of a test ban. The gathering agreed in principle that tests could be discovered through a world-wide system of listening posts. Soviet agreement on a network of control posts was an amazing surprise to Washington, although the conference's impasse over separating political from technical issues repeated earlier failures.

In August 1958 Eisenhower announced that the United States would agree to a one-year suspension of nuclear weapons while the talks were going on, provided the Soviets concurred and provided they would also agree to negotiate some effective future control. Eisenhower was able to counter the opposition within his administration by revealing that the U.S. suspension would not begin until after the completion of its latest tests in the Pacific. The Soviets agreed to the temporary ban, but insisted on going ahead with their own latest tests. These took place on November 2 and 3, several days after the temporary ban was to have started on October 31, 1958. However, Eisenhower agreed to adhere to the proposed moratorium. No further Soviet tests were held, and the ban continued on its temporary and shaky course.

A three-power conference[5] composed of the United States, Great Britain, and Russia opened in 1958 at Geneva on the future discontinuance of nuclear tests, with Americans hoping that some measures of political agreement would lead to general disarmament talks. But hundreds of sessions over the next three years led only to very minor understandings. Russian fears of attack from Europe were opposed to American fears of an attack from over the polar regions. The Americans insisted on a step-by-step disarmament. Basically, most of the attempts at reconciliation foundered on the Russian avoidance of a local system of inspection and an objection to penalties for violations, and the American insistence on a virtually absolute system of inspections backed up by a legalistic system of penalties to police the system. In actuality, both positions were somewhat behind the technological developments of the times, since more powerful atomic weapons, aerial photography, and more sensitive detecting devices were making the suggested inspec-

---

[5] France exploded an atomic bomb in February 1959, and thereby became the fourth member of the world's atomic club.

tions and the reaction to them increasingly outdated. Additionally, each test or atomic advance—or suspected advance—by one party invariably triggered a similar response by the other; this then caused a further reaction by the first party, ad infinitum. Although all estimates showed the United States leading in number of atomic weapons, neither the Soviet Union nor the United States would admit that it surpassed the other in advanced atomic weaponry sufficiently for "defensive" security. The march toward an eventual holocaust continued at only a slightly slower pace.

The failure to find nuclear and disarmament solutions was largely repeated in the effort to find mutually agreeable positions on the Berlin and unified-Germany problems. Russia had watched with increasing trepidation as West Germany was voted into NATO and began rearming for her troop contributions to that organization. When Adenauer demanded artillery fitted for firing nuclear shells and fighter-bombers capable of delivering nuclear bombs, Russian apprehension was increased even though the United States delivered the arms requested without relinquishing any nuclear capabilities to the Germans. In 1956 alarmed Europeans, including Adenauer's opposition West Germany parties, attacked the idea of German rearmament. British Prime Minister Anthony Eden sought to head off the incipient arms race by calling for the neutralization and unification of Germany. George Kennan's series of lectures over the BBC in 1957 also attacked the Acheson-Dulles-Adenauer policies by suggesting that the situations and circumstances of the late 1940s had changed considerably, and that our knowledge had similarly increased. German rearmament could never bring about free elections for a unified Germany, as Adenauer and Dulles insisted. On the contrary, Kennan said, a rearmed West Germany with missile bases on her soil would permanently nullify German reunification. He proposed, in a policy generally called "disengagement," that a refusal to give Germany nuclear arms be traded for a Russian neutralization of Central and Eastern Europe, and that opposing forces be drawn back from points of mutual friction. Dean Acheson, former Secretary of State, upheld the Dulles-Adenauer position in a heated rebuttal. He reiterated his previous views and insisted on the continued dangers of a Russian military advance on Europe or a possible new German-Soviet agreement. Dulles gave some indication, however, that he might favor the Kennan argument. He remarked coyly that "disengagement" was "a naughty word," and implied to Adenauer that a military neutralization of Central Europe was a prize worth seeking.

An additional variety of "disengagement" continued the threat to the unity of Western thought. The Foreign Minister of Poland, Adam Rapacki, suggested in 1958 an approach that would provide a nuclear-free zone in Central Europe. The so-called Rapacki Plan would have set aside Poland, Czechoslovakia, West Germany, and East Germany as a zone where the absence of any nuclear weapons would help to relieve the tensions of armed East-West borders. Dulles and Eisenhower, however, rejected the proposal. Dulles contended it would perpetuate tension because it accepted the continuance of a divided Germany. Both men insisted that it constituted too small a zone to add anything to the security of Europe.

Two other events of 1958 weakened the North Atlantic alliance. Charles de Gaulle moved into the presidency of France in June, announcing that his government would bring the bitter and divisive colonial war in Algeria to an end and grant independence to the African colony. Both the blast at American policy and the new direction of de Gaullist ambitions foreshadowed a stronger French leadership in European councils and even in NATO. That organization's membership also underwent an economic innovation that further strained the alliance. On March 25, 1957, six nations of continental Europe—France, West Germany, Italy, and the three Benelux countries—had bound themselves to the European Economic Community, or Common Market, to begin on January 1, 1959.[6] As these countries prepared themselves in 1958 for its establishment, it became evident that its goals and its makeup would have significant European results. The Common Market sought a powerful economic union by eliminating all tariffs and national restrictions within its membership over a period of 12 to 15 years, beginning a lowering of their national trade quotas and tariffs almost immediately. Thus the Common Market, as a solid economic unit, could establish uniform common tariffs against all outsiders. If it did not actually lead to a United States of Europe, as many hoped, it would at least set up a sizable economic power to offset the weight of the two superpowers, United States and Soviet Russia. Britain initially sought to join, but was rejected when she refused to give up her traditional and special economic ties to the nations of the Commonwealth. She thereupon formed in November 1959 the Free Trade Association, composed of Austria, Denmark, Great Britain, Norway, Portugal, Sweden, and Switzerland. They soon became known, in contradistinction to the "Inner Six" members of the Common Market, as the "Outer Seven." Although the two groups aspired to free trade with each other, the result was a split within the ranks of the North Atlantic alliance. The United States indicated a preference for the Common Market, since its economic power and potential for European unity were superior to that of the Outer Seven. Its efforts to bring the two groups together were unsatisfactory.

This rift among the allies required considerable patching up in the

---

[6] At the same time, the same nations also became members of the European Atomic Energy Community, or Euratom, devoted to a common development of atomic energy solely for peaceful purposes.

face of the crisis of the Berlin question, which Khrushchev presented in a new series of demands. Berlin was a persistent thorn for the Russians, since the stark contrast between the bustling Western sectors and the poverty-stricken Eastern sectors provided an embarrassing comparison for visitors and Germans alike. It was also a focal point for the escape of numbers of Germans intent upon leaving the German Democratic Republic (East Germany). Khrushchev may have also been influenced to renew the Berlin problem by Russia's undoubted achievements in space and rocket technology, hoping that concessions would flow from these accomplishments. He suddenly announced on November 10, 1958, that the Soviet Union wanted a new arrangement for the city of Berlin. The United States, Great Britain, and France were to withdraw their troops, leaving it a demilitarized city. Access to Berlin was to be negotiated directly with the German Democratic Republic (which none of the Western powers recognized). Failing to do so within six-months' time would result in the Soviets handing over control of Western military supply routes to their East German cohorts. Khrushchev added to these demands in January 1959, a suggestion that peace treaties for West and East Germany be considered. If the Western allies did not choose to do this, he said later, the Soviets would proceed in any case with their own separate treaty with East Germany.

Dulles, on behalf of the Western allies, rejected the Khrushchev demands and refused any recognition to the new East German state. If supply routes were blocked, Dulles said, the NATO powers would use military force. Khrushchev retorted that this would mean the beginning of World War III. The United States denounced the Russian intent to break the four-power commitment as a violation of her pledge to work for a unified Germany with Berlin as its capital. On the other hand, the Soviets pointed out that the United States had already violated her pledge of never again permitting Germany to become a military power by establishing her in NATO and giving her weapons with nuclear potential. Both the United States and Russia found in the Berlin question the continuing aspects of the Cold War, each attempting to manipulate the situation to her own interests. Eisenhower, at British Prime Minister Harold MacMillan's urging, agreed to call a summit meeting, provided both that the Soviet six-month ultimatum be withdrawn and that a meeting of the four foreign ministers be held first. The Soviets agreed, partly by insisting that their six-month time limit could not be regarded as an ultimatum.

Christian A. Herter, who had succeeded the gravely ill Dulles on his resignation some months before, represented the United States as the talks got under way in May 1959, in Geneva. After several weeks of meetings, the conference had to be temporarily adjourned for the sad occasion of Dulles' death by cancer on May 24. All four principals returned from Dulles' funeral in Washington to eight or nine more weeks of futile argument. The Western allies had modified their position slightly to permit free elections coming after a German unification instead of before. A limitation of armaments in some areas of Central Europe was officially confirmed, but the insistence on guarantees of access to the West Berlin sectors continued unchanged. The Russians still wished to consider the problems of Berlin access and a treaty for East Germany apart from any consideration of German reunification, and the conference finally broke up without any advance on the problem.

Despite the lack of success in the preliminary meeting, Eisenhower felt that the seriousness of the Berlin problem required high-level discussion. In July the President accordingly extended an invitation to Khrushchev to come to the United States, and also declared he would be willing to visit the Russian leader in Moscow. Khrushchev came to the United States in September 1959, in a jovial and convivial spirit that gained him a successful press. He insisted that capitalism and communism could peacefully coexist, addressed the United Nations, and obviously enjoyed himself in visits to Los Angeles and Disneyland and an American farm in Iowa. Amicable talks with President Eisenhower went on at Camp David, the secluded White House retreat in the Maryland mountains, where the Russian leader put aside all idea of time limitation regarding Berlin negotiations. This cleared the way for a four-power summit meeting, later scheduled for the spring of 1960 in Paris, but the seemingly peaceful "Spirit of Camp David" which emerged from the conversations did not actually mark any reconciliation on fundamental issues.

Preparations for the Paris summit meeting, which de Gaulle had asked be held on May 16, were blown sky-high by the fiasco of the U-2 incident. Khrushchev announced on May 5 that a high-flying American plane had been brought down May 1 over Soviet territory. The Eisenhower administration's reaction to this was a sad series of lies and misstatements which were soon revealed to the world as such. First to issue a denial was NASA, which said that the pilot had reported having oxygen trouble over Turkey and emphasized the weather instruments carried. The implication was that this was simply a weather flight in which the pilot might inadvertently have strayed across the Russian border. On the next day the State Department spokesman, Lincoln White, asserted that the pilot had lost consciousness because of oxygen failure and flatly declared: "There was no deliberate attempt to violate Soviet air space, and there never has been."

On May 7 Khrushchev shot this fabricated story down in flames. He displayed the evidence before Soviet deputies of having shot down the U-2, actually a high-flying photo-reconnaissance plane, some 1300 miles inside the Soviet Union near Sverdlovsk. Furthermore, he had both the captured pilot, Francis Gary Powers, who admitted that the flight was a CIA-sponsored espionage mission from Pakistan to Norway, and the captured films of Soviet military installations. After an uneasy silence in Washington, it was admitted that such "civilian" flights had been going on for four years, but it was maintained that since the Soviets had rejected the American open-skies offer in 1955 such flights over Soviet territory were deemed necessary. Khrushchev's responses were considered by world observers to be of moderate tone. He charged that the flights were deliberately arranged to disrupt the summit meeting, but declared Russia's friendship for the American people. He also declared his complete willingness to absolve Eisenhower of any guilt or even knowledge of the U-2 flight.

Secretary of State Herter's rejoinder, however, not only made a point of the President's original issuance of the aerial surveillance directives (which shocked the world press) but clearly implied that the United States must continue its violation of Soviet airspace. Since the President was thereby associated with the activities, this unfortunately left him personally open to Soviet attacks. The President followed by bearing down on Russian secrecy and repeating the need for the gathering of military information to prevent "another Pearl Harbor." Later, in a Chief-of-Staff position, Eisenhower took "full responsibility" for the actions of his subordinates in authorizing the espionage flights prior to the summit meeting, although he had no specific knowledge of them.

At the scheduled meeting in Paris Khrushchev dissipated much of the worldwide sympathy for his plight by belligerently demanding an apology from Eisenhower that the American President could scarcely afford to make. Eisenhower did admit belatedly that he had ordered the cessation of further flights, but Khrushchev railed against American "aggressive" acts and threatened to destroy any nation that permitted American espionage planes to use its airfields. Khrushchev thereupon withdrew his earlier invitation for Eisenhower to visit Russia, and suggested that any summit meetings be postponed for six to eight months.

Russia won a considerable world propaganda victory. The principle under international law of a nation's right to control plane flights over its own airspace was as old as the airplane and had never been questioned. The United States would obviously have reacted fully as violently had the same incident occurred in American skies, yet the American response was to deny Russia the same basic military security the United States would have insisted upon and to challenge the very basis of a nation's sovereignty. The shabby tissue of lies in the U-2 fiasco added a lack of credibility to other administration problems. Only the inexcusable shouting and personal abuse by Khrushchev in destroying the summit conference dulled the edge of a Soviet propaganda victory, and the summit issues remained unresolved.

The Middle East remained a continuing problem in administration eyes, particularly after the Suez diplomatic setback and the resultant vacuum created by British and French withdrawal from the area. The American-sponsored Baghdad Pact was weakened and Egypt's Nasser had been stimulated to increase his pan-Arab approach to power. In January 1957, Eisenhower went before Congress to ask that body's approval of a Dulles-sponsored Middle East Resolution similar in many ways to the Formosa Resolution previously granted. The "Eisenhower Doctrine," as it came to be universally known, requested authority to develop economic strength and programs of military assistance for the nations of the Middle East, and for the use of U.S. armed forces, when requested "against overt armed aggression from any nation controlled by international communism." It received a cold welcome both from the domestic press and the world press. The Eisenhower Doctrine passed in the House, even though a heavy volume of congressional mail was eight to one against the proposal, with bitter criticism of Dulles' belligerent "brinkmanship" policies. The Senate gave the Secretary of State the most grueling ordeal of his career. The headstrong courses that Dulles stood ready to use under a proposal many regarded as permission to declare war brought many overt indications of lack of confidence. Implied requests for his resignation mounted during his six days on the Foreign Relations witness stand. Final Senate passage came only after the presidential use of the armed forces was modified, and with the aid of Majority Leader Lyndon Johnson. Senator Wayne Morse's amendment against weakening Congress' war-approving powers found unusual allies, with such Democratic Senators as Hubert Humphrey of Minnesota and John Kennedy of Massachusetts joining Strom Thurmond of South Carolina and James Eastland of Mississippi and most Republicans to pass the resolution in March.

The freshly granted Eisenhower Doctrine was quickly put to use. The small Arab kingdom of Jordan, threatened internally by pro-Nasser Arab nationalists, appealed to the United States for help. Eisenhower ordered part of the Sixth Fleet to the eastern Mediterranean. The threat to intervene was defended by the State Department, not by any reference to the Doctrine's anticommunism, but by an insistence on policing "the preservation of the independence and integrity of the nations of the Middle East." With King Hussein's crushing of his opposition, the United States advanced him $30 million as a down payment on a replacement of the withdrawn British subsidy. In 1958 Egypt, Syria, and Yemen formed the United Arab Republic, with Nasser as its president, and united behind his policy of "positive neutralism" which favored the Soviet Union for its great willingness to support Arab nationalism. Dulles correctly feared that the wave of Arab nationalism would influence Lebanon, Iraq, and Jordan. Lebanon had long maintained good stability as a nation by maintaining a delicate political balance between the Moslems and Christians who were approximately equal in numbers. By common consent, such offices as the head of state and head of the armed forces were rotated evenly between the two faiths, with the Christian element pro-United States and pro-Western democracies, and the Moslems pro-Arab nationalist and pro-Nasser. President Camille Chamoun, a Maronite Christian, held elections in 1957 that were considered strongly rigged to give him the necessary parliamentary majority for a constitutional amendment permitting him to remain in office. Some Moslems took up arms, and a small-scale civil war broke out. Chamoun appealed to the Eisenhower administration for aid. Although the UN team of observers requested by Chamoun found little help for the rebels coming across the borders, administration sources spoke of the threat from Arab countries "dominated" by Communists. The "overt aggression" part of the Eisenhower Doctrine was not utilized, but Marines flowed ashore without incident at Beirut on July 15, 1958, the first of some 15,000 troops sent to Lebanon. At the same time, British paratroopers were dropped in Jordan to bolster Hussein's position. The Lebanese Army had cautiously refrained from supporting either side and the rebellion quickly quieted down when a special election brought to the presidency General Fuad Chehab, whom both sides were able to trust. American troops had all left by October.

At the same time the first Marines were being landed in Lebanon, a group of pro-Nasser army officers in Iraq had murdered the king and crown prince, overthrown the monarchy, and proclaimed the Republic of Iraq. The new leader, General Abdel Karim Kassim, quickly scrapped the links with Jordan and instead allied the new government with the United Arab Republic. Both the Soviet Union and the United States soon recognized the Kassim government, although Washington was shocked by the suddenness of the revolt and the split in the Baghdad Pact. Kassim completed this by formally withdrawing Iraq from the pact in 1959. With this key nation missing, the remaining nations reformed as the Central Treaty Organization (CENTO), and Dulles inaugurated bilateral military aid treaties with Turkey, Pakistan, and Iran. America's first armed intervention into the Middle East drew highly unfavorable responses from the underdeveloped world and the Arab world, and additional aid to the latter countries from Soviet Russia. It warned the Arab nationalist states that threats to Western oil resources touched a quickly responsive chord in American foreign policy. It was based upon Dulles' untenable assumption that Soviet Russia, as the world's second power, could actually be denied access to, and influence in, areas of strategic importance near her borders. The Russians, with renewed influence in Iraq and the United Arab Republic, demonstrated that neither a containment ring nor toppling dominoes had any relationship to the extent of Soviet influence. CENTO, like SEATO and NATO, was intended further to contain Russia and China, while the Eisenhower

Doctrine specifically applied the Truman Doctrine to the Middle East. Only a few Congressmen soberly considered the steady flow of their war-making powers to the presidency.

The ominous rumblings of crises soon to come plagued the Eisenhower administration in Southeast Asia. In Laos, which with Cambodia was stipulated by the Geneva Accords of 1954 to be neutral, a precarious balance of rival forces prevailed. Strongest militarily was the Pathet Lao, the pro-Communist guerrilla fighters who resembled the Vietminh in their nationalist attacks upon the Japanese and then the French colonial forces. Although elections under the supervision of the International Control Commission (India, Canada, Poland) were to bring about a coalition government, Dulles, the State Department, and the CIA worked assiduously to prevent an election which might return a pro-Communist or Communist government. An election held in 1958 in northern Laos returned 13 out of 21 pro-Pathet Lao province officials. In 1959, with large infusions of American funds, the Royal government was able to achieve better results in southern Laos elections, even in areas known to be dominated by Communists. The rightist government, with American advice and aid, then began a military campaign against the Pathet Lao and their supporters.

In 1959 and 1960 the Eisenhower administration poured such funds into Laos as to give it the highest per capita aid of any country in the world, but 80 percent of it went to a totally inept army. Large amounts corrupted politicians willing to be bought and badly inflated a primitive economy. American-dominated politicians had no popular support outside the well-paid army, and credit for the strong currents of anticolonialism nationalism went to the Pathet Lao. The latter, with some infiltration from North Vietnam and large infusions of guns and supplies from the Soviet Union—much of it airlifted from Hanoi—answered the rightist government's assault by counterattacks that routed the Royal Laotian forces. In 1960 the Pathet Lao steadily won more territory along the Laotian border of North Vietnam. By the time that President Eisenhower was ready to turn over his difficulties to his successor, the Pathet Lao held a threatening upper hand.

Secretary of State Dulles, with the support of Eisenhower and the National Security Council, was even more intent upon overturning the Geneva Accords where South Vietnam was concerned. Even while the Geneva agreements were still being discussed, a team of agents under the direction of Colonel Edward Lansdale,[7] an experienced counterguerrilla leader, was sent to undertake paramilitary operations against

---

[7] His exploits over the next few years were so legendary as to be fictionalized, in a sympathetic light, as the protagonist in Lederer and Burdick's *The Ugly American* and to be portrayed more critically in Graham Greene's *The Quiet American*.

the Vietminh. Shortly thereafter the Eisenhower administration committed itself to military, economic, and political support of South Vietnam
and became the only major power which refused to accept a political
settlement of the First Indochinese War. Insurgency opposing the Diem
regime revived strongly in 1957 and increased steadily in 1958 and 1959
in numbers and in the area of territory controlled. Despite intelligence
reports of the improbability of any lasting stability in the Diem regime,
the Eisenhower administration reiterated its objectives in 1958 and 1960
in language identical with 1954 and 1956. Any success of communism
would lead to the "loss" of all Southeast Asia and, through the domino
process, to other areas. Whether achieved through ballot or bullet, it
must be opposed. Financial aid to the Diem regime leaped upward
from $50 million in 1957 to nearly $300 million by the end of the Eisenhower administration. Although reports from Saigon to Washington were
pessimistic accounts of the jeopardy involved, Congress and the public
received only a picture of amazing and continuing progress. So well
was Diem able to cope with any insurgency in 1959 that a "phased
withdrawal" of American military advisers could begin in 1961, Ambassador Elbridge Durbrow and General Samuel T. Williams claimed. But
Diem, lacking in popular and political support, was able to maintain
a shaky military control only through increasing amounts of American
finances and additional American advisers. Although the Eisenhower
commitment was not a formal one which then committed other administrations (as Lyndon Johnson was to insist), the South Vietnamese government was an American creation which could lead only to growing
involvement.

In the Far East, only the repetition of a previous crisis gave pause
to the second Eisenhower administration. Quiescent for three years, the
Mao forces of mainland China revived suddenly in August 1958 their
heavy shelling of the off-shore island of Quemoy, held by Chiang's Nationalist troops. Their action was not without cause, since in the interim
Chiang had used American support and military supplies to mount an
intensive blockade of the mainland Chinese ports of Amoy and Foochow.
Both shelling and commando raids on the mainland were carried on
from Quemoy and the Matsus, while air strikes with American-supplied
planes were directed at Chinese mainland points from Formosa. But
President Eisenhower, persuaded by Dulles, sent warships withdrawn
from the Middle East to the Formosa Straits, and the Peking government
was repeatedly warned that military retaliation would take place if the
islands were invaded. On September 11, 1958, Eisenhower warned the
American public that the shelling was an "ambitious plan of armed
conquest," although both Chiang Kai-shek and Mao Tse-tung agreed
that the islands (and Formosa as well) were an integral part of China.

The domino theory was invoked to equate success in Quemoy for the Communist Chinese with domination of the Western half of the Pacific Ocean.

Both American public and editorial opinion rejected the administration position. It was pointed out that Chiang's commitment of fully one third of his army to these outpost islands was not so much a military blunder as a deliberate attempt to bind the United States more closely to his cause. Such previous supporters as the *New York Times* scoffed at the domino theory, and the *Wall Street Journal* and other Republican papers strongly objected to the idea of an American defense of Quemoy. In the face of such public criticism, Dulles was forced to retreat. He stated flatly that the United States had no commitment to aid Chiang in any attempt to regain the mainland. He admitted that he had acquiesced in the stationing of the troops on Quemoy, but thought it would not be wise to keep them there if a cease-fire could be arranged. When he went further, to the dismay of Chiang, and agreed that the return of the Nationalists was "highly hypothetical," the mainland Chinese suggested a cease-fire arrangement. In October, Dulles went to Formosa. He announced that the Nationalists would no longer use force to regain the mainland, and that the troops on Quemoy would be decreased. Dulles' brinkmanship over the isle of Quemoy and the resultant pledge of Russia to come to Mao's aid if he were attacked were strong factors in the elections of 1958 which retired such China Lobby old hands as Senators Knowland, Bricker, and Jenner. The crisis of Cold War, for the second time, had visited and left the Formosa Straits.

Decline of the Good Neighbor Policy

The United States' interest in Latin America has traditionally considered that hostile powers must be kept out of the hemisphere, and that the capital surplus of the United States must have outlets in Latin America. Latin Americans have not only resented the economic exploitation and the military intervention which frequently stemmed from these basic American considerations, but have chafed under the low priority of Latin American affairs in United States interests and the resultant periods of neglect. Roosevelt's Good Neighbor policy was some amelioration of these complaints, and a welcome relief from the post-Wilsonian military interventions of the 1920s. But it also demonstrated to some extent that Latin American interests were generally ignored except when events threatened United States interests. The Nazi threat in the late 1930s and then the war years stimulated American aid and friendliness. The Mexican oil nationalization was amicably resolved, and military missions and aid programs blossomed throughout Latin America. With the war's end, the Good Neighbor policy and American interest in the southern hemisphere declined precipitately. Truman and Acheson aggressively pushed private American capital investment, which Latin Americans understandably did not regard as "economic aid." The Cold War brought with it the fear of communism and added another basic consideration where Latin America was concerned: that any change of government too radically repugnant to the United States must be opposed, since such a political turnabout would cause the United States to lose face and jeopardize its influence elsewhere in the world. Whether the change in question was legally and constitutionally effected could not be permitted to stand in the way of this concept.

Such was the case in regard to the Central American Republic of Guatemala. The government of Colonel Jacobo Arbenz Guzman, duly elected in 1951, carried on much-needed reforms begun under the preceding Arevalo administration, particularly in land redistribution. The small force of Communists in Guatemala had minority representation in the Congress and had been given several bureaucratic posts. Arbenz sometimes sought advice from them, used them to promote anti-American demonstrations, and they were reputed to have a foothold in the growing labor movement. In 1953 the new Eisenhower Department of State strongly protested Arbenz' expropriation of several hundred thousand acres of unused land belonging to the dominating American corporation, United Fruit Company. The United States could not, under international law, question the right of any nation to expropriate foreign-owned property on its own sovereign soil. The only challengeable aspect was the amount of compensation for the expropriation, properly taken under the Agrarian Law of 1952. Here Arbenz had understandably based compensation on the absurdly low evaluation that United Fruit had itself originally used to conceal the land's true value and escape most government taxation. Arbenz offered 25-year bonds at the United Fruit tax valuation, and refused to take the dispute before the Court of Arbitration at The Hague. Dulles raised the cry of communism, and invoked the Tenth Inter-American Conference at Caracas, Venezuela in March 1954, where he forced through a resolution condemning international communism. Although Latin American nations did not share the American obsession with communism and considered American intervention a more likely menace, most countries reluctantly voted affirmatively rather than face the loss of American economic aid.

It was readily understood by Latin American nations that the United States was determined to get rid of the Arbenz government. A shipment of Czechoslovak arms to Guatemala in a Swedish vessel was denounced by Dulles as an Iron Curtain threat. He unsuccessfully requested permission from European allies to search their merchant ships if suspected of carrying arms to Guatemala. At the same time, mutual security treaties were hastily signed with Honduras and Nicaragua, and arms were flown to these nations. The CIA picked an Arbenz opponent, Colonel Carlos Castillo Armas, to set up a training base in Honduras and prepare a small army for an invasion of Guatemala and the overthrow of the Arbenz government. United States Ambassador to Honduras Whiting Willauer kept the Honduran government in line while the training went on. With the full approval of President Eisenhower, the invasion took place on June 18, 1954. Although Castillo Armas had only a few hundred men, several old American planes flown by CIA-hired Americans strafed and bombed Guatemala City in the deciding blow. The Guatemalan Army refused to support Arbenz, and Castillo Armas made a triumphal entry at the side of the American Ambassador, John E. Peurifoy. The Castillo Armas regime (he was assassinated by a member of his palace guard in 1957) promptly restored the lands of United Fruit, threw out the reforms of the past two governments, and resumed a strong-arm dictatorship. The United States, fearing Soviet sponsoring of an Arbenz appeal to the UN Security Council, effectively blocked Guatemalan access to that body. Both for this high-handed policy and for her use of aggression in one area while denouncing it in another, the United States was strongly criticized by her European allies. Latin America underwent renewed attacks of anti-Yankeeism, the fury of which was only made evident to Americans several years later.

Latin American nations had both economic and political grievances where their huge neighbor to the north was concerned. They objected to the fact that American business investment frequently was in extractive industries which stripped hemispheric natural resources and returned all the profits to the United States. They resented American tariffs or quotas levied against their agricultural products and feared more restrictions to come on important exports such as petroleum and wool. Although the United States had been generous with loans for Europe and Asia, its neighbors' needs for hemispheric development had been neglected. Many Latins actively resented the American military aid which helped to bring into power eight or nine repressive military dictatorships, which were then honored by medals and decorations from President Eisenhower. Several of these dictatorships, such as that of Perez Jimenez in Venezuela, had recently been overthrown by the people after bitter struggles.

Eisenhower had made some attempts to improve Latin American relations through speeches and occasional meetings with national heads. In April 1958, he dispatched Vice President Nixon and his wife to attend the inauguration of a constitutionally elected successor to Peron in Argentina. Following this, the Nixons were to make a well-publicized goodwill tour to seven other nations. But the Nixon tour was faced with numerous demonstrations. In two nations, Peru and Venezuela, these reached the stage of serious disorders. In Caracas, site of the recently overthrown and American-supported Jimenez dictatorship, mobs got out of police control and attacked his official limousine. The lives of the Nixons were in serious danger in this episode. The anti-American-ism directed against Nixon was clearly symptomatic of widespread Latin American nationalistic resentment. It was only exacerbated by Eisen-hower's rushing Marines to Caribbean bases, since this merely added the possibility of more armed intervention. Brazil's president wrote a conciliatory and apologetic letter regarding the Nixon incident and re-vived the idea of an inter-American economic development plan. The State Department, after a closer look at Latin American problems, de-cided that channels for developmental needs were indeed inadequate. The President sent his brother, Dr. Milton Eisenhower, on a fact-finding trip in July which again emphasized the legitimate economic needs of Latin America. The United States agreed to support the establishment of an Inter-American Development Bank, which it had long opposed and Latin Americans had repeatedly requested. The bank was chartered in 1959, with the United States furnishing $450 million of its initial $1 billion capital and Latin Americans furnishing the balance. The par-ticipation of the United States in such an enterprise not only revealed a turnabout from the Dulles and Humphrey refusals of the first Eisen-hower administration, but the financial involvement marked a further departure in American economic foreign policy. Both the Bank's estab-lishment and further efforts to undertake an aid program in Latin Amer-ica financed by the United States were energized by concurrent events in Cuba.

In that land, one of the genuinely revolutionary movements of the 20th century had taken place in 1958 and 1959. Cuba had been a thoroughly dominated dependency of the United States ever since 1898. American Marines were landed in 1906, 1912, and 1917 to ensure that the government was to American liking. The Roosevelt administration had abrogated the humiliating Platt Amendment during the Mendieta administration in 1934, but had nevertheless followed the Sumner Welles' recommendations for economic pressure and nonrecognition which brought down the government of his predecessor, Ramon Grau San Martin. In this episode and in other anti-American outbursts, United States aims had the full support of army colonel and long-time strong man in Cuban politics, Fulgencio Batista. Washington loyally supported such governments as that of Carlos Mendieta, which suspended all con-stitutional guarantees and used troops to suppress the general strike that reflected strong Cuban sentiment. Batista was constitutionally elected in 1940, although the ex-sergeant had actually controlled the government for many years before. After his presidential term ended in 1944, he continued to exert a dominating control. In 1952 Batista chose to overthrow the elected and constitutional government with the aid of army cronies, and was immediately recognized by the United States.

Economically, American corporations had long held a commanding position in Cuba. By the 1950s, Americans owned 40 percent of Cuba's primary resource, sugar; 80 percent of her utilities; and 90 percent of Cuban mining. A large part of the banking done and the food consumed in Cuba was handled through American corporations. Even the gambling in the plush Havana casinos was run by Miami-based racketeers. The American sugar quota favoring Cuban sugar was also a subsidy for American-owned sugar corporations, and could in any case be moved up or down as the United States Congress willed. Governments such as Batista's were thus of great importance in the protection of American interests and influence. Ambassador Earl E. T. Smith, an ostentatiously admiring friend of Batista's, stated the case very aptly when he told a Senate committee that the U.S. Ambassador to Cuba was the second most important man on the island, and occasionally of more importance than the president himself.

Cuban per capita income was one of the highest in the Caribbean area, but the booming economy concealed an aggravated maldistribution of income which found a small minority of well-to-do or wealthy individuals overbalanced by masses of people without even the most basic needs in health, food, and housing. The Batista dictatorship used terrorism and assassination to thwart any attempt at social reform or governmental change. Its continued ruthlessness and the miserable state of Cuban society alienated many of the lower economic classes, the students and intellectuals, elements of the middle class, and even a large part of the Batista army. An early leader for reforms and the struggle to depose Batista was Fidel Castro, a young lawyer. With his brother, Raul, and a small group, they had mounted an unsuccessful attack upon Moncada, an army stronghold, on July 26, 1953. Many of the group were executed, with the Castros and others imprisoned. Popular pressure brought about amnesty in 1955, and the Castro brothers went into exile in Mexico. There they trained a small band of other exiles, returning in the sloop *Granma* in late 1956. In December, a group of 85 which included Fidel and Raul Castro and Ernesto Guevara moved up into the Sierra Maestra mountains to begin a two-year guerrilla war against the Batista forces. Although popular sympathy in the United States favored the Castro forces (which called themselves the 26 of July Movement, after the Moncada assault), Washington furnished Pentagon advisers and arms to Batista for use against Castro until March 1958. By December Batista's supporters had melted away and Fidel Castro's Revolutionary Government assumed control on January 1, 1959.

The United States recognized the new government on January 7, and other nations followed suit. But Americans soon began to take a harshly critical view of the revolution. A prominent excuse was the punishment of war criminals by the Castro government. The full extent of the hired gangs of *pistoleros,* tortures, and murders carried out over the years by Batista's hated Military Intelligence Service (SIM) was not fully realized by Cubans until his forces were defeated. Then the relatives of those assassinated surged forward with their stories. Tortured bodies, skeletons, and torture chambers were exposed and pictured in the Cuban press. The Castro government in exile in the Sierra Maestra mountains had issued many promulgations, including promise of punishment for the commission of such crimes, and it proceeded immediately to act under these decrees. Some hundreds of war criminal trials, mostly of SIM personnel and army officers, were held, and many of those tried were executed. The American press and Congress reacted angrily, including suggestions that the Platt Amendment be restored and the sugar quota be cut or eliminated. What made Fidelistas seethe with fury even more than the suggested retributions was the fact that the American press, which played up the war trials, had never referred to the thousands of Cubans murdered by Batista, although this was common knowledge long before the Castro government came to power. Nor did the American press point out that most of the early tribunals[8] were carried out under Nuremberg Trials precedent, and that mob violence against hated public figures was sternly prohibited.

An additional critical view of the revolution by Americans arose out of the question mark regarding communism. Castro himself was not a Communist at the time of the revolution, but of vaguely Marxist and mixed beliefs common among Latin American radicals. American military intelligence reported to a congressional committee that Castro was neither a Communist nor considered by Cubans to be one. Although he consistently denied in the early stages that the revolution was Communist, American Cold War fears and the very atmosphere of revolution combined to form a ready label. Castro's later avowals of marxism and the moves toward Soviet friendship made the early distinctions academic to most Americans. The Communist party of Cuba was an anomaly. In earlier years it had actually been an ally of Batista, and enjoyed many favors until it lost his approval in 1953. In the first years of Castro's guerrilla warfare it had disapproved of the 26 of July Movement, and had not participated in the Castro call for a general strike in 1958. Thus its support for the 26 of July was largely passive. Nevertheless, it was the best-organized anti-Batista group and as such was then util-

---

[8] Even allowing for differences between Cuban and American judicial procedure, an unfortunate exception to the many orderly tribunals was the trial in January in the jammed Havana sports stadium of six military figures, four of whom were condemned to death, in an atmosphere best described as circuslike.

ized by Castro after his victory. Although it could in no way interfere with the base of his overwhelming personal popularity and had no share of early officialdom, its presence aroused apprehension. Revolutionary moves such as the arbitrary slashing of urban rents by as much as 50 percent were popularly ascribed, both in Cuba and the United States, to the Communists.

Castro's trip to the United States in April 1959, was a public success but a complete failure in American-Cuban official relations. Invited to make the trip as the guest of the American Society of Newspaper Editors, Castro spoke successfully to a variety of large audiences. President Eisenhower, irritated over the invitation, left on a golfing trip to South Carolina so that there could be no possibility of a meeting. Castro had a long talk with Vice President Nixon in the latter's office, after which Nixon suggested to his administration colleagues that Castro was probably a prisoner of the Communists and should be dealt with accordingly. His recommendation was for a force of Cuban exiles to be armed for an overthrow of the Castro government. The Fidelista promulgation in May of its Agrarian Reform Law increased State Department irritation with Cuba. In addition to some expropriation and land redistribution, the act also called for governmental co-ops to replace much of American and British ownership in such areas as sugar plantations and cattle ranches. Although again the expropriation itself was not debatable, the issue of compensation further widened the gap between the United States and Castro. Washington agreed that land reform was a desirable step in social reforms in its June 11 note, but insisted on immediate and "adequate" compensation. The Cuban government rejected the note, pointing out that the Batista regime had virtually denuded the nation of its cash reserves. The landowners, Castro replied, would have to be satisfied with 20-year 4.5 percent bonds.

By the end of 1959, congressional and administration threats to cut the American sugar quota coincided with large surpluses of Cuban sugar and a lowered world price. As the *Wall Street Journal* correctly prophesied on February 5, 1960, "European and U.S. credit sources are cracking down on Cuba and the Cubans have no other place to go than to Russia." A week later, after visits to the United States and Mexico, Soviet Deputy Premier Anastas I. Mikoyan arrived in Havana. Russia had been buying sugar from the Batista government, but in relatively small amounts. Aggressively seeking markets, she was glad to offer Cuba a $12 million credit at low rates, and to contract to buy 5 million tons of sugar at the world price, 80 percent of which would be in Russian industrial and farm equipment and other merchandise. In February and March repeated bombings of Havana and sugar plantations from planes flown by Cuban exiles from Florida fields exasperated the Castro government. More lands were expropriated (International Harvester, King Ranches of Texas); American telephone company workers were discharged. There seemed no further possibility of a reconciliation in Cuban-American relations. In July the United States sugar quota from Cuba was formally cut out by congressional action. New Secretary of State Herter attempted in August to get a strong anti-Cuban mandate from the OAS, but received only a vaguely worded declaration against intervention. CIA recommendations for an armed counterrevolutionary invasion similar to that of Guatemala had been accepted by the Chiefs of Staff and gained the approval of the Eisenhower administration in early 1960. During the spring and summer months the recruiting among the thousands of Cuban exiles in Miami and their training in guerrilla warfare by CIA experts was an open secret. Although the invasion was originally scheduled for November 1960, it was postponed for ultimate decision by the incoming Democratic administration, which had been briefed on the development. Two weeks before the Kennedy inauguration Eisenhower formally withdrew United States recognition from the Castro government, and the stage was set for the future Bay of Pigs fiasco.

The Cuban Revolution was not another Latin American coup, where only the actors change and the same play continues, but a social revolution of great depth and breadth of support. Modeled somewhat on the earlier Mexican Revolution, it was led by Fidel Castro far beyond the moderate limits he had prescribed earlier. Its anti-Americanism could scarcely have been avoided, given the fact of 60 years of overwhelming American political and economic domination. Added to this were the angry feelings of a denied nationalism, probably the most potent factor in mid-20th century developments, and the "revolution of rising expectations" common to all the underdeveloped nations of the world. Any wholly successful slashing of American economic ties could not fail to evoke strong American reactions, although those who advocated American aid to keep the revolution out of Communist hands were best able to cry "I told you so" in retrospect. On his trip to the United States, Castro stiffly declined to ask for aid (although he did so before the OAS in Buenos Aires) and the United States suspiciously declined to offer any. Khrushchev's later scoffing at the semisacred Monroe Doctrine and his unfortunate remarks on Russian protection of Cuba served to confirm the Cuban change of orbit.

Evaluation of the Eisenhower Years

The achievements of President Eisenhower and the first Republican administration since Herbert Hoover are readily definable. By his attention and prestige, his impeccable attributes of moderately conservative Republicanism and World War military stature, General Eisenhower as President was infinitely more able to bring about—or at least support—a compromise ending to a war against the ideological Communist enemy in Korea. No Democratic regime, given the frustrated climate of the 1950s, could have successfully brought off such an ending. Similarly, perhaps no move by the opposition party could have so effectively slowed down Republican Senator Joe McCarthy and the insane vitality of McCarthyism as could an administration and a Congress dominated by fellow Republicans. Although the 1960 summit meeting was blown up by the U-2 affair, Eisenhower's meetings with Khrushchev produced an equating of atomic war with mutual suicide and probably the early beginnings of coexistence. Ike's "open skies" and "atoms for peace" proposals were timid steps arising out of misconceptions of the gap between American insistence on absolute security and Russian fears of her immediate security. The United States, however, was a signatory together with the Soviet Union, Great Britain, France, Japan, Norway, Belgium, Argentina, Chile, Australia, New Zealand, and South Africa in the Antarctic Treaty signed in Washington on December 1, 1959. Approved by the United States Senate on August 10, 1960, by a 66 to 21 vote, the treaty provided for the maintenance of the region around the South Pole as a nuclear-free zone, subject to inspection without a veto. By his defeat of Taft and his neo-isolationist followers, Eisenhower assured a continuation of a foreign policy oriented toward Europe's defense and the support of UN principles. The Eisenhower administration must be credited with the final agreement on an Austrian peace treaty; and war was avoided, in spite of rather than because of Dulles' brinkmanship. Domestically, a major accomplishment of the Eisenhower administration was its acceptance for the United States of the social welfare program of the New Deal. It took the moderately conservative Eisenhower and the once-in-opposition Republican party to demonstrate in convincing fashion that the great social advances of the Democratic Roosevelt's years were an integral part of the American system, there to stay. Backhanded testimony to this came from the extremist John Birch Society's ludicrous denunciation of Ike as pro-Communist. And Eisenhower, the man of peace who feared the United States' development into an armed camp, pointed out to a largely indifferent public and Congress the many dangers of a growing military-industrial complex in his Farewell Address.

This having been said, little else of praise adheres to the works of the two Eisenhower administrations, although much that was praiseworthy remains for Eisenhower, the man. Even the aforementioned must be somewhat qualified. Eisenhower took a hefty swing at TVA, deflected largely by the Dixon-Yates uproar. His budget-obsessed administration displayed an alarming lack of concern for the low-income voter, cutting back the slum clearance program and subverting the mounting need for federal aid to a deteriorating national school system.

The turbulent war years and the Cold War tensions of the postwar years may have prepared the times for the Whiggish tactic of nominating a popular military figure, innocent of political ideas, whose approach would obfuscate the issues but who would symbolize integrity and provide unity, peace, and quiet. Yet not even Eisenhower's own party was united or expanded for long. In the electoral processes of the 1950s, Ike's great personal popularity continued, but the Republican party candidates for local and congressional office received increasing setbacks. "Modern" republicanism turned out to be modern only in name, and, lacking any program of action, was soon dropped. Many Democrats and Independents who voted for Ike drifted back to their original positions, their problems unsolved. Even in the traditionally Republican Midwest farm areas, the Eisenhower-Benson theory that farmers yearned to be free of their federal subsidy chains only served to alienate additional loyal voters. In the administration itself, "conflicts of interest" were no less acute under Eisenhower than under Truman and carried out on a higher level and a more grandiose scale. The Cabinet was of mediocre quality, and its general air of antiintellectualism was personified by Secretary of Defense Wilson's response to a congressional inquiry why he had not spent the $175 million appropriated for basic research: This was what you were doing when you did not know what else to do.

Ike's relations with Congress could not be counted a success, although that body's unrepresentative nature, its anachronistic procedures, and its domination by Democrats during his second term clearly did not help. But Ike generally refused to use his vast public support or the executive's persuasive devices to advance the administration's requests for legislation, even when conviction was strongest. Thus Congressmen learned that ignoring White House programs carried little possibility of retribution. On the other hand, Eisenhower negatively loomed over Congress with veto powers. In the last session of Congress alone, such measures as tentative steps in education, housing, and urban redevelopment were among those beaten down in the hail of 150 vetoes. The holy formula of bipartisanship was invoked to stifle congressional dissent in foreign policy, on the grounds that Russians and Chinese would otherwise think we were sorely divided. Thus additional congressional—particularly Senate—powers were yielded up to the Chief Executive in the Formosa and Middle East Resolutions,[9] in the latter even in advance of any defined problem.

Eisenhower's position on civil rights ranged from indifferent to peculiarly neutral. When, in the wake of the trauma of Little Rock, the

---

[9] To the Middle East Resolution, or Eisenhower Doctrine, bitter Latin Americans added their own "Dulles Doctrine": assumption by the United States of the right to overthrow any Latin American government of which it disapproved.

country needed leadership and a powerful voice speaking as a moral conscience of the nation, it received only reluctant action based upon a minimal interpretation of constitutional duties. Ike seemed to have no awareness how disheartening it was to those in both parties to accede to Joe McCarthy's demands that Eisenhower delete a favorable comment regarding his old friend General George Marshall during the 1952 campaign. As President, Eisenhower and Dulles then threw to the McCarthyite wolves whole sections of the State Department. Nor were blacks heartened by Eisenhower's attitudes. Responsible leaders of black communities sought, without success, an appointment with the President for the first five and a half years of his tenure before being granted an interview.

In foreign policy, the Eisenhower administration was characterized by quantities of rhetoric and thousands of miles of "personal" diplomacy, but remained no closer to solutions after eight years than it had been after the first year. It confused foreign policy with the threatened holocaust of "massive retaliation." It failed to see that threats to "liberate" Russian satellites and public statements seeking peace with Russia were completely self-cancelling. The confusions of Suez weakened a NATO already eroded by a European recognition that the Russians actually had no intentions, and probably never had had, of loosing armed hordes on the Western European democracies. CENTO and SEATO were weak imitations of the European Alliance, largely irrelevant devices to carry on the containment policy of Truman and Acheson. Eisenhower resisted extremist pressures to restore to Chiang and Rhee their revanchist claims, using American troops to make it possible, but he was politically unable to admit the reality of the People's Republic of China and suggest to Americans that the world's largest nation lived on the same globe as did the United States.

Ex-President Eisenhower quickly turned out a two-volume memoir, *The White House Years,* much of which accurately reflected the complacency of the Eisenhower administrations. Yet they were strangely remiss. No admission of mistakes, no errors of judgment ruffled the calm assertion of the account. Unpleasant events and comparisons were left out or given dubious interpretation. The fact that an announced policy of liberating the Eastern European satellites, when confronted by a series of uprisings from 1953 to 1956, was left naked of meaning before the world's gaze, was nowhere mentioned. There was no indication that, in the public shock and dismay at the palpable administration lies in the dismal U-2 episode, a credibility gap began to open between those who are governed and those who are charged with the governing.

Yet Ike remained, throughout, enormously popular. His warm, engaging grin and his innate decency were reassuring. His background and bearing inspired trust. The people of the United States ignored his experienced reflections on the military-industrial complex, but they voted him the most popular political figure in America before he was elected President, and they repeated the same judgment after he had left the presidency. But in the eight Eisenhower years no urgent problems of the country were moved materially toward solution by the White House or Congress. The nation drifted, opportunities passed. Demands long postponed were left for his successor.

Suggestions for Reading

To the surveys of the Eisenhower period mentioned in the previous chapter should be added Herbert Parmet, *Eisenhower: The Necessary President* (1973). Outstanding events of Ike's presidency are covered in Aaron Wildavsky, *Dixon-Yates: A Study in Power Politics,* (1961), and W. R. Willoughby, *The St. Lawrence Waterway: A Study in Politics and Diplomacy* (1961).

There are a number of useful works treating society and problems of the times. Tart comments are found in I. F. Stone, *The Haunted Fifties** (1964). A good summation is Eric Larrabee, *The Self-Conscious Society* (1960). Outstanding works aimed at various facets of the period are J. K. Galbraith's *The Affluent Society** and *American Capitalism: The Concept of Countervailing Power** (1958 and 1952, but revised and reissued); David Potter, *People of Plenty** (1954); David Riesman, et al., *The Lonely Crowd** (1952); and W. H. Whyte, Jr., *The Organization Man** (1956).

On civil rights, see J. W. Anderson, *Eisenhower, Brownell, and the Congress** (1964), for the 1957 Civil Rights Act. For the events following the *Brown* decision, see A. P. Blaustein and C. C. Ferguson, Jr., *Desegregation and the Law: The Meaning and Effect of the School Segregation Cases* (1957); Benjamin Muse, *Ten Years of Prelude* (1964); and G. T. Mitau, *Decade of Decision: The Supreme Court and the Constitutional Decision, 1954–1964** (1967). Martin Luther King, Jr., supplies his own important place in the Negro Revolution in *Stride Toward Freedom* (1958) and *Why We Can't Wait* (1964). The feelings of the Eisenhower administration are depicted in E. F. Morrow, *Black Man in the White House*" (1963). For other works on the Negro Revolution and the Warren Court, refer to the following chapter.

Most of the literature on foreign relations cited previously is relevant here. For the notorious incident that helped upset the summit conference, see David Wise and T. B. Ross, *The U-2 Affair* (1962). For other cloak-and-dagger activities, a highly favorable account is offered by a former official in L. B. Kirkpatrick, Jr., *The Real CIA* (1968). Far more critical are the works by two leading journalists, David Wise and T. B. Ross, *The Invisible Government* (1964), and by a disenchanted former Pentagon contact, L. F. Prouty, *The Secret Team* (1973).

For Latin America, the President's brother uses his trip as the basis for description of that area's deteriorating relations with the United States in

Milton Eisenhower, *The Wine is Bitter* (1963). On the Cuban problem, Hugh Thomas' comprehensive work, *Cuba* (1971) is valuable background. For Cuban-American relations see W. A. Williams, *The United States, Cuba, and Castro** (1962); Leo Huberman and P. M. Sweezy, *Cuba: Anatomy of a Revolution** (1960); Theodore Draper, *Castroism: Theory and Practice** (1965), and R. E. Ruiz, Cuba: *The Making of a Revolution* (1968).

All the works cited previously on Vietnam are applicable. To these should be added two comprehensive, yet compact, documentary collections, Marvin Gettleman, ed., *Vietnam: History, Documents, and Opinions** (2d ed. 1970) and M. G. Raskin and B. B. Fall, eds., *The Viet-Nam Reader** (1965). On Laos, see C. A. Stevenson, *The End of Nowhere* (1972); Arthur Dommen, *Conflict in Laos* (1964, rev. in 1971); and for a documentary, Nina Adams and Alfred McCoy, eds., *Laos: War and Revolution** (1970).

5

A New Frontier for the United States

The Election of 1960

THE growing disenchantment of the American electorate with the Eisenhower administration and the Republican party was watched with delight from the opposing Democratic camp. Only two presidential elections had been won by the Republicans since the Great Crash of 1929, both by Eisenhower, and only once—in 1952—had the GOP been able to field a majority in Congress. It was true enough that the nation had been kept close to the center of the political road by a strong coalition of conservative Democrats and Republicans in Congress ever since the end of the New Deal, regardless of Presidents, but the First Prize was sought none the less avidly for that. The elections of 1958 signaled to Democrats that the presidency in 1960 would probably be theirs. Even the popular figure of Eisenhower, who remained far ahead of his political colleagues in public opinion, would not have to be reckoned with. The Republicans had taken care of this themselves. With many of their number still smarting over four successive trips to the White House by Franklin D. Roosevelt, they had successfully maneuvered through Congress and the requisite number of states a 22d Amendment to the Constitution prohibiting a third term for any President.

The resultant climate in 1959 thus brought out a large crop of presidential hopefuls. Prominent among them were: Adlai Stevenson, the titular leader of the Democratic party as its standard-bearer against Eisenhower in 1952 and 1956; Senator John F. Kennedy of Massachusetts, the youngest of the group but with ample finances and a large and enthusiastic organization; Senator Hubert H. Humphrey of Minnesota, whose base of political power outside of his own region was furnished by his support for labor; Senator Lyndon B. Johnson of Texas, whose Senate power and authority were not very translatable in national terms and whose pose as a Westerner instead of a Southerner fooled no one; and Senator Stuart Symington of Missouri, whose support by ex-President Truman was now of dubious blessing. The Stevenson movement had many well-wishers among Democratic intellectuals and the party ranks, and a small national organization. Some followers emphasized the great integrity Stevenson had shown in discussing unpopular issues in the campaigns; party members remembered with gratitude his representation in 1956 when many friends of both parties begged him to forego certain defeat. But Stevenson, although declaring he was available, refused to strive for a nomination he had already been given twice. Kennedy and Humphrey thus established themselves as frontrunners by their seriousness in beating their way through the grueling primaries, while the Stevenson, Symington, and Johnson forces placed their hopes in a deadlocked convention which might then turn to a third candidate.

John F. Kennedy had one handicap which he shared with most of the other hopefuls: Only once before in history had a United States Senator moved from one end of Pennsylvania Avenue to the other. His two other handicaps—extreme youthfulness (he was 43) and his Catholic religion—were far more formidable, and the Kennedy organization was faced with the necessity of proving their candidate's national votegathering stature if the convention wheelers and dealers were to be impressed. Presidential primaries were ordeals exhausting both physically and financially, as Hubert Humphrey was soon to find out, and the Kennedy entries were thus carefully chosen. After an easy, but unimportant, win in early New Hampshire, Kennedy challenged Humphrey in the somewhat unpredictable state of Wisconsin. He won six districts, most of them with heavy Catholic registration, to Humphrey's four. While not exactly a great triumph for Kennedy, to political observers it was a poor showing for Humphrey in a neighboring state.

Both candidates moved on to overwhelmingly Protestant West Virginia, where Kennedy boldly raised the religious issue. He put great emphasis in numerous television appearances on his oath to uphold the separation of church and state and insisted that the tolerance of the American voter would not deny him office simply because of his religion. The Kennedy entourage, aided by Franklin D. Roosevelt, Jr.; the heavy television coverage in the final days; and finally the issue of "tolerance" were too much for a physically spent and financially outspent Humphrey. With the West Virginia vote heavily against him, Humphrey thereupon declared himself out of presidential contention. Kennedy went on to win Nebraska, Maryland, Indiana (unopposed) and Oregon, arriving at the Democratic convention in Los Angeles in early July 1960, with a generally admitted count of at least 600 delegate votes. The only hope other contenders had was to block the Kennedy movement for several ballots, hoping for its disintegration; but large-scale splits throwing additional votes to Kennedy in such important states as Pennsylvania and Illinois brought him 806 votes on the first ballot and his party's nomination for President. Lyndon Johnson followed with 409 votes, mostly from the South. Symington and Stevenson each had less than 100. Kennedy had obviously been the national favorite, and the convention, instead of carrying out its traditional private nominating process, had actually seconded the choice of public opinion. Much to the horror of many urban liberals and of labor supporters who remembered the Texan Senator's votes, the vice presidential nomination was offered to Lyndon Johnson as a means of corralling potentially anti-Kennedy Southern votes. Johnson accepted and the convention ratified the choice. The Democratic platform promised not to neglect the people's welfare as the Republicans had done, but to promote education and medical care insurance and to attack the unemployment problem. It belligerently blamed the Republican administration for a "missile gap," for failures in the space race, and for a general deterioration of American prestige throughout the world.

The Republicans, convening two weeks later in Chicago, were embarrassed from both external and internal sources. The United States had just staggered through the undignified incident of the U-2. The hoped-for summit meeting had then been cancelled. On the heels of this came a humiliating rebuff for President Eisenhower, when large and perhaps dangerous anti-American riots in Japan forced him to cancel his visit there. Internally, the GOP had been soundly and publicly called to task for the quality and direction of its leadership by a power in the party's Eastern Establishment. This was Governor Nelson A. Rockefeller of New York, whose tremendous 570,000-vote victory made him a figure to be reckoned with. His nine-point program for action in a public bill of complaints was an obvious indictment of the Eisenhower administration in everything from civil rights and lack of economic growth to the conduct of world affairs. Rockefeller had already refused the vice presidency as well as removed himself from presidential contention, but his candid and politically pungent remarks had to be taken into account, even though the platform committee had finished its labors, lest party disunity reach serious proportions. Nixon visited Rockefeller in New York and accepted the latter's "14 Points," which included such items as medical care for the aged and the promotion of traditional military forces regardless of the budget. It provoked screams of a "Munich" by the ultraconservative Senator Barry Goldwater of Arizona, but its essentials were finally fitted into the national platform.

Most unusually, the fight over the platform took precedence in the news media over the balance of the convention proceedings. But Nixon's nomination, with his control of the party's conservative machinery and the continued support of President Eisenhower, was a foregone conclusion. On the first ballot Nixon captured 1,321 votes, with 10 dissident Louisiana Republicans casting their votes for Senator Goldwater. With equal facility, the convention accepted Nixons' choice of Henry Cabot Lodge, Jr., the Ambassador to the United Nations, as the vice presidential nominee.

The two candidates waged a furious, physically punishing campaign that left few points in the United States uncovered, including the newly entered states of Alaska and Hawaii. Kennedy carried on a strongly personalized campaign, putting in maximum exposure in public appearances and on television before large and varied groups, and with heavy reliance on his large retinue of relatives and friends. His brother, Robert Kennedy, was the manager of the tour, and much of the strategy was decided by the Kennedys rather than by the Democratic National Committee organization. Kennedy sought to exploit what were considered the weaknesses of the Eisenhower administration. In a criticism of the manner in which the Republicans handled national defense, Kennedy promised to boost conventional forces. He repeatedly hammered away at a so-called "missile gap" said to exist between the Soviet Union and the United States. This was a much publicized fear in 1959, but the weight of later evidence in this clouded controversy did not adequately support such an alarmist presentation in 1960. Kennedy also took a strongly pugnacious stand against Castro and the Cuban Revolution, charging the Eisenhower administration with gross negligence.

The fact that Kennedy had edged out Theodore Roosevelt as the youngest presidential candidate in history was not a difficult factor, since Nixon was only four years older. Questions of experience and leadership were more difficult to face, since his youthfulness was an unspoken but present factor in such doubts. Kennedy could only point to his varied political experience and mention that he and Nixon entered national politics in the same year. The Democratic candidate's speeches reflected an economy of style and a touch of missionary zeal, and his "All-American Boy" attitude—as a critic described it—triggered responsive chords from large crowds and personal appearances. Kennedy's chief difficulty was his Catholic religion, and here, as in West Virginia, he preferred to meet it head on. In September Kennedy accepted a challenging invitation to appear before a Texas gathering of Protestant clergy and lay leaders, agreeing to answer any and all questions. At the meeting of the Greater Houston Ministerial Association Kennedy delivered a moving and compelling speech, frankly and fully explaining the position of a Catholic in a modern democratic society. He reminded them that even the Catholic bishops had gone on record as firmly committed to a separation of church and state, and pledged: "If the time should ever come—and I do not concede any conflict to be remotely possible—when my office would require me to either violate my conscience or violate the national interest, then I would resign the office." The questions directed to him were skillfully turned to his own advantage, and Kennedy emerged from the Houston challenge with national applause.

Nixon was necessarily bound to a defense of the Republican administration, but also sought in a variety of ways to bind himself tightly to the popular figure of Eisenhower. He called attention to the upgrading of the vice presidency in terms of the increased functions which had been added under Eisenhower, and placed persistent emphasis on the need for the continuity of that administration. But Eisenhower, much to his irritation, was scarcely ever called upon for advice and activity, and intervened with a barnstorming trip only on the last eight days of the campaign. Rather than exacerbate the tensions in his party, Nixon was vague and evasive on controversial issues, although seemingly there was not a great substantive difference in the public utterances of the two candidates. Nixon charged that reporters and some pollsters were so biased in their presentation that they helped to create a bandwagon atmosphere for his opponent. The complaint had merit, although since most newspapers were Republican owned, the editorial pages were balanced somewhat in the other direction. The innovation of the 1960 campaign was the agreement of both candidates to meet in "debate" on a national television hookup. Four such broadcasts were given in September and October before an estimated audience of 80 to 100 million Americans. They were not debates in the true sense of the word. None of the viewers actually learned a great deal more about the candidates' stands, but as a personality match the masterfully cool Kennedy scored heavily over the less concise, somewhat harried-looking Nixon. Additionally, Nixon's charges of inexperience leveled at his opponent were dissipated by the obviously even matching of the two performers in the questions thrown at them by reporters and news analysts. Polls indicated that the "Great TV Debates" were largely to the benefit of Kennedy.

All that most pollsters were willing to predict on the 1960 campaign was that it would be very close, and here they had never been more seerlike. Kennedy received only 112,881 more votes than Nixon out of more than 68 million total votes cast, and the issue in several states was in doubt for days. Minor parties kept either major party candidate from a majority, so Kennedy's winning percentage was 49.7 percent. In electoral votes, Kennedy received 303 from 23 states to Nixon's 219 from 26 states. The other state, Mississippi, cast its unpledged electoral ballots for Senator Harry Byrd of Virginia, as did eight unpledged electors in Alabama and one Nixon delegate in Oklahoma. Kennedy carried the day with the big states of New York, Pennsylvania, Illinois, Michigan, and Texas, and narrowly missed taking Nixon's home state of California. Although Johnson's influence had helped in the South, Kennedy still lost Florida in the Deep South and the border states of Virginia, Kentucky, Tennessee, and Oklahoma. National voting revealed a slight benefit for the Republicans in Congress and for Democrats in the statehouses. In the Senate the Republicans gained two seats to remain on the short side of a 64 to 35 margin, while in the House a Republican gain did not materially change Democratic control, 262 to 174. In gubernatorial races, the Democrats won 15 as against 12 for the Republicans.

There were several significant aspects of the 1960 presidential race. In the campaign itself Kennedy ran an intensely personalized campaign, both in appearance and appeal as well as at the decision-making level. His great reliance on a small and intimate group of advisers and workers both bore out a continuance of his congressional campaign styles and indicted a presidential reliance to come. The television meeting of the two candidates was unique, even though its format needed considerable improvement to be of future importance in American politics. The voting revealed that Kennedy's great strength in urban areas and among the minorities had given him the biggest cities and with them the largest states and their electoral vote. Balanced against this was a disturbing hint of racial influences on the electorate to come in the large Republican vote amassed by Nixon in the suburbs of the large cities of the South. The religious factor, while obviously important, was difficult to measure. Later polls indicated that many Catholics who voted for Eisenhower changed over to Kennedy, and that many Protestants normally Democratic had voted against a Catholic candidate. The candidate's astute father, Joseph P. Kennedy, was disappointed in the Catholic-Protestant split, and most analysts agreed that Kennedy probably suffered a net loss of 2 or 3 percent in the religious switching. Far more significant, however, was the fact that an intolerance in American politics had been laid to rest by the election of the first Catholic to the country's highest office. As Kennedy stated, he was not the Catholic candidate for President but a presidential candidate who happened to be a Catholic, and the nation had accepted him in this fashion.

John Fitzgerald Kennedy

The youngest man ever to be elected President, John Fitzgerald Kennedy came from a family of Boston Irish immigrants dating back to the many who were able to flee Ireland after the great potato famine of the 1840s. His paternal grandfather, Patrick Joseph Kennedy, was able by tenacious effort to promote one small saloon into several such establishments from a shoestring start, and to use this base of upsurging Irish power for political successes at the state and local level. His maternal grandfather, John F. ("Honey Fitz") Fitzgerald, was a dapper little man from the north side of Boston whose elevation to Mayor in 1910 moved him a social notch or two higher than his political ally, Patrick Kennedy. The latter began the process of moving his children out of the tightly circumscribed circles of the "lace curtain" Boston Irish. His son and the new President's father, Joseph Patrick Kennedy, went to Boston Latin preparatory school, a stronghold for centuries of New England Protestantism. Joe moved on to Harvard, despite Catholic frowns of disapproval, where with great determination he made the grade both academically and, with calculated effort, socially. He married Rose Fitzgerald, to the displeasure of "Honey Fitz," but the families were soon reconciled. The young Joseph Kennedy had already displayed talents of fiercely driving ambition, and of determination to get where he wanted regardless of obstacles. With family help, he was made president of a small East Boston bank. From there he went into World War I shipbuilding (where he met Assistant Secretary of the Navy Franklin D. Roosevelt), the early moving picture industry, assorted stock market and investment opportunities, and was quickly a millionaire many times over. An ardent supporter of Roosevelt in both 1932 and 1936, he was appointed the first head of the newly created Security and Exchange Commission and later the chairman of the Maritime Commission. In 1937 Joseph P. Kennedy reached a pinnacle of social success by his appointment to the prestigious Ambassadorship to Great Britain, the Court of Saint James.

Joe Kennedy was as determined as his father before him to expand his sons' education and acceptance. The four boys went chiefly to non-Catholic schools (but not the five girls). John F., born in May 29, 1917, was second to Joseph P., Jr., in age. He went to a Catholic school only briefly, and did his prepping at Choate, a select New England Episcopalian establishment. On his graduation, his father, wanting the benefit of diverse backgrounds and experiences for the young man, sent him to the London School of Economics where he was briefly exposed to the lectures of the famous Socialist professor, Harold J. Laski. But attacks of jaundice cut this short as it did his matriculation at Princeton, and on regaining his health Jack decided on Harvard instead. There he remained largely uninvolved in the student ferment of the depression years, majoring in government and reading widely in American history and biography. His senior honors thesis treated the British appeasement of Hitler at Munich as not solely to be blamed upon Chamberlain and Baldwin, but on the British people's preference for self-interest over rearmament, and on impersonal economic forces within democracy and capitalism. Titled *Why England Slept,* it was published in 1940 with parental influence, and the 23-year old found himself with a best seller and good reviews. Before his graduation, Joseph Kennedy settled a trust fund of more than $1 million on each of his children.

Pearl Harbor meant a Navy desk job for John Kennedy, but his father's pull got him his requested sea duty. This meant motor torpedo boat training school and command of a PT boat in the South Pacific. A Japanese destroyer rammed his ship in August 1943, and Kennedy's heroic efforts to save his crew won him the Navy and Marine Corps Medal and a Purple Heart. His aggravation of a previous back injury put him into the hospital and finally out of the Navy. The tragic wartime death of Joseph, Jr., his eldest brother, was one of several factors that turned Jack toward politics. In 1946 he chose the 11th Massachusetts Congressional District and, with a fiery crew of young supporters drawn from Harvard and the Navy, Democrat and Republican, and with local young workers weary of the corruption of Boston politics, won out with an impressive 42 percent in a field of ten candidates. Using the technique of a highly personal organization rather than relying on the party pros, Kennedy was returned twice more to Congress from the 11th.

In 1952, to the dismay of many friends, he took on the incumbent and redoubtable Henry Cabot Lodge, Jr. for United States Senator. By starting literally years ahead, Congressman Kennedy had made himself known throughout Massachusetts, using the same punishing technique of hundreds of personal appearances to the point of illness and renewed back troubles. But Kennedy won over Lodge in a year when Eisenhower beat Stevenson in Massachusetts and the Republican candidate for Governor edged out his Democratic opponent. Kennedy's margin evidently came from such successful tactics as the multitudinous tea parties staged by the Kennedy women, an edge in campaign funds, and his indefatigable stumping efforts. The following year Kennedy married Jacqueline Lee Bouvier, a lovely 21-year-old George Washington University student of wealthy Catholic background and previous training at Vassar and the Sorbonne. In 1958 Kennedy even accumulated Republican votes in achieving reelection to the Senate by the awesome margin of 874,000 votes, the largest edge ever given any candidate for any office in Massachusetts and the largest margin for any senatorial candidate in the United States in 1958.

Kennedy as Congressman and Senator was frequently difficult to pigeonhole as liberal or conservative. He consciously fought against being labelled and exhibited a consistent independence, but undoubtedly moved from a generally conservative position just to the right of center to a generally liberal one a little to the left of center in his 14 years in Congress. For many years his outlook, like his father's narrow basis for New Deal support, was a bread-and-butter liberalism. He supported such issues for his constituents as low-cost housing, higher minimum wages, and increased Social Security benefits, but remained uninterested or ambivalent on civil rights matters. In foreign policy, his early years were marked by a rigid anticommunism, and he attacked the State Department over Chiang's defeat in China as bitterly as any China Lobby member (although he later remarked that he wished he could "unsay" some of his 1949 speeches). He wanted a 75-group Air Force rather than the 55-group one that Truman requested. As Senator he attacked the United States' failure to recognize the powerful forces of nationalism, and worked for an American position of support for Algerian independence. He received severe criticism from liberals for his noncommittal attitude toward Joe McCarthy. He was in the hospital when the censure vote was taken and, although he voted against McCarthy friends and McCarthy appointments, he was held in some suspicion by liberals for some time after. Nevertheless, by 1957 and 1958 he was working more and more with liberal senators for liberal causes. He became more involved in the pending Negro Revolution, and introduced the first Senate bill outlawing the bombing of houses and churches. His abortive effort to defeat Estes Kefauver for the vice presidency in 1956 gave him renewed exposure and support for his graceful acceptance of the loss. He gained increasing stature throughout 1959 and 1960 both in the Senate and in the nation for the race he was to win in November of 1960.

Manning the New Frontier

The new President's technique had put heavy reliance on his personal organization to round up convention delegates and to formulate strategy and make major decisions during the campaign. These tactics and his use of the media had largely freed him from the usual party ties that find most presidential cabinets a faithful reflection of their partisan debts. Thus only half of the Kennedy Cabinet were politicians, and none of those was a national political figure such as a Hull in Roosevelt's Cabinet or a Byrnes in Truman's. The remainder were professional administrators, possessing technical rather than political qualifications. Both at the executive and advisory levels, the Kennedy administration could boast an unusual quantity of highly competent men of dedication and intellectual verve.

Kennedy was not concerned with partisan labels, but with ability to get things done and the drive and creativity to get them done with perception and perhaps needed innovation. He inevitably received and carefully sifted a great deal of advice and suggestions, both politically and administratively oriented. Family and advisers served both to recruit and to help weed out the potential office holders. Clark Clifford, counsel and advisor for President Truman and attorney for Kennedy as Senator when his authorship of *Profiles in Courage* was in question, prepared a lengthy memorandum on the many top-level jobs and the mechanics of filling them and then took part in the selection process. Finally, many men were interviewed personally—and many rejected after such close-ups—before the first appointments reached the announcement stage.

One of the chief Kennedy headaches was the Secretary of State choice. Two of the more prominent candidates were politicians. Of the two, Adlai Stevenson, as the erstwhile leader of the Democratic party, would under many other presidents have moved into the top Cabinet position. Stevenson himself probably expected such an offer, but he was told by Kennedy that the frictions brought about by his tart handling of national issues would negate any influence he might have had on Capitol Hill. Kennedy preferred instead that Stevenson's undoubted international prestige be put to good use as Ambassador to the United Nations. After some reluctance, based upon his need to know whom he would be working with in State, Stevenson accepted the lesser post. Senator J. William Fulbright's post as Chairman of the Foreign Relations Committee and his incisive positions in foreign affairs were attractive to Kennedy. He had been President of the University of Arkansas, and his influence in Congress would be an asset. Fulbright's segregationist stands in Arkansas, however, militated strongly against his acceptance by the nonwhite part of the globe, and he was reluctantly abandoned. Former Secretary of Defense Robert A. Lovett, an urbane Republican member of the Eastern financial "Establishment," was offered the post but declined, with a recommendation for Dean Rusk, president of the Rockefeller Foundation. Other recommendations from former Secretary of State Dean Acheson and Kennedy advisers helped to pinpoint Rusk's name. Biographical data revealed the son of a Georgia cotton farmer educated at Davidson College. A Phi Beta Kappa, a ROTC officer, and a Rhodes scholar, Rusk had been a professor of international relations and then Dean of Faculty at Mills College in California. His war service was largely in India, and postwar positions in the War and State Departments included the Assistant Secretaryship for Far Eastern Affairs. Impressed favorably with his reading of Rusk's articles and memoranda, Kennedy offered the 51-year old Georgian the job.

A young Republican administrator, Robert S. McNamara, was the subject of several recommendations for the Defense post. Closer examination disclosed a Phi Beta Kappa graduate in economics of the University of California who had attended the Harvard Graduate School of Business and then become an assistant professor of business administration at that institution. During the war, McNamara had been a consultant to the War Department on an Air Force control system. After the war, he was brought into the Ford Company as a business management expert, and moved with amazing speed through a series of promotions to become, at 44—on the day after Kennedy's election—the first head of the Ford Company outside of that family. Kennedy and his advisers were greatly impressed by McNamara's precision and conciseness, and by his unhesitating decision to sacrifice considerable financial stock benefits to assume the Secretary of Defense post for as long as he might be needed. A strong and vigorous administrator backed by a strong President, McNamara was a good bet to stamp out the internecine warfare of the Pentagon and curb its unruly generals and admirals.

To another Republican went the sensitive post of Secretary of the Treasury. As adviser to the President on domestic and foreign fiscal affairs, the confidence of Wall Street and international finance was acknowledged to be influential. C. Douglas Dillon, who had earlier impressed Harvard classmate Kennedy with his speeches on an advanced growth rate for the American economy, turned out to combine both the needed banker confidence and the willingness to promote progressive Kennedy economic measures. His appointment to the Kennedy Cabinet brought adverse comment from many liberals and Democrats, but was an example of how little Kennedy cared for partisan labels among high administrative positions.

Two appointments quickly decided upon were Commerce and Health, Education and Welfare. For the former, Kennedy chose the Governor of North Carolina, Luther H. Hodges, who then had the unusual distinction of becoming the only one in the Kennedy Cabinet born before 1900. Another Governor, Abraham Ribicoff of Connecticut, was one of the earliest of the Kennedy supporters. The first person of Jewish faith to be elected to Connecticut's highest office, he had made remarkable records in the improvement of the state's educational system while effecting tax-saving cuts in administrative costs that impressed even such fiscal conservatives as Virginia's Harry Byrd.

The appointment of Secretary of the Interior was based upon the fortunate combination of early Kennedy support and demonstrated competence for the job. Stewart L. Udall, a young Arizona Congressman, had accomplished the feat of leading the Arizona convention delegation away from Johnson and safely into the Kennedy camp. Young, enthusiastic, and a political scrapper, Udall was ready to defend progressive Western viewpoints on public power and the exploitation of public lands. A great favorite of liberals, Arthur J. Goldberg, was made the Secretary of Labor. Although he had been the national counsel for the AFL-CIO for some years, he was not the labor candidate nor among the names labor leaders suggested for the post. Goldberg lived up to his reputation as a labor-management mediator by successfully settling a New York City harbor strike within hours after being sworn in.

Agriculture, Justice, and even Postmaster General were among the more difficult appointments. Concerned more with a fresh approach to the farm problem than with the individual's background, Kennedy had rejected several of those proposed. He finally decided upon Governor Orville Freeman of Minnesota, a Midwestern liberal, not so much for his farm experience as for his practical get-it-done approach and innovative willingness to look actively for solutions to the farm surplus problem. John Kennedy was very anxious to have his brother Bobby become his Attorney General. Unaffected by the obvious criticisms, the President wanted not only his younger brother's undoubted talents and enthusiasm but his nay-saying critical abilities as well. The subject himself was the greatest doubter as to the propriety of such an appointment. He would have preferred Defense or State, and even spoke of running for Governor of Massachusetts, but finally yielded to his brother's insistence. The Postmaster General, instead of going to the politician occupying the National Committee chairmanship or some other deserving national politico, went to a California businessman, J. Edward Day. Once an Insurance Commissioner for Adlai Stevenson in Illinois, Day was chosen for his administrative and organizational abilities.

The youngest Cabinet in the 20th century formed the President's executive department heads, but a brilliant and relatively small Brain Trust and a devoted group of political associates made up an inner White House staff of advisers and liaison agents. The latter group, headed by such long-time political intimates as Kenneth O'Donnell and Larry O'Brien (and frequently known as the "Irish Mafia") filled important second-echelon posts such as Appointments Secretary and Congressional Relations Chief. A large number of academics occupied a variety of Special Assistant positions, with four or five foremost in an advisory capacity. Frequently considered the most powerful among a group which readily admitted that the name of the game was indeed power, was McGeorge Bundy, the Special Assistant for National Security Affairs. A Beacon Hill Republican, Bundy was a Yale math major of superb intellect who moved into the realm of foreign affairs and through professorial ranks at Harvard to Dean of Arts and Sciences at age 34. The National Security responsibilities of the witty and overbearing Bundy impinged on both State and Defense.[1] Bundy's deputy, Walt Whitman Rostow, was a Yale graduate and a former M.I.T. professor who had supplied Kennedy with "position papers" on defense matters during the campaign. A prominent Harvard historian, Arthur M. Schlesinger, Jr., who had received the Pulitzer Prize for his work, *The Age of Jackson,* was a Special Assistant for Research and Special Projects. Schlesinger functioned as a general troubleshooter and speech writer,

---

[1] His brother, William Bundy, Dean Acheson's son-in-law, moved from his position as a CIA Far Eastern expert to Deputy Assistant Secretary of Defense.

was frequently used on Latin American affairs, and quickly moved into the position of the semiofficial administration historian. Special Counsel Theodore Sorenson occupied a rather unique category. A liberal intellectual, the 32-year-old adviser who was number one in his University of Nebraska Law School joined Congressman Kennedy back in 1952, and had been Kennedy's number one idea man and traveling companion ever since that time. Sorenson performed a variety of chores, and had even researched much of *Profiles in Courage* for the bedridden Kennedy. His particular specialty was speech writing, and he had been so close to Kennedy for so long that his style of writing was an exact duplicate of the President's. Sorenson was valued for his political advice, and all domestic issues and bills received the Sorenson scrutiny. His close relationship as the President's alter ego made Sorenson one of the most influential advisers on politics and domestic affairs. Other advisors who were less prominent but often used included General Maxwell Taylor, whom Kennedy made his personal adviser on military affairs after the Bay of Pigs; Richard N. Goodwin, who was used on Latin American affairs from his State Department post; and Jerome B. Wiesner, the M.I.T. professor who was the President's adviser on science and nuclear affairs.

Kennedy's Cabinet was admittedly one of high calibre, with its bipartisanship as well as its high percentage of technicians and professional administrators marking it as unusual. Although Franklin Roosevelt was generally looked upon as the modern organizer of the Brain Trust, John F. Kennedy may have to be regarded as the institutionalizer of that system. Additionally, his advisers and immediate staff contained a higher proportion of academics than did any previous administration. In many ways the President's assistants were a reflection of the man who was the undoubted boss of the entire show. They were of keen intellect, tough, and power loving; they were generalists rather than narrow specialists, liberal rather than reformist, and practical and pragmatic rather than idealistic. But the Executive Department of government, however talented and enthusiastic, constitutionally had to deal with the legislative branch, no matter how jealous of prerogatives and politically contrary it was, in the business of forging national legislation.

The New Frontier Revealed

The new President and the 87th Congress took office as the United States was emerging from a short but sharp recession. In his first State of the Union Message to Congress, delivered January 30, Kennedy somberly noted that "the American economy is in trouble. We take office in the wake of seven months of recession, three and one half years of slack, seven diminished years of economic growth, and nine years of falling farm income." Several days later he presented a program which included federal spending to stimulate the economy and was designed to spur the national growth rate from its poor 3.6 percent to one competitive with Western Europe's 4 to 6 percent. Kennedy went to some lengths to defend the transition from surplus to deficit budget, including an insistence that the alleged surplus was the result of faulty, if not downright dishonest, estimates of the preceding administration.

Kennedy took a number of executive steps to relieve the slow-moving economy and asked Congress to enact a series of measures to help. He announced that he had reduced long-term interest rates on home mortgages, and released $724 million in highway funds in order to stimulate construction. The distribution of surplus food to needy persons was stepped up, and $258 million in veterans' life insurance dividends was paid in advance to put some purchasing power into the economy. Of the bills submitted to Congress as antirecession measures, the most controversial was the Area Redevelopment Act. Already twice vetoed by President Eisenhower, the legislation provided for loans and grants to depressed urban areas of chronic unemployment and to rural areas of underemployment and low income. In the 1961 version, the method of financing the bill provided the chief opposition. Senator Paul Douglas of Illinois and his cosponsors called for $389.5 million for loans and grants, to be financed directly from and by the Treasury. But fiscal conservatives and Congressmen jealous of their annual prerogative of voting appropriations (or not voting them) successfully knocked out this provision in the House. The Senate agreed to appropriations rather than the Treasury for funding, in order to get the measure passed, and Kennedy signed the bill on May 1, 1961. The Area Redevelopment Act set forth certain criteria, so that depressed areas had to show sharply declining unemployment statistics or persistent underemployment rates to be eligible for federal aid. The bill provided loans for the relocation of industrial plants, grants for the construction of public facilities, and vocational retraining and subsistence for those thrown out of work by closing or relocating industries. The Housing Act of 1961 and the Manpower Retraining Act of 1962 were also of aid as boosts to the economy.

Kennedy's other immediate requests were passed with only slight alterations. The Social Security amendments of 1961 provided for increased benefits and liberalized retirement regulations. Unemployment compensation pay, almost exhausted in some states, was extended for 13 additional weeks through an advance of federal funds, and temporary grants to the states provided further aid to dependent children. A minor victory was scored by administration forces in bringing about the first significant extension of the Fair Labor Standards Act of 1938 and its minimum-wage provisions. First introduced in 1960 by Kennedy as Senator, the bill called for raising the minimum wage from $1 per hour to $1.25 and brought into the bill's provisions nearly 4 million previously excluded workers. Powerful opposition against the inclusion of laundry workers forced the dropping of this category in order to pick up the votes of some 16 Southern Democrats and ensure the bill's passage. As finally signed in May 1961, the workers covered by minimum wage provisions increased from 23.8 million to 27.4 million, and the increase to $1.25 was arranged in steps between 1961 and 1965.

However, before any major reform legislation of the new administration could be passed, the formidable obstacle of the House Rules Committee had to be surmounted. The Rules Committee, with its majority of conservative Southern Democrats and Midwestern Republicans, was a principal agent of that coalition's ideology. Presided over by the elderly and autocratic "Judge" Howard Smith of Virginia, the committee effectively prevented civil rights or progressive social measures—all of which Representative Smith disapproved—from reaching the House floor for a vote. Speaker Sam Rayburn of Texas was committed to the Kennedy administration and to the newly formed liberal Democratic Study Group to get all major legislation out of the Rules Committee for consideration by the entire House, since he had failed to do so as promised the year before. Rayburn announced that a vote would be taken on his proposal to enlarge the Rules Committee from 12 to 15 members, with 2 Democrats and 1 Republican to be added. This would then provide a slim margin to outvote "Judge" Smith's coalition. Despite intensive lobbying efforts by the National Association of Manufacturers, the United States Chamber of Commerce, and other conservative groups intent upon preserving Smith's virtual veto powers over progressive legislation, the combined pressure of the Kennedy administration, the Democratic Study Group, and the personal buttonholing by Speaker Rayburn proved to be more influential by a close 217 to 212 vote.

The successful challenge to the powers of the Rules Committee was unusual in that it brought about a meeting between Democratic Representative Smith and the Republican leader, Representative Charles Halleck, and their publicly announced intention to continue a coalition that had functioned very quietly and with denials of its existence heretofore. The addition to the Rules Committee permitted the passage of more bills than before, but it was no panacea. Also, the stiff fight, the intensive persuasion used and the tensions aroused to generate a paper-thin five-vote margin, meant that such efforts would have to be reserved for the highest priority measures. Even then, a minor change of votes could mean failure.

The most important act of the 87th Congress, and a major triumph for the Kennedy forces, was the Trade Expansion Act of 1962. The reciprocal trade program inaugurated under Franklin Roosevelt badly needed updating to conform to the realities of the 1960s. As has been noted before, the establishment of Europe's Common Market formed a united trade group of some 275 million people, and its announced tariff changes for the near future would make it more difficult for American exporters without some changes in American trade policies. Kennedy proposed in January 1962 that the Chief Executive be authorized by Congress to negotiate trade agreements for a five-year period. These would include possible mutual reductions of up to 50 percent on entire categories of goods (rather than traditionally on separate items); the elimination of tariffs altogether on those products where the United States and the Common Market together displayed a genuine dominance by accounting for at least 80 percent of all world trade; and the dropping of nuisance tariffs of less than 5 percent. The innovative part of the proposal put aside the traditional protectionism of high tariff walls for weak and small industries in the United States which required the consumer to pay higher prices for the luxury of supporting such industries. Instead, government subsidies would take a different means of aiding those businesses and workers who were threatened by foreign imports. "Trade adjustment assistance" meant federal aid for an industry to change or diversify its product, and would finance the retraining of any employees who might be thrown out of work by such change. Eisenhower Republicans supported the tariff proposals in the weeks of hearings and testimony that followed, but objected to the trade adjustment program and tried to separate the two. Some business elements and the AFL-CIO opposed the bill, but the bigger export corporations and the financial world argued in its behalf. The only portion of the bill which was cut out, in action by the House, was the administration's attempt to extend the usual most-favored-nation status to Poland and Yugoslavia and thereby wean those nations away from the Moscow bloc. Kennedy signed the Trade Expansion Act in October 1962, calling it the most important initiative in foreign policy "since the passing of the Marshall Plan." The bill created a flexible instrument for negotiating favorable trade agreements for the United States in the face of rapidly changing world conditions.

The Kennedy administration and the 87th Congress also joined forces to produce housing bills, a controversial communications act, and some lesser domestic housekeeping legislation. The Housing Act of 1961 was the most comprehensive such measure since 1949, and aimed at reducing urban blight and congestion and improving housing opportunities for those with incomes of $6,000 and under. The bill authorized $2.55 billion for urban renewal and planning, and provided special grants and loan funds for the development of mass transportation facilities and "open spaces" in cities. The Senior Citizens' Housing Act of 1962 was especially designed for those elderly persons whose limited income made their access to home loans and similar credits all too difficult.

Kennedy's announced determination of achieving an American moon landing by 1970 spurred larger expenditures and activity for space and communication areas. Outlays for NASA increased from $916 million in 1961 to $1.8 billion in 1962 and $3.7 billion the following year. Budget funds were further stimulated by the first manned flights around earth, which saw Soviet Major Yuri Gagarin's flight of April 12, 1961, followed by United States Marine Lieutenant Colonel John H. Glenn's on February 20, 1962. The Satellite Communications Act of 1962 was based upon other technological developments in space. This resulted from man-made satellites which, positioned in space, could relay microwaves far beyond the barriers which the ground-level horizon had previously presented. The American Telephone and Telegraph Company proposal for a series of relatively low satellites which would receive microwaves from ground stations as they successively moved above the earth's horizons became the heart of the administration's so-called "Telstar" bill. In the Kennedy proposal, a private corporation chartered by Congress would have two types of stock in equal amounts, one type available to investors and the other only to communication companies. This meant that AT&T, the developer of the communications satellite, would assume the dominant financial position. Critics protested that most of the research funds leading to the satellite development had been federal funds and that therefore any such agency should be federally owned. A small group of Senators attempted to defeat the bill by filibuster on this account but were voted down. On July 10, 1962, the satellite successfully relayed television programs from the United States to Europe and vice versa, providing yet another step toward a common Atlantic community culture.

To its limited list of successes, the 87th Congress also added an increase in federal grants to combat water pollution and a refinancing of the interstate highway program. A slightly more stringent drug act was passed, prodded by the publicizing of the thalidomide scandal. This European tranquilizer was prescribed for pregnant women and resulted in a number of severely malformed babies at birth. Congress voted successfully on the 24th Amendment to the Constitution, which outlawed the practice of states levying poll taxes as a condition to exercise the vote. Anti–poll tax legislation had failed several times in the past, but even the filibustering efforts of Southern Senators failed to halt its passage on this occasion, and it was readily ratified by the requisite number of states.

In two areas, agriculture and tax reform, the administration sustained mixed results which were probably more defeat than success. The Kennedy administration brought some innovative ideas to its long-range proposals for cutting down on the dangerously mounting surpluses of farm produce, but Congress rejected most of them. The heart of the Kennedy program was the "supply management" technique, which was intended to keep farm products from becoming surplus storage inventories, while nevertheless maintaining farm income and helping to preserve the smaller farmer. Supply management abandoned the old acreage allotment plan, because scientific and technological improvements meant that farmers could use more disease-resistant seed and more powerful fertilizers to grow four times as much on an acre as previously. The radical departure was to base marketing quotas on a precise number of bushels of wheat, for example, based upon the farmer's history of production rather than on an acreage quota. This curtailment would prevent a surplus of wheat reaching the market, market prices would rise up to or beyond support levels, and the government would be saved the costs of storage and even some support subsidies. In addition, the administration bill called for the innovative inclusion of all farm products under such a plan, if various crop producers agreed by referendum, rather than the traditional six or seven major crops. Another new departure provided that curtailed acreage was to be taken completely out of production instead of simply being transferred to a different crop.

The supply management plan engendered heavy opposition. Some Midwestern Republicans and Southern Democrats refused to countenance any growth of federal or executive powers. Economically, livestock, poultry, and dairy interests feared higher prices for the feeds they had to buy, and some consumer-oriented urban Congressmen were dubious as to higher food prices. The Farm Bureau, representing chiefly corporate agriculture, lobbied against the proposal while the Grange and the National Farmers' Union, representing the smaller farmer, favored the bill. The conservative Southern Democrat-Republican coalition killed the supply management proposal in committee. All that finally remained of the Agricultural Act of 1961 was a continuation of that year's emergency measures to cut down on feed grain production (and wheat, also) by added inducements to farmers to take acreage out of production. Continuation of various minor provisions, such as a five-year extension of the special school milk program, was included. Kennedy again proposed a supply management bill in 1962, including provisions for land to be taken out of production and used for recreational purposes or the improvement of rural community facilities. Some of these land-use proposals were retained, but the same groups again repulsed the "harsh controls" aimed at reducing the growing surpluses. In direct contrast to the Eisenhower-Benson plan, which sought to lower price support levels and relax production controls no matter what its effect upon the average farmer, the Kennedy-Freeman proposal sought to protect farm profit margins on the smaller farmer while effectively halting surplus storage. Supply management was a rational approach to the farm problem, as the Truman-Brannen plan had been, but was forced to yield by special interests and by those opposed to extensions of federal authority.

President Kennedy was anxious to effect an overall tax cut to boost the economy. He delivered a special tax message in the spring of 1961 that nevertheless asked continuation of corporate income and excise taxes. At the same time, he proposed easier depreciation rules which would help industries modernize their plants and thus become more competitive internationally. To offset this loss of tax revenues he proposed a number of revisions which would close existing and much-abused tax loopholes. These included such items as taxation of American investments abroad; using withholding to insure taxes paid on largely unreported bonds and savings accounts; repeal of the $50 exclusion on dividend income; and limiting severely the enormous amounts deductible for entertainment, gifts, and travel described as business expense accounts. Congress extended the existing corporate and excise taxes readily enough, but never got beyond hearings on the controversial revisions in 1961. The Revenue Act of 1962, as the President signed it in October, bore little resemblance to the original Kennedy proposals. The investment credits designed to stimulate modernization of industry were cut back to about half of what the administration proposed, and the tax revisions suffered more heavily. In the face of an invasion of Washington by more than 1,000 owners of expensive (or expense-account) restaurants, Congress retreated into vague warnings that business deductibility expenses must be "directly related" to the conduct of a business and strongly substantiated by bills and records. Mild restrictions were placed upon American personal and corporate income from abroad. Provisions for repeal of the dividend income exclusion and for instituting withholding on dividend income and savings accounts were both defeated, aided by lobbyists against the latter item who deliberately misrepresented withholding to the public as a new and additional tax, instead of simply a new collection method. In signing the bill, Kennedy chose to comment optimistically on what little had been done, but a general tax cut would only come about under his successor.

The 87th Congress reserved its worst setbacks for Kennedy proposals in the field of federal aid to education and in health welfare. The President asked for an education bill that would give grants to the states for classroom construction and teacher salaries, furnish loans for college construction of libraries and dormitories, and create grants for four-year federal scholarships averaging about $2,800 each. No general school aid funds were to go to private and parochial schools. Ironically, the nation's first Catholic President and the Catholic hierarchy were at sword's points over the aid to Catholic schools provision, and great pressure was brought with general success on Catholic legislators to support the Catholic bishops rather than the President. Conservative Southern Democrats and their Republican allies successfully played off the religious issue against racial, financial, or federal power opposition. Representative James J. Delaney of New York, a Democrat and a Catholic, although one of those Democrats added to the Rules Committee to bypass the "Judge" Smith roadblock, voted with that group to kill the education bill in committee. The 1962 bill, to which Kennedy had added provisions for combatting adult illiteracy and for training handicapped children, met a similar fate. The only item that Congress rescued was the provision enacting Educational Television, setting up a five-year $32 million program to begin its funding in 1964. Congress also removed the anti-Communist oath and affidavit initially required in the National Defense Education Act, since 32 universities—among them the nation's most prestigious—had refused to participate in NDEA unless the oath taking was removed. The tangle of racial and religious issues was chiefly responsible for killing the education bills, although poor administration footwork and homework, plus a lack of presidential leadership, made the defeat possible.

A bill for which the President did make a sustained personal and political effort also sustained defeat. This was the Medicare bill, as HEW had dubbed it, which would have used the Social Security framework to provide medical insurance for retired persons over 65 years of age. Like other retirement benefits, it was to be financed by payroll deductions. Medicare was just as popular with young and old as Social Security had been originally, and opposed by much the same forces. Many Southern Democrats, most Republicans, and lobbies for health insurance firms and the powerful American Medical Association trained their heaviest guns on the bill. Labor and senior citizen organizations sponsored rallies for the bill throughout the country, with President Kennedy as one of the chief speakers. But the House Ways and Means Committee, under the direction of Chairman Wilbur Mills of Arkansas, prevented the bill from reaching the floor, and the Medicare provisions were defeated in the Senate by a 52 to 48 vote. The President publicly blamed the lobbying influence of the American Medical Association and, backed by most of the Democratic party, promised to make Medicare an issue in the 1962 congressional elections. The AMA in turn established their Political Action Committee, with its funds committed to defray the campaign expenses of candidates opposing Medicare.

Included in the wreckage left by the 87th Congress were defeats for mass transportation and the administration plan to elevate the Housing and Home Finance Agency into a Cabinet Department of Urban and Housing Affairs. When Congress learned that Kennedy planned to name the agency head, Dr. Robert C. Weaver, a black, as the first secretary this was enough to doom the proposal. A revival of the New Deal CCC concept as the Youth Conservation Corps was also defeated, although Kennedy founded the Peace Corps by executive order in March 1961. Also derived from New Deal antecedents, the Peace Corps use of young volunteer Americans to help the underdeveloped countries help themselves educationally and technically soon overcame its domestic critics. Foreign critics remained skeptical over its future usages.

Kennedy's relationship with the 87th Congress and the progress of administration programs were slowed by several factors. The strength of the conservative Southern Democrat-Midwestern Republican coalition was important. So, too, was the loss of leadership in both Senate and House brought about by Lyndon Johnson's transfer to the vice presidency and Sam Rayburn's removal by his death in November 1961 after having served as Speaker of the House longer than anyone else in history (17 years). Johnson's powers of organization and persuasion had been invaluable to the Democratic party. Their replacements—Senator Mike Mansfield of Montana and Representative James McCormack of Massachusetts—were not able to contribute the influence and experience of their predecessors. The anachronistic rules of Congress itself contributed. Despite Kennedy's efforts, the legislative record was of mediocre caliber.

Because of Congress' rejection of many of his major proposals, Kennedy decided to take an active hand in campaigning for Democratic candidates in the 1962 off-year elections. He carried out a vigorous electioneering against Republican "negativism," interrupted only by the emergencies of the Cuban missile crisis. How much the President's campaigning helped is difficult to evaluate, but results were generally favorable for the Democratic party. An ultraconservative, John G. Tower, became the first Republican Senator from Texas since Reconstruction, but voters removed two John Birch Congressmen from their California districts and turned down the bids of two others. Ex–Vice President Nixon was defeated in his Republican bid for the governorship of California, and a Kennedy ally, Democrat Robert F. Wagner, was reelected Mayor of New York City. The Democrats lost four seats in the House, shortening their margin of 259 to 176. They picked up four seats in the Senate, leaving the Democrats ahead 68 to 32. Since the first off-year elections traditionally resulted in a setback for a new administration, the results were considered to be the best for any administration since 1934.

Kennedy's mixed, liberal-conservative record received another addition of ambiguity on the occasion of his well-publicized battle with the steel industry in its unilateral decision to raise prices in April 1962. The administration had been continually urging that management and labor mutually resist raising prices and wages in order to curb the rising cost of living and also maintain the nation's export surplus by necessary price stability. Administration pressure helped bring about a noninflationary wage settlement in steel on March 31. But ten days later Roger Blough, chairman of United States Steel, called at the White House to announce that his firm and five other steel companies were raising their prices $6 per ton. Kennedy, taken completely by surprise, administered a tongue lashing to Blough which included the accusation that both the administration and the public had been "double-crossed" by the move. On television, Kennedy denounced the steel actions as "a wholly unjustifiable and irresponsible defiance of the public interest," and the administration went into action on several fronts. Kennedy announced that the Department of Justice and the Federal Trade Commission would both investigate the antitrust aspects of the case. Meanwhile, the administration successfully persuaded two large independent steel companies—Inland and Kaiser—not to raise prices. When these companies publicly agreed, the Defense Department ordered its contractors to buy their steel only from companies offering lower prices. When Bethlehem, one of the original price raisers, then announced that it would forego the price increase "to remain competitive," the others quickly capitulated. While some critics pointed to the incident as proof of Kennedy's antibusiness stand, other puzzled observers brought up contrary evidence in the Kennedy backing of AT&T on the Telstar bill, his unwillingness to touch the oil depletion loophole in the proposed tax revisions, and the approval of the Justice Department in the merger of Standard Oil of Kentucky with Standard Oil of California. Although Kennedy quickly moved to make peace with the steel industry, large segments of business remained suspiciously hostile. The alleged ambivalence of his tactics in 1961 and 1962 was more properly attributed to his lack of any doctrinaire position and his cool appraisal of the political art of the possible. Kennedy's clash with the giant steel industry and his full-scale counterattack remained a topic for public and journalistic discussion until it was superceded by the even more dramatic Cuban missile crisis of 1962.

Latin American Problems

The outgoing administration had left behind an unfulfilled legacy in the form of almost fully prepared plans and forces for an invasion of Cuba and the overthrow of Fidel Castro. During the campaign, Kennedy had taken a belligerent tone regarding the Cuban situation. He had taunted the Republicans for not having treated the Cuban problem and had promised he would do something for the "democratic opposition," although he carefully refrained from any specifics. Vice President Nixon, who had been urging military force against Cuba since April 1959 and knew of the impending invasion, was constrained by the secrecy of the CIA's Eisenhower-approved plans from answering Kennedy during the campaign. After his election Kennedy was briefed on the invasion plan but, despite his doubts, gave no contrary orders. At about the same time, the news of the preparations began to get into print. The CIA training of Cuban exiles at a Guatemala base first appeared in the United States in November 1960 in the *Hispanic American Report* published at Stanford University. The gist of this report then appeared as an editorial in *The Nation* during the same month. The Associated Press and the UPI, despite being told that it had appeared in Guatemala's *La Hora*, either ignored the story or presented routine denials from Guatemala's President. By January 1961, even though some self-censoring went on in the *New York Times* and the *Miami Herald*, news of the training activities and the planned invasion began to appear.

By April, Kennedy was advised by Allen Dulles of the CIA and by the Chiefs of Staff that the Cuban force was more than ready for the invasion, that its success was assured by the all-out support it would receive from Cubans themselves, and that further delays would be dangerous. Kennedy's advisers either agreed or were content to let the intelligence and armed services experts do the talking. Only Senator Fulbright, a confidant in his capacity as Chairman of the Foreign Relations Committee, openly opposed the plan. Kennedy reluctantly acquiesced to the invasion, but insisted that no official U.S. planes be used. Instead, B-26s with faked Cuban markings supplied by the CIA and piloted by Cuban exiles and American paid volunteers bombed Havana and various airfields as a preliminary to the invasion. At dawn on April 17, 1961 a force of some 1,300 landed at several points in the Bahia de Cochinos (Bay of Pigs) on Cuba's southern coast. They were met by far larger numbers of defenders, plus Castro's tiny air force.[2] The two jet trainers in the latter battered the supply vessels of the invading force, and Castro's army and militia soon surrounded and captured all but a handful of the surviving 1,200. Contrary to CIA expectations, the Cuban people made no move to rally to the invaders, and CIA agents and those believed sympathetic to an overthrow of Castro had been methodically rounded up several days before the landings took place.

The Bay of Pigs was an unqualified disaster, even if considered only technically. The CIA intelligence and planning was monumentally faulty.

---

[2] Castro was popularly attributed with a force of Russian MIGs, but the U.S. Naval Base at Guantanamo reported no such planes were operating in or near Cuba, nor were any reported seen at the Bay of Pigs.

The Cuban exiles trained by the CIA included no liberal reformist anti-Castroites, but were composed largely of ex-Batista supporters who could scarcely expect to find any wide support among the Cuban people. Enamored of their unusually easy success in the Guatemala episode, the CIA officials were supremely confident that it could readily be repeated. Washington correspondents were able to report before the invasion that Cuba was about to get "the Guatemala treatment," and that the CIA had placed Captain Manuel Artime, a conservative Spanish Catholic, in the role of Colonel Castillo Armas.

The invasion was also disastrous from a standpoint of press and public confidence, since they were systematically lied to by many of those responsible. On the same day that the American-planned invasion force landed at the Bay of Pigs, Secretary of State Dean Rusk told gathered newsmen: "The American people are entitled to know whether we are intervening in Cuba or intend to do so in the future. The answer to that question is no." Ambassador Adlai Stevenson was mortified to discover that the administration accounts he presented to the UN were obvious distortions. Although some sections of the press criticized the Bay of Pigs only in terms of its lack of military success, Senator Fulbright and many other critics insisted that there was no excuse for such an American-planned, American-financed, American-guided invasion force. It was pointed out that it was a clear violation of American treaty agreements and obligations, and that American domestic statutes prohibiting such invasion groups were similarly trespassed. American prestige and reputation suffered irreparable damage around the world, particularly in Latin America and among America's own allies. Contrarily, Castro reaped more benefits among his own people and other Latin Americans than any amount of propaganda could have given him. Like other revolutionary governments in world history, the Cuban government was immeasurably strengthened by its nationalistic fervor in repulsing counterrevolutionary forces. Americans sympathetically rallied around President Kennedy, however, and polls showed that his personal popularity rose to a higher percentage point than he had achieved as a presidential candidate.

In the wake of the Bay of Pigs disaster, the United States brought economic and diplomatic pressure to bear on Cuba. A ban on Cuban imports was imposed, and an embargo was placed on most items except food and medicine. An exception to the latter was made in 1962, when a ransom of the imprisoned invasion force was effected largely through the transfer of some millions of dollars of medical supplies. The United States sought to isolate Castro from his Latin American neighbors by urging OAS nations to expel him and cut off diplomatic and trade relations. Most Latin American nations were unwilling to take the latter step, and Cuban expulsion from the OAS was only obtained by numerous abstentions[3] on the vote and at the cost of increased resentment over American pressure tactics.

Actually, the Kennedy administration had planned to give Latin America a new and higher priority in American aid and attention. In an important campaign speech at Tampa, Florida, Kennedy had spoken of an *alianza para progreso*—Alliance for Progress—which he defined as a policy which would mean a common effort to develop the resources of the hemisphere, raise long-term development funds, and strengthen democracy and democratic opportunity in the Americas. He spoke of this program again two months after his inauguration to a White House assembly of the Latin American diplomatic corps, many of whom had not heard such hopeful words since Franklin Roosevelt. Secretaries of State Acheson and Dulles had been notably bored by Latin American affairs, and the Truman and Eisenhower policies were largely those of neglect. In the last years of the Eisenhower administration, however, the seeds for a future alliance were sown by the visits and reports of the President's brother, Dr. Milton Eisenhower. In September 1960 Under Secretary of State C. Douglas Dillon (soon to become Kennedy's Treasury Secretary) had also mentioned a $500 million U.S. development fund at an OAS meeting. Eisenhower had announced it in the United States, but the circumstances of the American reaction against Castro's revolution caused it to be viewed by American and European critics simply as a bribe.

Kennedy had recommended to Congress in March 1961 that it appropriate at least the $500 million authorized under Eisenhower. After the Bay of Pigs affair, there was far more willingness in Congress to expedite and expand an alliance, and in August the Latin American nations gathered in the Uruguayan resort of Punta del Este to consider the Alliance for Progress. On August 17 all Latin nations except Cuba signed the Act of Punta del Este, which became the charter for the Alliance. This provided at least $20 billion, to be spread over ten years, for aid in Latin struggles against poverty, illiteracy, and a chronic lack of indigenous capital. The funds were to come from the United States (more than half), from Western Europe, from international agencies and private sources. The Latin nations were to qualify themselves for such funds by undertaking needed reforms which would improve social conditions and stimulate economic growth. Unfortunately, effecting these reforms meant separating power and privileges from the wealthy oligarchy of Latin America which controlled most nations and thus presented a tremendous obstacle. The record of the Alliance showed only the most modest of successes in its earliest years and almost total failure thereafter. Largely a response to Fidel Castro, one of the few Latin

---

[3] Argentina, Brazil, Chile, Mexico, Bolivia, and Ecuador, representing three fourths of Latin America, abstained from the expulsion vote.

Americans ever to challenge United States' overwhelming dominance of all its neighbors to the South, the Alliance lost much of its urgency after the 1962 Cuban crisis was resolved.[4] The discovery that Castro could not readily export insurgency and the growing preoccupation with Vietnam also served to cut down interest in and funds for the Alliance.

The Bay of Pigs decided for many hesitating Cubans their allegiance to Castro rather than the U.S.-led right-wing Cubans based in Miami. The Cuban Communist party, once on the outside of the revolutionary movement, began to receive government appointments and to achieve integration with the 26 July Movement and other revolutionary groups. With the American blockade seriously hampering the Cuban economy, and with Cuba striving for an acknowledged role within the world bloc of Communist states, Castro explained to a mildly puzzled Cuban television audience on December 2, 1961, that he really had always been a "Marxist-Leninist." He revealed that as a student he had read up to page 370 of *Das Kapital*, and that he expected to remain a "Marxist-Leninist" all his life.

In 1962 the expansion of an earlier pact with Russia brought missiles to the island nation 90 miles off the southern Florida coast. The reasons for Khrushchev's decision are not completely clear. The OAS had expelled Cuba in February. Fears were rife throughout the island following waves of rumors regarding a second invasion, and surface-to-air missiles and even short-range missiles would aid Cuban defenses. For the Soviet head, however, the presence of the missiles as a bargaining point for some favorable solution to the Berlin problem may have been the prime factor. Other possibilities for the action would have to include the wish to upset the nuclear balance of power, even if only politically or psychologically; the presence of missiles as a trading point for an American promise not to invade Cuba, or even as a display to other Latin American nations that freedom from American dominance could be achieved and that Russian aid was more likely than Chinese.

In September 1962 Kennedy authorized U-2 reconnaissance flights over Cuba. These brought back photographic evidence of minor installations of rockets and short-range missiles that could properly be described as defensive. Although Kennedy was under strong partisan and media pressure regarding a missile buildup in Cuba, his photographic evidence of a lack of genuinely offensive weapons on the island reinforced his stand not to be pushed into precipitate action. The "private information" brought to his Senate critics by emotionally charged Cuban refugees

---

[4] As an alliance official facetiously put it in the first years of the organization: "We all know that there are only three categories of loans in the Alliance for Progress: very high priority, hysterical, and if-you-don't-make-this-loan-the-Communists-will-take-over-the-country." Cited in Jerome Levinson and Juan de Onis, *The Alliance That Lost Its Way* (1970), p. 113.

was of highly dubious value, but Kennedy made it clear that the United States would have to act if offensive weapons were installed in Cuba. Delayed several days by hurricanes, a U-2 flight on October 14 over areas not covered for several weeks finally revealed the presence of medium-range (1,000 miles) missiles at several sites. Other flights revealed more such missiles emplaced, plus work proceeding on sites capable of accommodating intermediate-range (2,000 miles) missiles. Kennedy immediately called a meeting of his advisers and the appropriate officials. Their suggestions ranged all the way from watchful waiting to invasions or full-scale bombing attacks. Former Secretary of State Dean Acheson and the Chiefs of Staff argued for a surprise bombing attack, but Attorney General Robert Kennedy, aided by Secretary of Defense McNamara, was more persuasive with the idea of a naval blockade which would turn back any further shipments of missiles or bombers. The blockade argument had the further advantage of permitting progressively more stringent measures still to be utilized if the blockade did not suffice. It also obviated the stigma which would inevitably be attached to the United States if what Robert Kennedy referred to as a "Pearl Harbor in reverse" were employed. President Kennedy went on the air on October 22 to inform the public of the missile sites and the naval quarantine to intercept further materials. The OAS, as usual, was informed rather than consulted, as were NATO and the UN. Kennedy asked Khrushchev to withdraw both the missiles and the bombers, and to abandon the establishment of launching sites. The President and his advisers then nervously settled down to await the Soviet response.

On October 24 a number of Russian cargo ships either changed course or halted at sea in the Atlantic far off the northern Florida coast. A tanker and an East German passenger ship, obviously incapable of carrying missiles, were permitted to continue toward Cuba without search. The blockade seemed to be working. Meantime, faint diplomatic signals were coming from Khrushchev and Russian officials, all pointing to a wish to avoid war and to find a way out of the situation. Russian diplomats were actively trying to enlist intermediaries everywhere, and Khrushchev's response to U Thant, the Secretary-General of the United Nations, was quietly accommodating. On October 26 a letter from Khrushchev was received by Kennedy which suggested an arrangement already known to be favored by the United States: The missiles would be removed in return for an American pledge not to invade Cuba. Since they were there solely for defensive purposes, the Soviet leader said, the American promise would remove any need for them. Before this could be answered, a second letter arrived from the Kremlin on October 27. It took a less conciliatory tone, and suggested that Russian missiles be evacuated from Cuba in return for the removal of U.S. missiles from Turkey. The proposal was not acceptable to Kennedy, and the confusion strongly suggested that Kremlin officials, and not Khrushchev, may have written the second letter.

Evidently the sage advice offered again by Robert Kennedy was that accepted, and the argument of the Chiefs of Staff for an air strike rejected. The President's brother suggested that the second letter be ignored and the American response be couched in terms applicable to the first letter received. The reply was drawn up promising not to invade Cuba if the missiles were quickly withdrawn, and requesting UN supervision of the withdrawal. It was emphasized that a Russian answer must be forthcoming immediately or the United States would be obliged to resort to military methods. Khrushchev confirmed the proposal within 24 hours and gave orders to dismantle the bases and ship the missiles and bombers back to Russia. The 1962 missile crisis came to a breathless halt, highlighted by a series of crucial episodes and decisions that carried with them the threat of nuclear holocaust.

President Kennedy wisely discouraged any administrative mention of "capitulation" or anything similar. He magnanimously referred to Khrushchev's "statesmanlike decision," realizing that the Soviet leader, whatever his reasons might have been, was backed into a dangerous corner from which it was to everyone's advantage to provide a viable exit. Frustrations, however, abounded. Cubans on their home island were no less exasperated than were Cuban exiles in Florida. Castro had not been informed of the solution, since the crisis had been a Russo-American confrontation which had pushed Cuba itself into the background. Castro reputedly swore in anger and privately denounced Khrushchev's "cowardly" behavior. The Cuban exiles, who had fondly imagined they were only days away from being restored to their property, were similarly exasperated. Although the various official and semi-official accounts of the Kennedy administration and the missile crisis later presented detailed accounts of the episode, they omitted the important factor of the mid-term elections, which were held several weeks after the Cuban crisis was resolved. Kennedy had been under severe partisan pressure to act militarily rather than diplomatically. He had made some stern public threats regarding offensive weapons in Cuba, and was thus committed to stern action. Lacking such action, a Republican campaign of "America's second humiliation over Cuba" would have put Democratic party candidates to rout as never before. Thus, one factor in Kennedy's "eyeball-to-eyeball" confrontation was that of domestic politics.

Cuba refused a UN surveillance of the missile withdrawal, and the United States therefore did not formally or publicly pledge not to be a party to future invasion. Evidently Kennedy never had any intention of invading Cuba, and public sentiment was also against such a move. Kennedy had achieved, at best, a propaganda victory over the Soviets (although Khrushchev, in obvious self-defense, had claimed the same in Moscow). What properly worried Kennedy was the fact that too many Americans would foolishly believe that thereafter all that was ever necessary to reverse a Russian move was to act "tough." The realization that no major power can be backed into a corner without an exit and thus be moved inexorably into war was a fact of international relations unknown to the average American. The cost of a no-invasion pledge for Cuba was not high, since the intent was lacking, but the admission of contemplated aggression did act to legitimize Cuban defense preparations. The solution of the crisis also carried with it an American acquiescence in a Cuban nationalist Communist regime. An additional probable consequence of the missile crisis was Khrushchev's fall from power two years later and a decline in his vigorous program of de-Stalinization. Kennedy brought the world face to face with a Third (or Last) World War. All U.S. bombers and missile crews were on "maximum alert." Plans had been made for the evacuation of Washington. Perhaps without the political factor, Kennedy might have conducted much of the episode in secret rather than in public. The question of an upsetting of the nuclear balance was psychological and political, never real, but Kennedy was aware that the distinction would be lost on most Americans as it would for much of the rest of the world. Fortunately, Kennedy acted cooly and with restraint. He insisted on the least provocative of retaliations, hoping that progressively harsher measures would not be necessary. Even the details of those initial measures were carefully supervised to remove any sources of friction, just as the final responses were rendered free of ill-advised crowing over "victory." Temperate and restrained reaction perhaps prevented many from realizing that the world had been uncomfortably close to nuclear destruction.

Cold War Becomes Armed Truce

Despite the Cuban facedown, the United States, during the brief presidential career of John Fitzgerald Kennedy, moved from a Cold War, with all its high tension, to a lower-pitched armed truce. It was not that Kennedy abandoned the policy of his predecessors in regard to the Soviet Union. He certainly continued a strong resistance to world communism, even accounting for increased American involvement in Vietnam and a large increase in the military budget, but as policy it was defused of its explosive Cold War emotionalism and apocalyptic rhetoric, its unyielding dogmatism and occasional near fanaticism. In what may have been Kennedy's finest hour, his American University speech,[5] he said that his administration would work to "make the world safe for diversity." This recognition of pluralism was in stark contrast

[5] "What Kind of Peace Do We Want?" (Speech delivered at The American University, Washington, D.C., June 10, 1963).

to the policy of the potent figure of John Foster Dulles, who considered neutrality as sinful as outright opposition. To make the point more force-ful, Kennedy explicitly renounced any intent of an enforced Pax Ameri-cana, and explicitly forbade any future diplomatic rhetorical hostility. It was evident that a more mature Kennedy was too much the historian, too lacking in Calvinistic impulses, to view the world simplistically in terms of a clash between the forces of absolute good and evil.

But Khrushchev as Soviet leader also made a contribution to a lower-keyed confrontation, even despite his ambitious adventurism—for what-ever reasons—in Cuba. He administered more Soviet might than Stalin enjoyed, yet deliberately and in fact presented a far less menacing figure. He made it quite clear that Russia had ambitions, and as a leader was perhaps even more challenging than Stalin, given the much greater Soviet resources. Yet he made it equally clear that accommodation and not nuclear disaster must be the framework within which the two oppos-ing powers must exist. Perhaps he helped to show this by making a more politically costly choice over Cuba (even though he was responsi-ble for creating it in the first place) than was required of Kennedy. In the wake of the Cuban crisis, it became apparent to many that Ken-nedy's world diversity and Khrushchev's coexistence were actually possi-ble. It was this recognition of global pluralism that put American-Soviet relations at least one remove from the Cold War. Confrontation under Kennedy certainly remained, but it became less emotional and more manageable.

Kennedy was concerned over a deterioration in Russo-American rela-tions following the Cuban crisis, and a periodic revival of Soviet intransi-gence over the Berlin question seemed likely to make matters worse. Although he had opposed a summit meeting, Kennedy decided that a conversation with Khrushchev over Berlin, Laos, and the possibilities of disarmament would help to clear the air. The meeting was arranged for June 3 and 4, 1961, in Vienna, with several days carefully set aside to talk with President de Gaulle in Paris on the way. The French capital was largely a conquest of Mrs. Kennedy's, with Parisians completely taken by her fluent French, her appreciation of the arts, and her charm and style. Her husband, without great success, attempted to assure de Gaulle of complete American commitment to the security of Europe. Trying to convince the French president of the United States' willingness to include nuclear weapons in such security, Kennedy was met with a cool recognition that any talk of pooling such weapons would still mean American control of them in fact.

Several days of blunt conversation helped to clear the air where Amer-ican and Soviet positions were concerned after Kennedy and Khrushchev came face to face in Vienna, but little was actually resolved. The two leaders were able to agree that there must be a neutralist government in Laos, but Khrushchev did not indicate great interest in a test-ban agreement. He insisted that such a ban was of secondary interest in the problem of world disarmament, and even suggested that talk of such a plan be merged with the concurrent negotiations on disarmament at Geneva. Berlin remained the Soviet leader's preoccupation and here he also displayed the greatest belligerence and emotionalism.

The erstwhile allies had their positions in Berlin as a result of the war's end in 1945. In 15 short years much had changed, but the stakes prevented either side from making any concessions which could reflect such changes. To the Russians, their ancient enemy and recent invader was again taking shape in West Germany, armed and industrially revived and finally a contributing member of NATO. Chancellor Adenauer, with his strong ties with the late Secretary of State John Foster Dulles, was supported by Dulles in his insistence that all of Germany be united under implacable anti-Communist control and that Germany's lost lands be restored. Such a policy posed nagging fears for Russian security. As for Berlin, it was the focal point of the German problem. It was an espionage and propaganda center deep within Communist East Germany; its access routes helped to reveal the weakness of the East German government; its prosperous presence siphoned off thousands of needed young and skilled Germans from the Communist East. Both Berlin and a powerful Germany were very real dangers to the Soviets.

For the United States, it was a matter of presence won by the sacrifices of the war against Nazidom, and a commitment to the West Germans. It also included an unwillingness to recognize the East German Communist regime or even admit that Germany might indeed become two separate nations for an unknowable length of time. Even the compromise of an international city under UN supervision was thus mutually impossible. But Kennedy's moderate and reasoned arguments at Vienna on the future status of Berlin met only impassioned complaints and harsh accusations. Khrushchev once before had threatened to sign a separate peace treaty with East Germany after a six-month grace period. He renewed this promise, insisting grimly that the United States and Great Britain would then have to make new access arrangements with East Germany's Democratic Republic. If the United States and Great Britain would join in such a treaty, Western troops—and Soviet ones—would be acceptable there under certain conditions, but the city's status must conform to its East German surroundings. Khrushchev warned again that if no multilateral change was forthcoming, Russia would sign a separate treaty in December and it would then be up to the United States to decide on war or peace.

Discussions in Washington over the American response followed, with Kennedy seeking advice from outside the administration as well. He finally accepted much of ex-Secretary Dean Acheson's simplistic and military-oriented thesis that the Berlin issue had to be treated as a test of wills. But the argument that any difficulty of access must be met by an armored division moving down the autobahn, which was the Acheson-Pentagon solution, was rejected. Instead, Kennedy sought to show American determination by a national broadcast in July which put many National Reserve troops on active duty and which proclaimed a hugh 25 percent increase in American military strength. New troop units were also moved into West Berlin, although this could only be a symbolic move, since even several divisions deep within the confines of East Germany would still be in a militarily untenable position.

In August the Soviets and their client state provided their own solution to the irritating enclave of West Berlin within East Germany's borders. Its prosperity had been in stark contrast to the drabness of the Eastern sector, and the daily total of 25,000 refugees of youth and skills who sought better economic and political conditions in West Berlin had become an unbearable drain on East Germany's resources. On August 13, a great wall was erected on the borders of East Berlin, cutting any further escape down to a desperate handful and erasing the ability of West Berliners to visit their friends and relatives on the other side. Tempers flared, both in Western Europe and the United States, but Kennedy ignored the wild advice to use tanks and bulldozers on the wall, pointing out that it was erected on East Berlin and not West Berlin territory.

Two weeks later, Khrushchev brought the three-year informal Russo-American moratorium on nuclear testing to an end by undertaking a series of nuclear bomb tests. The climax came in November, when the explosion of a 58-megaton weapon revealed to the world that the nuclear powers were now experimenting with weapons some 3,000 times more powerful than the blast that leveled Hiroshima. Kennedy responded with resumed nuclear testing in September, but, confident of American nuclear superiority, also attempted to revive the Geneva Disarmament Conference which had staggered to an end in July after several years of inconclusive meetings. In the war of nerves of summer 1961, the silly season manifested itself in the United States by a wave of fallout-shelter building. Kennedy had given some impetus to the craze by a vague suggestion that families consider such projects. It became an overnight but relatively short-lived obsession, with the smartest department stores of New York and Dallas offering a variety of luxury underground burrows. Some people announced their intent to move to relatively fallout-free areas in Alaska or Peru, and a Catholic clergyman reassured an agonizing parishioner that he would be justified in the protection of his loved ones by shooting those neighbors who might seek to crowd into his family shelter. Kennedy requested funds from Congress in November for federal aid in the construction of community shelters, but

Congress only appropriated funds for further research and surveys. Within 18 months the craze had subsided in the face of a great public apathy for an existence in the rubble and fallout of a nuclear-blasted world. The state of Oregon took a public stand by abolishing its entire "civil defense" operation as the fallout-shelter boom collapsed. Khrushchev again chose the summer tourist season to heat things up around Berlin in 1962 by harassing transportation and by handing over some Russian military functions to the East Germans, but the Berlin Wall had evidently removed some of the urgency from the situation and matters were not permitted to reach a climax.

The Eisenhower administration had also bequeathed to its successors a sticky problem in the newly emerging states of Africa, where the Congo, in the course of throwing off its Belgian colonialism, had involved the UN, the Soviets, and the United States. Although the Belgians had spoken hesitantly of a long-range program eventually leading to independence, violent anticolonial riots and world pressure were responsible for a hastily made decision to grant the Congo its independence on June 30, 1960, lest the very considerable Belgian economic interests be destroyed by continued stalling.

Independence brought instant chaos to the Congo, with Congolese assaults on their white Belgian officers and on white civilians. Nationalism in the Congo, as in many emerging African nations, was further complicated by strong tribal and regional allegiances. These feelings were exploited prior to independence by a cynical and Belgian-backed politician, Moishe Tshombe, who sought even before Congolese independence to achieve that status separately for Katanga Province, source of half of all Congo revenue. Within weeks after Congo's independence, Tshombe had proclaimed the same for the seceding province of Katanga, and had called upon Belgian paratroopers to return, together with forces from white Rhodesia, to support his claim of secession. Congolese Prime Minister Patrice Lumumba, as closely identified with militant African nationalism as Tshombe was with white colonialism, appealed in desperation to the United Nations to keep out the Belgians and prevent Katanga's secession. He also cabled Khrushchev "to watch hourly over the situation," and the Soviets had responded with several hundred technicians, trucks, and planes. Lumumba thought the UN was not acting quickly or aggressively enough, and turned increasingly toward the Soviet Union. President Kasavubu dismissed Lumumba, who was later kidnapped to Katanga and murdered, and the United States and the Soviet Union were engaged in a diplomatic shoving match as the Kennedy administration came into office.

Kennedy and some of his advisers were aware that any move to aid Tshombe would immediately be translated by the emerging nations of the world as a support of dying colonialism. There was also a fear of major Russian penetration. Without the unity to be brought about by a defeat of all secessionists, Congolese authority would succumb to rival tribal factions and a possible clash between their major power sponsors. The United Nations was thus the agency to be supported, and the Kennedy government stood behind the effort of UN troops to subdue Katanga. The UN offensive finally captured three quarters of Katanga, and Tshombe was deterred from his threatened destruction of remaining resources and facilities only by a threat of stronger U.S. military commitment to the UN forces and by indications that he could expect to play a prominent role in a united Congo. President Kennedy had also decided to lend American fighter planes if the UN requested them, but Tshombe halted the secessionist movement on January 16, 1963. Ironically, Tshombe, later premier of the Congo, put down the revolt of the African nationalist Gizenga group with direct military aid from the United States.

The Kennedy policy helped to preserve the Congo as a nation. Although both the United States and the Soviet Union intervened in the affair, the stress on the use of United Nation forces precluded any confrontation between those two powers and gave the UN its most successful peace-keeping operation. It was not done without cost. Dag Hammarskjold, the Secretary General of that body, met his death in a plane crash—which many UN members insisted could not have been an accident—over northern Rhodesia on his way to the Congo to plead for a diplomatic settlement. Nothing could be proven, and Hammarskjold was succeeded by the Burmese, U Thant. Khrushchev also exploited the UN turmoil by pushing for a three-person governing body for the UN (referred to as a *troika,* after the three-horse Russian sled arrangement) instead of its Secretary General. Khrushchev's plan called for the triumvirate to be composed of one diplomat from the Western bloc, one from the Communist powers, and one from a suitably neutral country, but it did not receive wide support.

Laos and Vietnam

The Geneva agreements of 1954 had stipulated that Laos and Cambodia were to be neutral. Laos, in particular, was regarded somewhat in the manner of a 19th century buffer state. The Kingdom of Laos bordered the People's Republic of China in the north. It stretched southward roughly parallel to artificially divided Vietnam, with pro-American Thailand to the west. But Laos never had the stability to accept the pressures from both sides which a buffer state is usually called upon to absorb. Ethnically, the Lao people were numerous in northern Thailand, and shared language and customs with Laos rather than their country of domicile. Thailand also feared and disliked the Vietnamese and thereby felt compelled to aid and support those Laotian groups more friendly to her than to the North Vietnamese. Laos was thus torn by Thai-Vietnamese historical rivalries in the post-Geneva period as well as by Cold War ideological differences. The Vietminh had their counterpart in Laos in the nationalist Pathet Lao. The pro-Communist Pathet Lao fought the Japanese occupiers (their neighbor, Thailand, collaborated with the Japanese during World War II), and then the French, with the aid and sponsorship of North Vietnam. Under the Geneva terms, China pressured the North Vietnamese to withdraw their troop aid to Laos so long as the United States did not try to establish military influence there. The Laotians were to integrate the Pathet Lao within the Lao community and to preserve strict neutrality.

Prince Souvanna Phouma set up a neutralist government and worked unsuccessfully to integrate the pro-Communist Pathet Lao areas into the central government. In 1958 he resigned, and a series of right-wing governments with CIA and American military mission support followed. General Phoumi Nosavan emerged as the strongman, benefited by U.S. antineutralist finances beginning in 1955. In 1959 and 1960 alone more than $90 million went to Laos, 90 percent of it for bolstering the Royal Army, which offered $130 per year to recruits, or more than twice the annual income of Laotians. In 1960 the neutralist Prince Souvanna Phouma was called back to head a coalition government, but General Phoumi, with strong CIA and State Department backing, continued to be the power in the Laos government. Phoumi ordered his troops to move against the capital, Vientiane, and Souvanna, fleeing northward, turned to the Russians and the Pathet Lao for support. The Soviets arranged a high priority weapons airlift from Hanoi to the Pathet Lao in December 1960. By the time Kennedy came into office the next month the Pathet Lao, with North Vietnamese help, had captured the strategic Plain of Jars and its airstrip and were spreading southward along the North and South Vietnamese borders.

Kennedy wanted no part of the Eisenhower-Dulles policy of recruiting rightist regimes to carry on anti-Communist crusades, although he evidently felt that the United States could not afford a public setback in Laos. In pursuit of a new policy of diplomatic moves, the President called for the support of a British plan for a cease-fire under the eyes of an international commission. He also delivered a television warning to the Soviets which suggested that U.S. intervention might be necessary if no cease-fire took place. United States naval forces were ordered to move closer to Laos, and a Marine helicopter force took up positions in Thailand close to the Laotian capital of Vientiane. A British-Soviet cease-fire proposal was accepted, and in May 1961 14 nations again met in Geneva to consider the neutralization of Laos. Both Kennedy and

Vietnam, Laos, and Cambodia

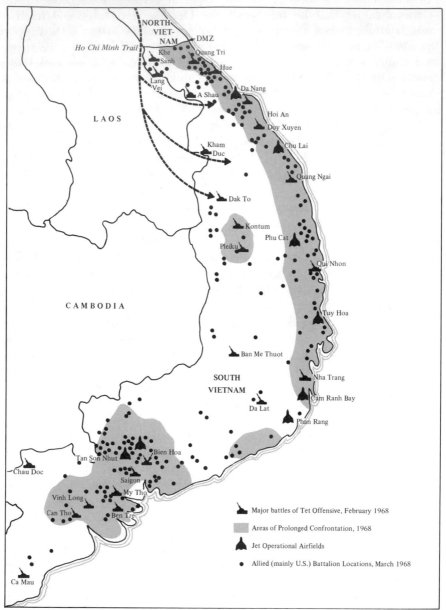

NORTH-VIET-NAM

Ho Chi Minh Trail

DMZ

Khe Sanh

Quang Tri

Hue

Lang Vei

Da Nang

A Shau

Hoi An

Duy Xuyen

Chu Lai

Kham Duc

Quang Ngai

LAOS

Dak To

Kontum

Phu Cat

Pleiku

Qui Nhon

CAMBODIA

Tuy Hoa

Ban Me Thuot

SOUTH VIETNAM

Nha Trang

Cam Ranh Bay

Da Lat

Phan Rang

Tan Son Nhut

Bien Hoa

Chau Doc

Saigon

My Tho

Vinh Long

Can Tho

Ben Tre

Ca Mau

⊾ Major battles of Tet Offensive, February 1968

▓ Areas of Prolonged Confrontation, 1968

▲ Jet Operational Airfields

● Allied (mainly U.S.) Battalion Locations, March 1968

Khrushchev agreed in Vienna to work for a neutral, independent Laos.
    The second Geneva Accords were signed in July 1962, and provided
for Prince Souvanna Phouma to head a tri-factional government of pro-
American right-wing royalists, neutralists, and pro-Communist Pathet
Lao forces. The 600 American military advisers were removed from

General Phoumi's forces, but the General refused to accede to the Geneva ruling that he relinquish the Defense and Interior Ministries which administered the army and police. Confident, that CIA support would eventually restore him to power, he withstood even President Kennedy's requests. It required the recall of some CIA personnel, the cutting off of all funds to his army, and several routs of his forces by the Pathet Lao before Phoumi would accept the provisional neutralist government. The North Vietnamese violated the Geneva agreements by retaining troops in Laos in support of the Pathet Laos, and the United States sent troops to Thailand to counter new Pathet Laos gains while it sought, behind the scenes, to create a new rightist-neutralist alignment in Laos. As 1963 ended, the United States was grudgingly supporting the same neutralist government of Prince Souvanna Phouma it had spent some seven or eight years and hundreds of millions of dollars trying to subvert.

In South Vietnam, Kennedy also inherited a deteriorating situation and soon moved to an even deeper commitment. In 1958 and 1959 the Vietcong, with peasant support engendered by their disaffection over Diem's repressive measures, had moved into widely expanded operations against the Saigon government. In 1960 the National Liberation Front (NLF) was established as the political agency of the Vietcong. Even Diem's army contained enough young officer dissidents to attempt an unsuccessful coup in 1960, and the civil war between Vietcong adherents and the loyal elements of Diem's army was steadily widening as Kennedy assumed office. Diem's government was also getting the worst of the struggle, with its control of South Vietnamese territory down to about one third by 1961.

In May of 1961, Kennedy sent Vice President Lyndon Johnson on a mission to bolster Diem and his forces. Johnson and Diem jointly announced from Saigon on May 13, that the United States had agreed to absorb the cost of increasing the Vietnamese army from 150,000 to 170,000, plus assuming the entire cost of equipping the approximately 140,000 men in the National Police (Civil Guard) and the Self Defense Corps. Johnson reported that the United States should "proceed with a clear-cut and strong program of action." In a speech delivered at Saigon, Johnson also fatuously proclaimed Diem as "the Winston Churchill of Asia." In response to a deterioration in Diem's position, both militarily and in morale, Kennedy sent two members of the White House staff in October for a further assessment. The reporting duo was composed of General Maxwell D. Taylor, Kennedy's military adviser, and Walt Whitman Rostow, one of the more belligerently militaristic of Kennedy's advisory group. The Taylor-Rostow report emphasized that there must be a firm, unambiguous military commitment in order to remove any doubts of United States support. It also recommended that, to counteract the many weaknesses of administration in Diem's government and a lack of offensive spirit in his army, the United States must insert American civilians and military at all levels in order to show the South Vietnamese how to be properly effective. The report also suggested that a force of 6,000 to 7,000 American troops be sent to the delta area where great floods were bringing havoc to the Vietnamese. The troops should include combat troops as well as engineer and logistical units, an "eyes only" cable to President Kennedy stated, and the humanitarian aspect of flood relief would nevertheless ensure a U.S. military presence which would show the seriousness of American involvement. The Joint Chiefs of Staff (JCS) had also advised a few weeks earlier that 40,000 U.S. troops would be needed "to clean up the Vietcong threat," but after the Taylor-Rostow assessment the Department of Defense joined with the JCS in a domino-theory report which recommended American commitment to preserving the Diem regime from the Vietcong and communism. It anticipated that no more than six divisions of American troops, or about 205,000 men, would be needed. Although the report spoke of the indigenous Vietcong and the need for counter-guerrilla operations in the countryside, it omitted reference to civil war and couched its recommendations in terms of aggression from North Vietnam.

Kennedy accepted the domino theory completely and defended it in press conferences, but he found a subsequent memo from the Defense and State Departments more to his liking. This argued immediate action in providing American helicopter, air reconnaissance, and special intelligence units, and providing advisers and equipment for training Vietnamese. Although it suggested that the sending of American combat troops could be deferred—which particularly suited Kennedy's ideas—it called for increased U.S. military personnel to organize and direct the added American participation. In December 1961, several American helicopter companies arrived in Saigon. Their 400 men brought the American military personnel to about 1,500 troops, or about twice the number permitted under the Geneva accords. The establishment of the United States Military Assistance Command, Vietnam, in February 1962 under General P. D. Harkins, marked a definite point of the United States' direct involvement in the new Indochina War. By the summer of 1962, American military personnel numbered 6,000 and were patrolling Vietnam's waters and rivers, flying South Vietnamese into battle in helicopters, and sometimes accompanying ground troops into combat. Inevitably, the casualties began and grew. By late 1963 American forces had increased to approximately 15,000 and the word "adviser" commonly appeared in print with quotation marks to indicate a description which no one was to take literally or seriously.

Diem proved a slippery and stubborn individual for the United States to deal with. He was determined to obtain an American commitment to his administration and to South Vietnam, since he did not consider he could exist without it. The other horn of the dilemma for Diem was that he not be put in a position of dependence. Such a turn of events would invite increased abuse from the militantly nationalist Vietcong, and might provide the final excuse for his restless generals to overthrow him. The United States tried to force Diem to undertake the needed reforms in his government and army, first by pressuring him and then by coaxing him. Neither course yielded any visible results. Diem's usual argument was that before reforms could be inaugurated he must first restore order, by which he meant that the sources of disaffection must be put down by force rather than treating their root causes. The Diem administration did inaugurate its Strategic Hamlet Program with American aid. Designed to move peasants into newly created villages to protect them from the Vietcong and ensure their loyalty to the central government, neither Diem's administrators nor American counter-insurgency officials took into account that the tactic had been practiced before by Diem and by the French. In each case, it provoked wide resentment and even active resistance from the peasants. The newest attempt, identified closely with Diem's brother Nhu, was equally ill-fated, with American officials attempting to push the program one way and Diem and his brother insisting on their own methods and priorities.

Once South Vietnam as a client state had received full United States commitment, it became obvious that no pressure on Diem could bring about reforms, as Diem was shrewd enough to recognize. The lesson that passionate ideological commitment will inevitably mean that no pressures (short of a traumatic scrapping of the entire commitment) can be brought to bear on a client state's rulers was not lost on Diem's successors as well. Diem's situation deteriorated rapidly in 1963. A key element was his reaction to the Buddhist religious protest against his repressive regime. Diem's ruling Catholic minority had consistently denied any voice in governmental affairs to the large Buddhist majority by increasingly authoritarian measures and with increasingly alienated popular support. At a protest demonstration in Hue on Buddha's birthday, May 8, Diem's police killed nine persons and wounded others. The situation was worsened by raids against Buddhist temples carried out under Diem's brother Nhu. The United States disassociated itself from Nhu and his actions. On November 1, 1963, after considerable maneuvering which had U.S. sanction and encouragement, a group of generals led by General Minh overthrew Diem and his brother. The two slipped away from the palace but were captured and murdered the following morning. The new government was recognized on November 8, but American complicity in the coup only deepened the commitment to South Vietnam, even as the failure of Diem's military and the Strategic Hamlet Program became more evident.

A total of nine governments were to succeed each other in Saigon in the next twenty months. Each was of short duration; each was composed basically of the same conservative social and political elements that Diem represented. The war became increasingly Americanized. In 1962, the *New York Times* reader could find out that Americans flew 30 percent or more of that year's 50,000 sorties in which entire areas were scorched with napalm fire bombs or drenched with crop-killing chemicals to destroy the peasant backbone of Vietcong support. By the end of 1963, an estimated 15,000 American "advisers" were in South Vietnam, with a limited combat role and the beginnings of casualty lists. The Vietcong were estimated to be composed of some 15,000 to 20,000 activists, with a reserve support of some 100,000 and peasant sympathizers of many times that number. That the guerrillas were indigenous to the area, South Vietnamese fighting the Diem and subsequent Saigon regimes with weapons which they were largely able to capture, was admitted by General Harkins in a 1963 press conference stating that the guerrillas were not being reinforced or supplied systematically from North Vietnam, China, or anywhere else.

Although Kennedy as Senator was thoroughly dubious of the success of an Indochinese government that lacked popular support, and was initially skeptical of the domino theory, by the second year of his presidency he dismissed the former premise and embraced uncritically the domino argument. The tarnishing of his image in the Bay of Pigs, Vienna, and Berlin incidents was widely interpreted as responsible for his hard-line approach to Vietnam. To Kennedy and his advisers, the wars of national liberation that Khrushchev had promised to aid had already begun. The Battle for Vietnam was a battle for American security, since any movement, however minor, from the non-Communist (or "free") realm to one led or dominated by Communists diminished the United States. From Rostow to Rusk or McGeorge Bundy to MacNamara, or whether through the occasional advice from Henry A. Kissinger, Harvard's Defense Studies Director, or the still potent suggestions of Dean Acheson, President Kennedy's advisers insisted on the use of dominant American force in traditional containment views. Vietnam was a testing ground, where the Communist world was to see that attempts to increase their hegemony or influence would be opposed around the globe.

But the civil war in Vietnam, the existence of which had ample evidence and critics domestic and foreign to argue its being, was an assumption that could not be tolerated. The Kennedy administration, like its predecessor, rejected a neutralist solution, and Secretary of State Dean Rusk repeatedly asserted the deliberate fiction of a separate South Vietnam as an outcome of the Geneva Accords. "Aggression" became a key word, and the support for the Vietcong among the people was negated or announced as only won at pistol point. Walt Rostow, with General Maxwell Taylor the counter-guerrilla expert of the Kennedy staff, asserted in an address to a Special Warfare graduating class at Fort Bragg that the need of a popular government or a popular cause in order to win a revolutionary war was "at best" a "half-truth." This negating of the political factor clashed with the fact of 30 years of Vietnamese national struggle for independence, whether against French colonialists, Japanese invaders, or regimes supported by American troops and money. The binding motivation among the Vietcong and the National Liberation Front, for Communist and non-Communist alike, was nationalism. By imposing a Cold War containment strategy on Vietnam, by insisting on forcing it into the ill-fitting mold of a Free World-Communist World issue, the Kennedy administration ensured both a further escalation and a final defeat of American forces.

Kennedy and the Negro Revolution

The ferment of World War II offered blacks a great opportunity to press for improvement in their rights and social treatment at the same time that the moral issue involved in combatting Nazi racism brought new recognition to the justice of their demands for full civil rights. The nature of the enemy and the growing frustration of blacks combined to bring about the greatest black militancy yet experienced. Although it was frequently met by race riots and repression, it heightened the obvious disparity between democratic myths and realities in America's second-class citizenship for its blacks and helped to enlist larger numbers of whites and liberal organizations in postwar civil rights movements.

By the 1950s, desegregation of the armed services was announced and largely implemented. In partisan terms, all but the Southern wing of the Democratic party was firmly committed to civil rights for blacks. The historic milestone decision of the Supreme Court on desegregation in 1954, while impressive, was also frustrating when its "all deliberate speed" failed to keep pace with heightened black expectations. The Civil Rights Acts of 1957 and 1960, although the former was the first such legislation in 87 years, were restricted to voting rights and did not produce notable results from the passive Eisenhower administration. Black identified more with the inspiration furnished by the young Baptist minister, Martin Luther King, Jr., in the Montgomery, Alabama, bus boycott in the winter of 1955–1956. Strongly influenced by the concept of nonviolent resistance he found in reading Thoreau and Mahatma Gandhi, King had formed amazing solidarity among his constituents to achieve a hard-won victory. Although it took an NAACP legal action to wrap up the desegregation principle achieved by the bus boycott, the example of mass community action carried out without violence was a tremendous stimulation to the black insistence on full, first-class citizenship. The NAACP's legal and congressional approach, although it accounted for considerable valuable groundwork, became too slowly paced for the rising expectation of blacks.

In February 1960, an incident occurred in Greensboro, North Carolina, which even more directly marked the beginning of a new and revolutionary phase of the black quest for civil rights. Four students from the black North Carolina Agricultural and Technical College requested and were denied service at a downtown lunch counter. They remained stubbornly but quietly in their seats until the lunchroom closed, and their example led to a wave of similar "sit-ins" and other nonviolent protests. Groups more disposed to the full implementation of such tactics rather than the NAACP's courtroom procedures sprang up. These included the Congress of Racial Equality (CORE), and the Student Nonviolent Coordinating Committee (SNCC), with the active spread of sit-in tactics. By 1960 the beginning Negro Revolution had broken through the formidable black barriers of apathy and fear and had summoned numbers, energy, and political pressure in unprecedented terms in pursuit of full civil rights for American blacks. As is common in revolutions, the strength and the impetus came not out of the depths of dispair but out of the aroused hopes and partially satisfied expectations. As some of the obstacles were overcome, the impatience and the certainty of right formed a wave of the future which would not recede until all barriers to complete membership in American society were removed.

As a Senator, John Kennedy had established himself as a proponent of civil rights, but his attitude was considered to be one of concern rather than deep commitment. Facing the rigors of the 1960 nominating convention and against the background of the recent sit-in incidents, Kennedy recognized the weakness of his public posture and moved to make his commitment better known. At the convention he called for a strong civil rights plank and joined with other Democratic Senators in condemning the Republican foot dragging in the field of civil rights. But it was in the campaign itself that Kennedy spelled out the depths of a commitment to the black drive for full citizenship that could not be misunderstood. In state after state Kennedy referred to blacks' lack of equality in American life and cited specific measures he intended to take. He pledged more appointments in all areas of federal service, more action protecting the black's right to vote than the Eisenhower administration had taken, and executive action in such fields as housing.

Perhaps a dramatic incident during the campaign was more of a signal to blacks than any platform promises. In October Reverend Martin Luther King, Jr., and 52 other blacks were arrested for a mass sit-in requesting restaurant service in Rich's Department Store in Atlanta. After all the others were released, King was not only held in jail but was sentenced to four months in prison on the technicality of not having a Georgia driving license, a typical example of the police harassment that Southern states were using against black leaders. Although Eisenhower's Department of Justice composed a draft requesting the release of the imprisoned minister, neither the President nor Vice President and presidential candidate Nixon acted to use the draft. Kennedy was notified of the incident while in Chicago and spontaneously picked up the phone to call Mrs. King and express his deep concern and, if necessary, his intervention. Bobby Kennedy followed up the next morning by telephoning a plea to the Georgia judge who had sentenced him, and on the next morning King was released on bail. The Reverend Martin Luther King, Sr., also a Baptist minister, had previously come out for Nixon on anti-Catholic grounds. But Kennedy's action changed his mind. He announced that he had "a suitcase of votes" that he was going to "dump in the lap" of Mr. Kennedy. The incident was widely and intensely publicized in black circles, and undoubtedly helped pile up a heavy black vote which could easily have accounted for the slim margin of victory in states such as South Carolina, Illinois, and Michigan.

As President, Kennedy intended to use both his executive powers and his position of moral leadership in the nation to demonstrate the need for eradicating racial prejudice. This approach not only suited Kennedy's activist concept of the presidency, in stark contrast to his predecessor's passivity, but was sure to prove more fruitful for the first year or two than risking the stubborn opposition of southern Congressmen on all Kennedy-initiated legislation. A black newspaperman, Andrew Hatcher, became a White House public relations secretary. Another, Carl Rowan, was appointed Deputy Assistant Secretary of State for Public Affairs. A strategic appointment was the naming of Robert C. Weaver to the post of Housing Administrator, although Kennedy's wish to name him to head a new Cabinet post—the Department of Urban Affairs and Housing—was a major factor in the congressional defeat of the proposal in 1962. Kennedy acted to make a black Foreign Service officer, Clifton R. Wharton, the United States Ambassador to Norway, the first of several such appointments. George Weaver of AFL-CIO became Assistant Secretary of Labor, and John Duncan became the first black Commissioner of the District of Columbia. Five blacks were made life term judges by President Kennedy, including Thurgood Marshall,[6] who later moved up to the Supreme Court.

---

[6] Marshall was the NAACP attorney who successfully argued the landmark decision of *Brown* v. *Board of Education* before the Supreme Court.

At his first Cabinet meeting Kennedy made it clear that he expected positive and immediate action throughout government agencies to promote equal opportunity in federal employment. Kennedy was also sharply aware of the unfavorable impact of race in international affairs. Diplomats from the new nations of the Third World were encountering Jim Crow attitudes in the nation's capital, and a special staff in the State Department's protocol office was set up to assist African diplomats in their search for housing. All the Kennedy appointments were not without drawbacks. Critics thoroughly disapproved of such judicial appointments as Judges Elliot, West, and Ellis in the Fifth Judical Circuit. Of these, however, probably only J. Robert Elliott of Georgia had a public record that made his judicial reactions fairly obvious. United States Attorney General Robert Kennedy also made some unfortunate appointments as U.S. District Attorneys through poor political advice, but more than made up for them by his equally intense commitment. Attorney General Kennedy greatly increased the number of black attorneys in the Justice Department, appointed the first black U.S. District Attorneys ever to hold office, and sternly pursued court action in desegregation cases.

Several events in the national news in 1961 and 1962 marked both the course of the Negro Revolution and the Kennedy role in it. Black-white organizations such as CORE and SNCC, more militant than NAACP, were impatient with many of the manifestations of segregation that hung on in the South. One that irked many was the interstate transport system. Here, although train or airline passengers were not subject to segregation en route, the waiting room, restaurants, and restroom facilities in interstate bus terminals, train stations, and airport terminals throughout the South were still in a Jim Crow category. First CORE, and then SNCC and King's Southern Christian Leadership Conference sent groups of blacks and whites, many of them students, into the South to break down these resented barriers. Calling themselves "freedom riders," they proceeded through several states in their own buses, challenging segregated terminal facilities on the way. In the spring of 1961 the CORE group, led by James Farmer, an ex-NAACP official who was a cofounder of the newer organization, finally ran into serious trouble in Anniston, Birmingham, and Montgomery, Alabama. One of their buses was burned, and the freedom riders were repeatedly attacked and beaten by mobs carrying clubs and iron pipes. Governor John Patterson first refused to accept calls from the President or the Attorney General, and finally promised appropriate action. But the Montgomery situation got out of hand and Attorney General Kennedy sent in 600 deputy federal marshals, the first of several occasions when federal marshals or troops were required to preserve the law and order which state or local officials were unable or unwilling to uphold. The Attorney

General followed through by securing a ruling from the dilatory Interstate Commerce Commission prohibiting segregation in all interstate facilities, and by instituting prompt suits against all municipalities that did not immediately comply.

A situation with even more bloodshed developed in the neighboring state of Mississippi over desegregation in higher education. James Meredith, a black Air Force veteran and native Mississippian, had been rejected when he first applied for admission to the University of Mississippi in 1961. The NAACP filed suit on grounds of racism, and the case moved over a district judge and to a favorable decision in a Circuit Court by June 1962. During the summer Supreme Court Justice Hugo Black upheld the Circuit Court. Governor Ross Barnett, referring to the federal courts as "illegal forces of tyranny," inflamed the state with his intemperate language and his Calhoun-like doctrines of 19th-century nullification. In September, when Meredith and a small group of federal marshals arrived at Oxford for registration, Barnett, flanked by student mobs, rejected Meredith's application. Attorney General Kennedy immediately had University officials cited for contempt of court and an injunction barring interference served on the Governor from the Fifth Circuit Court. Notwithstanding, Barnett physically barred Meredith from the campus, as the mobs were expanded by nonstudents and segregationists from several states and grew increasingly riotous.

President Kennedy was anxious to find a way out of the dilemma without using military means, but Governor Barnett, after a variety of devious moves and assurances, eventually left no room for anything else. Kennedy addressed a national television appeal to the imperatives of resisting defiance of courts and Constitution, and particularly asked the students of Mississippi to honor their state and university. Instead, the mob, further swollen by outsiders and displaying rifles and shotguns, attacked the federal marshals with stones and bottles as soon as night came. The marshals initially did not respond to the attack, but finally fired tear gas at a mob numbering several thousand. Federal troops, dispatched from Memphis by helicopter, finally brought the battle under control. Several hundred persons were wounded, many of them the federal marshals. Two individuals were killed by rifle fire, one of them a French correspondent from the European press. Meredith was duly registered the next morning and was accompanied to classes by marshals for many months afterward. Despite threats against his family and acceptance by only a part of the faculty and none of the students, Meredith grimly stayed on until his graduation in 1963.

The first two Kennedy years were more litigation than legislation as far as the impatient black militants were concerned. Kennedy had tested the climate of Congress and was fully aware that a civil rights bill had no chance of passage. Cautiously, he decided to wait, since any premature antagonisms among southern Democrats would also imperil his trade expansion acts and his hopes of getting a new Department of Urban Affairs established. A bill setting up the new Cabinet post was killed in the House Rules Committee, and an enabling provision with the same purpose was rudely defeated in the House of Representatives in early 1962. Even the executive action in federal housing was not undertaken until November of 1962, after the urban affairs and housing legislation had been decided. Then Kennedy finally issued an executive order prohibiting discrimination in housing. Such presidential powers only extended to units directly insured by the federal government, and thus comprised merely 15 percent of residential mortgage holdings.

Black impatience with the slow pace of executive action moved their revolutionary movement into new violent clashes in the hostile South. Reverend Martin Luther King, Jr., was leading a series of sit-ins and demonstration marches in April 1963 to protest the continuing discrimination in restaurants and employment practiced in Birmingham, when their persistence finally triggered police retaliation. Police Commissioner Eugene "Bull" Conner obtained an injunction against a march scheduled for Good Friday, April 12. King and other leaders were arrested and the blacks threatened by police dogs. Demonstrations and arrests both multiplied. On May 2 and May 3 hundreds of parading black students met the worst attacks of all. Bystanders threw bricks and glass, and police used fire hoses and finally unleashed savage police dogs on the marchers. Few photographs have had more sickening impact than the one of May 5 which appeared in newspapers around the world showing a police dog with fangs bared leaping at a frightened black woman. Bull Conner's police dogs and fire hoses aroused the conscience of white Americans as few other events had done.

For blacks, their standing up to such weapons, their courage and persistence in the face of police and official harassment, was the stimulus for dozens of similar operations and sit-ins throughout the South. Another crisis in higher education presented itself when a federal judge ruled on May 21, 1963, that the University of Alabama must admit two blacks to its June summer session. Governor George Wallace threatened to "bar the entrance" of such an enrollment. Although President Kennedy warned Wallace against such a course, the Governor personally blocked the doorway to the black students and federal marshals. Kennedy immediately federalized part of the Alabama National Guard, and Wallace slipped away when they appeared on the campus. The students were promptly registered, and that evening Kennedy made one of his most stirring speeches to a national television audience. After sternly committing himself as well as the office of the presidency to the proposition "that race has no place in American life or law," Kennedy mentioned the legislation which he would send to Congress. He admitted that this alone was not enough, but that the problem must be solved "in the homes of every American." It was not a regional or a partisan issue, he went on:

> We are confronted primarily with a moral issue. It is as old as the Scriptures and is as clear as the American Constitution. . . . Now the time has come for this nation to fulfill its promise. . . ."

The Civil Rights bill which Kennedy sent to the 88th Congress on June 19, 1963 was the most comprehensive such bill ever drawn. Accompanied by a forceful message as strong as his television address of the week before, the proposed legislation called for a ban on discrimination in all places of public accommodation which could possibly come in contact—however lightly—with the interstate commerce clause. This was the general area which had drawn the most resentment and the largest sit-ins, and could be applied to all but the smallest operations. This section of the bill was complemented by further provisions which gave the Attorney General's office authority to press for desegregation of public education regardless of whether the United States was brought into action by a suit or not. In this way, the absence of a suit occasioned by either a lack of means or a fear of reprisal on the individual's part could be remedied by watchful federal action.

Many blacks, despairing of congressional willingness to act on such a bill, suggested that their recently successful sit-in tactics be used in the galleries of the Capitol itself. But this brought outcries from friends of the bill as being counter-productive, and the idea of a demonstration took on the more readily supportable form of a national, peaceable march to and in the nation's capital. The March on Washington for Jobs and Freedom, as it was finally described, was the most amazing demonstration yet experienced in the movement for equal rights. Numbering a quarter of a million people, young and old, black and white, they had the support of almost every religious denomination in the United States and represented every state in the Union. Although there was some trepidation in Washington, the President publicly praised and supported the enterprise and unofficially aided with park police and federal facilities. August 28, 1963, the occasion for the largest public demonstration the nation's capital had ever seen, was nevertheless a completely disciplined gathering. With A. Philip Randolph at their head—whose prerogative in this position was soundly based upon his similar efforts extending over several decades—they moved from their encampment on the Washington Monument grounds to the Lincoln Memorial. There the outstanding speech was the impassioned and memorable delivery of Martin Luther King, Jr., whose moving repetition of "I have a dream" furnished a powerful theme of hope for the day when all Americans might be as one in equality and brotherhood. Significantly, the march displayed not only solidarity of blacks and whites and virtually all religious sects, but was the first public recognition of the concept that jobs and an end to poverty must form the basis for any lasting racial equality.

Although it became increasingly obvious that Kennedy's stand on blacks and civil rights was jeopardizing his political future in 1964, he insisted on pressing forward. Signs of a so-called white "backlash" in Northern suburbs, based upon "too fast" a push, were coupled with damaging reports of the probable loss of several Deep South states. "K.O. the Kennedys," as the Mississippi slogan had it, left no doubt of Deep South feelings or who had performed most ably in the cause of the black movement. Bull Connor's dogs and Governor Barnett's antics had caught the ear and eye of the country, but Kennedy had seized the day to rally the moral conscience of Americans and lead the way to the most advanced legislation yet in the area of civil rights. His approach had frequently to be adjusted to political ends and means, but it was soundly based on the morality of the cause and the American dream. His legislative proposal, labelled together with his address to Congress as "the Second Emancipation Proclamation," was to be a prodigious landmark of human rights, even though it was stalled in Congress as Kennedy took off in November for Dallas and tragic destiny.

Suggestions for Reading

The election of 1960 is carefully covered in T. H. White, *The Making of the President* (1960). A far-better-than-usual campaign biography is J. M. Burns, *John Kennedy** (1959). Comprehensive memoir-historical works by two participants are A. M. Schlesinger, Jr., *A Thousand Days: John F. Kennedy in the White House* (1965), and T. C. Sorenson, *Kennedy* (1965). Recollections by his advisers are well done in Kenneth O'Donnell, *Johnny, We Hardly Knew Ye* (1973). See also Pierre Salinger, *With Kennedy* (1965). The Kennedy family is the subject of R. J. Whalen, *The Founding Father: The Story of Joseph P. Kennedy* (1964), and has some revealing background. The political Kennedys are the topic of Henry Fairlie, *The Kennedy Promise* (1973). See also L. H. Fuchs, *John F. Kennedy and American Catholicism* (1967). Valuable also are Tom Wicker's *Kennedy Without Tears: The Man Beneath the Myth* (1964), and his *JFK and LBJ: The Influence of Personality upon Politics** (1968). R. E. Neustadt, *Presidential Power** (rev. ed. 1969), also touches on Kennedy in the presidency.

On the Kennedy advisers, Patrick Anderson, *The President's Men** (1968) covers those of recent presidents. See also Stan Opotowsky, *The Kennedy Government* (1961), and Lester Tanzer, ed., *The Kennedy Circle* (1961).

For economic policies, consult Seymour Harris, *The Economics of the Kennedy Years* (1964), and Walter Heller, *New Dimensions of Political Economy* (1966).

Kennedy's difficulties with Congress can be seen in J. M. Burns, *The Deadlock of Democracy: Four-Party Politics in America* (1963). Valuable collections are A. D. Donald, ed., *John F. Kennedy and the New Frontier* (1966), and A. Nevins, ed., *The Burden and the Glory* (1964).

Signs of the times are set forth in W. L. O'Neill, *Coming Apart: An Informal History of America in the 1960s* (1971), and in Edward Quinn and P. J. Dolan, eds., *The Sense of the 60s* (1968). For American society, personalities, and issues under Kennedy and Johnson, see I. F. Stone, *In a Time of Torment* (1967). A hard look at American poverty and evidently of seminal influence on Kennedy is Michael Harrington, *The Other America* (1962). See also Herman Miller, *Rich Man, Poor Man* (1964).

The foreign policy of the Kennedy administration is ably presented by a participant in Roger Hilsman, *To Move a Nation* (1967). An adviser who was more influential under Johnson supports his views in W. W. Rostow, *The Diffusion of Power* (1972). Newer and more critical looks at Kennedy foreign relations are R. J. Walton, *Cold War and Counter-Revolution* (1972), and Louise FitzSimons, *The Kennedy Doctrine* (1972). For the Bay of Pigs, see H. B. Johnson, *The Bay of Pigs* (1964), and Tad Szulc and K. E. Meyer, *The Cuban Invasion: The Chronicle of a Disaster* (1962). Robert Kennedy supplies an insider's account of the later Cuban missile crisis in *Thirteen Days* (1971). Elie Abel, *The Missile Crisis* (1966), is a friendly journalistic description. A variety of judgments are found in R. A. Divine, ed., *The Cuban Missile Crisis* (1971). Kennedy and the UN is a relationship explored in R. J. Walton, *The Remnants of Power: The Tragic Last Years of Adlai Stevenson* (1968). The stubborn difficulties which beset the Alliance for Progress are recounted in W. D. Rogers, *The Twilight Struggle: The Alliance for Progress and the Politics of Development in Latin America* (1967). Its failures are dissected in Jerome Levinson and Juan de Onis, *The Alliance that Lost its Way* (1970). The many works on Laos and Vietnam cited in the preceding and in the following chapters serve to cover the Kennedy experience as well.

6

Democratic Continuity

Kennedy: The Third and Final Year

THE 88th Congress which met in January 1963, was considered to be a Democratic triumph, since its slight improvement in Democratic numbers was the best off-year record posted since 1934. The new Congress also reflected some gradual geographical shifts, in that Senate Democrats had increased their representation in the Midwest and Far West while declining slightly in the South. Senate Republicans had suffered some attrition in the Midwest and Far West, but had offsetting victories in the Northeast. A parallel movement was also noticeable in the House, and in both branches a newer and younger political generation was evident. Their political elders still held the reins, however, and their antiquated procedures were a source of frustration to the underrepresented newcomers of both parties. In the more aggressive House, the liberal Democratic Study Group, which had forced a temporary enlargement of the powerful Rules Committee, made that enlargement a permanent part of the congressional structure in 1963. The same group was also instrumental in adding two administration supporters to the important Ways and Means Committee. Younger and livelier Republicans had long been dissatisfied with the stodgy and do-nothing leadership of Charles A. Halleck of Indiana. Although they did not yet feel capable of unseating Halleck himself, they made their feelings known by defeating Halleck's man for Chairman of the Republican Conference and putting Representative Gerald R. Ford of Michigan in his place. Efforts in the Senate for better committee representation of newer members and of areas other than the South generally met with defeat, but

248

the issue of institutional reform had begun to crystallize in Congress for the first time since 1946.

President Kennedy's rapport with the 88th Congress was considerably greater than had been the case with its predecessor, although it still refused to give him all he asked for. The State of the Union message delivered in January stressed the need for tax reduction and tax reform, and the details submitted to Congress a few days later carried on Kennedy's proposals incorporated in the Revenue Act of 1962. That act had granted considerable tax relief to business. The 1963 proposals, therefore, emphasized tax help for the consumer, particularly through reduction in income taxes. Corporations would also receive tax reductions, which were defended as promoting economic growth. Additionally, Kennedy sought several long-range reforms, including capital gains changes, increased taxation on oil, gas, and mineral-extraction companies, and a tightening of the depletion allowances for oil and gas. Reforms which would result in a loss of tax revenues but would furnish relief for lower-income classes included greater deductions for dependents, allowing deductions for child care and change of employment moving expenses, and tax credits for persons 65 or older.

The administration tax bill received the usual attacks. Business blasted it for not giving bigger cuts in the upper-income brackets "to promote investment." Labor insisted that the cuts for low-income persons were grossly inadequate. Many Congressmen were loath to vote for those reforms which would sacrifice tax revenues, because of the spending levels of the government budget. In the Ways and Means Committee, many of the reforms disappeared. The petroleum industry, as usual, was successful in having the depletion allowances restored to their original percentages. However, the bill which was reported out did contain most of the income tax cuts requested by Kennedy as well as many minor and modified reforms. The attempts to give persons 65 and older a tax credit and special medical-expense deductions were defeated, as was the blocking of a tax loophole for charitable deductions used by wealthy taxpayers. In this somewhat modified form, the bill passed the House but bogged down in the Senate, from where it was to emerge to passage in virtually the same form next February as the Revenue Act of 1964.

A subject dear to President Kennedy's heart received amazingly expansive treatment from the first session of the 88th Congress. This was the entire field of education, the topic which occupied more of the President's time and talks than any other domestic issue. Capitol Hill did well enough in this area to be dubbed by many the "Education Congress of 1963." Although the President's education proposals had been largely defeated in 1961 and 1962 by combinations of conservative Republicans and Democrats—frequently joined by a Catholic hierarchy angered over aid only to the public schools—he bounced back to the attack in 1963. Some of the emphasis was shifted to higher education, since the Justice Department suggested that such federal aid would be constitutionally possible. This opinion was based on the fact that college attendance, regardless of religious sponsorship, was not mandatory; nor were standards of admission required by law or states required to furnish free education to all comers. This approach proved to be the basis of a later favorable Supreme Court decision, and proved a valuable vehicle for wide support. The Higher Education Facilities Act of 1963 readily cleared both the House and Senate, and authorized a five-year program of federal grants and loans for construction or improvement of public and private higher-education facilities. Its $1.2 billion provided matching grants to the states for construction and improvement of undergraduate academic facilities, grants to construct graduate schools and cooperative graduate centers, and loans to private institutions for similar activities. The same Congress also approved an extensive Kennedy vocational educational measure, extensions of the impacted areas school aid, and an extension and expansion of NDEA authorizations. When scholarship aids in the Higher Education Act were stricken out, Kennedy increased such funds in the act which approved NDEA extension. The "Education Congress" also enacted bills which provided for an attack on mental illness through new community treatment centers, and for medical- and dental-school construction.

Congress posted its share of refusals also. It permitted some expansion of existing programs such as housing and air pollution control, but rejected outright (as it had also in 1962) administration attempts to establish mass urban transportation development. Rapid transit measures for the congested District of Columbia area were similarly disapproved. While many other education measures were passed, the religious and segregationist opposition to federal aid for elementary and secondary schools prevented any such legislation from being enacted. Occasionally, Kennedy resorted to executive order or took advantage of older legislation to forward his attacks upon poverty-stricken regions. An example was his creation of the Committee on the Appalachian Region, headed by Undersecretary of Commerce Franklin D. Roosevelt, Jr., to work up vocational training and public works projects for this area of severe and chronic unemployment.

A general aura of prosperity and a relieved moving away from the brink in 1962's missile crisis created an atmosphere of vastly reduced tensions between the United States and the Soviet Union in 1963. A rift between the Soviet Union and the People's Republic of China which had deepened by mid-1963 may also have contributed to the possibility of better Russo-American relations. President Kennedy made this evident in a masterfully statesmanlike speech ("What Kind of Peace Do We

Want?") delivered June 10, 1963 at American University in Washington. Calling to the attention of his audience the dangers of nuclear holocaust and the mutual abhorrence of war shared by the United States and the Soviet Union, he remarked:

> Let us reexamine our attitude toward the Cold War. . . . We must deal with the world as it is and not as it might have been had the history of the last 18 years been different. . . . And if we cannot end now our differences, at least we can help make the world safe for diversity. For in the final analysis our most basic common link is that we all inhabit this planet. We all breathe the same air. We all cherish our children's future. And we are all mortal.

This challenge to "find solutions that now seem beyond us" met a quick and favorable response from Premier Khrushchev. He readily pledged Soviet adherence to Kennedy's announcement that the United States would ban nuclear testing in the atmosphere as long as other nations similarly refrained. Kennedy was able to announce that the moribund discussions on disarmament would be revived on a three-nation basis in a July Moscow meeting. The President named Undersecretary of State W. Averell Harriman, an old Moscow hand, and the conferences began on July 15, with Lord Hailsham representing Great Britain. The tentative treaty was quickly concluded. It provided for a ban on any further nuclear testing in the atmosphere, in outer space, or in the water. Although Khrushchev had originally demanded that any treaty include a ban on underground testing as well, he finally agreed to the American version.

The task of selling the Test Ban Treaty to the nation and particularly to the Senate and the military then commenced. Kennedy made another effective address to the nation after agreement had been reached in Moscow. Speaking of mankind's struggle to "escape from the darkening prospect of mass destruction on earth" since the advent of nuclear weapons, he likened the agreement to "a shaft of light cut into the darkness. . . ." He soberly noted that "This treaty is not the millennium. . . . But it is an important first step—a step toward peace, a step toward reason, a step away from war". A bipartisan organization, The Citizens' Committee for a Nuclear Test Ban, also drummed up support among business and professional leaders. Within two months, public support for the treaty grew impressively. The military and their powerful allies in the Senate proved far more difficult. The Air Force generals were the most adamantly opposed, and the Air Force Association, composed of air force personnel and the defense contractors, lobbied strenuously against it. Kennedy's aide, General Maxwell Taylor, understood the treaty's basis of American nuclear superiority and was able to convince some of his colleagues. Many others were brought to support the treaty by Secretary MacNamara's testimony before a Senate hearing which brought out not only America's huge missile superiority but also the plans for even more of an increase in weaponry. When the Senate ratified the Nuclear Test Ban Treaty on September 24, 1963 with a vote of 80 to 19, a breakdown of the dissenters showed 11 Democrats—all except one from the ranks of the Southern conservatives—and 8 Republicans, all except one from the West.

The treaty was regarded as a valuable clearing of the air between the United States and the Soviet Union and helped transform the Cold War into a less-frenzied confrontation. It was more of a victory for the United States, however, since there was a clear understanding and admission from both sides that the treaty stabilized a position of nuclear superiority for the United States and one of nuclear inferiority for the Soviet Union. This admission was costly to Khrushchev's future. Coming on top of his backing away from the Cuban crisis, his giving in to the American point of view on continued underground testing, accompanied by the Senate hearings disclosing American missile superiority and plans for enormous expenditures to widen the gap further, all undoubtedly added up to the major factors sending Khrushchev into political oblivion within the next 13 months. The cost of selling the Test Ban Treaty to the American military was also high. Kennedy pledged to the Chiefs of Staff in the Senate hearings, partly because of his own willingness and partly to get them to accept the treaty ". . . comprehensive, aggressive, and continuing underground nuclear test programs" and the resumption of nuclear atmospheric tests if deemed essential to national security, even though this meant abrogating the treaty. The military chiefs were also sold by the fact, ably illustrated by Secretary MacNamara, that unlimited testing would more readily enable the Soviet Union to close the American-Russian gap, whereas underground testing (requiring far more expense and technical experience) would ensure protracted American superiority. The underground testing clause, although Kennedy deplored unlimited testing in that environment, turned out to be the loophole which focused intensified efforts on moving the arms race underground and thereafter actually escalated it. All development and testing which American scientists once thought only possible in the atmosphere was successfully moved underground and even new weaponry (such as MIRV) perfected in the new environment. Within five years of the signing of the limited Test Ban Treaty, the underground permission clause brought about an actual increase rather than a decrease in nuclear testing.

The Nuclear Test Ban Treaty was quickly signed by 101 of the world's nations. China refused to sign on grounds that the agreement was a Soviet-American conspiracy to prevent China from becoming a world power. France's de Gaulle also refused to sign, emphasizing the privileged nuclear positions of the two superpowers and insisting that the treaty did not actually reduce world armaments. Kennedy sought his compliance through the promise of aid for French underground testing, but de Gaulle was adamant. The Nuclear Test Ban Treaty rested upon strong majority support in the United States, Japan, and other nations made aware of the dangers of continuing atmospheric testing. It was undoubtedly aided by the trauma of the Cuban facedown. It was not only the first nonproliferation pact ever signed, but also marked the first time that the two superpowers had reached a major formal agreement. In the context of 1963, regardless of the meaning for the future of its dangerous underground loophole, it had to be accounted a new and major step towards a lessening of Russo-American tensions and world peace.

But Kennedy's speech in June "for diversity" evidently alarmed the Adenauer administration in Germany, and Kennedy decided to make a European trip to emphasize the basic American commitment to Europe and promote "a united Europe in an Atlantic partnership." His visit to Germany, England, Ireland, and Italy was an unqualified personal success. The President's reaction to the Berlin Wall was an impassioned speech to a huge and almost hysterical public audience. Likening freedom to the citizenry of Berlin, Kennedy said he was proud to claim: "Ich bin ein Berliner." ("I am a Berliner.") But the German desire to be admitted to some kind of nuclear membership or a sharing of nuclear decision making, as a prestige symbol to offset the British nuclear possessions and the newly independent French nuclear position, was not satisfied.

The most widely discussed vehicle for sharing of nuclear responsibility was a multilateral force (MLF), which was finally envisioned as a special group of some twenty-five naval vessels armed with Polaris missiles and manned by mixed crews made up of at least three different nationalities. Promoted domestically by a coterie within the State Department and by the Navy (the Army and the Air Force had no MLF role and were predictably negative), it was intended to give our European non nuclear allies a feeling of participation in nuclear decisions and to promote European unity and Atlantic partnership. The MLF concept had first been discussed in the Eisenhower administration, and its most zealous proponents on the European scene in 1963 were General Lauris Norstad, commander of NATO, and Thomas K. Finletter, the American Ambassador to NATO. Both saw in MLF a chance to adjust NATO to the changed conditions of the times. But just as economic growth made the Marshall Plan and European dependence on the United States a thing of the past, so had changed military circumstances made NATO obsolescent. If there had ever been a possibility of a Russian sweep through Western Europe in the postwar 1940s—a dubious proposal at best—there were extremely few Europeans who would admit to such a likelihood in the nuclear deterrent climate of 1963. NATO, originally formed to prevent such a happening, seemed to have institutional instincts for survival that were probably stronger than the necessity for its continued existence. The MLF, it was hoped, would breathe new life into NATO in addition to its other desired results. Great Britain and Italy, however, were negative, and France openly derisive. The small nations also made it clear that the MLF concept was really a sham where their "decision sharing" was concerned, since neither Congress nor the White House intended to give up sole American control of any group nuclear trigger. With the President cautiously skeptical, and the Adenauer government's voice the only one eagerly raised, MLF died a not-too-lingering death.

In order to ensure against any approach to war by the two super-powers because of misinformation or a misunderstanding of intentions, the two nations agreed in August 1963 to the establishment of a "hot line" between Washington and Moscow. This new arrangement for in-stant communication was actually a teletype via London and Helsinki, with instant coding and decoding by American and Soviet electronic equipment in each capital. Looking hopefully into the future, Kennedy could see the possibility of Soviet-American accord on a civil air agree-ment and perhaps a consular treaty. No one could peer down the road to Dallas at the terrible tragedy to come.

Assassination of a President

As the election year of 1964 neared, Kennedy and his advisors gave increasing attention to the strategic problems that might handicap the President's second-term ambitions and expectations. A lesser one was the Democratic party split in the Vice President's home state of Texas, where the liberal elements (represented by Senator Ralph Yarborough) and the strong conservatives (led by Governor John Connally) were at such loggerheads as to emperil that state's electoral votes in the Demo-cratic column. A flying trip to Texas and to Florida was decided upon for the latter part of November 1963. Kennedy counted on the Vice President's ties with both factions and the favorable spotlight of the presidential trip to bring unity to the warring Democrats of Texas.

Of the several Texas cities where Kennedy talks were planned, Dallas had already established an unenviable reputation. In 1960, while carrying the campaign banner of John Kennedy, Lyndon Johnson and his wife were spat upon and threatened by a screeching mob of ultraconservatives in the lobby of a downtown hotel. This same pathological hatred for Eastern international liberalism was manifested in even more virulent form and only a few weeks before the presidential visit. The occasion was a talk by Ambassador Adlai Stevenson on United Nations Day, when a noisy contingent of General Edwin A. Walker's superpatriots not only harassed and interrupted Stevenson's talk but spat upon him and banged their picket signs on the head of the UN Ambassador as the police escorted him to his car. Handbills picturing the President of the United States and denouncing him as "Wanted for Treason" also appeared throughout the city.

The Texas trip started auspiciously enough. San Antonio, on November 21, was extremely enthusiastic. The President spoke at the dedication of Aerospace Medical Health Center at Brooks Air Force Base on the nation's determination to penetrate the mysteries of outer space. After a brief stop in Houston for a dinner in honor of Congressman Albert Thomas, the presidential party moved on to Fort Worth to spend the night. President Kennedy addressed the Fort Worth Chamber of Commerce at a breakfast appearance on November 22, mentioning the Liberator bombers produced there, one of which his late elder brother had helped fly from its Fort Worth production line. The party then emplaned for Dallas, where Kennedy was scheduled for a luncheon speech at the Dallas Trade Mart, in which he intended a keynote of increased American military and scientific strength for vigilance rather than aggression.

November 22 was a colorful fall day in Dallas, with morning clouds having yielded to a bright sun at midday when the presidential motorcade set out from Love Field. Presidential aides thought the reception from the crowds on the outskirts of Dallas was friendly enough but somewhat reserved in their greeting. But in downtown Dallas the crowds were huge and visibly enthusiastic. The motorcade, with Governor Connally sitting next to the President in the big, open Lincoln that conveyed them and their wives, turned off Main Street and briefly onto Houston Street. It then turned left onto Elm Street and down a slope leading to the new triple underpass of Dealey Plaza. As it passed the eight-story building of the Texas School Book Depository, rifle shots were heard faintly, but distinctly, over the crowd's noise. President Kennedy, with blood pouring from wounds in the head and neck, pitched over into his wife's arms. Governor Connally also collapsed, with a bullet wound in the back. As the crowd screamed in panic, the President's car, with siren wide open, streaked for nearby Parkland Memorial Hospital. The best efforts of a hastily summoned team of expert physicians were futile. At 1:00 p.m. John Fitzgerald Kennedy, fourth President of the United States to fall at the hands of assassins, was pronounced dead.

In 1963, John F. Kennedy was a greatly beloved President. His youth, his quick smile, and splendid vitality, moreover, were reassuring symbols to Americans and non-Americans alike of a people brimming with new energy and confidence, moving with a fresh approach to the solution of their problems. The anguished news of his sudden death seemed to have an impact on every American. Cars were pulled to the side of freeways and people gathered on streets to listen to the erratic and confused radio reports. People broke into tears and sobbed openly. Others dropped to their knees in prayer or accosted strangers, hoping for a denial of the terrible news. Newspaper and television station switchboards were deluged with frantic calls. Church bells rang slowly in every city, and many people filed into the church closest at hand. A gong suspended trading in the stock exchange, all sports events were cancelled, theatres declined to show their Friday night performances. The United Nations session was brought to a halt, and flags everywhere moved to half-mast. In Washington itself, crowds gathered in front of the White House, gazing dumbly and sadly through the iron fence at the deserted mansion. Waves of grief seemed to have paralyzed the whole nation. The mourning around the entire world was literally unprecedented in history.

Searching for a man unaccountably missing from his recently acquired job in the Book Depository, the Dallas police took into custody one Lee Harvey Oswald minutes after the suspect had fatally shot the first officer who had accosted him. Oswald, an ex-Marine with sharpshooter classification, had attempted to rid himself of his American citizenship while living in Russia. An unstable and frustrated individual equipped with only a superficial knowledge of Marxism, Oswald finally left the Soviet Union. With his Russian wife, he returned to the United States to a succession of jobs which he either quit within a short time or from which he was fired because of his quarrelsome nature. But Oswald never lived to reach a courtroom. On Sunday, November 25, Dallas police planned to move Oswald from the police department to the county jail. The press was notified, and television cameras were set up for a national broadcast. But when Oswald appeared manacled to two officers, Jack Ruby, the owner of two small "strip joints" and friendly with many police officers, stepped close to Oswald and shot him at point-blank range in full view of millions of television viewers. Oswald died on the operating table, and Ruby soon went on trial for murder.

The incoming 36th President, Lyndon Baines Johnson, moved quickly to appoint a special investigating commission consisting of seven public figures of suitably bipartisan status. Its very reluctant head was Chief Justice of the United States Earl Warren. The other members were Senators Richard B. Russell (D.) of Georgia and John Sherman Cooper (R.) of Kentucky; Representatives Hale Boggs (D.) of Louisiana and Gerald R. Ford (R.) of Michigan; Allen W. Dulles, former head of the CIA; and John J. McCloy, former adviser on disarmament to President Kennedy. The commission's report, commonly known as the Warren Report, was issued in 26 volumes on September 27, 1964. Compiled by the commission's staff of investigators, researchers, and attorneys, it concluded that Oswald was "acting alone and without advice or assistance." Jack Ruby, the report stated, was also on his own and neither individual was part of "any conspiracy, domestic or foreign." For motivation the report cited Oswald's disturbed youth, his avowed commitment to Marxism, his resentment of all authority, and his profound alienation from the world in which he lived. These characteristics, plus his known hostility toward his environment and his proclivity for violent acts all added up to an individual whose character was that of a man "capable of assassinating President Kennedy."

Before the Warren Commission Report was even published, a variety of publications seized upon the many puzzling aspects of the case to titillate or further confuse the public. With the publication of the commission's report, however, a number of critics studying its 26 volumes were easily able to pinpoint its many contradictions, inconsistencies, and omissions. In the wave of critical works which followed, it was considered significant that the commission did not have access to the important autopsy photographs and X rays, and that the report of the FBI agents witnessing the autopsy did not match the commission's findings. Most critical works were able to offer stiff arguments against the commission's "one bullet" theory which held that the bullet striking the President in the neck was also the same bullet which entered Governor Connally's back and exited through the Governor's wrist and thence into his thigh. Several critical works presented substantial refutation of the lone-assassin theory by means of the varying motion of the President's head in the available films as an indication of bullets striking from the front as well as from the rear. Supported by painstaking measurements of the distances and angles involved and with analyses of bullet trajectory and impact, these works were the target of a counterattack defending the commission's report. Largely *ad hominem* attacks upon the character and motivation of the author rather than upon the evidence of argument used, these then provoked additional responses. Publications challenging the findings of the commission far outnumbered its defenders, with the media and the press generally supporting the Warren Report. Its critics were able to question seriously its conclusions yet were frustrated in their inability to advance additional evidence. The effect of unresolved questions persisted. Several years after the publication of the commission's report, polls revealed that fully two thirds of the public had grave doubts as to its conclusions.

Evaluation of the Kennedy Administration

No President in American history was seen and heard on radio and television more than John F. Kennedy. He was the first President whose press conferences were televised live, and such public conferences far outnumbered those of his predecessor or of his two successors. Even Franklin Roosevelt, that assiduous and skilled employer of the radio as media, did not bring the agents of the mass media into the privacy of his office or his home as did Kennedy. The White House was the subject of an unprecedented volume of news and human interest coverage. In many ways, it came as a relief from the stuffiness of the Eisenhower administration. The Kennedy family was about as close to a royal family as the United States ever had, and although it was a target for the bitter and critical wrath of some, it was a delight for many more who were willing to be charmed by a young and vigorous President and an attractive wife. The Kennedys, with wealth and youth, political power and international glamor, were natural copy for the press. Their connections with the worlds of art and literature and high fashion increased the coverage afforded the White House residents, and President Kennedy brought this to new heights by making himself and his official activities supremely accessible to the public media. The image projected was that of youth and energy, of fresh winds of change, of the addressing of American and world problems with verve and courage. It was an image that reached most Americans and summoned increasing public support for the Kennedy program. As one partisan critic complained, "An administration which can turn the rocking chair into a vitality symbol can do anything with image."

The image was not translated fully where innovative and corrective legislation was concerned. The New Frontier brought about the Peace Corps and the Alliance for Progress, but it backed off from the oil depletion issue in tax reform and settled on a mild drug-control act rather than the more stringent one that investigative exposures called for. The Trade Expansion Act of 1962 was a major achievement, but efforts towards farm legislation, civil rights, and federal aid to education all bogged down in Congress. Kennedy cannot completely escape blame for the New Frontier's legislative failures, particularly since—with unusual lack of caution—he had announced that he was going to be a "strong" President. Much of the congressional contact was left to the Kennedy staff—to many Congressmen, a young and pushy lot. Kennedy himself, although he cultivated individual Senators and Representatives, had little taste for the political type as such and neglected the necessary bargaining over desired legislation. In the Bay of Pigs affair, he ignored the politician's good sense and sensitivity (of Fulbright and Stevenson) for the disastrous advice of the technical "experts." Although his projected image was one that mustered wide popular support, he rarely went over the heads of a recalcitrant Congress to the public as others had successfully done before him. At a time in American governmental history when the President had unprecedented executive power, Kennedy was cautious in its domestic use. Although Kennedy did not dare introduce a civil rights bill until 1963, the Negro Revolution received the moral support of the White House in the press and on national television. Despite a potential loss of votes even in the urban North, Kennedy identified himself personally with black civil rights goals, and the enforcement of court decisions received strong executive backing.

Critics sometimes could not decide whether Kennedy was conservative or liberal, but the seeming ambiguities in some domestic actions more properly reflected a lack of doctrinaire policy than a switching of ideologies. (Kennedy insisted as a politician that he was neither, but for the purposes of historical consensus he is consistently adjudged as being of a liberal persuasion in his years of the presidency.) When Kennedy assailed the steel industry in no uncertain terms, an antibusiness judgment was hastily rendered. But Kennedy went on to take a definitely probusiness stand on Telstar, and the merger of giant Standard Oil of Kentucky with supercorporation Standard Oil of California was unopposed by the Kennedy Department of Justice.

President Kennedy made no secret of the fact that he infinitely preferred the realm of foreign affairs to domestic ones, but it was also in this area that his administration was most replete with paradox, ambivalence, and ambiguity. Two weeks after General Eisenhower had warned the nation of the dangers of the military-industrial complex, Kennedy revealed plans to enlarge and expand America's already dominant military capacity. Although he found on assuming office that the "missile gap" of the campaign was wholly fictional, he announced he would "accelerate our entire missile program." Although presidential adviser Walt Rostow insisted to the Russians that the Kennedy-enlarged deterrent was actually only in the higher interests of peace, the Soviets understandably accelerated their own rearmament. Kennedy acted to forbid belligerent generals and admirals from making speeches affecting the nation's foreign policy. But this curtailment was vastly offset by an expansion of the militarization of American global reactions. Instead of the limited nuclear reaction of the Dulles days, the United States moved to an expanded ability to intervene militarily against any small conflagration on a distant continent. The "brush-fire" concept and the military and social science tactics of counter-insurgency became key characteristics of the Kennedy administration. The President also inaugurated—over the protests of the generals—a Special Forces group distinguished by the green beret that gave them their popular name. It was under the Kennedy administration that the armed forces were greatly expanded and military spending leaped upward.

In some ways, decisions of the early Kennedy administration reflected far more understanding of the Third World than those of its predecessor. It was a relief to many to see the United States lined up with the emerging nations by voting in the United Nations against the feudal colonial position of Portugal regarding Angola. The Congo incident took a healthier and less emotional direction than had been the case under Eisenhower. The Cuban Bay of Pigs affair, although damaging, was saved from proportions of long-range disaster by Kennedy's caution. Concurrently in Laos, Kennedy seemingly sought to rewrite history by indicating that it was the Communists who tried to subvert a shaky neutrality rather than the American CIA. Despite threatening military chess moves, Kennedy was finally willing to accept a 1962 Geneva agreement for a renewed neutrality status for the war-weary Laotians. The 1962 missile crisis over Cuba produced the most dangerous moment for the world of the postwar years. Despite an unfortunate "him or me" egocentrism, Kennedy avoided the equally dangerous course of pushing Khrushchev into an impossible corner and took the advice (chiefly from brother Robert) which resolved the affair without conflict rather than the irreversible military strike suggested by the Pentagon.

By 1963, Kennedy was moving toward détente with the Soviets and a nuclear treaty. His American University speech was not only his finest hour but the first presidential speech in nearly two decades to draw back from the concepts of the Cold War. On that historic occasion, he asked the nation to reexamine its attitude toward the Soviet Union, reminding soberly that "No government or social system is so evil that its people must be considered as lacking in virtue." He insisted that the United States did not seek a *Pax Americana* "enforced on the world by American weapons of war," and called upon all men to "help make the world safe for diversity." The Nuclear Test Ban Treaty and such measures as the sale of wheat to the Communist nations and the precautionary "hot line" were steps in that worthy direction.

Although Vietnam may not have been one of the most time-consuming issues of the Kennedy administration, the disclosure of the Pentagon Papers and other once-secret documentation on the conduct of that war have required it to be so considered, and the historical verdict has not been wholly kind to the Kennedy presidency. In a war in which American national security was never at stake, Kennedy ignored sound advice from experience painfully gained. General Douglas MacArthur, with the Korean adventure firmly etched in his memory, warned against sacrificing even one American soldier on the Asian continent. General Charles de Gaulle, whose nation was still recovering from the bloody and futile losses of the French armies in Vietnam, warned Kennedy not to become entangled. Neither piece of advice was accepted. Where Vietnam was concerned, Kennedy relied heavily on Walt W. Rostow, Chief of State's Policy Planning Council; McGeorge Bundy, Presidential Adviser on National Security; and General Maxwell Taylor, Presidential Military Adviser, with Secretary of Defense McNamara and his deputies furnishing strong aid and support, and Secretary of State Rusk and his deputies in a less-prominent position. The "hardnosed pragmatists," as the White House circle of advisers saw themselves, proved to be power advocates for the solution of every problem. American power, plus American technology and American efficiency, furnished all the possible components for resolving any crisis around the globe. President Kennedy took the position that the fall of every sparrow of a nation anywhere in the world to communism, or to nationalism dominated by communism, was of primary concern to the security of the United States. His advisers, strongly influenced by Khrushchev's speech on "national liberation wars," ignored the lessons of nationalistic resistance in Vietnam. The American version of counter-insurgency, with massive doses of men and aid, only served to make Diem and his successors more and more dependent on the American. To the "crisis managers," or "defense intellectuals," as their critics dubbed them, Vietnam was a "testing ground" with results of mortal global significance. Although the Kennedy administration knew very well that no infiltration had taken place from North Vietnam by 1963, and had no evidence whatever of Soviet or Chinese military aid to the Vietcong, its spokesmen refused to face the obvious fact of a Vietnamese civil war. Secretary Rusk persistently spoke of "aggression from the North," and sorely abused the Munich analogy in describing the situation.

Neither Kennedy nor his advisers ever questioned the American right of intervention or American globalistic assumptions. They accepted the Eisenhower domino theory not merely on a regional basis but on a world scale. The traditional policies of Communist containment were pursued, even where the United States addressed itself to the unattainable goal of the "freeing" of one country by another. The military, once dispatched by civilian authority, contributed to the ensuing downfall of American policy in Indochina. Problems, in their view, were only solvable by the application of more men and more firepower. The "can do" training of the military was largely responsible for the refusal at higher echelons to accept any field report not firmly optimistic in tone and content. An incredible and unreal aura of official optimism was thus sustained in Pentagon, State Department, and White House.

The Kennedy administration policies toward Southeast Asia were ambiguous. Kennedy was cautious, and he wished to control and end the war through political means rather than military ones. Against this must be weighed the fact that he introduced the first heavy weapons and the first contingents of combat troops, and firmly voiced his refusal to withdraw. American troops in Vietnam moved upward from the 600-odd approved by the Geneva Accord to 16,000 by the end of 1963. Elsewhere, Kennedy clearly wished to preserve peace, but he accepted the Achesonian view that negotiation can only be successfully carried out over a gun barrel twice as large as one's diplomatic adversary. The

Peace Corps and the Alliance for Progress were innovations that drew the world's admiration. So, too, was de-escalating the Cold War to a calmer confrontation by divesting it of its evangelical and apocalyptic rhetoric, even while American global assumptions and traditional containment tactics and beliefs remained the same as before.

The tragedy of Kennedy's assassination blinded his contemporaries to some extent. His tragic death cut short the realization of many aspirations and left both hopes and doubts unresolved. He used stirring prose: "Now the trumpet summons us again"; "Ask not what your country can do for you." His style, his refreshing lack of pretense and pomposity, attracted the young as never before. To both Americans and Europeans, the future seemed a bright, hopeful glow on the horizon for the first time since the war, and the fog of doubt closed in again with his passing. The spirit of the period perhaps stood for more than did the record of the period. If it was an era of great expectations rather than concrete accomplishments, it was to many the promise of great deeds that lived on to illuminate the memory of the days of Kennedy. Historically, the assessment of an administration of only two years, ten months, and three day's duration must tend toward the unique Scottish legal verdict of "not proven."

Lyndon Baines Johnson

Trauma always accompanies the passing of presidential powers when the Chief Executive dies in office. But at no time was it ever more in evidence than when the presidential plane bore both the body of John F. Kennedy and the newly sworn-in President, together with their respective aides and families, back to Washington. To Kennedy's staff, it was incredible that Johnson and his aides should be giving orders. They felt that even the swearing in of Johnson before the plane left Dallas was unnecessary and in undignified haste. Johnson's aides carried the sores and the humiliations of the bitter convention defeat of 1960 by Kennedy forces, and three years of disparaging remarks directed from the Kennedy circle to and about Johnson and his assistants. The new President left no doubt in the minds of the red-eyed and inconsolable Kennedy staff that the reins of authority had passed from the dead to the living. Many of the Kennedy people continued to regard Johnson as an interloper, an unfortunate and temporary phenomenon. To these irreconcilables, the only reality was a ticket in the following year headed by the heir apparent, Robert F. Kennedy. To Johnson, the various Kennedy officials and advisers represented two kinds of sorely needed continuity. One kind was the obvious and necessary carry-over of nationally vital information and policy. The other, less obvious but no less vital, was an assurance to the American people that with Kennedy advisers and officials still very much in evidence the transition was one of smooth and undisturbed continuation. Thus Johnson commanded or cajoled, in order to prevent a disturbing wholesale exiting of talent, to help him in the early months of his presidency.

Lyndon Baines Johnson was born August 27, 1908, in the south central Texas community of Stonewall, to Rebekah Baines and Samuel Ealy Johnson, Jr. Sam Johnson was a cotton farmer, cattle dealer, real estate agent, and local politician, none of which provided the family with more than a very modest subsistence. Young Lyndon resisted his mother's wish for higher education by several years of odd jobs after high school graduation in Johnson City, but finally consented to attend Southwest State Teachers' College at San Marcos, Texas. His attendance was noteworthy for establishing him as a young man of excessive brashness and aggressiveness, with a short temper and a flair for political organization. After graduation, he taught at Sam Houston High School in Houston for a year, where his fierce competitiveness and insistence upon perfection drove his new debating teams to the Texas State finals. Lyndon Johnson seized the opportunity to campaign for the reactionary Richard Kleberg of the fabulous King Ranch spread, who won a seat in Congress, as a meal ticket to Washington. Installed in the nation's capital, the 23-year-old Texan began the instant friendship and brain-picking techniques which were to be so useful to him over his political career of nearly four decades. Pushed out of his job when Kleberg found that his young assistant was planning to run for his seat, Johnson's prestigious congressional friends Maury Maverick and Sam Rayburn secured for him the state directorship of the New Deal's National Youth Administration.

In 1937 Johnson won out over five opponents in a special election to fill the Tenth District congressional seat by clever and energetic pro-Roosevelt tactics, and returned to Washington. He won reelection each time until 1948. In the House, Lyndon Johnson displayed the same pushy aggressiveness that had marked his earlier successes and an unerring discovery of the sources of power. By injecting himself into newspaper pictures and a train ride with President Roosevelt while in Texas, Johnson received Washington favors as the President's "protégé." For his constituents, the young Congressman assiduously cultivated a host of New Dealers among the various executive agencies. The Senate was always Johnson's goal. Running in 1941 as a strong Roosevelt man, Johnson lost in the Democratic primaries to the colorful and conservative "Pappy" O'Daniel and quickly began a move away from the politically damaging New Deal image. In 1943 the Congressman's wife (once Claudia "Lady Bird" Taylor) used a portion of her inheritance to buy a run-down Austin radio station, KTBC. With Federal Communications

Commission permission, the station extended its broadcast time, quadrupled its transmitting power, and became affiliated with the television operations of the Columbia Broadcasting System. Quick profits were plowed back into cattle, land, and bank stock. By 1948 Johnson was able to tell a few friends that the net worth of the family holdings was $1 million. In that year Pappy O'Daniel made it known he would resign from his Senate seat and Johnson, with new and powerful alliances forged with oil and aircraft interests, jumped into the primary. He won by 87 questionable votes out of nearly 990,000 cast. In the legal challenges that followed, Johnson's attorneys, Abe Fortas and Alvin Wirtz, with aid from the Truman administration, were able to keep Johnson's name on the ballot. An easy defeat of the Republican opposition brought "Landslide Lyndon," as his new colleagues promptly dubbed him, into the United States Senate.

The 81st Congress, convening in January 1949, had changed from Republican dominance to Democratic along with Harry Truman's upset victory. The 40-year-old Senator from Texas was able to get seats on the powerful Armed Services Committee and on the Interstate and Foreign Commerce Committee, which carried great weight with the Federal Communications Commission. His tremendous drive and his aggressiveness were quickly made evident, although his brashness and noisiness were subdued to fit the newly tailored role of freshman Senator. His staff received the full brunt of the Johnson violent temper, the insatiable demand for the same 14- or 16-hour days that he put in himself, and the insistence on a complete "loyalty" down to the type of necktie to be worn. The young Texan's drive for the source of power led him to Senator Richard B. Russell of Georgia, whose lofty niche in the Senate hierarchy was devoted to his twin goals of white supremacy and an enormous military machine. His new protégé role under Russell found Johnson supporting the Southern filibuster against civil rights bills, which Russell led, and generally opposing the largely unsuccessful Fair Deal program of President Truman. It was a position far more suited to the growing conservatism of the state of Texas. Johnson also convinced any doubting colleagues of his new position in accord with the oil and gas industry by leading a successful Senate attack to reject Truman's nomination of Leland D. Olds, a consumer-oriented commissioner, to another term as Chairman of the Federal Power Commission.

Majority leader and party whip, the number one and two jobs in the Senate, were powerless and thankless tasks in the postwar period, with strings being pulled behind the scenes largely by Russell of Georgia on the Democratic side and Taft of Ohio for the Republicans. Largely pushed by Oklahoma's Robert Kerr, with whom Johnson shared in common gas and oil interests and investigations of their slim votes for Senate victory, the Texan was given the post of party whip. From this vantage point he was able to head a subcommittee on defense preparedness, from which he blasted Truman's "makeshift mobilization" for the Korean War. The cultivation of defense measures, contracts, and knowledge Johnson found far more to his liking than his necessary oil and gas chores.

When Eisenhower entered the White House in 1953 with a narrowly Republican Senate, Johnson maneuvered himself into the post of minority leader. With the coming of a Democratic victory two years after, Johnson was assured of the majority leader's position. From both posts Johnson worked to consolidate his authority and to ally himself with all hues of Democratic and Republican ideology. He invoked the well worn rule of favor returning by getting favorable committee assignments for new Democratic Senators Kennedy of Massachusetts, Mansfield of Montana, Jackson of Washington, Symington of Missouri, and Gore of Tennessee. He also decided to make out of Senator Hubert Humphrey of Minnesota a willing and loyal lieutenant. Johnson's relations with Eisenhower were cordial. He never made the mistake of opposing the enormously popular White House tenant solely for partisan reasons or in support of legislative efforts sure to be defeated. Close and friendly relationships with the Senate's Republican leaders were assiduously cultivated. At the same time, Johnson forged a series of links with liberal Democrats by working for bills he could afford to support, such as on housing, social security, minimum wages, and farm legislation, even while protecting his Texas base of support by voting for oil and gas matters and against civil rights.

Steadily Lyndon Johnson worked to make the Senate majority leadership the most powerful position on Capitol Hill. The majority whip's post was beefed up with a special office and staff as an aid to the majority leader and given to his ally, Senator Earle D. Clements of Kentucky, who had valuable contacts with both liberal and conservative Democrats. The moribund Democratic Policy Committee was revitalized as a board of party strategy serving to reinforce Johnson's control over the Democratic membership. An effective "intelligence service" was set up under Senate Clerk Bobby Baker to inform Johnson how every Senator could be expected to vote on a given issue. Johnson worked largely behind the scenes, preferring not to show his hand. He was adept at setting up a smoke screen of despair to lull the opposition into complacent somnolence while he actually held on to a four-vote margin, as in the successful passage of the Housing Act of 1955. He delighted in secrecy of maneuver and legislative legerdemain. Idealistic lost causes found no support, but the politics of consensus thrived. Johnson's amazing control and its use in cooperation with the Eisenhower administration led to criticism from national Democratic circles, but Johnson was able to show that such control could also defeat extremely bad legislation such as the 1958 bills attacking the Supreme Court and the entire federal judiciary system.

With the election of 1958 a large group of liberal Senators moved into the Johnson domain, yet refused to yield to the Majority Leader's threats or blandishments. The "Johnson System" fell upon unhappy days in 1959 and 1960. Johnson's efforts to trim liberal social legislation sufficiently to get it by a newly bumptious and veto-prone Eisenhower did not please the President and thoroughly displeased many Democratic Senators. As 1960 began, Lyndon Johnson again planned a presidential role for himself. He had already flirted briefly with the idea in 1952, when a deal with Richard Russell for President and himself for Vice President never got off the ground. In 1956 he was an avowed candidate, but his support was completely Southern and inadequate as well as obviously regional. Johnson also found out at the 1956 convention that the powerful princes and barons of the Senate could command few, if any, followers at a national convention. Johnson agonized so much in 1959 over the factionally torn fabric of Texas Democratic politics that his commitment finally came too late in 1960 to give his candidacy whatever chance it might have had originally. Badly beaten by the Kennedy organization, Johnson was dutifully offered the vice presidential nomination. Somewhat to the surprise of the Kennedyites, Johnson eagerly accepted.

As Vice President Johnson was quickly thwarted in his plan to exercise continued control over the Senate when his erstwhile colleagues let him know that his role in that body could no longer be anything more than the largely honorary duties his new position required. Expanding on the duties Eisenhower gave his Vice President, Kennedy assigned Johnson to the chairmanship of the Space Council, made him Chairman of the new President's Committee on Equal Employment, and gave him a staff to aid in his innovative executive duties. In foreign affairs, Kennedy also built upon the Eisenhower-Nixon idea of vice presidential assistance by assigning Johnson to an unusual 11 tours abroad, from Berlin to Senegal and from Jamaica to Saigon. In Asia, Johnson made an excellent impression on India's Nehru and sent back a report stoutly upholding the domino theory and calling for positive American action in Vietnam and Thailand. But he was not the Johnson whom friends knew as the strongest and most powerful leader of the United States Senate in its history. He had put himself under iron discipline. No word of disapproval or cavil regarding the Kennedy administration or family was permitted his staff or himself by Lyndon Johnson, even though his relations with Robert Kennedy were on the edge of disruption. Johnson had decided that his best—perhaps only—chance lay in eight years of painful subordination which might then lead to the JFK accolade as his successor. And in early November 1963 Kennedy had replied in an emphatic affirmative when asked if he wanted Johnson on the ticket with him in 1964.

The Shift in Personnel

John F. Kennedy's death had been far too traumatic for the nation and the transition too perilous for Johnson to follow Harry Truman's example of a clean sweep of White House staff and Cabinet members. Instead, he used his very considerable powers of persuasion and an unusual humility to keep many of the Kennedy advisers for a suitable period of time. Ted Sorenson, one of the top Kennedy men, was the first to leave in February 1964 in order to write a book on the Kennedy administration. Pierre Salinger, the outgoing Press Secretary, lasted only a few months longer. His place was taken by George E. Reedy, one of the few non-Texans in the Johnson circle. Reedy had been on the Washington staff of United Press International, where he had come to know Senator Johnson and admire his talent for getting things done. Another departure in the early spring of 1964 was Arthur M. Schlesinger, Jr., the historian in residence. Schlesinger had yielded to the blandishments of Johnson to stay. But in the four months he remained he received no jobs to perform, and it was evident that he had been temporarily retained solely as an assuring symbol of the ideological liberalism of the Kennedy regime. The gap in the role of White House intellectual was filled by Eric F. Goldman, the Rollins Professor of History from Princeton University. Goldman managed to remain nearly three years in a somewhat subdued capacity. The 1965 White House Festival of Arts planned by Goldman proved to be something of a liability when several participants made their antiwar stands strongly known. Observers dated Goldman's departure from the intense displeasure manifested by President Johnson after the arts episode. His place in turn was taken by John Roche of Brandeis University, a staunch supporter of the war in Vietnam.

Some of the Kennedy circle remained for several years as part of the Johnson administration. McGeorge Bundy, a prowar advocate under both Kennedy and Johnson, left in 1966. His position as Special Assistant for National Security was filled by Walt W. Rostow, Chairman of the State Department Policy Planning Council, one of the most consistently warlike advisers even from the earliest Kennedy years. Walter Heller, Chairman of the Council of Economic Advisers, successfully remained in the same capacity for several years. Adlai Stevenson, Ambassador to the United Nations, continued in that post. Although he had evidently been given to believe that he would play a more important role in the Johnson scheme of things, he was actually relegated to the extreme outer limits of the presidential circle. Although nettled by the gambit that Johnson used to persuade Kennedy men (his own staff were not quite of the same superior level, he indicated) the Johnson men quickly moved into the White House. Probably the most outstanding of Johnson's advisers, both in ability and influence, was Bill D. Moyers, a protégé since 1954. A University of Texas graduate in journalism, Moyers had studied religious history on a fellowship at the University of Edinburgh and had begun preaching in a small Texas Baptist church before he got another Johnson call to help campaign in 1960. As Executive Assistant, Moyers at 26 years of age with several years of Peace Corps experience behind him quickly became Johnson's closest adviser on policy. His duties ranged from the writing of speeches to writing of much of the Democratic platform of 1964, and from a major part in that campaign to the driving force behind much of the legislation that came to be known as the "Great Society." Moved to Press Secretary in 1965, Moyers finally left in 1966 over his increasing distaste for the Vietnamese War.

Other Texans who were a part of the White House staff were Walter W. Jenkins, Jack J. Valenti, and Horace Busby. Jenkins had a long and close relationship with Johnson and served as his trusted Chief of Staff for White House Affairs. Valenti was a young and ambitious Texan who had gone through the Harvard Business School into a partnership in a Houston advertising and public relations firm. An early and fervent admirer of Johnson, Valenti served in a variety of public relations and odd-job categories with full presidential confidence. Horace Busby, a newspaperman who had long worked for Johnson, drafted Johnson speeches and maintained commercial and congressional contacts as one of Johnson's Special Assistants.

Not on the presidential payroll but very importantly behind the scenes as advisers were Abe Fortas and Clark M. Clifford. A bright young New Deal lawyer in the Interior Department, Fortas had been Johnson's savior as attorney in the contested 87 votes of 1948. Since those days, Fortas had become an established Washington figure in the legal firm of Arnold, Fortas, and Porter. The firm's formidable list of corporate clients was balanced by a Clarence Darrow-like willingness to undertake the unpaid cause of the little man. Abe Fortas had the distinction of winning the landmark *Gideon* v. *Wainwright* case before the Supreme Court, and of being the first person Johnson called in the chaos of Dallas. Clark M. Clifford, formerly an influential Truman adviser and since then one of the best-known corporate lawyers in the country, had advised Johnson unofficially before. Both men were vastly experienced in the complex power structure of the nation's capital. Both supported the Johnson position of an escalated combat role in 1965 for Vietnam.

Both men were frequently called upon for advice in an unofficial capacity until Johnson nominated Fortas for an Associate Justiceship of the Supreme Court, and appointed Clifford to the post of the declining-in-favor McNamara as Secretary of Defense.

Within two years virtually all the Kennedy men had left the new administration and so had most of the early Johnson figures. Moyers' place was filled by the competent and influential Special Assistant Joseph A. Califano, Jr. George Reedy and Horace Busby had moved on to less man-killing posts. Walter Jenkins' arrest on a morals charge had necessitated his resignation. The turnover of these and many others marked Lyndon Johnson as probably the most demanding and most difficult employer known to Washington, a reputation going back to his earliest congressional days. A man of fiery outbursts and sadistic temper, Johnson was reputed to have given vitriolic and public tongue-lashings to all of his aides at one time or another in words, as some expressed it, "never even heard before." He expected not only a close and indiscriminate loyalty, but insisted on domination of the individuals' lives and even their wives' lives to an unparalleled extent. White House assistants were expected to be as close to the telephone and as readily responsive at 3:00 A.M. as at 9:00 A.M. or 8:00 P.M. Despite the vituperations, Johnson showed an affectionate and solicitous side to those who worked closely with him. He could make a gift of an automobile to an assistant smarting from the sharp presidential tongue, or show up unexpectedly with Ladybird at an assistant's wedding anniversary. Nevertheless, the pressures and the devouring demands Lyndon Johnson levied upon his White House staff usually outweighed other factors enough to keep its personnel in a continuous turnover. The inner circle of advisers considered themselves as "pragmatists," actually meaning they were not dogmatically either liberal or conservative. President Johnson, in the opinion of Washington observers and those of his aides who had been part of the process, was not disposed to hearing "no" from his advisers, and the nay-sayers quickly found themselves relegated to the outer extremities of the presidential advisory circle. The Johnson staff was the largest of its kind up to that point in presidential history. Despite the fact that it was generally adjudged to fill an operative and liaison role rather than a strongly advisory one, it had several members (notably Moyers and Califano) who would rank with the best of the Kennedy and Franklin Roosevelt groups.

In his Cabinet, Johnson had decided to retain Dean Rusk as Secretary of State, even though his resistance to a Kennedy détente with the Soviets was evidently behind a well-known decision to replace him after a Kennedy reelection in 1964. Rusk's prestige, coupled with a retiring and unaggressive stance, fit very well as subordinate to a strong-minded President in foreign affairs. Rusk, with a background of State Department Far East experience under John Foster Dulles, was a consistent hard-liner who almost invariably supported the Joint Chiefs of Staff and usually formed military solutions on diplomatic approaches. Increasingly, Rusk was also content to let the Department of Defense control decisions and policy where Indochina was concerned. In the popularized designations of Capitol Hill and the public, Rusk was decidedly hawkish.[1] Having State Department functions continually eroded by the Department of Defense and the President helped to bring about a noticeable decline in the prestige of Secretary Rusk, in spite of Johnson's other efforts to bolster it.

Johnson admired the efficiency with which Robert S. McNamara ran Defense matters. He remained a favorite until his long-delayed reservations about Johnsonian policy in Vietnam came to the fore, when he was displaced by presidential adviser Clark Clifford. Three Cabinet members of early Kennedy days remained until the end of the Johnson administration. Secretaries Stewart Udall of Arizona in Interior, Orville Freeman of Minnesota in Agriculture, and Willard Wirtz of Illinois in Labor all wished to remain. Their political credentials were uniformly good, and Johnson was particularly enthusiastic about the abilities of Wirtz in the Department of Labor. Douglas Dillon, the Wall Street Republican whom Kennedy chose as Secretary of the Treasury, gave notice of wishing to leave by early 1965. Henry H. Fowler, a Virginia Democrat who had been most effective in lining up business community support for several Kennedy measures, was moved up to replace him from his post as Undersecretary. Attorney General Robert F. Kennedy was the first of his brother's Cabinet to leave. Relations between Johnson and Bobby Kennedy were strained and coldly correct. When Kennedy decided to leave in September 1964 to run for the Senate in New York State, his chief deputy, Nicholas deB. Katzenbach, was named in his place. In 1966, Katzenbach moved into the State Department as Undersecretary and his place was taken by Ramsey Clark, a Texas Democrat. His father, Associate Justice Tom C. Clark, resigned from the Supreme Court in order to avoid any conflict of interest with his son in the Attorney General's post.

Secretary of Commerce went through the most changes (four) of any Cabinet position. After Luther Hodges resigned in 1965, his first successor, John T. Connor of New Jersey, remained in the post the longest—from January 1965 to February 1967. The post of Health, Education, and Welfare held by Anthony Celebrezze until his departure in 1965 was filled first by John W. Gardner, a New York Republican,

---

[1] "Hawk" and "dove" were used, in frequently an oversimplified way, for those who favored or opposed more warlike measures in Vietnam. President Johnson especially disliked the less-used "dawk," which connoted a strange bird going in both directions simultaneously.

and then by Wilbur J. Cohen, a Maryland Democrat. Two new Cabinet posts were created during the Johnson administration. A Department of Housing and Urban Development, defeated under Kennedy partly because of his potential nominee, was created in 1965. Named to the post by Johnson in January 1966 was Robert C. Weaver, whom Kennedy had been expected to nominate. Weaver, a Harvard Ph.D. and a black, became the first of his race to attain Cabinet rank. The 12th and newest Cabinet post to be created was the Department of Transportation. Approved by Congress in 1966, its first Secretary was Alan C. Boyd, a Florida Democrat.

The Early Lyndon Johnson Administration

In his emotional first address to the Congress after the funeral of John F. Kennedy, Johnson followed his predecessor's inaugural remark, "Let us begin," with an appropriate "Let us continue." He asked that Kennedy's civil rights bill and tax reduction proposal be enacted, and mentioned his long association with the Congress and his high regard for that body. Johnson knew well enough that the honeymoon period between new Presidents and Congress is relatively short, but he also knew that there were signs in the fall of 1963 that the Kennedy legislative program was beginning to move in Congress. With the tremendous emotional impact of Kennedy's death coupled with his own knowledge of congressional manipulation, he was sure that the major components of the New Frontier could reach completion. A new, suitably Johnsonian title had to be found for the program, however. The phrase which soon identified the goals of the Lyndon Johnson administration was the "Great Society," first enunciated in a speech at the University of Michigan on May 22, 1964. "The Great Society rests on abundance and liberty for all. It demands an end to poverty and racial injustice, to which we are totally committed in our time." The Great Society program was amplified and explained in more specific detail after Johnson's overwhelming victory in the elections of 1964, but his beginning on it in the first year of the presidency was an auspicious one.

Lyndon Johnson succeeded in getting passed more of the Kennedy legislative program in one year than the Kennedy administration had been able to do in nearly three years. The emotional impact of the Kennedy assassination had much to do with this success, but Johnson's knowledge of Congress and his willingness to phone and confer endlessly with Congressmen, to cajole and wheedle and threaten them, was a prime factor. Additionally, the need for much of the proposed legislation and its long delay contributed to a reservoir of willingness and reluctant acquiescence. Johnson scored his first victory only two days after the Kennedy funeral. Kennedy had eagerly responded to nibbles from the Soviet Union regarding the purchase of wheat, hoping that commercial exchanges would expedite a détente between the two powers. Offered to Congress and the public in the more palatable guise of selling off part of the huge wheat surplus, it drew the angry opposition of conservative Republicans led by Senator Karl Mundt of South Dakota, an unrelentingly hard-line anti-Communist. Mundt's group also piously disguised their viewpoint, so as not to displease their farm constituents, by attacking financing through the government Export-Import Bank. Although Mundt evidently had enough votes to block the wheat proposal originally, Johnson's insistence on pushing it to an immediate reconsideration not only drew upon all the success factors noted above, but added to these the powerful "vote of confidence" motive which contributed to a 57 to 35 defeat of the Mundt bill.

The earliest major enactment of the Kennedy carry-over program was the Revenue Act of 1964. Proposed to Congress in early 1963 on the Kennedy assumption that tax policy instead of public works could be used to promote economic growth, it called for considerable tax cuts for both individuals and corporations, coupled with tax reform measures. Although the concept of tax cuts to release consumer dollars received understandably warm support from all sides, there was little agreement over which group should get the biggest cuts. Similar controversy over the proposed tax reforms carried consideration of the bill into 1964. As it was finally signed into law on February 26, 1964, it changed the span of income tax from the previous 20 percent in the lowest brackets up to 90 percent in the highest bracket into a 16–77 percent reach for 1964 and a 14–70 percent for 1965 (as compared with the Kennedy suggestion of 14–65 percent). More taxation for the highest bracket than Kennedy recommended was necessitated by the refusal of Congress to permit offsetting reforms. Tax reforms such as a limitation on individual itemized deductions and a curtailment on unlimited charitable deductions were defeated. The attempt to plug up the loophole of a depletion allowance for the oil and gas industry was buried at the request of those corporations, and had never had Lyndon Johnson's support. Congress would not accept a proposed reduction in the capital gains rates for corporations. However, the bill tightened tax rules on stock option plans favored by the business community, and aided individuals by newly allowable deductions covering the expense of moving to a new location for work and for expenses incurred by a working taxpayer for the care of children. A corresponding lowering of the withholding rate from 18 percent to 14 percent resulted in higher paychecks beginning in early March 1964.

Kennedy had asked Congress in 1962 for federal aid to meet the increasing public demand for the improvement of mass transportation facilities. It was obvious that only government capital assistance could provide the necessary impetus in most areas, and the increasing tendency of heavily urbanized or suburbanized areas to cut across the jurisdictional lines of cities and even states made the federal government the appropriate agency. But Congress' reluctance to extend federal responsibility into still another sphere—particularly one with built-in financial losses—accounted for the measure's delay. The Urban Mass Transportation Act of 1964 avoided the pitfall of suggesting rail transportation specifically, since this had brought out the road construction, rubber, and petroleum industries in loud opposition. It remained silently neutral as to whether localities should utilize rail or bus systems, authorizing a piddling $375 million for a three-year period (less than one week's cost of the Vietnam War) in federal grants for construction, improvement, and experimentation in transit services. In this fashion it drew the support of business groups and city and state governments, and was chiefly opposed only by those objecting to government expenditures. Despite its inadequate financing, the bill had to be considered a landmark in a long-overdue examination of the scandalous conditions which put American mass transportation in a third-rate category among the world's industrialized nations.

Poverty in the United States was officially discovered only in the 1960s. Kennedy came face to face with it campaigning in the Appalachian region of West Virginia, and was strongly influenced by Michael Harrington's moving *The Other America*. But it remained for Lyndon Johnson to declare a "War on Poverty" and make it the most highly publicized portion of his Great Society program. Johnson's very considerable legislative triumph in this regard was in the passage of the Economic Opportunity Act of 1964. Although it included several components offered before by Kennedy and defeated, and again received heavy Republican opposition (Senate, 22 to 10 against; House, 145 to 22) it was signed into law in August by the President. It set up the Office of Economic Opportunity within the Executive Office, to which Johnson named John Kennedy's brother-in-law R. Sargent Shriver, Jr., formerly in charge of the Peace Corps, as its head. One of the act's provisions set up a Job Corps, based upon earlier Youth Conservation Corps proposals and with historic origins in the New Deal's Civilian Conservation Corps. Young men and women from 16 to 21 could enroll in training centers in both rural and urban areas to receive education, vocational training, and useful work experience. Forty percent of the corpsmen were to be assigned to conservation projects, and all would be paid living and travel allowances and $50 per month.

Title VI of the Economic Opportunity Act of 1964 provided for a special group of workers organized around the suitable acronym of VISTA (Volunteers in Service to America). This section of the act envisioned trained workers assisting state and local programs in providing community services to rural and urban poor, Indians, migratory workers, and other disadvantaged groups. Based upon previous proposals such as the 1963 National Service Corps and intended as a domestic counterpart of the Peace Corps, it carried—at Southern Congressmen's insistence—a stipulation that VISTA recruits would not be referred to any state without the consent of its Governor. Most innovative and controversial portion of the act was Title II, the Community Action Programs. This attempted to set up community programs to develop employment opportunities and improve performance and motivation by involving "maximum participation" by the poor themselves. This directly threatened local politicians who saw their power being diminished, and to a lesser extent provoked the opposition of professional social workers and city officials over this "amateur" invasion of their domain. Attempts by the poor to gain a voice in antipoverty councils or other city organizations alarmed officialdom, and the mandate for "participation" was soon emasculated. The Economic Opportunity Act had no effect on large segments of the poor such as the sick and aged, the handicapped, or the families abandoned by a wage-earning father. Its funding at $800 million, or about 10 percent of the annual cost of the Vietnam War, was criticized as more fitting for a minor skirmish than a major war against poverty. Nevertheless, it constituted a new departure for governmental action and focused attention upon a heretofore unadmitted and unadmissible problem of American society.

In 1963 civil rights legislation, on which Kennedy had deliberately withheld action so as to have southern support for other bills, could no longer be put off. The issue of black rights produced a national domestic crisis in the United States, evidenced by a series of well-organized black demonstrations and boycotts throughout the country. Kennedy had introduced a bill in early 1963 limited largely to protection of voting rights and authorization of federal assistance to areas desegregating their schools. By June, however, the bill was broadened to include allowing federal programs to be cut off in areas of discrimination, and also provisions for bringing government suits to desegregate schools, guaranteeing blacks access to public accommodations. Blocked by Chairman Howard W. ("Judge") Smith (D. Va.) of the House Rules Committee in November, it was the topic of President Johnson's first address to Congress following Kennedy's assassination. "No memorial oration or eulogy could more eloquently honor President Kennedy's memory than the earliest possible passage of the civil rights bill for which he fought so long," Johnson said.

The Civil Rights Act of 1964 made dramatic history, not only for its lengthy debate but because the Senate for the first time finally voted to end a filibuster over civil rights. The bill could not have been passed without partisan Republican support. The bill's proponents were organized in their tactics and in their grouping into shifts for floor debate and voting, as the Southern civil rights opponents had always been in the past. In the House of Representatives, nearly all of the 122 amendments offered by the bill's opponents were rejected. In the Senate, the bill's supporters surprisingly were able to put the legislation on the calendar rather than be required to route it through the notably anti–civil rights chairman of the Judiciary Committee, Senator Eastland of Mississippi. After 74 days before the Senate, during which only minor modifications were added, a vote of 71 to 29 sustained cloture (closing off further debate). The House quickly adopted the Senate version, and President Johnson signed the Civil Rights Act of 1964 into law on July 2. A sign of the changing times was reflected in the general election of 1964 several months later. None of the 12 Southern Democrats who dared to vote *for* the bill was defeated although one third of the Republicans who had opposed the bill in the House *were* defeated for reelection.

The most far-reaching civil rights legislation since the Reconstruction period, the act in some instances went even further than the 1963 proposals. Blacks were specifically guaranteed access to such public accommodations as hotels, motels, restaurants and places of amusement. In addition to authorizing the federal government to sue to desegregate public facilities and schools, the Justice Department was also given permission to enter pending civil rights cases. Provisions to protect blacks' right to vote and to cut off federal funds of discriminatory programs were included. Most companies and unions were required to grant equal employment opportunity. The Civil Rights Commission received new powers and its life was extended by four years. The act also called for the establishment of a Community Relations Service to help areas work out their civil rights problems, and Johnson appointed the moderate ex-Governor of Florida, LeRoy Collins, to head the new bureau. The new law itself was well received throughout the South, even though tensions in race relations continued to account for tragedies.[2]

Lyndon Johnson had other lesser successes and a few disappointments, both in and out of Congress, in his first year of office. A Kennedy foreign aid bill had been passed by the Senate but was hung up in the House. The amount was batted down from a requested $4.5 billion to $3.3 billion, then down to $3.0 billion and back up to $3.6 billion. But the obstinacy and inaction of the House were seen as a dire threat to his reputation by Johnson. All absentee Congressmen were ordered

---

[2] Indicative of the strong feelings that existed was the remark of the militant leader of SNCC, Stokely Carmichael, regarding passage of the Civil Rights Act, "This is a white man's bill. I knew as a human being that I had those rights all the time."

by the Speaker to get back for a December 24 vote, and Johnson gave an eggnog party for all on the night before. The vote next day was a satisfying 189 to 158 for passage. The margin of victory evidently did not come from the fraternally offered eggnog so much as it did from Johnson's dispatching military jets to transport those Democrats who could be counted on to vote for the bill, although the press continued to carry stories on the Johnson congressional wizardry. He was not able to get Medicare proposals past Chairman Wilbur Means of the House Ways and Means Committee or to gain House approval of a bill to relieve the poverty-stricken area of Appalachia, however. Without a Vice President, Johnson was also more concerned than usual about legislation covering presidential succession. But any attempt to circumvent 72-year-old House Speaker McCormack, who was the legal successor at the time, would evidently have been considered an affront, so it was silently postponed.

Johnson was able to score a public success in his first year on the knotty problem of a railroad strike. In April the railroad unions struck the Illinois Central. The basic problem was technological job displacement, with the railroads dead set against further featherbedding. The unions sought desperately for job security, but also pointed out that the railroads must assume some of the social costs of technological progress rather than put the entire burden on the displaced individual. Johnson pried an additional 15 days out of the two antagonists and then closeted them in the White House where he could give them an occasional pep talk and use his admitted powers of personal and official persuasion. With only hours to go before a national strike deadline, the unions accepted an agreement which would eliminate firemen on freight diesel locomotives, but only through normal attrition means. The railroads, assured by Johnson that their unrelated complaints regarding freight rate regulation and tax depreciation would receive sympathetic treatment, acceded. A triumphal Johnson spread the good word immediately to the nation by television.

A considerable minus rather than a plus went on the presidential balance sheet with the development of a scandal over an erstwhile Johnson protégé. The individual involved was Robert G. (Bobby) Baker, a cocky young South Carolinian whom Johnson moved up from a page boy to the powerful office of Senate Democratic Secretary and who ran the knowledgeable, if unofficial, Senate "intelligence" bureau. The Senate Rules Committee turned up evidence of insurance policies and advertising peddled through Baker to Senate figures, where handsome "kickbacks" were the rule. Testimony before the committee concerned the mysterious ways in which Baker's $19,612 salary was transmuted into a reputed $2 million fortune, and led through a tangle of bank loans, concessions, and land and real estate deals. Johnson denied any improper connection regarding his insurance policies or his television properties, and the committee report revealed a feeble follow-up. Voters, according to polls, did not consider the Bobby Baker case a serious liability for presidential contender Lyndon B. Johnson in the fall of 1964. He had evidently piled up such a substantial number of pluses that other polls revealed no other contender close to him for reelection to the presidency.

The Election of 1964

Planning for the presidential race in November quietly began very early in the year. Abe Fortas, Clark Clifford, and Jim Rowe, a former FDR aide and now also a powerful Washington attorney, remained Johnson's chief advisers. Although their experience in political campaigns was slight, their advice on presidential imagery and strategy was both cogent and influential. The Washington press, which was well aware of Johnson's reputation for bad temper and irascibility, was assiduously wooed with everything from a garden party on the White House lawn for their wives and children to a series of intimate, news-relaying breakfasts and luncheons. The public received a series of impressions intended to show Johnson as a friendly, average, man-in-the-street American. This portion of the image campaign had to overcome an early setback when Johnson during a walk with reporters, picked up his pet beagles by the ears, drawing yelps from the presidential dogs and outraged cries from dog lovers. But this was soon erased. Johnson repeatedly accosted tourists through the White House gates, chatting with them in folksy style. Frequently they were invited for walks with the President, much to Secret Service dismay. They were also invited to personally conducted tours through the White House, which was referred to as *"your* house."

White House incidents gave the public a picture of Johnson the economizer. Early in the year the President had ordered that the lights be turned off in the presidential residence when not actually in use, thereby saving an alleged "couple of thousand dollars a month." While some outcries deplored the loss of the nighttime beauty of a national building, a surprising number of somewhat defensive letters to newspaper editors spoke approvingly of "the principle of the thing" as an economy measure. Critics spoke of the new LBJ as "Light Bulb" Johnson. Continuing the personal economy, Johnson announced that he had ordered the Pentagon to reduce the number of official limousines to ten.[3]

The political polls of spring, private and public, showed Johnson

---

[3] One enterprising reporter checked with the Pentagon and found that the number of limousines assigned to officials before the presidential order was also ten. (Cited in Alfred Steinberg, *Sam Johnson's Boy* (New York: 1968, p. 669.)

far out in front of any of the Republican hopefuls. They also revealed that, regardless of which Democrat his name might be coupled with on a national ticket, his lead was not measureably affected. It meant that Johnson could easily choose whomever he wished. The big barrier here was the Kennedy heritage, boldly personified by Attorney General Robert F. Kennedy. Although the two had worked closely together on the Civil Rights Act, the Johnson forces never lost their uneasiness over a possible Kennedy putsch. An unresolvable personality clash also effectively precluded Bobby Kennedy as a Johnson choice. Johnson supporters sought quietly to have delegates to the national convention sign a pledge that Johnson would have "a free choice" to name his own running mate. Although most potential delegates acknowledged that this generally happened in practice, enough of them objected to a blank-check release from their selection function to scuttle the pledge.

Secret emissaries suggesting a Kennedy withdrawal statement were received with indignant refusals. Johnson's advisers then suggested a personal confrontation with Kennedy and a candid admission that he could not be the President's choice. The public later received the rather transparent decision of Johnson that no member of his Cabinet "or those meeting regularly with the Cabinet" could be spared for vice presidential duties, thereby knocking out such dark horses as Adlai Stevenson and Sargent Shriver along with Bobby Kennedy. Johnson's old friend, Senator Hubert Humphrey of Minnesota, thereupon became the leading candidate, although Johnson chose to play a cat-and-mouse game until the last moment. At the Democratic convention in Atlantic City in August, Johnson and Humphrey were duly nominated. More notable were the black Mississippi witnesses before the Credentials Committee telling of the beatings they had suffered in their attempts to register and vote. The Freedom Democratic party, as the largely black delegates from Mississippi called themselves, insisted that they be accepted instead of the regular lily-white delegation. As a painful compromise between legality and morality, the committee accepted two of the Freedom party as voting delegates. It also required the Mississippi delegation to pledge allegiance to the national ticket and further stated that in 1968 and thereafter no delegations would be accepted from states with racist practices. The walkout of Mississippi and Alabama constituted the final, small, rear-guard action of now largely acquiescent Southern states to the fact of desegregation.

The foremost Republican machine to begin cranking up for 1964 immediately after the paper-thin defeat of 1960 was the well-organized group of staff members and supporters of Nelson A. Rockefeller, popular Governor of New York State. Rockefeller had proved himself a very capable administrator. A man of high principle, the Governor and his family supported black education and the causes of Dr. Martin Luther

King by their donations. A hard-line militarist in foreign policy, Rockefeller had nevertheless supported the United Nations and the Test Ban Treaty in the best tradition of Eastern Establishment republicanism. Rockefeller's divorce in 1961 had not hurt him; he had retained the gubernatorial chair in 1962 by more than half a million votes. His candidacy was formidable until his remarriage in 1963 to Margaretta "Happy" Murphy, a divorcee volunteer member of the Rockefeller political organization. Not only was the remarriage disliked by many, but the fact that the Murphy children remained with the father as the price for a divorce made the situation more difficult politically. Even the Hudson River Presbytery censured the pastor who performed the Rockefeller marriage. From a commanding lead, polls soon showed a bad slip to second place behind Senator Goldwater of Arizona.

Barry M. Goldwater, the son of a Jewish pioneer and a Protestant mother, grew up and prospered in the booming frontier economy and phenomenal growth of Phoenix. Within the Republican party's conservatism, Goldwater's 19th century economic individualism and Social Darwinism could only be accounted as ultraconservatism. Such beliefs were attractive to many, including political amateurs, who resented what they called the "me, too" line of many losing eastern Establishment Republican candidates. The Nixon-Rockefeller pact and the "advanced" 1960 platform which stemmed from it was the focus for an early drive undertaken by the frustrated primitive elements of the Republican party. This movement selected Goldwater even before he finally announced his candidacy in January 1964, and had begun lining up delegates in 1963.

Failure to take the Goldwater candidacy seriously and the large early lead taken by Rockefeller combined to narrow the field of Republican aspirants. Governor George W. Romney of Michigan had attempted some national image-making in the late 1963, but little or no support materialized. Richard M. Nixon, stigmatized by a 1962 defeat for Governor of California on top of his narrow loss to Kennedy two years before, sought desperately to stay as neutral as possible in the hope that a deadlocked convention would turn to him once again. Governor William W. Scranton of Pennsylvania, dismayed that Goldwater's vote against the Civil Rights Act of 1964 would portray the party of Lincoln as an anti-black party, made a late and futile stop-Goldwater movement. The only other possibility was Henry Cabot Lodge of Massachusetts, who was urged to come home from his post as Ambassador to South Vietnam by General Eisenhower. But the General had obdurately refused his public endorsement to any Republican candidate and, after an early primary victory in his native New England, the Lodge campaign had wound down.

Goldwater's win in California had actually put him over the top in pledged delegates, since his supporters had already gathered up most of the Southern votes and delegates from those many states which did not hold primaries. At the Cow Palace in San Francisco, Goldwater received more than the 655 votes needed for nomination before the roll call was even completed the first time. He promptly named as his choice of a vice presidential nominee, the ultraconservative Representative William E. Miller of Buffalo, New York. Allegedly an infighting debater of great prowess, Goldwater stated that one of the foremost reasons for Miller's choice was "he drives Johnson nuts." In his acceptance speech Goldwater struck hard at the more moderate and liberal wings of his own party and set the tone for his forthcoming crusade: "Extremism in the defense of liberty is no vice! . . . Moderation in the pursuit of justice is no virtue!" Goldwater's "extremism" was to plague him throughout the campaign and would drive many of his party into the camp of his Democratic adversary.

Governor George C. Wallace of Alabama began in the primaries as though a three-cornered presidential race might take place. Wallace's appeal was a simple anti–civil rights (meaning anti-black) bigotry, and his calls for "law 'n order" and denunciations of "violence in the streets" were readily decoded as opposition to the black demonstrations over civil rights issues. In the spring primaries, Wallace successfully demonstrated the racism and insecurity latent in the blue-collar working class areas of the industrial North. The Alabama Governor had piled up 34 percent and 30 percent respectively in Wisconsin and Indiana, with strong support from Polish, Italian, and other ethnic groups. But with Goldwater's strong stand against the Civil Rights Act, Wallace's backers convinced their man in July that he must withdraw rather than draw upon Southern votes that would otherwise surely go to the Republican favorite.

In the campaign, Goldwater insisted on polarizing as many voters as possible rather than pitching his appeal to the broad middle spectrum. He attacked TVA in Tennessee and Social Security before the oldsters of Saint Petersburg, Florida. He admitted he knew nothing of farm problems, but insisted that farm subsidies must come to a complete halt. A 1961 remark was revived, when the Chicago Tribune quoted him as saying that the country would be better off if "we could just saw off the Eastern seaboard and let it float out to sea." In foreign policy, Goldwater sometimes presented a terrifying image. His 1962 publication, *Why Not Victory?*, took an extremely casual air regarding the use of nuclear weapons, and the Senator later advocated giving American generals the field control over their use. He was also tagged with previous militaristic remarks, such as stating before the assembled Military Order of the World Wars in reference to the Pentagon situation, "I say, fear the civilians—they're taking over." In the campaign, his concept of the American world mission was simplistically and belligerently stated as "the removal of Communists from power wherever they hold it."

In August the Goldwater supporters attempted their only effort at uniting all wings of the party with a meeting near the Eisenhower home, accompanied by statements from Goldwater that he as candidate accepted the Eisenhower-Lodge foreign policy concepts. He also pledged support for Social Security and promised not to read out of the party those who were not fully committed to him. But the unity was short lived and, in any case, ineffective. Not only his campaign utterances, but statements in his essay *The Conscience of a Conservative,* and previous remarks as a Senator combined to form a negative public image. As the campaign progressed, more and more Republicans openly refused their endorsement or made it clear that their support was purely nominal.

With Goldwater as a target, Johnson's task was the relatively simple one of ensuring that everything his opponent said was promptly used against him. An early threat to the Democratic candidacy were the black ghetto riots. The simmering economic and social conditions of the inner-city black slums—removed even from areas of more prosperous black residency—erupted in the hot summer of 1964 with terrifying suddenness. Triggered frequently by a police assault on an individual black, or by the rumors of such a happening, riots began in New York's Harlem and Brooklyn and spread through New Jersey ghettoes in Jersey City, Elizabeth, and Paterson, and on into Philadelphia in a chaotic orgy of window smashing and looting of stores. However, Johnson acted immediately with a variety of investigative pressures, financial threats, and political persuasion. Black civil rights leaders were told to use their influence to help channel the destructiveness of black social and economic resentment into constructive political registration drives, and the black slum areas gradually quieted. Democrats greatly feared a "backlash" supposedly generated among white voters by the riots and civil rights advances, but the feeling was evidently not as intense or as enduring as observers had thought.

Republicans hopefully believed they had an issue for an attack upon administration corruption and credibility when Walter Jenkins, Johnson's chief assistant on domestic affairs and an old associate, was arrested in October on a morals charge. But on October 15 Soviet Premier Nikita Khrushchev was removed from office, and on October 16 the Peoples' Republic of China exploded a high-intensity nuclear device. The Jenkins affair was quickly relegated to the back pages in favor of foreign policy matters. Here Johnson confined himself to vague commitments to peace—for strong defenses, yet with a willingness to negotiate with the Soviet Union on international affairs. Vietnam—soon to become the overriding issue—was seldom even mentioned, although the public impression of a peaceful and quiescent Johnson was in stark contrast with a belligerent and militaristic Goldwater.

On November 3, 1964, Lyndon Johnson could truly lay claim to the previously joking nickname of "Landslide Lyndon." By the tremendous margin of 61 percent of the total vote, and with 43 million votes arrayed against Goldwater's 27 million, Johnson had registered the greatest percentage as well as the greatest margin of victory ever received by an American president. Goldwater had carried only the Deep South states of Mississippi, Alabama, Louisiana, Georgia, and South Carolina, and had narrowly won in his home state of Arizona. All the rest went to Johnson, with percentages ranging from Hawaii's 79 percent and New England's average 71 percent to 57 percent in normally Republican Kansas, Iowa, and Nebraska.[4] Congressional results were equally disastrous for the Republicans. Those who had divorced themselves from Goldwater were usually successful, while his warmest congressional supporters suffered numerous defeats. The only exception was in the Deep South, where Republicans elected five Representatives from Alabama and one each from Georgia and Mississippi. In the Senate, the balance was to be 68 Democrats and 32 Republicans. The House of Representatives, with 295 Democrats versus 140 Republicans, had the lowest Republican level since 1936.

The election returns readily settled the claim that a great "silent vote" was available to the first ultraconservative who offered a "clear choice." Certainly Senator Goldwater had a hard-core band whose devotion to primitive principles transcended any partisan or political gain, but their numbers were not significant at the national level. What was more noteworthy in the history of presidential elections and partisan politics was the sharp break with precedent made by the Goldwater forces. The election of 1964 was an unusual one and a critical one because of the departure of a major party from the broad, mainstream political current to a position hugging the right bank. This broke the rules that politicians had observed for several generations, with resounding and perhaps predictable results. The chief innovation of the 1964 election was the technological introduction of the Network Election Service by the combined forces of the three major broadcasting chains and the Associated Press and United Press International. These vote-counting resources, aided by computerized vote analysis, were able to give the television viewer a projection of the total vote based on small fractional returns that proved uncannily accurate. Most importantly for the immediate future, the election carried in such a wave of Democrats as to erode seriously the Southern Democrat-Western Republican con-

---

[4] Johnson won 44 states and the District of Columbia, which was voting for the first time for President as a result of the 23d Amendment, for 486 electoral votes against Goldwater's 52.

servative coalition and opened the gates to a reservoir of social legislation that had been penned up for years and even decades.

Suggestions for Reading

All of the works on Kennedy cited in the preceding chapter are applicable. To these should be added T. C. Sorenson, *The Kennedy Legacy* (1969). Additional monographs are Grant McConnell, *Steel and the Presidency—1962* (1963), and J. F. Heath, *John F. Kennedy and the Business Community* (1969).

On Kennedy's assassination, see *A Concise Compendium of the Warren Commission Report* (1964). The Warren Commission's findings are disputed in E. J. Epstein, *Inquest: The Warren Commission and the Establishment of Truth* (1966), and Mark Lane, *Rush to Judgment* (1966). An exhaustive analysis is presented in Albert H. Newman, *The Assassination of John F. Kennedy: The Reasons Why* (1970). A detailed recreation of the event is William Manchester, *Death of a President* (1967).

Lyndon Johnson's own memoirs of the presidency as he saw it are in *The Vantage Point: Perspectives of the Presidency: 1963–1969* (1971). The Johnson administration as seen by a White House adviser and historian is E. F. Goldman, *The Tragedy of Lyndon Johnson* (1968). Louis Heren, *No Hail, No Farewell* (1970) is the same period seen through the eyes of a British correspondent. An early look is Rowland Evans, Jr. and Robert Novak, *Lyndon B. Johnson: The Exercise of Power** (1966). See also Hugh Sidey, *A Very Personal Presidency: Lyndon Johnson in the White House* (1968). An excellent collection is M. E. Gettleman and David Mermelstein, eds., *The Great Society Reader** (1967). Two works by former Johnson staff members are George Reedy, *The Twilight of the Presidency** (1970), and Harry McPherson, *A Political Education* (1972). A critical biographical study is Alfred Steinberg, *Sam Johnson's Boy* (1968). Revealing looks at Johnson as Vice President are in Tom Wicker, *JFK and LBJ** (1968), and Leonard Baker, *The Johnson Eclipse* (1970).

An early work on Johnson's foreign policy is P. L. Geyelin, *Lyndon B. Johnson and the World* (1966). Critical and perceptive are Theodore Draper, *Abuse of Power** (1967), and J. W. Fulbright, *The Arrogance of Power** (1967). For the Dominican intervention, see Theodore Draper, *The Dominican Revolt* (1971); Jerome Slater, *Intervention and Negotiation* (1970); and A. L. Lowenthal, *The Dominican Intervention* (1972). The ambassador has written his own account in J. B. Martin, *Overtaken by Events* (1966).

A number of works are valuable for understanding the Warren Court and its significant decisions of the 1960s. An outstanding anthology is R. H. Sayler et al., eds., *The Warren Court* (1968). Excellent on the Chief Justice is J. D. Weaver, *Warren: The Man, The Court, The Era* (1968). See also Leo Katcher, *Earl Warren: A Political Biography* (1967). The constitutional approach is explored in A. M. Bickel, *The Supreme Court and the Idea of Progress* (1970); P. B. Kurland, *Politics, the Constitution, and the Warren Court* (1970); and Archibald Cox, *The Warren Court: Constitutional*

Decision as an Instrument of Reform (1968). See also C. H. Pritchett, *The Political Offender and the Warren Court* (1969), and R. C. Catner, *The Apportionment Cases* (1966).

For the election of 1964, see the detailed account by T. H. White, *The Making of the President 1964* (1965) and a good anthology, Harold Faber, ed., *The Road to the White House* (1965). See also R. J. Huchshorn, *Republican Politics: The 1964 Campaign and its Aftermath for the Party* (1968), and R. H. Rovere, *The Goldwater Caper* (1965).

7

The LBJ Brand

The Great Society

THE SECOND State of the Union message that Lyndon Johnson delivered before the packed chambers of the House of Representatives on January 4, 1965, differed somewhat in tone from his first such effort of 1964. No longer was Johnson in the position of pressuring legislators to enact a Kennedy program with the momentum of a tragic assassination. Now Johnson was requesting that the remaining Kennedy items and his own emphasis on the War on Poverty be carried through without delay. To this he added an expanded aid-to-education program. The phrasing and tone were self-confident, assured; and the momentum now came from the stunning margin of 15 million victory votes.

Johnson's message to the new 89th Congress was replete with the politics of consensus which was to be a hallmark of the LBJ efforts, and Congressmen were lauded with a variety of buttery phrases. But they also were given a relatively long list of legislative matters, and they were under no illusion regarding the action that was expected of them. There were an amazing 91 new members in the House, of whom 71 were Democrats. In general, they were young and eager to take a hand in the social welfare legislation that had been piled up for a number of frustrating years. Even the formulas for making up the usually conservative Rules and Ways and Means committees in the House were liberalized by the exuberant new membership, putting larger numbers of the majority Democrats on these frequently obstacle-like committees. Coupled with another change which gave the Speaker the power to call out of the still stubborn Virginian "Judge" Smith's Rules

Committee any bill it had not acted on after 21 days, the House in the 89th Congress stood ready to act as quickly as the Senate.

The themes that came through most clearly from the President were health, classrooms, cities, and conservation. Medicare, perhaps the most important of these and initiated by Kennedy, reached the Congress immediately after the State of the Union address in early January. The administration bill was the relatively simple provision for the mandatory hospital care of those 65 and over through Social Security, such as had been regularly defeated ever since Truman's time. The opposing American Medical Association, sensing the flood tide favoring some such concept, introduced its own bill covering doctors' services as well, but requiring individuals to finance the entire program through private insurance companies. The Republicans also introduced a bill which would provide supplemental care, but still clung to the voluntary concept and financing through insurance companies. By putting together some features of each of the three proposals, Congress effectively undercut the negative lobbying of the AMA and actually broadened the scope of the legislation considerably beyond the Johnson administration's hopes. Medicare, as finally passed in July 1965, was kept entirely under Social Security and was to be financed by a slightly larger deduction to be placed in a separate fund. All persons 65 or over were eligible for up to 90 days of hospital care and 100 days of posthospital nursing-home care, with small deductible amounts. Supplementary benefits, which were voluntary and cost the individual $3 per month, would cover 80 percent of doctors' services. In the same bill, Social Security benefits were also increased by 7 percent.

In the field of health, Congress enacted the major part of the President's proposals. These included authorizations for federal grants establishing regional medical programs for an attack upon heart diseases, cancer, and strokes; renewals of federal grants for community mental health centers; and expansions of programs for health research facilities and scholarship aid for needy medical students. The Medical Library Assistance Act provided matching grants for the building of medical library facilities and for the expansion of such services. Congress also posted a first with a weak Cigarette Labeling and Advertising Act requiring a cautionary statement on the health hazards of cigarette smoking to be stated on the package. But inasmuch as the bill preempted infinitely more stringent regulations set up by the Federal Trade Commission (which would have required health hazard warnings in *all* advertising media), the legislation was appropriately considered a victory for the tobacco industry's lobbying. Nonetheless, it was a precedent-setting act which was to bear further legislative and regulative fruit.

Johnson was fond of referring to himself, with excellent grounds, as the "health and education President." In the latter area, he scored a major triumph with federal aid for elementary and secondary schools. Because most private, parochial schools were religious in nature—chiefly Catholic—previous efforts had foundered on the separation of church and state issue. A new formula centered around the child-benefit rather than the school-benefit thrust of a 1947 Supreme Court decision.[1] When this was combined with the recent and popular antipoverty impulse, the successful untangling of a decades-old Gordian knot had been found. Drawn up under Lyndon Johnson's watchfully paternal eyes, the Elementary and Secondary Education Act of 1965 went to Capitol Hill with alleged instructions "not to change a single comma." It was passed with very little more than such a change, despite the attempts of conservatives who objected both to the expenditure of funds and to the increasing role of the federal government. So well laid was the new basis for the legislation that debate was largely limited instead to the formula for providing the aid. The bill was designed to aid school districts with impoverished children, which was thought to mean between 90 to 95 percent of the nation's counties. Funds would go through the states to the school districts and school boards on the basis of the number of children from low-income families times 50 percent of the state average expenditure per school child. This was objected to because it would give wealthier states a larger share of the funds, but the administration supporters argued successfully that it would give such areas as the South and Appalachia larger percentage increases even if not in absolute figures. Additionally, it was pointed out, the percentage formula better took into account the wide disparity among the states in the cost of education.

By abandoning the traditional approach of direct aid and aiming instead at districts with low-income families, the Elementary and Secondary Education Act became the first general school aid legislation in the nation's history. Private schools, whether religious or not, benefitted from this approach in several ways. They were able to participate in "shared-time" projects wherein special subjects were taught to combined public-private school audiences, and in educational television usage. Title II of the bill provided authorization for purchases of textbooks and library materials which also could be loaned to private and parochial schools.

Hard on the heels of elementary and secondary education legislation came the Higher Education Act of 1965, which put great emphasis on scholarship aid for needy students. The act authorized federal scholarships and also encouraged loans for scholarships from state or private

---

[1] *Everson* v. *Ewing Township,* which upheld the constitutionality of a New Jersey law providing state bus transportation for parochial schoolchildren because the benefit went to the individual child rather than the school.

sources by subsidizing the interest costs. Funds were authorized to improve the academic quality of developing institutions—mainly small black colleges—and additional funds were made available for general classroom construction. The most controversial part of the bill was the Teacher Corps, first proposed by Senators Edward M. Kennedy of Massachusetts and Gaylord Nelson of Wisconsin. Under Title V of the act, a corps of skilled teachers and young apprentice teachers could be assigned to improve education in slum schools through federally financed scholarships. Congress also passed in 1965 an act establishing a National Foundation on the Arts and the Humanities. Long opposed in Congress, the act finally set up a counterpart to the Science Foundation to develop for the first time a national policy supporting the arts and humane letters. Although President Johnson had labeled the efforts of 1963 as the "Education Congress," the title more appropriately belonged to the 89th Congress of 1965–1966 for its significant breakthroughs in the elementary and secondary educational areas and its innovations and expansions in higher education.

Johnson's large Democratic majority accounted for major advances in the area of public housing. Late in 1965 Congress approved as a new Cabinet position the establishment of a Secretary of Housing and Urban Development (HUD). Introduced and defeated several times under Kennedy, the growing problem of urban deterioration and inadequate housing had attracted increasing attention and support. The new position absorbed the Home Finance Agency, whose administrator, Robert C. Weaver, became the nation's first black Cabinet member on assuming the new secretaryship in 1966. The Housing Act of 1965 was easily the most far-reaching legislation in the field of housing and urban development since the Housing Act of 1949 under Harry Truman. The bill expanded and extended urban renewal programs and provided grants covering the major cost of community health and recreation centers. Municipalities were given funds for urban beautification and low-income homeowners could get grants for home repair and improvement. The most innovative feature drew the most opposition. This was the rent supplement provision, based upon the principle that public housing was not only insufficient to meet the demand, but that its concentration of solely low-income families might germinate additional ghettoes. Under the act, those families who qualified for public housing and who had been displaced by governmental action (urban renewal, highway construction, etc.) or were living in "substandard housing" or were elderly or handicapped were eligible. They could seek private, standard housing, where the government would subsidize that portion of the rent in excess of 25 percent of the individual's income. (For example, if the income was $400 per month and the rent came to $125 per month, the federal subsidy paid to the renter—not the rentee—would be $25 per month.)

The supplement provision was also expected to stimulate construction of private housing.

The Great Society emphasis upon the poor and on urban aid was equally visible in the Demonstration Cities and Metropolitan Development Act of 1966, better known as the "model cities" act. The model cities approach sought to go beyond the traditional physical treatment of slum building removal by combining with it antipoverty and educational projects. The aim was to tackle social as well as the physical problems of blighted areas and change thereby the total environment of previously slum sites. Only a relatively few cities could qualify under the rigid standards, and their own contributions would then receive matching federal grants.

Many members of the clergy joined with blacks and students in the voting protest march from Selma, Alabama, to the capital at Montgomery, March 21, 1965. It was soon broken up by Alabama state troopers. (Wide World Photos)

Despite the advances made under the Civil Rights Act of 1964, the black right to vote in the Deep South was still largely denied by racist sheriffs and voting registration officials. To illustrate this predicament to the nation, Dr. Martin Luther King chose Selma (Dallas County), Alabama. In the county, 14,400 whites and 15,115 blacks were eligible to vote, but those successfully registered to vote included 9,542 whites and only 335 blacks. Registration was permitted only two days monthly, and the applicant was required to fill in more than 50 blanks, write from dictation a part of the Constitution, etc., etc. King organized nonviolent demonstrations and marches in January and February 1965, and the nation's temper was aroused when Wallace's state troopers clubbed and gassed demonstrators. Police shot and killed one black, and in March white thugs clubbed to death Reverend James Reeb of Boston, one of the many ministers of all faiths who rallied to the black cause at Selma. Governor Wallace reneged on his promise to give the Selma-to-Montgomery marchers protection, and President Johnson swiftly nationalized the Alabama National Guard. On March 25, the last day of the march, four Ku Klux Klan members shot and killed Mrs. Viola Liuzzo of Detroit, a volunteer civil rights worker.

A tidal wave of national indignation mounted against Governor George Wallace, the fatal brutalities, and the Selma practices. The administration quickly submitted to Congress the Voting Rights Act of 1965, which provided for direct federal action to enable blacks to register and vote. The act, finally signed into law in August, gave the Attorney General the power to appoint federal registration officials where voter activity had fallen below certain specified levels. These areas included Alabama, Georgia, Louisiana, Mississippi, South Carolina, Virginia, 28 counties in North Carolina, and miscellaneous counties in several far western states. Literacy tests and similar qualifying devices were suspended, and criminal penalties were provided for interference with voter rights. Allied with this measure was the passing of the later Civil Rights Protection Act of 1968. Originally designed to lend protection to civil rights workers and to those exercising their right to vote or work or use public accommodations, an amendment turned it into the first open-housing act of the 20th century. As enacted into law, it prohibited discrimination in the sale or rental of housing and was aimed at covering some 80 percent of all housing within two years of its passage. Favorable action on the bill came as somewhat of a surprise, but the assassination of Dr. Martin Luther King on April 4 and the subsequent rioting in more than 100 cities evidently had an effect on the final voting.

Lyndon Johnson was chiefly responsible for a major reorientation in American national values. He had written a book, *A Nation of Immigrants,* in which he took up the cudgels for doing away with the racist basis which had dominated American immigration laws and quotas since post–World War I. These new concepts were incorporated in the Immigration and Nationality Act of 1965 and virtually pushed through Congress by the President's insistence. Instead of country by country quotas, largely based on racial superiority concepts favoring Northern European nations at the expense of southern European and Mediterranean countries, the Johnson reform act merely set overall quotas for the Western Hemisphere and for the rest of the world. Productive skills were emphasized. Immigrant totals were raised somewhat, and provisions were broadened for relatives of persons living in the United States.

President Johnson's impatient prodding of Congress produced a variety of other legislation. One of the earlier bills passed in 1965 was Johnson's own first reform measure, the Appalachian Regional Development Act, aimed at aiding this economically depressed area to emerge from its backwardness and poverty. The area covered included portions of Georgia and Alabama northward through a large part of Pennsylvania and a dozen counties in southern New York (West Virginia was the only state entirely covered). More than $1 million was authorized in federal funds to be used to provide the primary facilities needed—principally roads and health and vocational aids—for a basic expansion of the subnormal economy of the region. The Public Works and Economic Development Act of the same year extended this concept to other depressed areas.

Congress attempted to reduce consumer prices and further stimulate the economy by repealing $4.5 billion in excise taxes. In 1966 the growing popularity of consumer support resulted in the beginning of safeguards against deceptive packaging and labeling practices. More controversial were the Traffic Safety Act and the Highway Safety Act. These were enacted after much crusading spadework by Ralph Nader, a young Connecticut lawyer who had served as a Department of Labor consultant. Impetus for the bills' passage came with the disclosure of General Motors' private detective harassment of Nader. A new Cabinet post, the Department of Transportation, was created in 1966, and administration of the new Highway and Traffic bills as well as other national transport matters was placed under the newly created department.

Johnson's own little "era of good feeling" quickly expired, and the torrent of legislation—the greatest outpouring of social welfare and reform enactments since the New Deal—slowed to a trickle. Even by the end of 1966 a discernible cooling of public opinion could be noted. The years of 1967 and 1968 were poor ones for the Lyndon Johnson regime, with the nation's approval of the President down to its lowest level since the Korean War and the 90th Congress largely unwilling to produce Johnson-sponsored legislation. A variety of factors accounted for the great turnabout. In Congress, resentment built up steadily over the Johnsonian prodding which sought to elevate the President to a super–New Deal reputation. Additionally, the off-year elections of 1966 had changed the heavily Democratic complexion of Congress, with Republicans gaining back 47 seats in the House and 3 in the Senate. The business community, which gave a large measure of support to Johnson in 1964, by 1967 resentfully considered it was not being consulted enough and was moreover worried over profit squeezes and the possibility of controls.

More important factors in Johnson's decline were the war in Vietnam and the accompanying student and black riots and rebelliousness. Moral indignation, alienation, and a loss of confidence both in society's values and the administration's credibility were the compelling reasons. Young people, more and more of whom adopted long hair and "sloppy" clothing, wondered what kind of a nation and society could support and pursue genocidal tactics on a small nation 10,000 miles away and of no danger to American security. No small part of their dismay was caused by the loss of American lives in such an immoral conflict and the expenditure of billions of dollars that were badly needed at home. For the blacks, the civil rights acts had aroused expectations in housing, education, and employment that had not kept pace with voting rights. To the ghetto dweller the slights and handicaps of racism were an everyday occurrence, and the sharply higher unemployment for blacks gave youths, as a black spokesman declared, "nothing to do but throw rocks."

Surprisingly then, when the phrase itself had fallen somewhat in public favor, several new measures were added to the Great Society in 1967 and 1968. One of these authorized more than 1.7 million units of housing for low-income families to become home owners by subsidizing a portion of the mortgage costs of interest, taxes, and insurance premium. This extensive housing act went through Congress because of special considerations. The foremost of these dated back to the preceding year, when administration efforts to aid ghetto dwellers with a bill for rat control were greeted with jeers and ill-timed jokes from the floor of the House. These came largely from the conservative Southern Democrat-Republican coalition, and took the form of heavily accented pleas to "vote down this rat bill *rat* now." The public storm of reaction to such misdirected humor, with ghetto fires and riots in the background, made it virtually impossible for even the most conservative Representatives to appear "antiurban" on the Housing Act of 1968.

In the field of consumer protection, Congress in 1968 passed one of the toughest consumer bills in its history. This was the Truth In Lending Act, long opposed by banks, department stores, and credit agencies. The bill required lenders and creditors to give their customers full, honest, and comparative information on the costs of the credit they were buying. Although it made no attempt to limit the charge for credit, it did force the creditor to tell his customer exactly what he was paying for credit charges in dollar terms and on a uniform, annual basis so that he might make valid cost comparisons between the installment plans of competing banks and credit agencies.

By late 1967 and in 1968 the term Great Society was no longer mentioned by the administration, but its record of accomplishment was a formidable one. Like Kennedy's New Frontier, the Johnson Great Society favored a balanced economy above a balanced budget. It sought, through slashing excise taxes and other measures, to stimulate and expand consumption as a necessity for increasing investment and overall growth. It tried—although with limited success—to boost employment. It hoped to move in this direction, yet avoid inflation, but mounting war expenditures created ominous inflationary undercurrents. Whether in education, housing, or urban problems, a concern for the lower-income brackets was a dominating characteristic of the Great Society. It not only extended the New Deal activities of 1935, but went far beyond them in education, civil rights, and in treating urban problems. The education legislation broke the barriers of decades to extend federal aid to elementary and secondary systems. The civil rights movement accomplished more in legislation during the Johnson years than in any previous period in the 20th century. Urban redevelopment, housing, and transportation all made important and significant gains.

There were shortcomings and disappointments as well. The great expectations deriving from civil rights progress paradoxically contributed to some of the worst relations between blacks and whites in a hundred years. It seemed that an excessive amount of the funds intended to improve the equality of opportunity among the poor found its way into state, local, or federal bureaucracy. The highly touted Appalachian and allied aid could more accurately have been described as a kind of gigantic pork barrel, since the great majority of the funds went into road-building projects rather than for direct retraining or employment help to the area's disadvantaged. The House Appropriations Committee successfully emasculated the rent supplement provision in the Housing Act and other authorizations by severely curtailing the funds necessary to implement such programs successfully. Regardless of these and other disappointments, various poverty programs were begun. The federal government's commitment to the disadvantaged, despite its handicaps and drawbacks, seemed evidence of an irreversible course.

Foreign Policy of the Johnson Administration

Although United States foreign policy under Lyndon Johnson was overwhelmingly dominated by the Vietnam War, it was in many respects a continuation of the basic approaches that the United States had adopted following World War II. The greatly expanded concern with Southeast Asia at the expense of Latin America was an obvious exception. The Johnson administration continued to look for settlement of the armaments race. It carried on the program of American economic aid coupled with the supply of American arms to the underdeveloped nations or those considered to be faced with threats, internal and external. It also sought to continue the policy of expanding international trade, although with limited success. In spite of many continuing policies, the Johnson administration was increasingly faced with challenges to the orthodox assumptions regarding American hegemony around the world and the United States' role as the only appropriate global policeman. A shift in tone and attitude away from the Kennedy policies occurred in Latin America, and one of the earliest domestic challenges to the American role of world policeman came as a result of American intervention in the troubled affairs of the Dominican Republic.

U.S. Arms Sales and Grants, 1952–69
(in millions of dollars)

	Grants	Sales	Total
1952............	$ 4,440	$ 532	$ 4,972
1953..........	1,965	230	2,195
1954..........	1,323	82	1,405
1955..........	2,556	98	2,654
1956..........	657	174	831
1957..........	1,283	663	1,946
1958..........	1,381	340	1,721
1959..........	1,318	853	2,171
1960..........	1,034	963	1,997
1961..........	1,450	630	2,080
Ten-year total	$17,407	$4,565	$21,972
1962..........	1,314	1,485	2,799
1963..........	958	1,483	2,441
1964..........	728	1,260	1,988
1965..........	721	1,766	2,487
1966..........	695	1,798	2,493
1967*..........	541	1,946	2,487
1968*..........	400	1,929	2,329
1969*..........	390	1,530	1,920
Eight-year total	$5,747	$13,197	$18,944

* 1967 figure was preliminary; 1968 and 1969 figures were Committee estimates.
    Source: House Foreign Affairs Committee *Congress and the Nation, Vol. II, 1965–1968* (Washington: Congressional Quarterly, Inc., 1969), p. 87.

Some of the Kennedy-to-Johnson shift was occasioned by Johnson's appointment of Thomas C. Mann, a Texas lawyer and diplomat who had been Ambassador to Mexico, to Assistant Secretary of State for Inter-American Affairs. He was also given charge of the Alliance for Progress and had Johnson's ear on all things Latin American. Where

Kennedy had been very reluctant to work with the military leaders of Latin American coups, Assistant Secretary Mann stressed "stability" above all, and considered that military regimes might best preserve it and hopefully would move on to democratic reform. In March 1964, a military coup ousted Brazil's President Goulart. A military government deliberately suppressed democratic government in Brazil, insisting that it could only institute major economic reforms under Army control. The United States gave strong support to the military regime of General Castello Branco. However, where Kennedy had tried to move military regimes toward both economic and democratic reforms, Johnson's Assistant Secretary insisted that economic development might require an interim loss of democratic processes. Nor were Johnson's unilateral statements on the occasion of the lesser crisis—a flareup in United States-Panamanian relations—accepted by Latin American leaders as a continuation of the Kennedy principles or tone.

A major crisis in Latin American affairs actually contained more continuity between the Kennedy and Johnson administrations than had the lesser ones. This was in the affairs of the Dominican Republic, where perhaps the longest and cruelest tyranny in Latin American history had come to an end in 1961 with the assassination of Dictator Rafael Trujillo by some of his own disaffected henchmen. In the ensuing turmoil, Kennedy had made it clear that he hoped for a democratic regime but, with the shadow of Cuba hanging over him, would accept anything as a second choice rather than a "Castro-type" government. In December 1962, in a constitutional election, the Dominican people had chosen as their President Juan Bosch, an anti-Trujillo exile and a nationalist non-Communist intellectual. The State Department cordially detested Bosch, as did Ambassador John Hartlow Martin, as "arrogant and erratic." White House circles did not approve of Bosch, holding to the stereotyped view that all anti-Communist liberals in Latin America were too naïve to be able to resist eventual Communist domination. The White House favorite was Joaquin Balaguer, a "moderate" and uncorrupted politician who had been Trujillo's puppet president. The Pentagon and American military attachés also disliked Bosch, and worked closely with the older Dominican generals. It was this latter group which overthrew the duly elected Bosch and his constitutional government in October 1963, setting up in his place a Dominican businessman, Donald Reid Cabral.

President Johnson moved to recognition of the military junta in December 1963. Younger Dominican Army officers, angry at the ousting of Bosch and the new constitution, began a counter-coup on April 24, 1965. With vast support from the urban populace, many thousands of whom seized arms from Army depots, a civil war began. Johnson quickly decided to intervene, sending in Marine units and then large components of the 82d Airborne Division. The President announced that the troops were only to protect American lives, but as correspondent Philip Geyelin of the *Wall Street Journal* observed, "The full weight of the U.S. Government on the scene had been committed to blocking the rebellion (of the Constitutionalists) before it was 24-hours old."[2] The rationale for the intervention soon changed. The panicky staff of the American Embassy (now under Ambassador W. Tapley Bennett) had produced a list of 58 Communists, which reporters were soon able to prove was wildly untrue. Names on the list included Communists who were dead or in jail and even the names of notable and undoubted anti-Communists. Nevertheless, the White House switched its intervention reason from the protection of American lives to a prevention of a "Communist takeover."

The United States poured in the amazing amount of 22,000 troops (not including another 10,000 naval and air support troops in a task force just offshore). Allegedly these were neutral, but their disposition was such as to cut the Bosch Constitutionalist forces in half, leaving the "Loyalist" forces (as Washington dubbed them) able to concentrate their strength on one half and then the other of their opposition, and to reverse their initial defeats. Marines also fought through civilian defenders in setting up an armed corridor as a "security zone" through the middle of the capital city of Santo Domingo. Troops from the Organization of American States (OAS)—chiefly Brazilians—were brought in to preserve peace. In a subsequent election in 1966 Bosch, who campaigned only from his home by radio, was surprisingly defeated by Joaquin Balaguer.

The intervention was clearly and specifically in violation of the OAS charter. That organization, unconsulted regarding the intervention and then muscled into acquiescence and token occupation troops to lend a tardy legitimacy to the intervention, was discredited by its willingness to follow State Department directives. The American Embassy and its officials in the Dominican Republic proved itself, at best, poorly informed, and severely handicapped by its bitterly anti-Bosch position. Although the Communist threat was something less than negligible, such a potential was a major consideration in American domestic politics. Johnson's "No Second Cuba" theme evidently offset all the undoubted intervention disadvantages and long-range anti-American costs. The Johnson administration's critics challenged more stoutly than ever the negativism of anticommunism as a policy and the concept of America as world policeman. They were outraged by the excesses of his gunboat proclivities, and the credibility gap widened as a result of the shifting

---

[2] Cited in Jerome Stater, *Intervention and Negotiation: The United States and the Dominican Revolution* (New York, 1970), 25.

justifications offered by the White House. Johnson and his ex-Kennedy advisers, however, considered the operation a success since it had accomplished what the administration had set out to do.

The distraction of Vietnam and the shifted emphasis of American foreign policy toward the Far East accounted not only for less diplomatic activity with European allies, but a straining of relations even where such activities were undertaken. The Multilateral Force (MLF), a ghost passed on by the Kennedy administration, was even less convincing in 1964 regarding American intent to share nuclear controls with an integrated Europe. De Gaulle's fierce objections intimidated even West Germany, the only country which had really supported the American idea, and Johnson prudently let this dubious project expire silently.

De Gaulle also contributed to the increasing decline of NATO, although there were other factors. The European nations were in the midst of a prosperous period which they intended to enjoy, and they complained strongly of the costs of the armed forces the United States demanded. Russia was obviously not the threat she was considered to be in the postwar years or even at the time of the Korean War. It was equally clear that the American policy of "unitary control" (translated as unilateral American control) meant that European nations would never share control of atomic weapons but would nevertheless still be under an American nuclear umbrella for continental Europe.

Americans cordially detested France's de Gaulle, although his nationalism was probably no greater than that of the United States. His diatribes against "Anglo-Saxon" domination (meaning the United States and her strong ally, Great Britain) were symptomatic of European states which wished merely to get along with Washington rather than be highly dependent upon America and American whims. To Americans, accustomed for decades to prompt acquiescence or, at worst, grudging cooperation from Western Europe, de Gaulle's nationalism and independence were sheer intransigence and anti-Americanism. The feeling mounted with French recognition of the Peoples' Republic of China in 1964. French land and air forces were ordered out of all NATO commands in 1965 (naval forces had already been withdrawn), and in the following year de Gaulle told NATO itself to be gone from French soil within a year. In 1967 the NATO headquarters bureaucracy moved to the more internationally friendly atmosphere of the Belgian capital of Brussels, with France still technically a member but not a participant.

Although always complicated by the overriding issue of Vietnam, the two nuclear superpowers edged toward closer accord despite several complications. When the belligerent President Nasser of Egypt and his Arab allies went to war again with Israel in 1967, Johnson and Premier Kosygin quickly agreed not to become involved in support of their respective protégés. The Israelis, in any case, wound up the so-called

Six Days' War in such short order as to have minimized any chance for the two great powers to clash. Kosygin came to the United Nations in New York to denounce Israel's "aggression," and the question of a meeting between Kosygin and Johnson arose. The former suggested his New York base; the latter his home grounds of Washington. As a compromise, both men agreed to meet at the halfway point of Glassboro, in southern New Jersey, on the grounds of Glassboro State College. There the two heads of state conversed in the home of the college president on June 23 and June 25. Kosygin wanted an Israeli rollback first with other considerations to follow; Johnson insisted on the reverse order. In the same manner, Johnson insisted that North Vietnam, in effect, indicate its surrender before he would halt the bombing. Kosygin insisted the bombing halt must come first and the negotiations later. As a summit meeting, it served no useful purpose except to keep the two powers in diplomatic contact and to reveal American public enthusiasm for a relaxation of tensions with the Soviet Union.

Relations between the United States and Russia improved with the final ratification in 1967 of a treaty providing for the operation of consulates in each country. The agreement was actually made in 1964 by the White House, but the necessary Senate ratification was postponed until 1967. The Consular Convention aroused some controversy, with ultraconservative groups such as Liberty Lobby, Young Americans for Freedom, and the American Legion actively lobbying against the treaty. The administration pointed to the improvement of relations, the greater protection for American tourists and travelers in Russia, and additional diplomatic windows from which to observe Soviet society. A push toward ratification came from moderate Republicans headed by Senator Thurston B. Morton of Kentucky. When such Republican leaders as Minority Leader Everett Dirksen of Illinois and Senator Bourke B. Hickenlooper of Iowa changed their position from opposition to support, the convention had more than the necessary two-thirds votes to pass, 66 to 28. The terms of the treaty, in addition to providing the basis for future mutual decisions on the establishment of consulates, gave diplomatic immunity to consular officials and employees. It also required each country promptly to notify the other of the detention or arrest of a citizen of the other country. Largely symbolic as part of the Johnson administration's efforts to improve relations with the Soviet Union and Eastern Europe, it was nevertheless the first bilateral treaty ever consummated between the United States and the Soviet Union.

In international trade developments, Congress finally completed negotiations for the Kennedy Round of tariff cutting. Dating from Kennedy's passage of the Trade Expansion Act of 1962, such negotiations had to be completed before June 1967. Despite new and strong protectionist attempts by such industries as steel, textiles, and chemicals, the final bargaining reduced duties an average 35 percent on some 60,000 items in exchange for similar slashes by other countries. Affecting some $40 billion in world trade, it represented a triumph for both the American consumer and American export business. Administration attempts to expand trade with Eastern European Communist countries, however, were blocked by a Congress that was more influenced by Vietnam and other East-West crises than by Johnson's plea for increased influence and improved relations with the Soviet satellite nations.

Two points of friction hampered but did not offset an overall improvement in nuclear disarmament and Soviet-American relations during 1968. The first occurred early in the year, when the U.S. intelligence collection ship *Pueblo* was captured by a more heavily armed North Korean warship. According to U.S. officials, the *Pueblo* was 25 miles offshore in international waters, although it was later admitted to be somewhat closer. The North Koreans insisted that it was "an armed spy boat" and had intruded into their territorial waters. Negotiations were carried out through the year at Panmunjom, resulting in the release of the crew after a U.S. official signed a statement admitting guilt for the incident. The United States made it clear the signing was purely an expedient to gain the men's release, and the North Koreans retained the ship. The Navy quickly opened a court of inquiry to answer the unresolved doubts raised by the vessel's capture.

Another setback to United States-Soviet relations came in the summer of 1968, when Russian troops invaded Czechoslovakia to put down what Moscow described as a counterrevolutionary plot aided by "external forces." By no means a movement against communism, the Czechs were simply seeking greater independence from Russian hegemony and freedom of speech and press. From the Soviet standpoint, such a liberalization evidently posed a possibility of spreading to other satellite states, but the excessive military weight of their reaction was roundly condemned by virtually all leaders in the Western political world. Two months previously, President Johnson had formerly approved the establishment of direct New York-Moscow air service by Pan American World Airways and the Soviet national airline Aeroflot. Flights began in July, when Johnson was also able to announce the beginning of talks on the reduction and limitation of nuclear arms.

The product of four years of tentative drafting and negotiations at the 18-Nation Disarmament Conference at Geneva, the nuclear nonproliferation treaty was finally approved by the United Nations General Assembly in June 1968. The treaty was signed in July by the United States, Russia, and 60 other nations, but its necessary Senate ratification was seriously hampered by the Czechoslovakian crisis. Under the terms of the treaty, the spread of nuclear weapons was banned by a provision which forbade those nations possessing nuclear weapons to transfer to any other nation nuclear explosive devices or control over them, nor could nuclear powers assist or encourage in any way the manufacture of such devices elsewhere. For their part, the nonnuclear signatories agreed neither to manufacture such weapons nor to receive them. Controversial Article III contained the safeguards which were finally accepted by all the signatories in order to ensure that nonnuclear states were not diverting nuclear energy from peaceful uses to the manufacture of weapons. Since it did not include safeguard inspections for those nations already possessing nuclear weapons, the article bypassed an area characterized by lack of any agreement between Moscow and Washington. The nuclear possessors were bound only to pursue disarmament negotiations, and the smaller nations were satisfied by treaty provisions ensuring their access to the peaceful uses of nuclear energy. Despite Johnson's urging, the Nuclear Nonproliferation Treaty was not ratified by the Senate until March 1969, after the election of President Richard M. Nixon.

The treaty was another stride forward in international nuclear accord, and a sizeable addition to the Johnson administration's policy of lessening Soviet-American tensions. The treaty, plus such factors as a growing similarity of interests and a mutual wariness toward the Peoples' Republic, helped move the two powers into increasing accord. Nevertheless, tensions arising out of the agonies of the Vietnamese War remained to plague American relations with Russia.

Vietnam

The legacy in Vietnam which Kennedy left to Johnson, and Johnson to Nixon, was a losing one, just as was the one bequeathed by Eisenhower to Kennedy. It was a losing policy because it pursued the will-of-the-wisp goal that the United States could endlessly uphold global commitments to all reactionary governments beseiged by the most powerful and dedicated forces of mid-20th Century—nationalism and anticolonialism. It was a losing policy because it practiced the self-deception that equated "freedom" or "Free World" solely with anticommunism and completely ignored the costs, domestic and otherwise, of such a course; losing because it ignored the basic fact that no nation can hand over the priceless gift of independence to another nation, no matter how lavish it may be with its own money and men; losing because it persistently sought a military solution to a situation that cried out for a political reckoning. In the 1950s when McCarthyism was rife and even the liberals were vying to display their own brand of anticommunism, Ngo Dinh Diem became the protégé of such conservative forces as Cardinal Spellman, Allen Dulles, and John Foster Dulles. But he was also accepted by such liberals as Justice William O. Douglas and Senators John F. Kennedy and Mike Mansfield as a nationalist noncommunist alternative to those Communist forces under Ho Chi Minh which had seemingly preempted the nationalist and anticolonial feeling of the Vietnamese people.

Escalation in Vietnam

	U.S. Armed Forces in South Vietnam*					
	Dec. 31, 1963	Dec. 31, 1964	Dec. 31, 1965	Dec. 31, 1966	Dec. 31, 1967	Dec. 28, 1968
Total	16,300	23,300	184,300	385,300	485,600	535,500

	U.S. Military Casualties from Hostile Action				
	1964	1965	1966	1967	1968	Jan. 1, 1961 through Dec. 28, 1968
Killed	147	1,369	5,008	9,378	14,592	30,614
Wounded†	1,039	6,114	30,093	62,025	92,820	192,582

	South Vietnam Military Casualties from Hostile Action				
	1964	1965	1966	1967	1968	Jan. 1, 1961 through Dec. 28, 1968
Killed	7,457	11,243	11,953	12,716	16,353	73,848
Wounded†	17,017	23,118	20,975	29,448	54,739	169,429

* Figures are rounded and do not include armed forces stationed on seas around or on islands outside of Vietnam.

† U.S. figures include both the seriously wounded, who required hospital treatment, and the less seriously injured, who did not require hospital care. The totals of those requiring hospital care are: 1964, 522; 1965, 3,308; 1966, 16,526; 1967, 32,371; 1968, 46,799; 1961 through 1968, 99,786.

‡ These figures, compiled by the South Vietnamese government, include only persons seriously wounded who required hospital or extensive treatment.

Source: Department of Defense, *Congress and the Nation, Vol. II, 1965–1968* (Washington: Congressional Quarterly Inc., 1969), p. 53.

By the time that Kennedy became President, Diem's repressive and corrupt regime was opposed by anti-Communists no less than by those remaining Communists hidden in the villages. Several non-Communist attempts at assassination and overthrow had failed, and the National Liberation Front (NLF), which was largely but not wholly Communist, began a guerrilla civil war against Diem. Diem continued to receive American aid and funds from Eisenhower and Kennedy, and successfully resisted the efforts of both to bring about needed reforms. American military personnel rose from some 4,000 in 1962 to 16,300, including Green Beret units, at the time of Kennedy's death in 1963.

In the campaign of 1964 Johnson promised not to expand the war in Vietnam. To Goldwater's denunciation of a "no-war" policy, Johnson was content to ask the largely agreeable electorate, "Whose finger do you want on the nuclear trigger?" with clear implications of the dangers inherent in the excitable belligerency of the Goldwater digit. Yet Johnson secretly planned for a variety of prosecutions of the war effort long before the election campaign. The Pentagon Papers exposed Johnson's approval in January 1964 of a covert plan of operations to be carried out by the CIA, the South Vietnamese, and American armed forces against North Vietnam. Military planners long before the election were drawing up lists of North Vietnamese bombing targets. Also, in early June McGeorge Bundy had drawn up a resolution for Congress to approve which would give the President a free hand in Vietnam without consulting with or explaining to members of Congress. For implementation and sympathetic agreement, some incident that could readily be exaggerated and dramatized was necessary.

The skeletal structure of such an incident became briefly visible in August 1964, and the Johnson administration lost no time in fleshing it out with alarming details. The destroyer *USS Maddox* was attacked by North Vietnamese patrol boats on August 2. The *Maddox* suffered no damage, and her subsequent action destroyed a number of North Vietnamese vessels. The *Maddox* was not "on routine patrol," as Secretary McNamara insisted, but on a secret mission with the CIA to provoke North Vietnamese reaction for intelligence gathering purposes, and was admittedly within North Vietnamese territorial waters. Two nights later and joined by the *C. Turner Joy,* the patrol was allegedly attacked without provocation in international waters of the Gulf of Tonkin by North Vietnamese PT boats. The *Turner Joy* insisted that she was under attack, but the patrol commander on the *Maddox* reported that the freak weather effects of a pitch-black, stormy night and inexperienced sonarmen probably were the cause of *Turner Joy's* alarm. No visual sightings were made by the *Maddox,* and neither ship had any damage or hits to show for the alleged incident. Nevertheless, President Johnson immediately ordered "retaliatory" air attacks on North Vietnam, and rushed the long-prepared resolution before Congress. It gave him a virtual blank check on Vietnam, authorizing him to "take all necessary measures to repel any armed attack against the forces of the United States and to prevent further aggression." The Senate endorsed the resolution by an 88 to 2 vote, with Senators Morse and Greuning opposed. Many Senators regretted their "yes" votes, particularly after the Foreign Relations Committee hearings. They were also disturbed by the insistence of Nicholas de B. Katzenbach, Undersecretary of State, that the so-called Tonkin Gulf Resolution was the "functional equivalent" of a declaration of war. The Tonkin Gulf affair widened the Johnson credibility gap, since the administration was repeatedly caught denying or distorting evidence which soon came out in Senate hearings. It did, however, give Johnson the leeway he wanted to pursue his war aims.

Several attempts were made in this early stage of the war to bring the participants together for discussions which might end the hostilities. In the winter of 1964–1965 U Thant, Secretary General of the United Nations, was active in setting up a site for talks in neutral Burma's capital city of Rangoon. Although Hanoi expressed interest, the Johnson administration refused to participate. The President publicly indicated a willingness to enter discussions, but the American note which went to Hanoi insisted on an end to North Vietnamese "aggression" and ignored negotiation attempts. President Johnson clearly was moving toward an escalation of the war and, as a former White House aide later remarked, "The very word 'negotiations' was anathema in the administration."[3]

In February 1965 Johnson, freshly armed with an impressive mandate from the electorate and a blank-check resolution from Congress, seized upon a Vietcong attack to mount heavy "retaliatory" bombing raids against North Vietnam. This marked a noticeable turning point in the war, and undertook the policy actually suggested by Johnson's opponent in the 1964 presidential election, Senator Goldwater. The incident in question occurred at an American air base at Pleiku, where enemy guerrilla rocket attacks killed 8 Americans, wounded 108 others, and destroyed 7 planes.[4] Though these bombings in early 1965 were described as "retaliatory," it soon became clear that they were the planned beginning of a constant and protracted United States air war against North Vietnam. President Johnson denied that this was so, but all the military arrangements were being made and Johnson, himself, it was later disclosed, was calling the initial targets. The bombing got under way in February, and Johnson responded to critics in March by escalating and Americanizing the war and ordering the first American combat troops—3,500 Marines—into the war zone. More Marines, Air Corps, and Army units rapidly followed, bringing U.S. troops in South Vietnam up to 180,000 by the end of 1965.

The sustained bombing, according to the Pentagon, would bring Hanoi to the negotiating table in six to ten weeks at the most. In April Johnson offered peace with economic aid for North Vietnam, but his

---

[3] Cited in David Kraslow and Stuart H. Loory, *The Secret Search for Peace in Vietnam* (New York, 1968), 91.

[4] A similar attack had taken place at the American air base at Bien Hoa on November 1, 1964, killing 5 Americans and destroying or damaging 27 planes. But this was one week before the presidential elections, and no "retaliation" took place.

The Vietnam War, 1966

VIETNAM
1966

☐   U.S. Base

──────   U.S.-Built Highway

••••••••••   Railroad

refusal to deal with the NLF effectively negated the proposal. Spring, summer, and fall passed without any move by Hanoi toward a negotiating table. In December the President agreed to a long bombing pause to give the North Vietnamese ample diplomatic time for contacts and meetings. Simultaneously, he sent a bevy of personal representatives on whirlwind diplomatic tours of three continents to reassure the world of his willingness to talk peace. At the same time, American military assaults on land were stepped up and the number of American troops in South Vietnam was sharply increased. Hanoi responded by insisting that the bombings, including napalm and toxic chemicals as well as explosives, must be halted before any solution could be arranged. After 37 days Johnson resumed the regular bombing in January 1966, insisting that Hanoi's reply precluded any negotiated settlement. By the end of 1966, United States troop numbers reached 380,000; in 1967, the number moved past the half-million mark. As American troops and bombing increased, North Vietnam responded by sending more North Vietnam regulars to fight alongside the Vietcong guerrillas in the South.

The administration strategy insisted that more men and more bombing sooner or later must triumph by technical superiority and weight of resources, not taking into account the very reduced leverage that such tactics have on a well-supported guerrilla movement. It insisted that a continuing American buildup would convince Hanoi and the NLF that time was not on their side, not taking into account the grim nationalistic determination that had kept many Vietnamese fighting against prior invaders from Japan and France, or for the vastly lesser needs of an agrarian society and of guerrilla warfare. Nor was the large Army of the Republic of Viet Nam (ARVN) a great help, with high desertion rates and a general unwillingness to fight for a series of unpopular regimes in Saigon. It became evident to many critics that this was a war that the United States could not win, even though its huge weight of numbers in South Vietnam meant that the Vietcong could not win either.

Johnson and his military and White House advisors nevertheless stressed a military solution where increasingly it was evident that a political answer precluded and outweighed all others. Bomb tonnage moved into incredible statistics. By the early months of 1968, American bombs dropped on North and South Vietnam exceeded the total dropped by the United States and its allies on all of Europe during all of World War II. The bombing took on genocidal aspects. With the wholesale bombing of villages in South Vietnam suspected of harboring Vietcong and the toxic chemicals used to defoliate large areas for the same reason, the question arose as to whether the United States was willing to kill or destroy the people and country in order to "save" them from communism. American casualties in this effort rose alarmingly, and produced

Vietnam, 1968. A paratrooper of the 101st Airborne Division guides a medical evacuation helicopter into a small gap in the heavy foliage to pick up casualties. (Wide World Photos)

far more serious complaints. By the end of 1968, over 30,000 Americans had been killed and nearly 200,000 wounded. To keep track of military successes in a war in which traditional capture of territory was not a factor, the enemy bodies left on the field of action became a new and gruesome criterion. The "body count," under the pressure from military commands for battlefield units to use such means to display their efficiency, became not only an additional brutalizing factor but a prevarication from platoon to division level. A shocking example of war brutality was disclosed in the little village of My Lai 4, where members of Charlie Company, 1st Battalion, 20th Infantry, indiscriminately shot, bayonetted, or machine-gunned several hundred old men, women, children, and babies in a systematic and meaningless massacre.[5]

The escalation of the war was paralleled by increasing conflict between the war's supporters, now known as "hawks," and its critics,

---

[5] Known to only a few in 1968, it received public attention chiefly in 1970. The resultant pressure forced military hearings to follow.

or "doves." By 1967 it had reached proportions of internal divisiveness and bitterness probably surpassing any domestic reaction over American foreign policy in history. The dovish groups could not at first reach their full potential because of their diversity of argument. Dove positions ranged from a wish to stop the bombing to a passive withdrawal of United States forces into protective enclaves, and from an insistence upon a forced coalition government for Saigon to complete American withdrawal. Some arguments were based wholly upon practical concepts which placed the cost in money and lives far beyond any possible political or military gain. Others mentioned the $30 billion drain per year. Still others were motivated solely by humanitarian considerations based upon the endless slaughter. Other groups, particularly on academic campuses, challenged the entire assumption of the legitimacy of American intervention in conjunction with one or more of the other points of view. Church action groups and clergy of Protestant, Catholic, and Jewish faith were unusually active in antiwar efforts, with young Catholic priests and nuns notably outspoken in dissent. They drew increasing public support, much of which sprang from the fact that the war's actual deaths and sufferings were brought, by means of television, into American living rooms for the first time in history.

The administration had its hawkish defenders. A notable group which zeroed in on the growing reluctance of Secretary McNamara to support continued bombing was the Preparedness Subcommittee of the Senate Armed Services Committee. It included Senators Stennis, Symington, Jackson, Cannon, Byrd, Smith, Thurmond, and Miller, all known for their hard-line military views and Pentagon associations. They echoed the views of the military, which insisted that the failure of bombing tactics was simply because it was neither heavy enough nor sustained enough, and because of "civilian" control.[6] This position ignored the evidence of unremitting Vietcong and North Vietnamese activity, and CIA reports on the ineffectiveness of bombing on some types of targets.

The administration itself had no dearth of stoutly hawkish spokesmen. Foremost among these were Secretary Dean Rusk, advisers Walt Rostow and McGeorge Bundy and, on occasion, Johnson himself. The military largely spoke through their congressional allies, although it should be noted that a number of retired generals heatedly criticized American intervention and its policies. A common prowar argument rested on the assumption that Vietnam was a "testing ground" for the defeat of communism. The whole world, according to this theory, must therefore see that the United States would persist in bringing about the downfall of any such Communist, pro-Communist, or Communist-aided effort.

---

[6] The Defense Department History of United States Decisionmaking on Vietnam, *The Pentagon Papers*, (Boston, 1972) Gravel Edition, IV, 197.

As Walt Rostow, one of the theory's most tireless exponents, phrased it, if the United States could just "get on with the job, the struggle might be the last confrontation of the postwar era." A more simplistic version was that which Johnson himself used to ex-Senate colleagues who must have known better. This apocalyptic version was, "If we didn't stop the Communists in Vietnam we'd soon have to stop them in Hawaii or San Diego." Dean Rusk insisted that North Vietnam must cease its "aggression," ignoring the civil war and Geneva Accords aspects of the struggle. Rusk was more notably associated with the use of the Munich analogy, in which the circumstances and participants were all severely wrenched out of historical context to try to show that Vietnamese or Chinese expansionism was akin to the Nazi stance before Munich, and that "appeasement" would only bring an avalanche of Asiatic and perhaps even world conquest efforts. General Westmoreland was brought back to the United States by the administration to reassure the public that the enemy "is clearly losing" and "the end begins to come into view," although the latter phrase sounded to critics like the optimistic French generals and their unfortunate phrase just before Dien Bien Phu of "the light now visible at the end of the tunnel." The new Ambassador to South Vietnam, Ellsworth Bunker, reported back to Washington that the South Vietnamese were making steady progress with the war, and Vice President Humphrey returned from a Pacific tour to herald the success of American policy on all fronts. Johnson sought to picture himself as one heroically mediating between hawks and doves. While it is true that Johnson did not accede to all Pentagon and Vietnam field requests, by 1968 doves within the administration were as rare as carrier pigeons. Lyndon Johnson did not relish nor long endure dissenting opinion.

By 1967 the hawks were desperately describing the increased number of antiwar marches, sit-ins, and demonstrations as "giving aid and comfort to the enemy." North Vietnam and the Vietcong, so this argument went, would see such dissent (although always present in all of America's wars) as a sign that the United States might cease her military efforts and thereby prolong the war. Extreme right-wingers insisted that any opposition to the war was no less than treasonable behavior. But the continued bombing stirred up hornets' nests on academic campuses. Where civil rights issues brought groups of students and faculty into peaceful marches and demonstrations, the continued bombing and slaughter of Vietnam brought not-so-peaceful onslaughts by co-ed masses of students against the police and a bold march on the Pentagon itself. The Johnson bombing tactics not only called out angry swarms of young people to fuse with the previous smaller civil rights groups, black and white, but put the finishing touches on a politicizing of the American student.

In the last two years of the Johnson administration, South Vietnam became an increasingly larger headache. Air Marshal Nguyen Cao Ky, who had come to power after some eight different governments in less than two years, embarrassed American officials by his outspoken regard for Adolf Hitler. During the American elections of 1966, Marshal Ky called for an invasion of North Vietnam and hinted strongly that China might have to be dealt with also. It was an alarming exhibition of the supposed puppet actually tugging at the strings, and the incongruity of his position had to be explained to Ky. In 1967 a South Vietnamese election took place which observers and journalists described as having been thoroughly rigged, but it brought the more diplomatic General Nguyen Van Thieu up to the presidency and demoted Marshal Ky to the vice presidency. Far more difficult to deal with, however, both in credibility and in military response was the Vietcong Tet (New Year) offensive of January 1968. It was preceded by announcements from Rostow at the White House that captured documents foretold the imminent and complete collapse of the Vietcong. Yet the Tet offensive was the most destructive enemy attack of the war. Surprise strikes against Hué and Saigon, carried out by infiltrated troops and supplies, badly disrupted American plans. Parts of Hué were controlled by the Vietcong for days, and in their dislodging American artillery and bombing smashed much of the revered cultural relics of the ancient capital city. When troops were rushed to the cities under attack, the Vietcong took over ever larger sections of the countryside. To General Westmoreland's explanation of Tet as a "last gasp" of a defeated enemy simultaneously with his request for another 200,000 troops, even the more willingly credible found their support of the administration and the war effort exhausted. Assurance from the military that the Vietcong effort "left the enemy on the ropes" fell on unfriendly ears, and even erstwhile supporters wondered about the efficiency of American intelligence and the loyalty of a Saigon regime that could not prevent such mass infiltration of men and supplies.

By March, Lyndon Johnson added his name to the casualties of the Vietnamese War. The mood of the country was bitter. The forthright war critic, Senator Eugene McCarthy of Minnesota, scored surprisingly well in the New Hampshire primary and looked like a winner in Wisconsin. The popular Robert Kennedy had announced his candidacy. Polls showed Kennedy leading the President nationally, and a private poll showed Johnson a big loser in California. On March 31, Johnson appeared on national television and announced both a partial bombing halt in Vietnam and his complete withdrawal from the presidential race. This was followed by the announcement that "peace" talks would soon begin in Paris, but both civil rights issues and Vietnam had left segments of American society in a far from peaceful mood.

The Continuing Negro Revolution

In the short span of half a dozen years, the black protest movement underwent amazing and momentous changes of direction. From the 1960 seminal sit-in by four young black college students at a Woolworth lunch counter in Greensboro, North Carolina, and a protest climate dominated by the genteel NAACP, legalism, and nonviolence, the movement had flowed powerfully into channels of black nationalism, "black power," revolutionary organizations, and protests couched in violence and riot.

Black organizations reflected the directional changes. The Student Nonviolent Coordinating Committee (SNCC), which Martin Luther King helped to found in 1960, moved to a militancy which belied its original title. Not only did advocates of nonviolence lose leadership control, but whites were frequently displaced by blacks in the organization hierarchy. The larger NAACP and the Urban League also displayed more black and fewer white leaders and officials and were pushed by the pressure of events to a far more militant position than ever before. At the revolutionary extreme were the Black Panthers, founded in Oakland, California, in 1966. The Black Panthers, who espoused a vaguely Marxist-oriented revolutionary philosophy, worked for black control of the inner city, where they sponsored free lunches and classes in black nationalism and separatism for poor black schoolchildren. Although their relatively strict social discipline and their avowed militancy toward traditional police methods required unusual dedication, their numbers and chapters grew throughout the nation's larger ghettoed cities.

The birth of "black power" and its variety of connotations for both blacks and whites dated from an episode of 1966. James Meredith, whose 1962 enrollment at the University of Mississippi precipitated riot, deaths, and the presence of federal troops, sought to encourage Mississippi black voting registration by walking to the state capital during primary election week. Meredith hoped to demonstrate that it was now harmless to display such intentions, but an assassination attempt wounded him. Martin Luther King and Stokely Carmichael, militant chairman of SNCC, immediately rushed to Mississippi to continue the march. While King continued to preach nonviolence and integrationist goals, Carmichael drew sharp response to his passionate advocation of black separatism and the potential of violence as represented by the slogan of "black power." To many whites, the phrase conjured up only the possibilities of violence or complete black control of political units or institutions. It represented a confusing variety of feelings in many different areas for blacks. In politics, it meant concentrated and independent action where blacks were predominant, instead of following or even working with white political groups. A black political party was not out of the question. Economically, it meant independent black business enterprise, but it also covered cooperatives for the ghettoes and rural South, and the use of economic boycott power to better working conditions or force the hiring of black personnel in previously all-white department stores. To some it meant black control of ghetto schools. To the Black Panthers it meant that only blacks from the local ghetto should make up that area's police force. Generally, it seemed to stand for an independence which ranged from self-help to belligerently retaliatory violence, and from sources of racial pride to means for racial unity.

Offshoots from this potent phrase expanded the concepts of black nationalism and separatism. Alongside "black power" stood "black consciousness," "black is beautiful," and "cultural nationalism." Found most often in the school systems and on higher education campuses, these slogans carried with them both a new awareness and a new urgency. In the elementary and secondary schools or among children at this age level, it meant an intense interest in African and Afro-American culture, folklore, art, music, and dress. In higher education it resulted in demands for the inclusion of "African Studies" in the curriculum and a heightened interest in and awareness of the role of blacks in American history. Reaction in higher education circles ranged from intensified recruiting in universities of black faculty and black students to demands from the latter group for completely separate dormitories and other facilities.

Relatively, blacks could point to impressive advances in political influence and to continued advances for individuals of their race in the middle 1960s. Edward W. Brooke, the Attorney General of Massachusetts, became in 1966 a Republican Senator from his state and the first black in the United States Senate since Reconstruction. In 1967, Thurgood Marshall, the brilliant NAACP attorney of *Brown* v. *Board of Education* fame, was moved by President Johnson from a Circuit Court post to the Supreme Court. Blacks occupied places in the Cabinet, on the Federal Reserve, and in high posts throughout the federal government. In Alabama, their combined weight had not been able to defeat Mrs. Lurleen Wallace (Governor George Wallace's wife was his means of getting around the constitutional prohibition against succeeding himself), but it was now evident that their votes could mean the difference in a close race. Their concentration and strong support by whites carried a black candidate to the mayor's office in such cities as Cleveland, Gary, and the District of Columbia. The civil rights acts of the 1950s and 1960s meant that blacks were no longer questioned in facilities and accommodations previously denied to them. The courts continued to expand questioned areas. In school desegregation, a district court ruled that Alabama state officials must not interfere with the court's desegregation plan, and also declared the state's tuition grant law unconstitutional. In Florida and Louisiana suits, the Supreme Court ruled in 1965 that

Blacks Move North and West, 1940–70

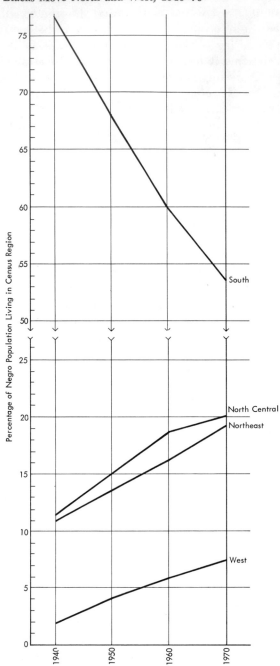

"delays in desegregation of school systems are no longer tolerable," thereby discarding the 1955 standard of "all deliberate speed." In voting rights, the 1966 decision of *Harper* v. *Virginia State Board of Elections* said that a state poll tax violated individual rights guaranteed by the 14th Amendment. To further demonstrate its attitude on the rights of individuals, the Court by a 9 to 0 vote in 1967 in *Loving* v. *Virginia* declared that the state's law prohibiting the marriage of individuals of different races was also an unconstitutional violation of 14th-Amendment rights.

Residential Changes by Blacks and Whites, 1950–70

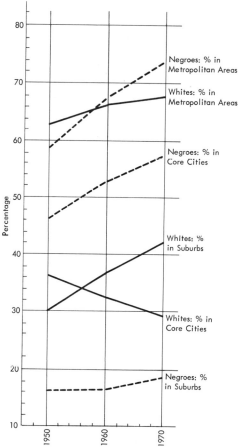

Yet somehow the gains never really matched the rightful expectations. The black population not only increased faster than did the white population, but its geographic shifts reflected rapid movement from South to North and from rural areas to urban locations. In 1910 only 10 percent of the nation's blacks lived outside the South; by 1966 the percentage was up to 45. In the same period, blacks living in urban areas moved from 25 percent to 69 percent, or 15 million blacks. The city proportion had virtually doubled over the last 20 years in some of the largest northern cities. Two thirds of Washington, D.C. was black. This shift was accompanied by a white flight to the suburbs, leaving even more segregated communities and inner-city black ghettoes. It was true that many urban blacks had moved upward into well-paid jobs, but such gains were always proportionately far behind the statistics showing upward economic movement for whites. Black urban unemployment was at a rate double that of whites and mounting even higher in the 1960s. The job training programs were inadequate and a further disappointment. Even the industries which might have provided jobs were steadily moving away from the cities. A hard core of millions of unskilled, undereducated, urban black poor were left in the ghettoes of all the largest American cities. They lived in rat-infested housing such as no middle-class white family could possibly imagine. Inadequate sanitation and public services combined with ignorance and poverty to create monumental health problems.[7] Poor urban transportation interposed difficulties in access to distant jobs, and the dreary cycle of inadequate education or training and the environment of despair effectively blocked any breakout from the ghetto. The entrapped millions were very ready to blame whites for their ghetto imprisonment. The accumulated frustration and disillusionment seemed to reach its heights in the summer months.

With such a fuse, the smallest spark sufficed. On August 11, 1965, a white patrolman stopped a weaving car in the black Watts district of Los Angeles and gave the black driver a sobriety test. Out of this incident grew one of the worst urban uprisings in American history. It occupied six days of rioting, arson, window breaking, looting, and destruction; 34 were killed, 856 injured, and damage approached $200 million. More than 3,100 were arrested, and 15,000 National Guardsmen and 1,000 law enforcement officers were needed to restore order. A similar riot on a lesser scale occupied Chicago at the same time, and in 1966 the pattern was repeated in diminishing statistics in Cleveland; Jacksonville, Florida; South Bend, Indiana; New York City; and again in Chicago. The following year saw no cessation; in fact, it included a new kind of violent protest on black college campuses. Here, also, an incident such as student arrests by white policemen set off days of rioting. Hundreds were injured and several police officers and black students killed in disturbances at Fisk University, Nashville, Tennessee;

---

[7] Although the United States ranked a poor No. 8 among the industralized nations of the world in the key medical health statistic of infant mortality, the black rate in the United States was twice that of the white race.

Jackson State College, Jackson, Mississippi; and Texas Southern University, in Houston, Texas.

The summer's rioting of 1967 spread into some 65 cities. The worst of these occurred in Newark, where one of the worst ghettoes in the North had drawn bitter and futile remonstrances to municipal authorities. Excessively high unemployment, housing shortages, and the plans to condemn 50 acres of slum area for a new medical school were triggering factors in five days of rioting which included sniping and fire bombings. The toll included 25 dead, 725 injured, 1,462 arrested, and property damage of $15 million reported. In Detroit, scene of several serious 20th century racial clashes, an incident centering around white police and a black "speakeasy" set off a wave of 4,000 fires together with sniping and looting. Police and National Guardsmen were unable to control the situation, and the President acceded to Governor George W. Romney's request for federal troops. The ghetto outbreaks were not racial riots but violently irrational explosions of resentment and frustration. The *Washington Post* correctly analyzed them as "not revolutionary or homicidal, but purposeless and suicidal."

Detroit, July 25, 1967. Violence gains momentum as the police begin to move into 12th Street at Clairmont. (Wide World Photos)

Two such summers brought severe political repercussions. "White backlash," which referred to the inclination of many whites to insist that politicians employ even more repressive measures, was frequently mentioned. Instead of attacks upon causation, there was an all-too-general willingness to invest community funds in armored cars and police riot equipment as a solution. Reference to the orderliness of past ethnic ghettoes such as Irish and Italian urban slums readily overlooked the overwhelmingly dominant factor of color and racism which blocked the mobility of black ghetto dwellers. As President Johnson pointed out, many of the gains in black progress and race relationship were seriously set back by the riots. The newer polarization brought in its wake the assassination on April 4, 1968, of the Reverend Martin Luther King, Jr., who was in Memphis, Tennessee, to lead a march in support of striking sanitation workers. His assassin was James Earl Ray, a white prison escapee who was apprehended two months later in London and finally tried and convicted in 1969. King's death also set off a wave of angry, riotous response in spite of the efforts of black leaders. Disturbances ranging from sporadic vandalism to arson, looting, and full-scale violence broke out in more than 100 cities across the United States.

King had been planning a "Poor People's Campaign" in Washington to bring to the attention of Congress the plight of the nation's impoverished. Taken over by Reverend Ralph D. Abernathy, King's successor as head of the Southern Christian Leadership Conference, the "camp-in" on the Washington Monument grounds in May was notable largely for the assemblage of blacks, whites, Chicanos, and Indians which came by caravan from various parts of the country. From their shantytown base of plywood and canvas, named "Resurrection City, U.S.A.," the poor people's representatives carried on a largely futile lobbying effort. Despite large, peaceable demonstrations of support from thousands of middle-class whites in a June 14 march, the reactions of Congressmen and the continued demonstrations, although nonviolent, brought a police closing of Resurrection City on June 24.

The Negro riots inevitably brought out assertions of conspiracy and communism, but no sober second looks were able to support such theories. The eight-member panel named by California's Governor Edmund G. Brown to investigate the Watts riot, and headed by former CIA Director John A. McCone, emphasized the deadening sense of despair which pervaded the black community in ever breaking out of their ghetto-determined status, and a "spiral of failure" among those blacks who had migrated to Los Angeles since World War II. In addition to recommended programs for job and education improvement, the McCone panel warned of the white community's ignorance of and complacency toward the conditions of black life.

In 1967 President Johnson named a commission headed by Governor Otto Kerner of Illinois to investigate riot and violence causes. The *Report of the National Advisory Commission on Civil Disorders,* released in 1968, had some exceedingly sharp words for the lawlessness and violence of many police forces both as contributory factors and in their attempts to check the onset of riot behavior. The commission investigation unequivocally ruled out any "organized plan or conspiracy" as causation or any direction "by any organization or group, international, national, or local," although it did acknowledge that "militant organizations" created "an atmosphere that contributed to the outbreak of disorder." The report's most condemnatory language, however, was levelled directly against white America. The basic and underlying cause of urban riots, which had "long permeated much of American life," was the "white racism" of American society itself, the report stated. White America's lack of concern and segregationist practices accumulated the explosive components of unemployment, inadequate housing and education, and ghetto life. These complaints, plus police practices, were found to be at the top of the list of ghetto grievances and common to almost every riot area. Finally and flatly, the commission stated: "This is our basic conclusion: Our nation is moving toward two societies, one black, one white—separate and unequal."

The Kerner Commission's report's firm insistence on America's white racism as a basic riot cause was not fully accepted by those who could see only the immediate damage and loss results. Its recommendations for the expenditure of both political will and funds were effectively throttled by the tensions and cost of the continuing Vietnamese War. By 1968 the nation was faced with a partially understandable paradox that revealed the progress of blacks to be greater than in any other decade in history, yet showed race relationships as among the worst of any in the American experience. And the Johnson administration's strong attempts to combat poverty and the lack of civil rights at home were considerably offset by the effects of its escalated war policies abroad.

Evaluation of the Johnson Administration

The steep, plunging graph of the Johnson popularity in the public polls went from the phenomenally high point of the 1964 elections to the depths of 1967's rejection with dizzying speed. Few administrations have accomplished such nose dives, and there was little doubt that the Johnson administration was in serious trouble by 1967. Its legislative output in 1965 and 1966 had been prodigious, outranked only by the historical achievements of Roosevelt's New Deal. Much of the Johnson production was an extension of those social welfare beginnings, but with innovative additions in poverty and urban areas, modifications such as rent subsidies in housing legislation, and its own distinctive progress in education and civil rights acts. In 1965 Johnson had been hailed variously as a legislative wizard and a congressional ringmaster with a sure touch of the whip. With the backing of a large public mandate and the benefit of his undoubted skills in manipulation, he had pushed through legislation that had been logjammed all the way back from the Truman era into the Kennedy regime. The beginnings of a poverty program under Kennedy became part of the enactments under the distinctive LBJ emblem of the Great Society, ranging from Appalachian aid to urban opportunity programs. Medicare, blocked since Truman's request in postwar days, broke through to provide the elderly with needed low-priced hospital care. Federal aid for underfunded secondary and elementary education, wrecked heretofore on the shoals of sectarian bickering, sailed through Congress on the new principle of aid to all poor schoolchildren rather than to the particular educational institution itself. The beginnings of consumer legislation and environmental laws appeared.

But both the congressional manipulation and much of the legislation had dubious defects which were to mar the progress and the future influence of the Johnson production. The ringmaster's whip that the media raved about and Johnson's frantic pushing of legislation with one eye cocked on historical record-breaking quickly brought many Congressmen to the point of angry stubborness. The "hurry-up-and-pass-it" insistence of 1965 helped to cancel out legislative progress in 1966 and 1967. Some legislators were actively determined to demonstrate to the press that it takes Congress as well as the Chief Executive to complete the passage of legislation. The War on Poverty legislation, probably the most publicized of all, suffered more than any other for several reasons. It was never funded to the extent necessary to do such a Herculean task. Between 1964 and 1967 the entire program was voted some $6.2 billion, or less than 1 percent of the gross national product, and by 1967 Congress had cut this down to less than one quarter of 1 percent of the gross national product. Johnson took a strong stance for both guns and butter, but Congress would vote funds for Vietnam only at the expense of needed domestic programs. Billed as an urban cure-all, a vast amount of the funds and activities actually benefitted middle-class suburbs more than they did the ghetto poor. The money went for civil defense boondoggles, for airports and extensions of water systems, for freeways. Much of it went to the professional social municipal worker and the welfare agencies and into more jobs for the local bureaucracy. Rural areas received even fewer crumbs, drawing protests from 17 Senators that the Office of Economic Opportunity neglected large areas of rural poverty. Even the specifically allocated Appalachian aid went either to new federal bureaucrats for administering the program, or was spent for roads, dams, and airports which could be only of the most indirect help to the Appalachian poverty stricken. Johnson's idea of selling the War on Poverty as a free enterprise money-maker only briefly drew the support of the business community, and this tactic could never guide the nation toward the long, hard, and probably sacrificial road of poverty eradication. For many of these reasons the young found the War on Poverty to be lacking in moral ammunition. They found it at least insincere and at worst, corrupt, and refused to participate. Even the Johnson era of civil rights, which was preeminent in the 20th-century history of the movement, was diminished by the exacerbations of unmet expectations, the draft, and the huge defense outlays that combined to reveal new and deep chasms between white and black as Johnson prepared to abandon the White House in 1968. Of the brave War on Poverty enactments only the shell of innovation and recognition remained, and the pall of inflation and the Vietnamese War hung over all the LBJ domestic legislation.

But it was in the field of foreign policy that the Johnson administration made the monumental errors that divided American society and shook the public faith in government. It was here that the incredible prevarications of the Johnson administration made a veritable chasm out of the credibility gap. The phrase itself was only coined by newsmen during the LBJ era, but most Americans could trace its existence back to the U-2 incident under Eisenhower. Here the United States government was caught in a series of blatant lies to its own citizens as well as to the world. In the progress of this doleful phenomenon through the intervening administrations and into that of Johnson's successor, Nixon, the Kennedy administration output on the Bay of Pigs made the U-2 statements look like the work of children, and the Johnson administration then carried the process further to new and unenviable heights.

The persistent private and secret war of the CIA in Laos and Cambodia under Eisenhower, Kennedy, Johnson, and then Nixon was just as persistently and flagrantly denied by each succeeding administration. From the bizarre and grotesquely distorted statements on the reasons for intervention in the Dominican Republic to the denial of peace feelers from Hanoi (which, once disclosed, were then dismissed as "not meaningful") Johnson and his advisers and officials told the American public a long series of untruths. Since they were largely after-the-fact announcements, they could not be readily defended where national security was concerned, but they played an influential part in a general mistrust of government. Even Johnson's campaign remarks on Vietnam went far beyond the allowable bounds of campaign exaggerations, as the public found out.

Johnson and his spokesmen sought to give foreign policy on Vietnam a basis of continuity and universal acceptance. President Johnson himself repeatedly mentioned Eisenhower's famous letter to Diem as a source of continuity and "commitment." Yet the *quid pro quo* portions of the letter were not mentioned and, as most students of American government realized, no administration can "commit" another to policies unless they are treaties constitutionally ratified by the United States Senate. Even in the use of the SEATO treaty for administrative propaganda purposes, it was not true to represent American membership as requiring the United States to send troops and planes to defend a signatory. The Rostow doctrine that a solution of the Vietnamese question would preclude all future confrontations was frequently advanced, but met increasing refusal of acceptance. The Rusk efforts to tie in other nations to American policy with an "identity of basic purpose" were more recognizably echoes of messianic conviction from the American past than solidly forged links of mutual agreement with allies. Johnson's actual continuity was the Cold War, the Truman Doctrine of containment of Russia and China, and the American insistence on global containment of revolutionary movements. Johnson was not willing to reverse this concept, and its fearful cost in Vietnam finally caught up to Johnson and the nation.

Many of Johnson's critics sought to find the basic causes for his failure in his personality. They ascribed it to the Texas parochialism, or the habitual secretiveness, or the long-time political willingness to distort or withhold the truth, and an inability to communicate. Johnson exhibited many symptoms of insecurity despite his assertiveness. He thought the eastern press was unfair to him because he was a Texan, without recognizing the ample reasons he afforded the media other than his Texas nationalism. He was sure that the intellectuals were unfair to him because of a snobbish distaste for his vulgarities. He could not realize that if he had been able to end what they thought of as a disgraceful war by the use of four-letter words the dove intellectuals, like Lincoln requesting some of Grant's liquor for his other generals, would have gladly contributed some words of their own for the solution of additional problem areas. Johnson, his critics had to admit, did display diplomatic potential in deciding on euthanasia for the moribund MLF project, in smoothing out the abrasive American contacts with de Gaulle, and in further pursuit of a détente with the Soviet Union. But pushing the country to new limits of military interventionism and destruction and to a new magnitude of governmental prevarication in so doing proved a far overbalancing factor.

The Johnson administration was part and parcel of the changing and turbulent times of the "Convulsive 60s" both as participant and contributor. It was affected as a recipient by those landmark decisions of the Supreme Court which put both congressional districts and state legislature on a basis of equitable population, removing them from their older domination by underpopulated rural areas. The earliest earthshaking decision was *Baker* v. *Carr,* which stated that the urban dwellers of Tennessee were being deprived of 14th Amendment protections by the stubborn refusal of the Tennessee legislature to reapportion itself after several decades of federal census changes between rural and urban areas.

In 1964 the *Reynolds* v. *Sims* and allied cases furnished guidelines requiring both houses of a state legislature to apportion themselves solely on a population basis. As Chief Justice Warren succinctly explained, "Legislators represent people, not trees or acres." In 1963 the Court struck down the county unit rule, another device to ensure rural domination, in *Gray* v. *Saunders*. Conservative Congressmen could also see one of their margins of control crumbling in the 1964 *Wesberry* v. *Sims* decision, which had a similar and far-reaching impact on the makeup of the House of Representatives, by ruling that henceforth all congressional districts must observe equal population bases. Led by Senator Everett McKinley Dirksen (R., Illinois), they sought unsuccessfully in 1965 and 1966 in both houses of Congress to lessen the impact of the Court's rulings through legislation or constitutional amendments. The "one man, one vote" principle meant that congressional districts which required an urban legislator to care for and seek reelection from 450,000 voters while his rural counterpart had only 85,000 or so constituents were effectively outlawed.

The divisiveness of American society reached new heights during the Johnson administration, and much of that was readily traceable to the escalation of both the war and the credibility gap. One measure was the unusually high number of young men who took the grave decision to desert from the armed forces or to forestall the draft by exiling themselves in Canada or elsewhere outside the United States. Although statistics are unreliable here, the desertion rate in 1970 was 52 per thousand, or more than twice that of the Korean War, while draft evaders were estimated at nearly 100,000. Such a high incidence could not be blamed on flaws in the American character since, as historian Henry Steele Commager pointed out, "there was neither large-scale desertion nor draft evasion in World War II, and the national character does not change in a single generation."

The changed values of college and high school students, manifested in everything from long hair styles and marijuana smoking to campus rebellions and antiwar marches, were frequently the result of a dissatisfaction or even complete rejection of American society. In good part, it was a complaint against the mores of a war improperly begun and immorally waged; against social effects ranging from neglect of America domestically to the militarization of society and a brutalization of the war-tested young men. It was also composed of the complaint of individuals against an increasingly mechanized society which was ruled by its technology rather than ruling it for humane ends; which characterized the individual only with a number; and which so polluted its environment as to bring closer the question of its imminent end. The key word for most young and some old was "alienation." An older generation felt itself out of touch more notably than over the usual gap between generations. It supported the presidential war much more readily, either because of having fought in a previous one and thus insisting on the same for the following generation, or because "the President knows more about it than we do," or because of fear of losing American prestige. But by 1967 and 1968 more of the older generation found itself on the antiwar side, either quietly or overtly. Parents were unwilling for their sons to be drafted, or they were concerned by the steady inflation coming from war expenditures, or their television sets brought increasingly unbearable sights into their living rooms. The division in the nation was a deep one, not readily bridged.

Lyndon Johnson did not impress his mounting number of critics as the man for the newly emerging times of the Convulsive 60s. In the latter 1960s he seemed more a politician of pre–World War II days, traditional in mode and approach, unwilling and unable to face new political manifestations. His Cold War crusading rhetoric was delivered in pre-Kennedy primitive exhortations. Where his political rejection was concerned Johnson never knew what hit him, so to speak. He considered it was the nation at fault, not himself, and vainly cited the country's previous election support for wartime Presidents without recognition or awareness of the unique place of the Vietnamese War in American annals. A new wave of political and social rebellion was forming in 1967 and 1968. Neither Lyndon Baines Johnson nor his evident candidate for the presidency were a part of that rebellion which, frustrated and many-channelled in 1968, was to break upon the American 1970s with historic force.

Democratic Rejection: The Election Year Surprises of 1968

The presidential year 1968 saw a dramatic succession of surprises, some of them tragic, and an election fervor and excitement which, at least up through the conventions, surpassed the past half century of American experience. A full year before the elections it seemed a somewhat unexciting conclusion that the incumbent President would probably face the Republican Governor of Michigan, George W. Romney. But the surprises began early, and neither "sure" candidate was in the picture on November 5, 1968.

In the fall of 1967 came the first, overt opposition to Lyndon Johnson. Senator Eugene McCarthy, a Minnesotan and a mild-mannered intellectual who had been a former instructor in his state's Saint Thomas College, announced that he would enter four presidential primaries to demonstrate that his strong dovish views on Vietnam would be more palatable to the public than the hawk's-eye view of the war held by Johnson. His candidacy was scornfully dismissed by the political pros. In his

State of the Union speech in January 1968, the President indicated strongly that his hard line on Vietnam was little changed. If Hanoi demonstrated its "good intentions" he would reduce the bombing, but the insistence on the determination of the United States to dispose of all "aggression" and thereby retain world credibility for the willing use of American power around the globe left no doubt of the military victory demand.

The Tet offensive of early February in Vietnam was a serious blow to the administration's "we're-winning-the-war" publicity. In the face of the Vietcong victories, even though achieved at high costs in casualties, the Pentagon's attempted selling of the offensive as a harbinger of defeat only produced less credibility. Little more than a month later the President received a stiff jolt in the March 12 New Hampshire Democratic primary. Eugene McCarthy had rallied a small army of energetic workers, most of them young, against the full weight of the state's Democratic establishment working for Johnson and had managed an amazing 42 percent to the President's 49 percent and an actual majority of the New Hampshire delegates. The strong vote behind the antiwar policies of a virtual unknown brought another surprise to the nation when Senator Robert F. Kennedy of New York (his residence had been changed several years ago from Massachusetts) announced on March 16 that he would be a contender for the presidential nomination. Kennedy said his race would be based upon new policies, ". . . policies to end the bloodshed in Vietnam and in our cities, policies to close the gaps between black and white, rich and poor, young and old, in this country and around the world."

The greatest surprise of the year came on March 31, when Johnson on national television took himself out of the race for the presidential nomination. He stated that his withdrawal might reduce the divisiveness in the nation and he could thereby concentrate on ending the war. It was a move that Johnson had evidently been considering for several months. Not until April 27, after it was no longer possible to enter any of the presidential primaries, did Vice President Hubert H. Humphrey enter the field with Johnson's blessing. The Vice President, noted earlier for his civil rights and labor support, had by 1968 become an acceptable Johnson substitute to the party conservatives, especially in the South. His position on Vietnam was fully as hawkish as was Johnson's and another strong supporter, President George Meany of the AFL-CIO. Humphrey's enthusiasm for American intervention in Indochina dated back to the Truman and Eisenhower administrations and, as he told *U.S. News & World Report* (May 27, 1968), "If Nixon and Humphrey should be the candidates in the general election, I don't think our views of the war would be far apart."

Heading into the primaries, the Democratic party was soon revealed to be in far more trouble than complacent party heads had realized. Gallup polls taken in 1940 and again in 1967 on party support showed the Democrats stable over the years at 42 percent and independent voters from 20 up to a formidable 31 percent. Although years of prosperity had attracted some business and previously Republican support, the Democratic party had grown conservative and remote from the grass roots and the public pulse. But the expanded, educated middle classes included many—of both the parent and their offspring student generation—who increasingly questioned the Establishment orthodoxy on such values as the American position in the world, or domestically on rights for blacks and the poor, or on the neglected environment. With its economic ties to the Democrats loosened by a more pervasive prosperity, the new politics of this group skeptically questioned both the quality of American life and the willingness of candidates to take constructive and specific action in its improvement. The Vietnamese War made inroads into this group. As Indochina devoured more and more men, money, and resources, these voters were joined by some of the business community as well as all the civil rights, antipoverty, and environmental forces, black and white, whom the war's fearful drains had pulled together.

Eugene McCarthy's victory in the Wisconsin primary on April 2 was followed by the shocking news of Reverend Martin Luther King's assassination in Memphis, and the resulting wave of riots lent new urgency

North Philadelphia Railroad Station, June 8, 1968. Crowds lined the rails and every rail station to wave farewells to the train carrying Robert F. Kennedy's body. His brother Edward Kennedy stands on the rear platform. (Wide World Photos)

to the issues of civil rights and urban housing. When McCarthy and Kennedy finally met in Indiana, Kennedy was the winner. He repeated his performance in the Nebraska primary. Where the McCarthy pitch was to the audiences of the late Adlai Stevenson, Kennedy made special efforts to woo ethnic groups, the urban areas, the poor and lower-middle classes. In Oregon, where these elements were not so numerically strong, Kennedy suffered the first defeat of his short campaign.[8] After a close victory over McCarthy in California, Robert Kennedy was shot in the head on June 5 in Los Angeles' Ambassador Hotel ballroom by a Jordanian immigrant who thought him to be pro-Israel. Kennedy died the next day. Crowds estimated at several million either followed the funeral procession at Saint Patrick's Cathedral in New York, stood crying alongside the railroad tracks on the route to Washington, or crowded silently behind the funeral cortege as it moved slowly to the hillside in Arlington where his brother was buried. The entire nation was in a state of shock and many echoed mentally the puzzled and bitter phrase of a weeping man as he watched the funeral train slowly part the grieving crowds, "What kind of a country is this?" The cry represented the shame felt over the assassinations of Robert Kennedy's brother before him and the more recent murder of Martin Luther King. It indicated the nation's deep doubt regarding its assumed political stability and democratic processes.

The Republican route to the convention was less divisive, although the early front-runner was displaced. Governor George Romney had begun his campaign in November 1967 as a war critic with the support of some leading Republicans. But neither his war position nor his organization drew the necessary audiences or finances, and he withdrew in February. The new and more solidly established front-runner was Richard M. Nixon, who had spent considerable effort in altering his previous image. No longer the surly gubernatorial loser of 1962, when the press was shrilly blamed for his political downfall, the "new" Nixon was poised and smiling. Working out of his New York law offices, where he had taken up residence after the California defeat, Nixon had worked assiduously and successfully for Republican congressional candidates in 1966 and had strongly supported Goldwater in 1964. He moved confidently into the New Hampshire primary, and then to victories in Wisconsin, Indiana, Nebraska, and Oregon. He avoided only his old home state, where Governor Ronald Reagan, ostensibly not a candidate, was nevertheless using the California delegates as a base to seek support from the Goldwater wing of the party. In April, Governor Nelson Rockefeller of New York announced his availability as an alternative choice to Nixon. Although considered a liberal on civil rights, Rockefeller's

---

[8] It was in fact the only political defeat ever suffered by any Kennedy since John F. first entered Massachusetts politics in 1946.

stand on the Vietnamese War took the same hard-line position held by Nixon, Johnson, and Humphrey. But Nixon's lead through victories in the primaries was too large at convention time for Rockefeller's advertising campaign to overcome.

On the way to the Democratic convention at Chicago in August, polls consistently showed McCarthy as the choice over Humphrey. But the Vice President, remaining quietly in the background, rounded up the delegates. In many states these were chosen or picked with little reference to public wishes or after public debate on the issues. But the city bosses, the courthouse crews, the state and federal bureaucrats, the labor spokesmen, and all those making up the party organization controlled the delegate and convention structure easily enough to ensure Humphrey's nomination. Platform efforts by McCarthy and Senator George McGovern of South Dakota to adopt an antiwar plank were thwarted by the President's personal call insisting on a strict support of the administration position. The McCarthy-McGovern and other liberal groups achieved their only success in liberalizing the party rules on convention procedure and the procedures for the choice of delegates for future conventions.

The tight administration grasp on the proceedings was quickly demonstrated. At 2:00 A.M. Wednesday morning, the Johnson-Humphrey leaders sought to hold a debate and vote on the Vietnam issue so that television screens would not reveal the angry divisiveness within the party. The permanent chairman, Representative Carl Albert of Oklahoma, refused to recognize a motion from a McCarthy delegate to postpone but, when the convention floor erupted into angry tumult, recognized a similar motion from the Chicago party boss, Mayor Daley. Mayor Daley's workers, chiefly from the Sanitation Department, also poured into the galleries with apparently improper convention credentials. Around the Amphitheatre, where the convention was held, thousands of police, National Guardsmen, and federal agents set up the most stringent security arrangements in the history of American presidential conventions. The extensive barbed-wire fences around the convention hall and the numerous security checks gave rise to the joking nickname of "Stalag 68" for the convention. President Johnson thought better of appearing, the first incumbent in several decades to miss such an occasion. Television viewers saw police control of demonstrators erupt into violence in which enforcement officers indiscriminately gassed antiwar groups and well-dressed onlookers alike at the Conrad Hilton Hotel. Police anger at hippie insults resulted in uncontrolled head cracking and gassing of the fleeing crowds which the Daniel Walker report to the National Commission on the Cause and Prevention of Violence could only characterize as a "police riot." Reporters and television personnel, occupied in publicizing both the machine-made decisions in the convention and the police actions outside, seemed to be a special target for police clubs.

Humphrey's nomination was never in doubt, with 1,762 votes to McCarthy's 601 and McGovern's 146. Even the traditional attempt to bring the party together after the presidential nomination was frustrated. Chairman Albert, despite obvious opposition to the suggestion on the floor, gaveled through a motion of false unanimity. Humphrey quickly announced that his choice for the vice presidential nomination was Senator Edmund Muskie of Maine. In full agreement with the Humphrey platform, Muskie was a Catholic of Polish background expected to lend the ticket "ethnic" strength.

By contrast, the Republican convention in Chicago was a plodding affair. The threat to Nixon by Rockefeller did not materialize, with party regulars remaining unmoved by public polls showing the latter with a better chance to defeat Humphrey in November. Of more seriousness behind the scenes was the challenge from Reagan, with some support from the Deep South delegates. Observers credited the work of Senator Strom Thurmond of South Carolina for turning a large part of the Southern tide to Nixon. Commentators referred to the "Southern Strategy," explained as promises by the winning candidate to ameliorate the federal position toward southern states and Southern feelings on desegregation and resented Supreme Court decisions. It also included some needed favoritism for the South's textile industry.[9] Although denied in specific terms, the Thurmond-Nixon combination was evidently part of a general Republican tactic to move the South more solidly into the permanent base of the Republican party. Nixon's choice for a running mate surprisingly was the little-known Governor of Maryland, Spiro T. Agnew. A newly ultraconservative spokesman, Agnew's choice enraged liberal Republicans, but southern Republicans and Agnew's border-state position overruled them.

The Nixon campaign was the best-financed campaign organization in Republican history, and profited from the Nixon errors of the hectic campaign of 1960. The Republican candidate cultivated an impression of dignity, at the same time linking himself with an Eisenhower-like restoration of order and stability in government such as Ike had used effectively against another Democratic administration. Nixon's distrust of television as a medium because of its merciless disclosure of personality in 1960 was overcome by concentrated professional attention on the art of TV appearances. Nixon the candidate became a packaged commodity of the advertising world's skillful manipulation. Humphrey denounced "packaged politics" as a substitute for the issues, but Nixon's carefully coached appearances and the image projected with endless

---

[9] See Reg Murphy and Hal Gulliver, *The Southern Strategy* (New York, 1971).

60-second television spots undoubtedly played an important role in America's first electronic election.

Nixon's personal appearances generated considerable enthusiasm. He had obviously written off the blacks and the inner cities, leaving these to Humphrey. His speeches were directed at white suburbia and the "forgotten" Americans who worked hard but saw their way upward blocked by inflation and taxes. The speech which evoked the best response and thus saw constant repetition was directed to the nation's plight under two previous Democratic administrations:

> ". . . when the strongest nation in the world can be tied down in a war in Vietnam for four years with no end in sight; when the nation with the greatest respect for law is torn apart by unprecedented lawlessness; when the richest country in the world can't manage its own economy; . . . and when the President of the United States of America for the first time in history cannot travel . . . to any major city in the country without fear of a hostile demonstration, then it's time for a new leadership for the American people. . . ."

Nixon did not say what contributed to the causation of American problems or how he would solve them, but the war's inflation and impact on domestic affairs presented a ready target. On ending the war itself, Nixon dodged policy discussion as jeopardizing the peace negotiations in progress in Paris, or seemed to indicate what the Press soon called a "secret plan," which he said could not be revealed.

Hubert Humphrey's chief task was to show some measure of independence from the unpopular LBJ. He had some success by carefully hedged statements in a September 30 television address from Salt Lake City which considered that a cessation of the bombing of North Vietnam could be "an acceptable risk for peace." He made the usual demands of Hanoi and assurances to Saigon, but was aided when on October 31 President Johnson announced "it was now safe" (without explanation) to cease the bombing. Humphrey's foremost asset was his own unquenchable verve and his dogged optimism, which kept him unflaggingly on the speech circuit. His underdog role enlisted grudgingly increased support. Humphrey was most effective against Nixon in pointing out the refusal of his Republican opponent to debate the issue with him, and in criticizing Nixon's alliance with Thurmond and "extremist elements" in the South.

An unusual element of the 1968 campaign was the candidacy of former Governor of Alabama George C. Wallace on the American Independent Party ticket. Wallace directed his remarks to "the little people," whom he insisted were tired of the federal government telling them "when to get up in the morning and when to go to bed at night." He also insisted his candidacy stood for "law 'n order in the streets."

Both of the symbolic utterances were readily translatable, the former directed against the federal desegregation laws, and the latter against blacks. The recent image of Wallace standing in the doors of the University of Alabama and the activities of his state troopers on the Selma march was readily understood by his listeners despite his denials of being a racist. He titillated his audiences by inveighing against the "pointy-head intellectuals" in Washington, and used a somewhat Jacksonian approach to assure the average man that his wisdom was far more accurate and trustworthy than that of the experts. Wallace exploited a disaffection with bland partisan politics and a lack of national leadership, and his racist attacks were shrewdly directed to the lower-income whites whose economic status made them more vulnerable to the allegedly fast rise of blacks and to direct competition for jobs and housing. But by late October Wallace's repeated stand had lost much of its emotional impact, and the blacks and antiwar students he had denounced began a noisy retaliation at his meetings. Both major candidates attacked Wallace. Humphrey denounced Wallace's "strategy of organized hate," and warned of the effects of his deliberate inflaming of prejudice. The Republicans were more covert in their assaults on Wallace in the South, although they particularly enraged the Alabama governor in reference to his short stature and previous judgeships by insisting that he should be called "LBJ—Little Bitty Judge."

September poll figures showed Nixon with 43 percent, Humphrey 31 percent, Wallace 19 percent, and 7 percent undecided. Nixon's voter support remained static during the remainder of the campaign, with Humphrey making steady progress at the expense of both Nixon and Wallace. In late October and early November, the polls showed scarcely a percentage point between Nixon and Humphrey. The Democratic candidate's dogged campaign and Nixon's refusal to debate him accounted in part for Humphrey's pulling nearly even. Some Democrats who first opposed him were reconciled by what they thought to be a less Johnsonian attitude on the war. Some voter uneasiness among independents over the "old" Nixon image and avoidance of issues prevented the Republican candidate from picking up extra support. Spiro Agnew's lack of knowledgeable background was soon evidenced in his bumbling statements, and observers could not credit him for any added strength on the Republican ticket. In sharp contrast, the cool, calm utterances of Edmund Muskie seeking party unity against the opposition earned him a national respect as well as the place of foremost contender for 1972. In October Wallace named Air Force General Curtis LeMay as his running mate. But LeMay's previous threat to bomb North Vietnam "back to the Stone Age," and his continued bluster regarding the atom bomb's conceivable use probably lost Wallace more votes than it gained.

On November 5 Richard Milhous Nixon became the 37th President of the United States by one of the narrowest margins in history. He failed to win a majority, defeating Humphrey and Wallace by 43.4 percent of the popular vote to 42.7 and 13.5 respectively. The total number of votes cast dropped to 61 percent of the eligible electorate, reflecting a general distaste for all three candidates and the siphoning off of votes for smaller parties not tabulated nationally. Of the 73,211,562 votes cast, Nixon received 31,785,480, Humphrey 31,275,165, and Wallace 9,906,473. Nixon's 301 electoral votes were sufficient for his election, followed by Humphrey's 191 and Wallace's 46, although many races were so close that even the electoral count was in doubt for several days. Nixon won four big states by narrow margins—California, New Jersey, Ohio, and Illinois. Humphrey took the industrial states· of New York, Pennsylvania, and Michigan, and added Minnesota, Texas, and most of the Northeast. Nixon made nearly a clean sweep of the West except for Washington and Hawaii, and won most of the border states except West Virginia and Agnew's Maryland. Wallace's victories were limited to the Deep South states of Arkansas, Mississippi, Alabama, Louisiana, and Georgia. His strategy had always been to take enough electoral votes to throw the election into the House of Representatives as a means of extracting concessions from the eventual winner, but this looking backward to 1824's experience was never close to realization. As a third party, Wallace's American Independence party received less voter support than such previous contenders as the Progressives in 1924 or the "Know-Nothings" in 1856.

Nixon's "Southern Strategy" was not successful in the Deep South, but if Wallace had not been on the ticket these states probably would have gone to him. More than offsetting this, however, was the probability that several additional and more important industrial states would have gone to Humphrey had Wallace's name not drawn 6 to 8 percent in such states as Illinois and Ohio. Nixon's hairline victory did not extend to his party's candidates for Congress, although Republican governors moved into 31 state houses. In Congress, Nixon, like Eisenhower, was unable to bring at least one of the two houses in with him. Republicans gained five seats in the Senate, bringing them from a 37 to 63 division up to 42 to 58, but their heavily financed efforts in the House of Representatives changed only four seats out of the 435-seat membership.

The structure of both the major parties appeared heading for trouble. Resentment over the undemocratic system of choice of convention delegates was shared by both parties, although of major dissonance only among the Democrats. Neither seemed particularly responsive to the wishes of the electorate, if preconvention sentiment in public opinion polls favoring Rockefeller over Nixon and McCarthy over Humphrey was accurate. This tight rule by the party pros was particularly under attack among the Democrats, with reforms advanced by the McGovern Commission soon to be accepted grudgingly or with qualification in a large majority of the states. In 1968 public confidence in the political process itself, as well as in the two major parties, was seriously eroded. A rebellion was brewing among young voters and concerned citizens everywhere for more equitable and less corrupt politics, for participatory democracy. The prolonged vicissitudes of the Vietnamese War, the assassinations of Martin Luther King and Robert Kennedy, and the fierce resentment over the Boss Daley tactics both inside and outside the Chicago convention hall all helped to swell the demand for a new kind of leadership in American politics.

Suggestions for Reading

The works on Johnson mentioned in the preceding chapter are recommended here as well.

Much of the works on foreign policy are confined to the Vietnamese War. For the varying views of participants see Townsend Hoopes, *The Limits of Intervention** (1969); Chester Cooper, *The Lost Crusade* (1970); and General Maxwell Taylor, *Swords and Ploughshares* (1972). A critical account of the origins and history of the war is David Halberstam, *The Best and the Brightest* (1973). A comprehensive collection of documents is M. E. Gettleman, ed., *Vietnam: History, Documents, and Opinions** (1970). The most comprehensive source materials are in *The Pentagon Papers** (1971). Valuable for understanding are background works such as Bernard Fall, *The Two Vietnams** (2d rev. ed. 1967); Joseph Buttinger, *Vietnam: A Dragon Embattled* (2 vols. 1967); and Robert Shaplen, *Road from War: Vietnam 1965–1970* (1970). The Tonkin Gulf episode is treated in J. C. Goulden, *Truth Is the First Casualty* (1971); Anthony Austin, *The President's War* (1971); and E. G. Windchy, *Tonkin Gulf* (1971). Other events are described in Don Oberdorfer, *Tet* (1971), and Seymour Hersh, *My Lai** (1971). See also Frank Harvey, *Air War—Vietnam** (1967); David Kraslow and S. H. Loory, *The Secret Search for Peace in Vietnam** (1968); Franz Schurman, P. D. Scott, and Reginald Zelnick, *The Politics of Escalation in Vietnam** (1966); and the excellent work by Raphael Littauer and Norman Uphoff, editors of Cornell's Air War Study Group, *The Air War in Indochina** (rev. ed., 1972). For widely differing views regarding domestic criticism, see A. M. Schlesinger, Jr., *The Bitter Heritage** (1966), and Noam Chomsky, *American Power and the New Mandarins** (1969). On Laos, see Wilfred Burchett, *The Furtive War** (1968).

For arms control, see W. B. Bader, *The United States and the Spread of Nuclear Weapons* (1968). An introduction to the space race is Walter Sullivan, ed., *America's Race for the Moon* (1962). See also Norman Mailer, *Of a Fire on the Moon* (1970) on the astronauts.

For the continuing Negro Revolution, consult the various works by black leaders. Foremost among these are Eldridge Cleaver, *Soul on Ice*° (1963); Stokely Carmichael and C. V. Hamilton, *Black Power*° (1967); M. L. King, Jr., *Where Do We Go from Here: Chaos or Community?*° (1967); Julius Lester, *Look Out, Whitey!*° (1968); James Baldwin, *The Fire Next Time*° (1963); and Malcolm X, *Autobiography*° (1965). See also J. H. Clark, ed., *Malcolm X, The Man and His Times*° (1969).

On the riots in the urban ghettoes, see Robert Cornot, *Rivers of Blood, Years of Darkness* (1968), and W. S. Murphy, *Burn, Baby, Burn: The Watts Riot* (1966), for the Los Angeles riot, and H. G. Locke, *The Detroit Riot of 1967* (1969). The violence in American society was probed by a number of reports and anthologies. See especially H. D. Graham and T. R. Gurr, *The History of Violence in America*° (1969); *Report of the National Advisory Commission on Civil Disorders*° (1968); Thomas Rose, ed., *Violence in America*° (1969); and Richard Hofstadter and Michael Wallace, eds., *American Violence: A Documentary History*° (1970).

On Mexican-Americans, see Faliciano Rivera, *The Chicanos* (1972); Edward Simmen, ed., *The Chicano: From Caricature to Self-Portrait* (1970); and Stan Steiner's works, *La Raza* (1970), and *The New Indians* (1968).

8

The Return of Richard Nixon

The Nixon Administration

THE Richard Nixon who as 37th President of the United States made the Inaugural Address on January 20, 1969, had not been expected even to return to politics after a severe drubbing in the California gubernatorial race of 1962. Neither friends nor critics thought it possible, especially coming as it did on the heels of the greatest loss of them all—the presidency—in 1960. But Nixon the man and Nixon the politician—and most Americans saw the two images blended together inextricably—was a persistent, compulsive, guileful, and politically hardworking duality. The violation of his written promise to his wife after the 1962 debacle not to run again for public office was evidently always a strong likelihood, given the life meaning that politics held for this man. Many felt they did not know the "real" Nixon, or even if there was one. An inner-directed, well-insulated, essentially humorless person, Nixon remained a loner, enigmatic and aloof, even as a lifelong politician. Unlike Hoover and Eisenhower, Nixon was the first Republican in half a century to make it into the White House as a machine politician, a genuine pro.

Richard Milhous Nixon was born January 9, 1913, in Yorba Linda, California, although the family home was, for the most part, in nearby Whittier. His parents were Frank Nixon and Hannah Milhous, migrants to the West from Ohio and Indiana respectively. His mother was of the rare breed of Irish Quaker, and the boy was raised in his mother's faith. The Nixon family fortunes were meagre. Even when their lot was somewhat improved the entire Nixon family toiled as though poverty were just around the corner. Everyone, including Dick and his four brothers, shared the daily work load. The boys were encouraged to be serious and self-reliant, and play was frequently regarded as taking precious time away from work. The powerful virtues of a work ethic were an important part of the boys' early training.

A hard worker in school as well, something of a loner, Dick continued his home chores without complaint. Excellent marks in high school were achieved through application rather than any brilliancy, and the notion that hard work could make up for any and all other deficiencies was implanted early. A fluent and tireless debater, Dick won a scholarship award and chose the local Quaker Whittier College. His energy and capacity to learn brought him various student and academia honors and a boost into Duke University Law School. Continued hard work, for which he was noted, graduated him high in the class of 1937. Several years of successful law practice and the position of Assistant City Attorney of Whittier followed.

In 1940, Nixon married Thelma "Pat" Ryan, a Whittier schoolteacher, and during World War II he worked briefly in OPA and then as a Navy officer. In 1946 he jumped into an underdog campaign against avid New Dealer Congressman Jerry Voorhis in the usually Republican and newly gerrymandered 12th District of California. Nixon used Voorhis' ties with labor to impute ties with Moscow, and housewives' complaints against wartime controls furnished additional material with which Voorhis was toppled. Nixon's sponsorship in HUAC of Whittaker Chambers for the Hiss case during the Cold War years brought him national publicity. He utilized the anti-Communist theme of the postwar years to defeat the well-regarded Congresswoman Helen Gahagan Douglas for a California Senate seat. Mrs. Douglas, although a vigorous foe of communism and also of Henry Wallace's Progressive party, was subverted through "soft on communism" tactics and the labeling of "The Pink Lady." Nixon defeated her in a smear campaign which saw both sides straining political hyperbole to the point of incredulity. The Hiss case and the California Senate victory propelled Nixon into vice presidential consideration and years of frustration and impatient subordination to Eisenhower. After losing narrowly to Kennedy in 1960, a 1962 Nixon gubernatorial race against Democrat Edmund "Pat" Brown—also a losing effort—was described as "the dirtiest campaign in California history." Attempting to use again the "soft on communism" theme, Nixon had found it did not work and after the election bade a bitter political "farewell forever" tirade to an astonished group of journalists. His subsequent move to New York and legal affairs never deterred him from stumping the country in 1964 and 1966 in an indefatigable speech-making support of Republican congressional nominees, with resultant influence in party circles.

During the campaign Nixon had said:

I have always thought this country could run itself domestically without a President. All you want is a competent Cabinet to run the country at home. You need a President for foreign policy; no Secretary of State is really important. The President makes foreign policy.

The Secretary of State appointment probably reflected this concept. It went to William P. Rogers, once an Assistant Attorney General under Eisenhower, and an old friend of Nixon's. The rise to highest importance of Dr. Henry Kissinger as Presidential Assistant for National Security affairs further reduced the Secretary of State position to overseeing internal organization matters. Secretary of Defense was given to Melvin R. Laird, Republican Representative from Wisconsin. Notable for support of military spending, Laird was expected to reverse the McNamara policy of bringing the military under tight civilian control. A Chicago banker, David M. Kennedy, became Secretary of the Treasury. He yielded the post in 1971 to an ambitious bipartisan Texas Democrat, ex-Governor John M. Connally. The Attorney General was John N. Mitchell, of the law firm of Nixon, Mudge, Rose, Guthrie, Alexander, and Mitchell. Mitchell's advisory duties ranged far beyond the Attorney General's department, and he was credited with playing an important role in the Southern Strategy and other political gambits. His place was taken in 1972 by his deputy, Richard G. Kleindienst, an Arizona protégé of Barry Goldwater's who was confirmed only after prolonged Senate conflict. The Cabinet appointments were entirely from corporation ranks and upper-echelon Republican politicians. Moderately progressive by Republican standards, it included former Governor of Michigan George Romney as Secretary of Housing and Urban Development, and former Governor of Massachusetts John A. Volpe as Secretary of Transportation. Perhaps its most notable feature was its singularly high rate of turnover, which saw a change of occupancy for all posts except State and Defense at least once during Nixon's first four years.

The Nixon White House and advisory staff had several collective characteristics. Very few of his aides had previous government experience. Many were from among his previous campaign associates or friends from his law practice days in New York. An unusual number were advertising agency executives, with four from the same Los Angeles firm. They shared a strong view of the corporate ethic, and Washington pressmen considered their group focus to be firmly to the right of center. The Nixon staff was larger than any of its predecessors and operated more as specialty squads on foreign policy, domestic policy, political affairs, and administration and speech making.

Easily the foremost of Nixon's advisory appointments, both in stature and in influence, was Dr. Henry A. Kissinger, ex-Harvard professor. A boyhood refugee from Hitler in 1938, when his father, a Jewish professor, was expelled, Kissinger's political hero was Prince Metternich of Austria. Kissinger admired the way in which this foremost practitioner of Europe's balance-of-power doctrine managed to confine European diplomatic processes to an elite handful of virtually autonomous foreign ministers. Kissinger was identified with principles of world stability, firm counterrevolutionary action, and American global primacy. An individual capable of considerable personal tact and charm and with great powers of persuasion and argument, Kissinger was also described in the press as "arrogant," and "abrasive." He soon built up a personal staff of 110 aides in the White House and assumed a commanding influence more potent in foreign policy than the Secretary of State.

Nixon dropped the titles of Press Secretary and Appointments Secretary as having too much influence on the presidency. Ronald Ziegler, a former campaign aide, was only permitted to report as Press Relations Assistant that material released by the President, and the latter position was relegated to that of schedule keeper. John D. Erlichman, also a former campaign aide, occupied an extremely influential post as the President's Assistant for Domestic Affairs. Other key assistants who saw the President daily were Bryce N. Harlow, an Eisenhower congressional lobbyist, and H. R. Haldeman, a long-time associate, as Counsellor to the President. Under Kennedy, the O'Connors, O'Briens, and other ethnically recognizable assistants were dubbed by the irreverent Washington newsmen as the "Irish Mafia." Under Nixon, the many assistants with names such as Kissinger and Kleindienst, Erlichman and Haldeman, Klein, Shultz, and Ziegler, were quickly labelled "the Berlin Wall" or "the German General Staff." Most of the high-level patronage jobs went to white, male Republicans, and criticism was levelled at the lack of appointments from the ranks of women and minority groups. A higher number of Southerners received patronage appointments than under other recent Presidents. The Nixon administration was clearly aimed at stability rather than any change, and the President and his advisers moved to meet the challenges of the new administration with calm confidence.

Nixon and the Domestic Scene

In his inaugural address, Nixon had pleaded for unity and had asked that "we stop shouting at one another." For its part, he said, "government will listen." But in his continuing relations with Congress, as well as in his policies with the national economy and the nation's highest court, elements of a shouting match persisted. Nixon was a minority President, with something less than 50 percent of the country's votes. Nixon added to his handicap by a disinterest in and an inadequate knowledge of congressional liaison. Despite his numerous years both in the House and the Senate, Nixon had no penetrating knowledge of congressional ways. Further, his aides were without experience either in policy making or in politics, and were inclined to view Congress as a distasteful and frequently hostile gathering to be manipulated or intimidated.

President Nixon's earlier years had some element of the usual honeymoon period in them, perhaps since few new dramatic proposals were offered. In part, Nixon seemed to go along with the continuity of many Johnson urban programs. However, the firing or forced resignations of upper-echelon officials in the Office of Economic Opportunity, in the legal services to the poor programs, and in the open-housing division of HUD indicated that the Nixon administration intended to reverse the thrust of the Johnson poverty program. In an economy drive, Nixon also closed more than half of the Job Corps training centers, and suggested legislation which would remove job training from federal control and hand it over to the states. It soon became apparent that Nixon had abandoned any emphasis on the urban elements and the poor for the innocuous abstraction of a "better quality of life" for "all Americans."

While President Nixon had mentioned new proposals such as welfare reform and sharing federal revenue with the states, he did not actually present Congress with a comprehensive legislative program until January 1971. In his State of the Union address, he included those items among what he described as his "six great goals": revenue-sharing; a government reorganization which would combine twelve Cabinet functions within eight new groupings; a national health insurance program; environmental initiatives; welfare reform; and a full-employment economy. The "great goals" were largely unrealized. The White House never really pushed for a reorganization of government, and Nixon himself vetoed several of the most important environmental bills, including the most comprehensive of all—the Federal Water Pollution Control Act of 1972. Congress, however, promptly overrode his veto. In welfare reform, Nixon officially introduced the new concept of a guaranteed minimal income in his family Assistance Program. While conservatives balked at both the principle and the expenditures, liberals and moderates objected to its regressive elements, which included a minimal support far below what government statistics listed as a bare subsistence level. Additionally, Nixon soon requested a slowdown of any consideration of the proposal. The health insurance goal, when it became evident that it favored private insurance firms and preserved the doctors' fee system, received little action in Congress. A "full-employment economy" was more a matter of rhetoric than of reality. Unemployment moved from about 3.5 percent in 1968 to a steady 6 percent neighborhood in 1972, and administration economists insisted that a 1 percent reduction in that figure might have to be considered a reasonable resting place for the American employment rate.

Thus the revenue-sharing plan was the only one of Nixon's "great goals" to be accepted, and this came only after years of modification and struggle. The concept was neither as new nor as "revolutionary" as Nixon labeled it, since it had a fervent advocate in the Eisenhower years in Senator Bob Taft, Sr. It also appeared in the Republican platform of 1952. As President Nixon first presented it, revenue sharing would have ended federal expenditures in such programs as urban development, transportation, job training, and rural development. Funds would be turned over to the states, but with no guidelines whatsoever as to how they might be spent. The flaws in this presentation were quickly challenged. Many public opinion leaders and more than a few Congressmen noted that, with all its faults, the federal government was still far more responsive to the needs of the people and with a better record of efficiency and honesty than state and local governments. They also pointed out that minorities and disadvantaged groups frequently had no champion other than the federal government. Opposition also came from fiscal conservatives opposed to a system in which one level of government raised funds but turned them over to another governmental entity without any control over how they were expended.

The magnet of federal funds proved irresistible to many state and local governments unwilling or unable to raise their own money. A modified bill, the State and Local Fiscal Assistance Act of 1972, was finally enacted. As compromised between House and Senate, the act set aside $30.2 billion in a special trust fund to be distributed regularly throughout a five-year period retroactively beginning on January 1, 1972. A Senate version favored smaller states at the expense of larger, more urban states. The House bill reversed this, and a compromise permitted a state to use whichever formula gave it the most. In compromises over the formula to be used, such factors as population, tax effort, and income level eventually favored poorer, central-city areas and poor, rural areas over the more affluent suburbs. One third of the funds went to state governments and two thirds, using the same deciding factors, was allotted to local governments. A weak system of "priorities" was given for guidelines in spending the money, and race, ethnic, and sex discriminations were forbidden in any program funded wholly or in part by the revenue-sharing funds. So that states would not take the opportunity to reduce their own payments to local governments, a penalty clause would automatically reduce the states' federal share by an equal amount for such transgressions.

In areas such as national security, Nixon achieved a mixed bag of defeats and victories. His presidential commission on an All-Volunteer

Military (the Gates Commission) reported that the draft could be ended in 1971, but Nixon disagreed. He insisted that the Pentagon required a two-year extension of the draft system beyond its 1971 cutoff date. A strong congressional movement sought to limit the extension to one year, but lost to the administration proposal by a slim two-vote margin in the House. The bill envisioned the beginning of a volunteer system of armed forces as of July 1, 1973. However, conscription could be resumed by Congress, and all Selective Service procedures—from yearly lotteries to preinduction physicals—remained on the books. An even closer vote gave Nixon a hairline victory in supporting the administration's Safeguard antiballistic missile system (ABM). This was the so-called "thin system" which supposedly was required for a possible attack by China. When the Army sought to locate the nuclear warheads near major cities, home owners united with those who claimed the ABM system was a prime example of wasteful Pentagon spending to block funds for construction. A 50 to 50 tie vote in the Senate, however, defeated the move. Nixon soon advanced to an even broader ABM system. Administration supporters argued that the further nuclear development would encourage the Russians, in the ongoing Strategic Arms Limitation Talks (SALT), to accept nuclear limitation more readily. Congressional and public opposition, including many scientists, insisted that it would only spur on the Russians to matching efforts and needlessly complicate the SALT discussions.

Administration opponents were more successful in refusing to vote funds for the enormously controversial supersonic transport (SST) so desired by the aerospace industry. The administration argued that to refuse funds would jeopardize jobs in the aerospace industry, and that the governmental monies already advanced would thus be wasted. Its antipollution opponents insisted that the prototype's 1,888 mile per hour speed had already demonstrated shock wave reports of such property damage as to preclude its flight over land. Fiscal opponents argued against government subsidy to aircraft builders and cost overruns which inevitably required still more tax funds, and a Senate vote of 52 to 41 denied the $290 million requested. Where funds for the national defense were concerned, however, Congress approved late in 1972 a staggering $74.3 billion for the Defense Department's 1973 appropriation. This was the largest sum ever granted any governmental unit in the nation's history.

Some of the lesser cracks in the facade of American society were plastered over with constitutional amendments. After many years of argument had set up a supporting ground swell of public opinion, Congress finally voted a 26th Amendment to the Constitution which would lower the age for exercising the right to vote to 18 years. Quickly ratified by the states, it went into effect in time for the 1972 presidential elections. Similarly, a proposed amendment first attempted nearly half a century earlier was overwhelmingly favored by Congress. This was the Equal Rights for Women Amendment, which was passed in 1972 and sent on to the states for ratification as the 27th Amendment with a proposed effective date of 1974. In the inflammatory area of antibusing arguments, the Senate refused to pass the highly restrictive provisions embodied in the House version of the Higher Education Amendments of 1972. The Senate's refusal prompted President Nixon, during the heat of the 1972 campaign, to threaten "going to the people" for the generating of pressure sufficient to pass a constitutional amendment which would incorporate strict antibusing provisions. Another unsuccessful attempt at amending the constitution was a move to restore prayers to the public schools by that method, but it had little support in Congress.

Although Congress in the earlier Nixon years was generally adjudged to be conservative in tone and action, the President's more fundamentalist right-wing supporters considered that their wishes were felt only in such areas as crime control and Supreme Court appointments. In the former category, Congress passed a variety of laws aimed hopefully at "crime in the streets," several of which alarmed legalists for their possibly unconstitutional assault on First and Fifth Amendment safeguards. The Comprehensive Drug Abuse Prevention and Control Act of 1970, while it unified a patchwork of narcotic and drug laws and reduced the penalties for simple possession of marijuana, also drew strong criticism for its "no-knock" search provisions. The District of Columbia Criminal Procedure Act of 1970 was intended to act as a "model" package which, if effective, could then be used across the nation. The bill lowered to 15 years the age at which a juvenile charged with a felony could be tried as an adult, and authorized a life sentence for a person convicted of a third felony. It not only approved additional no-knock searches, but authorized up to 60 days of pretrial detention if the defendant was pronounced too dangerous to be released on bail.

President Nixon made no secret of his intention of shifting Supreme Court membership safely to the right. When Chief Justice Earl Warren retired, Nixon appointed Warren E. Burger as the nation's 15th Chief Justice. Burger had little or no legal reputation, but had been an important political organizer for the Eisenhower-Nixon ticket of 1952 and had eventually received appointment to the U.S. Circuit Court of Appeals for the District of Columbia. With the resignation of Justice Abe Fortas after the acceptance of outside fees from questionable individuals, Nixon's choice for a replacement, Judge Clement F. Haynsworth, Jr. of South Carolina, was the cause of one of Nixon's worst congressional defeats. Some of the objection to Haynsworth came from labor and civil rights leaders. The necessary margin of the 45 to 55 roll-call vote came from those who balked at Haynsworth's insensitive judgment in participating in cases where his financial interests may have been involved. Those objecting included all three Republican Senate leaders. The President's second choice for the Fortas vacancy was an even unhappier one. The nominee was Judge G. Harrold Carswell of Florida, and his violently segregationist views both in and out of court were amply documented. In addition, his extraordinarily high reversal rate while on the bench, many of them unanimous, called his judicial competence into serious question. Although it was first considered doubtful that the Senate would have the stomach for a second rejection, several months of airing the facts of the Carswell nomination finally brought about a 45 to 51 negative vote. Nixon fumed at Congress for an allegedly "anti-Southern" bias and obviously considered the Senate action a personal insult. His third choice for the Fortas vacancy, Judge Harry A. Blackmun of Minnesota, was soon thereafter unanimously confirmed by the Senate.

Nixon had insisted, in the heat of the extended busing and antibusing controversy, that he wanted "strict constructionists" for the Court. This was never meant literally, but was a readily recognized symbol for reversing the direction of the Warren Court in matters of segregation and civil rights. The strictest constructionist of them all—Hugo L. Black, 85, and scarcely an object of approval for the Nixon administration—retired in 1971. The almost simultaneous retirement of Justice John Marshall Harlan, 72, gave Nixon two more appointments. President Nixon attempted to bring forward Herschel Friday, an Arkansas ultraconservative, and Judge Mildred Lillie, a much reversed lower-court judge of Los Angeles. These suggestions were sharply rebuffed by the conservative American Bar Association. Nixon thereupon appointed William H. Rehnquist of Arizona, an Assistant Attorney General, and Lewis F. Powell of Virginia, a former president of the ABA. Rehnquist's segregationist remarks in the past were the subject of several days of debate before both appointments were approved by the Senate in December 1971. By 1972 the Nixon court thus became a reality. Only three justices ideologically in the Oliver Wendell Holmes tradition remained—Douglas, Marshall, and Brennan—and all three gave signs of imminent retirement.

Even more intense public interest was generated by the problem of steady inflation and the Nixon approach to it. President Johnson's steeply rising military expenditures and deceptive budget estimates were a major factor in the nation's continually accelerating inflation. President Nixon not only inherited this legacy but added to it by continuing the Johnsonian tactics and military expenditures. By the third year of his administration, Federal Reserve constraints had slowed the rate of inflation. But neither stability nor a needed downward trend were at hand, unemployment was at the abnormally high rate of 6 percent, and the average consumer's wage raises were less than the rise in cost of goods and services.

Congress had in August 1970 passed the Economic Stabilization Act, giving the President authority to take action to stabilize prices, rents, and wages. Nixon had consistently opposed the idea, and had stated that he would not use such authority or methods. But on August 15, 1971, faced with increasing inflation, a worsening foreign trade balance, a sizeable international payments deficit, and a growing loss of public confidence, President Nixon took to national television to tell of his imposition of a 90-day price-wage freeze, effective the same day. At the same time, he announced the repeal of the 7 percent automobile excise tax, and moved forward one year the $50 increase in personal income tax exemptions originally due to become effective January 1, 1973. The sagging U.S. dollar abroad was attacked by a new 10 percent surcharge on imported goods, the cessation of gold sales at $35 an ounce to foreign central banks, and suspension of the dollar's convertibility into gold (see Foreign Affairs). After the 90-day freeze, Nixon warned the nation, a second phase would begin in which guidelines would be set up for wage and price increase requests and committees established to administer them.

Greatest complaint came from organized labor, one of whose leaders referred to the freeze as "Robin Hood in reverse—robbing the poor to pay the rich." This was based upon the fact that there was no control on profits, and made the point that employers, with a direct stake in holding wages down, were a far more effective vehicle for that purpose than for policing their own price structure. Political critics also pointed out that executive pay benefits such as stock options, incentive bonuses, etc., remained unregulated. In a period in which indexes reflected rising profits, the working man could be expected to bear much of the burden of price-wage controls.

Under "Phase II," beginning in November 1971, a Cost of Living Council, a Price Commission, and a Pay Board set a 5.5 percent guideline for average annual raises. Advance approval for projected price or wage increases had to come from the appropriate body. Although wholesale prices showed some decline during the freeze, there was little evidence of substantial results.[1] Early 1972 still showed an annual inflationary rise of 5.3 percent, or about the same rate permitted for salary rises. The administration goal of a 2 or 3 percent annual inflation was nowhere in sight, but there were evidences of some halting of the rate of upward climb. President Nixon had moved within a year from a position of little intervention in the economy to the most radical economic controls ever experienced outside of national emergencies. Although the high

---

[1] France, the Netherlands, and Canada had all tried price-wage controls within the past decade with little or no luck.

unemployment rate continued, public polls indicated some willingness to try price-wage controls further. The Nixon action effectively removed the economic issue from the Democratic arsenal of attack, but the national economy moved into the Nixon second term with further inflation still a serious threat.

Nixon and Foreign Affairs

A wartime and military expenditure economy also largely accounted for a worsening of the position of the American dollar on the international scene. The United States dollar emerged from World War II as the strongest of the world's currencies. But by the late 1960s it had been considerably weakened by U.S. inflation and the great drainage of dollars caused by the Vietnamese War expenditures and vast overseas military commitments. In addition, American products faced stiff competition from a revitalized West Germany and Japan whose goods could be bought in undervalued marks and yen. The dollars flowing abroad out of the United States were no longer exceeded or even matched by dollars coming into the United States from abroad, and the American government was thus faced with a persistent deficit in its balance of payments to international holders of the U.S. dollar. United States gold reserves shrank steadily as dollar holders presented them for payment in gold, and the United States sought to pressure foreign governments into hanging on to their exchange dollars. By 1970, there were more surplus dollars held abroad than there were gold reserves to pay for them at the pegged price of $35 an ounce.

In terms which were strongly resented by other nations, Secretary of the Treasury Connally demanded that they must help the United States reverse its balance-of-payments deficit by revaluing their own currencies and by assuming a larger share of the international defense burdens carried by the United States. Many nations had been antagonized by the 10 percent surcharge on foreign imports Nixon had announced, since it was in violation of the General Agreement on Trade and Tariff (GATT) and was considered unjust and an unnecessary regressive move toward protectionism. Most nations thereupon took the position that their currencies would not be revalued until the United States removed the surcharge and, in addition, considered the drastic step of revaluing the dollar.

President Nixon met with Premier Georges Pompidou of France in December 1971, and agreed to break the impasse by devaluing the dollar. At a meeting of ten large industrial nations of the world in Washington, the United States devalued the dollar 8.57 percent by raising the price of gold from $35 to $38 an ounce. West Germany and Japan, with whom the United States had the most severe deficits in trade and international payments, agreed to revalue their currencies from their beneficially cheap rate upward 13 and 17 percent respectively. Nixon thereupon declared the temporary 10 percent surcharge on imports to be ended. The International Monetary Fund placed the new currency values in effect, and Congress acted quickly to grant President Nixon the authority to change the price of gold from the rate it had occupied for almost 40 years. The American consumer was unaffected domestically by devaluation of the U.S. dollar. However, he would now find that his dollars abroad would buy less Japanese textiles, German autos, or British and Italian shoes. Fewer yen, marks, pounds, or lira would then be presented for payment in American dollars. At the same time, buyers abroad, whether German, Japanese, Italian or British, would find that their currency now would buy *more* American dollars than heretofore and American products would thus be more competitive on world markets. Like Herbert Hoover before him, President Nixon sought to pin the blame for American financial difficulties on "international speculators" who were "waging an all-out war on the American dollar." But inflation and swollen military and war expenditures ceaselessly funneled abroad were the primary cause for the crisis of the American dollar internationally. Money traders took advantage of the crisis to profit from trading in the dollar as they did during crises with the pound, the franc, or the mark. They were an effect of the crisis but scarcely a cause of it.

Overwhelming successes, however, were scored in breakthrough areas of American foreign policy, with the United States seeking historically important friendly relations with the People's Republic of China and further détentes with Soviet Russia. President Richard Nixon, not too long before one of the nation's most ardent anti-Chinese anti-Communists, made in 1972 the first state visit in U.S. history to a country with which Washington had no diplomatic relations. It constituted an amazing reversal of foreign policy.

Nixon had cautiously pursued the Lyndon Johnson suggestion of reducing tensions with mainland China by hints conveyed through the Rumanian government and by the easing of minor restrictions on Chinese travel and trade. Contact between the Peking government and Washington, other than the ambassadorial talks held largely in Poland from 1955 to 1970, was first signaled by the cordial invitation in 1971 to the American champion table tennis team playing in Japan to visit mainland China. The invitation was promptly accepted, and on April 10, 1971, the team, with several wives, four officials, and a small group of newsmen became the first Americans allowed into China since the People's Republic was established in 1949. The "Ping Pong diplomacy" was recognized as a serious and planned step in new Chinese foreign policy. It evidently included considerations such as Peking's belief that a Republican administration more nearly represented "American capitalists" and would also be better able to effect a turnabout in the hostility of Sino-American relations. It certainly contained some consideration of new Chinese-Russian enmities, and undoubtedly was concerned with Chinese entry into the formal world of international affairs.

The visit of the Ping Pong diplomats quickly led to several other developments, including a reciprocal invitation. The White House announced several days later that a 20-year embargo on trade with China would be lifted, visas for visitors would be expedited, and currency controls relaxed. More importantly, two months later Henry Kissinger, the President's foreign policy adviser, flew secretly from Pakistan to Peking to set up Nixon's historic trip. It was announced on July 15, 1971, that the President would journey to Peking some time in early 1972. The approving reception on the domestic scene of the planned Nixon visit was the best indication that cessation of official American-Chinese hostility was an idea whose time was, if anything, overdue.

President Nixon's trip to China from February 21 to 28, 1972, was a television spectacle and diplomatic tour de force which undoubtedly helped his election later in the year. It marked a more rational course for the United States both in Asia and in international affairs, with the probability of diplomatic recognition in the offing. It also opened the door to the American trade that Pacific Coast interests and others had long been requesting. Chinese pressure on Hanoi to help end the Indochinese War was evidently an American hope that could not be clearly recognized. For the People's Republic, the American visit and its implied support was the slight extra push needed for the necessary vote of admission to the seat marked "China" in the United Nations General Assembly and Security Council, from which Chiang Kai-shek's Taiwanese government was expelled. Although the fact of Chinese sovereignty over Taiwan was perhaps the one thing that both Chiang and Mao could agree upon, mainland China was evidently willing to postpone to some more distant date the resolution of conflict with Chiang's Nationalists.

The Soviet Union was perhaps understandably suspicious about the nature of both United States and Chinese motives after Nixon's visit to Peking was announced in 1971. Accordingly, the President also announced that he wished to prepare a summit meeting in Moscow for May 1972, and would also confer with leaders of Great Britain, France, and West Germany. The Moscow meeting, from May 22 to May 31, 1972, took place in an atmosphere of cordiality even though the United States had just inaugurated a policy of bombing and mining the North Vietnamese port of Haiphong and had damaged Soviet vessels in the process.

The Moscow summit meeting centered on an arms limitation treaty and a series of agreements regarding trade, space, and environmental problems. On May 26 Nixon signed the Arms Limitation Treaty, consummating the initial Strategic Arms Limitation Talks (SALT) which had been carried on in Helsinki and Vienna since November 1969. Under the terms of the treaty, the two nations limited themselves to one ABM site for the nation's capital and only one additional ABM site for the protection of an ICBM field. Under the terms of an additional executive agreement, the two nations agreed to cease the deployment of any further new offensive weapons systems, although permitting any improvement in "quality" of those existing. The fact that a freeze would leave the United States with slightly fewer missiles than the Soviet was cause for complaint among right-wing groups in the United States. However, since Multiple Independently Targetable Reentry Vehicles (MIRVs) were already deployed on many American missiles, it gave the United States a 5,700 to 2,200 edge over Russia in the actual number of separate nuclear warheads available. This statistic, plus a continued American technological superiority, brought a ready 88 to 2 vote in the Senate to ratify the Arms Limitation Treaty.

Richard Nixon became the first United States President ever to pay a state visit to Moscow, but this historic first was not matched in importance in any great slowing down of the nuclear arms race. The treaty set a limitation on the number of missiles, but no limit on the number of warheads each could carry. By 1977, it was estimated, the United States would possess nearly 10,000 warheads and the Soviets, desperately trying to catch up technologically to the American MIRV system, would have some 4,000. Each warhead in the American MIRV system was separately targeted, and each was capable of completely destroying an entire large city. In 1963, President Kennedy had difficulty in getting a nuclear treaty past the Pentagon until he agreed on an underground development clause as a loophole. Similarly, the 1972 treaty had the blessing of Secretary of Defense Laird and the Chiefs of Staff because of the key clause permitting unending qualitative development of American weapons systems in a climate of superior technology and a huge and willing weapons industry. President Nixon made it clear that the United States was unwilling to accept any actual parity in nuclear weapons. The signing of the accords might be regarded as the first step toward a legal codification of coexistence between the two differing social systems, but it also marked a Russian willingness to accept a junior partnership in a bipolar nuclear balance of powers. The arms race was diverted into channels more qualitative than quantitative, but scarcely arrested; and burdensome military costs continued at the same high level.

An optimistic note was furnished by a series of amicable agreements between the United States and Russia. These provided for a space flight in 1975 to be undertaken jointly, and mutual prohibitions on the harassment of each other's naval units on the high seas. Other accords were reached for cooperation on environmental protection, for coordination in research on cancer and heart disease, and for American wheat sales and other trade with the Soviet Union. In nuclear accords, another minor step had been taken in 1971, when the Senate ratified and the United States signed the International Seabed Treaty. The 85 signatories (excluding France and the People's Republic) agreed to prohibit the deployment of nuclear weapons on the ocean floor outside national 12-mile territorial limits. The two great nuclear powers also agreed to resume SALT, Phase II, at Geneva, based upon the 1972 Moscow treaty.

The Nixon administration gingerly approached problems in the Middle East and in South Asia. It sought to maintain a delicate balance between continued support of embattled Israel without unduly antagonizing the Arabian oil nations or bringing on a confrontation with their occasional ally, the Soviet Union. The Nixon policy, in favoring the military government of Pakistan over the democratic government of India, was the target of critical invective because of the bloodthirsty attempts of Pakistan to suppress the nationalistic freedom aims of the Bengalis of East Pakistan, who announced their independence as the nation of Bangla Desh. The frequently duplicitous statements and activities of the Nixon administration on behalf of the Pakistani military dictatorship were criticized domestically within the same context of world condemnation of Pakistani army atrocities in Bangla Desh.

In its world view, the Nixon administration became the first to recognize both the fact of the Chinese revolution of 1949 and the persistent historical evidence showing the Soviet Union to have abandoned revolutionary movements around the world when in its national interests to do so. Accordingly, China and Russia were viewed more as nation states than as ideological centers of a world conspiracy. Both nations, it was recognized, had domestic considerations which might make them susceptible to attractive trade offers. The Kissinger-Nixon foreign policy clearly put Europe into sharpest diplomatic focus and moved the United States into a balance-of-power accommodation. Latin America, Africa, and the Third World nations were pushed into the background, and reliance upon and participation in United Nations activities was muted. In Southeast Asia, however, military-diplomatic policies which seriously affected American relations around the world continued throughout the first Nixon administration.

Indochina—Four More Years of War

Richard Nixon, as Vice President under President Eisenhower, was belligerently disposed to intervene with American troops to bail out the failing French efforts in Indochina. He remained in the front ranks of those demanding a military victory, lest ". . . creeping communism will become galloping communism throughout that part of the world." He consistently supported Johnson's attempts to gain a victory through troop and bombing escalations, but in the campaign of 1968 he finally deferred to growing American antagonism toward the war by promising the electorate a "secret plan" for a quick end to it. The secret plan was never disclosed. In 1969 Dr. Kissinger smilingly told angry students that if the war were not concluded within another 12 months, their return and their protests would then be justifiable. The war and American casualties showed no signs of abating, and American tempers became noticeably shorter.

It became apparent that the Nixon administration, no less than the Johnson administration, had as a goal a military victory which would leave the Saigon government intact and in nominal sovereignty regardless of whether it had the allegiance of South Vietnamese or actual control of its territories. The means, however, were modified by the announcement of Secretary of Defense Laird that South Vietnamese armed forces would be stepped up from their lesser role of internal security to a full-scale combat status capable of carrying on the war in place of American troops. Any sizeable withdrawal of American forces was contingent upon the ability of South Vietnam to carry on the American combat role, a policy which soon became better known as "Vietnamization." This attempt to mollify American public opinion by substituting Vietnamese combat deaths for American ones was also supplemented by attempts to have President Thieu hold national elections and by a meeting of reassurance between Nixon and Thieu at the big United States air base on Guam.

While on his Pacific tour at Guam in July 1969, Nixon also announced a "new" departure for the basis of United States Asiatic policy. The precise meaning of the formula was shrouded in ambiguity, and was set forth only unofficially in a Guam press conference, with additions and some clarification soon visible in subsequent presidential addresses to Congress and in Department of Defense reports. The "Nixon Doctrine" (or "Nixon-Kissinger Doctrine," since Dr. Kissinger was recognized as the chief architect of the Nixon administration's foreign policy) expanded the idea of Vietnamization to the point of "Asianization" for the future. It announced not only initial troop withdrawals from Vietnam, but also lesser numbers to be moved out of South Korea, Japan, Okinawa, and the Philippines. The Nixon-Kissinger Doctrine did not mean any abandonment of U.S. bases or the U.S. presence in the Pacific, as the President made clear. It did mean that in the event of insurgency against pro-American regimes, the United States would shoulder much of the economic and military supply burden and furnish air and naval assistance, but the Asian nation would be expected to exercise more "self-help," particularly in supplying the necessary ground troops. In the President's more aseptic phrase, "Asian hands must shape the Asian future." As American Ambassador Ellsworth Bunker commented more candidly on Vietnamization, it meant changing "the color of the corpses."

The Nixon-Kissinger Doctrine actually represented only minor changes in decades of American policies in Asia and the Pacific. Decisions to utilize American air and sea power but not to commit American land troops in Asia had long been accepted by the American military, with heightened awareness furnished by (and with support from) MacArthur in Korea. President Eisenhower's insistence that wars in Asia should be "Asians against Asians" was implemented by an early but intensive "Vietnamization" carried on by Secretary of State Dulles. American willingness to defend Asiatic countries beyond their own primary responsibilities had been stated by Secretary of State Dean Acheson in 1950, although Acheson had included support from the United Nations where Nixon promised only unilateral nuclear reaction from the United States if it should be deemed necessary. The doctrine made clear that a less hostile China nevertheless was still part of a military containment structure. The Nixon emphasis on American vital interests in Asia and on retaining all treaty commitments made it apparent that the doctrine was an updated version of continuing post–World War II policy. It precluded American ground casualties by the use of "indigenous" troops and stepped-up American military technology, but it retained a strong distaste for insurgency and sufficient bases from which to cope with it when the need arose.

Despite President Nixon's assurance that complete success was just around the corner in Vietnam, the war became the cause of more and more public opposition. Critics insisted that the same blindly optimistic reports that had characterized past years were still being given credence. The goal to many seemed less one of withdrawal and negotiation than one of insistence upon a military victory and the sustaining of a corrupt, reactionary, and poorly supported regime in Saigon. Dr. Henry Kissinger, who had infinitely more importance, responsibility, and influence than did the Rostows or McBundys and other advisers of the Johnson-Kennedy era, gave no more awareness than his predecessors of the nature of Vietnamese culture, Vietnamese nationalism, or the long-lasting Vietnamese will to fight. In an interview for Look, Kissinger deplored the dissent of the young, stating that "Conscientious objection must be reserved for only the greatest moral issues, and Vietnam is not of this magnitude." But the deaths and wounding of millions and the wrecking of both North and South Vietnam by more bomb tonnage than was used in all of World War II was accepted by many, both young and old, as a moral issue of inescapable magnitude.

Student rallies on October 15 constituted the largest antiwar demonstrations to date, but an even larger one was planned for Washington on November 15. Nixon promptly sought to move public opinion to his support by a television speech which posed two artificially simplistic alternatives as the only possible choices. On the one hand, Nixon stated, were the administration proposals of victory and "a just peace through a negotiated settlement"; on the other, "precipitate withdrawal" would bring massacre for the Vietnamese, and defeat and humiliation for the United States. By leaving out the many alternatives already advanced and by insisting that only disaster and national disgrace could be brought about by his critics, Nixon effectively gained the support of those he termed "the silent majority." He was also aided by the Vice President's heavy-handed speeches. Most alarming of Agnew's comments was his proposal that dissenting students be removed from society "with no more regret than we should feel over discarding rotten apples from a barrel." Some 250,000 people nevertheless converged on Washington for the largest of all antiwar demonstrations. There were few gatherings of any size or consequence for the opposition view, but a noteworthy one was the march in downtown Manhattan of hard-hat construction workers bearing signs of support for President Nixon and demanding full prosecution of the war. Not since Civil War days had the country been so completely polarized.

By early 1970 President Nixon had announced several troop withdrawals, bringing American peak strength from its February 1969 high-water mark of 542,500 men down to less than 500,000. But on April 29 Nixon revealed that South Vietnamese troops with American support had invaded Cambodia. Although Nixon insisted that the United States respected Cambodia's neutrality, his announcement the following day said that American combat forces would be a part of the invasion. The rationale given was a necessity to clean out Vietcong and North Vietnamese "sanctuaries" serving as bases for attack. The administration decision was defended as an accelerated means by which the withdrawal program could be expedited and the war ended with a just peace.

To some of the steadily increasing number of those opposing the war the Cambodian invasion could only be regarded as a widening of the war, regardless of administration semantics. Most serious reaction to the Cambodian decision occurred on more than 400 university campuses around the nation. One confrontation resulted in a disaster unparalleled in American annals, when four students were shot and killed and nine others wounded by a panicky National Guard facing a demonstration at Kent State University in Ohio. Perhaps even more shocking where the chasm dividing American society was concerned was the pronouncement of many that the killings of those in opposition to national war-making policy were justifiable.

In spite of the strong national reaction to the Cambodian invasion, Nixon was persuaded by Saigon and the American military to undertake an invasion of Laos in early 1971. The tempting target was a cutting of the so-called Ho Chi Minh Trail, down which men and supplies for the Vietcong and the North Vietnamese moved through the thick jungles parallel to the Vietnamese border. The Air Force bombings, despite continual optimistic reports, had no better success in curtailing the traffic on the Trail than had been the case, by Air Force admission, with similar primitive supply routes in the Korean War. A ground invasion by ARVN troops supported closely by U.S. tactical planes was therefore mounted, supported by arguments that if Vietnamization was to work, the ARVN troops must show their worth as combat forces.

The protestation of Secretary Laird to Senate members in February 1971 that "we have not widened the war. To the contrary, we have shortened it." was not well received. The barrages of semantic confusion loosed by the administration and the Pentagon in the wake of controversial moves into Cambodia and Laos served rather to goad war critics to new heights of opposition. They pointed with some scorn to the insistence from the White House that the invasion of Cambodia was actually only an "incursion." They refused to consider planned bombing raids as different from or less innocuous than "protective reaction strikes." A bizarre example of administration-tortured semantics was the revelation before a congressional committee that the CIA assassinations of suspected double agents in Indochina did not use the term to fit the deed but spoke rather of "elimination with extreme prejudice."

It was doubtful that the two invasions were successful enough to overbalance the increased domestic opposition to the Nixon policies. The Cambodian invasion found no enemy "headquarters," but it did succeed in uncovering and destroying large stores of food and ammunition which must have considerably set back Vietcong and North Vietnamese operations in the area. The Laos invasion was perhaps even more counter-productive. Far from showing the mettle of the South Vietnamese troops who were supposed to make Vietnamization workable, it showed the American television public pictures of ARVN troops fleeing in such panic from their North Vietnamese adversaries as to cling desperately to the skids of departing helicopters and to abandon their own wounded along the roads. Moreover, it aroused for the first time powerful pressures for a complete withdrawal deadline from even the more moderate and conservative members of Congress. The Cambodian venture brought forth the bipartisan Cooper-Church amendment seeking to inhibit military activities in that region. Although its ambiguous terms made it ineffective, the 58 to 37 majority for its passage gave clear indication of the national disenchantment with the war. In the more pro-Nixon House, many conservative Congressmen came out strongly for a positive ending date for complete withdrawal of American troops. In March 1971, the House failed by only one vote, 101 to 100, to set an absolute deadline for such withdrawal by the following December 31. Additionally, the American public's credibility gap regarding its own government widened. Public opinion polls after Laos revealed the almost 50 percent of all Americans did not believe the White House insistence that no American troops were being used in the invasion, and the same percentage said that they were unable to believe anything the administration said about any aspect of the Vietnam War. The Nixon attempts to conceal operations which were subsequently disclosed, the transparent and unconvincing semantics, and the citizen's view on his television of a war that was being widened instead of "shortened" combined to bring the steadily growing public credibility gap to chasm proportions.

The first of several gruesome incidents of the Vietnam War was disclosed just after the Laos invasion. First Lieutenant William L. Calley, Jr., 28 years old, was convicted on March 29, 1971, by an Army court-martial of the premeditated murder of 22 defenseless civilians in the village of My Lai 4 on March 16, 1968 in South Vietnam. Calley was the platoon leader of a unit from the American Division which was charged with the wanton machine-gunning of hundreds of Vietnamese old men, women, and children. Secretary of the Army Stanley Resor and Army Chief of Staff General William Westmoreland, with the backing of Defense Secretary Laird, had investigated the episode carefully and found ample evidence of murder. A court of Vietnam combat officers then had the painful duty of prosecuting Calley. Of the two choices for punishment to fit the crime they chose the lesser sentence of life imprisonment.

The My Lai 4 disclosure was the first of several such to pinpoint the brutalization of American troops fighting in a war for which they had little stomach and among a race of color and an alien culture they all too frequently considered to be of little human value. Fighting a guerrilla war in which their fellows were frustratingly picked off by Vietcong who might be later tilling the fields as innocent farmers, their nervous instinct was sometimes to kill indiscriminately whether village inhabitants in a suspected zone were old men or women with babes in arms. The outcry that resulted over Calley's sentence found the war-hawks defending Calley as a hero who carried out his orders to kill, while the doves insisted that Calley was a scapegoat for the sins of administration and Pentagon officials and four-star generals. The Army, which had carried out the judicial proceedings with scrupulous objectivity, quietly decided to meet the fierce public clamor by releasing Calley from a prison confinement to the more comfortable restriction of his own quarters. Nixon, however, sensing the strong public tide of sentiment which sought to elevate Calley to heroic stature, intervened to announce the decision as his own after secretly testing congressional feelings. The President's announcement that he would personally review the case "before any final sentence was carried out" was an intervening prejudgment that gave the Army review board, which still had to hear the evidence and judge the court's verdict, an impossible task. An indication of deeply felt Army sentiment was the letter to Nixon from Captain Aubrey M. Daniel, the chief prosecutor in the Calley Case. Captain Daniel gravely deplored the tragedy possible "if political expediency dictates the compromise of such a fundamental moral principle as the inherent unlawfulness of the murder of innocent persons." The President, Daniel said in the long letter to Nixon later made public, did not provide the moral leadership which the nation should have to face a moral issue beyond compromise.

The Nixon administration made no substantial moves toward peace in Vietnam for several years. The Vietcong negotiator at the continuing but futile talks in Paris offered an eight-point plan in September 1970 which included political talks with any South Vietnamese government which did not include President Thieu or Vice President Ky. Since the basis of the White House continuance of the war was the support of that same regime, the proposal was rejected. So, too, was a Nixon proposal of October 1970 which avoided mention of the political settlement which constituted the core reason for 18 years of Vietcong opposition to the Saigon government. Critics of the government's Vietnam policy insisted that a military solution to keep a corrupt Saigon clique in power had already exacted an impossible price from American society in 45,000 American dead, the expenditure over $100 billion in defending the poorly supported Thieu regime, and the continuing exacerbation of American domestic problems of inflation, racial tension, and urban blight. Nixon proposals of late 1971 in the wake of increased public and congressional opposition to the war included a cease-fire, but still without prior political settlement. Since any laying down of arms by the Vietcong before such a settlement would have meant their incarceration by South Vietnamese national police forces, they understandably refused.

In the spring of 1972 Nixon went far beyond his predecessors in ordering the mining of Haiphong harbor in North Vietnam and the bombing of civilian sectors in the North Vietnamese capital city of Hanoi. Congress was not consulted, and the decision was evidently a personal presidential one. Although supply cuts for North Vietnamese and Vietcong troops were admittedly negligible and city bombing was no more able to bring the North Vietnamese nation to its knees than had intense German and British bombing in World War II, there was a note of accrued war weariness apparent on both sides in the renewed talks between the Nixon administration and North Vietnamese representatives. By October Dr. Kissinger was able to announce that willingness to change previous proposals of both sides had produced "peace at hand," although denying that the October date had anything to do with the November elections. But the hoped-for signing date of October 31 came and went and the negotiating continued. With an overwhelming victory in November behind him and exasperated with the slow pace of the Paris talks, Nixon ordered full-scale B-52 bombings of North Vietnamese civilian areas shortly before Christmas. The decision was evidently made without consultation with advisers or the military. The unparalleled ferocity and personal vindictiveness of the attacks brought outraged responses from many of the President's previously stoutest Republican supporters. In a representative press reaction the *Los Angeles Times* described it as ". . . directing against a small Asian country a rain of death and terror that to the whole world makes the United States of America appear a barbarian gone mad."

The B-52 onslaught not only provoked the strongest protests from political friend and foe alike, but resulted in unmatched destruction of the big planes by North Vietnamese missiles and an upturn in American casualties and prisoners. Renewed and stronger domestic pressure brought the bombing to an end December 30. Nixon was finally able to announce on January 23, 1973, that a cease-fire agreement would be signed on January 27 by North Vietnam, South Vietnam, the Provisional Revolutionary Government (Vietcong), and the United States. (Sadly and ironically, the announcement came less than 48 hours after the death from a fatal heart attack of former President Lyndon B. Johnson.)

It was considered most unlikely that a brief intensification of the bombing induced the North Vietnamese to move closer to a peace agreement, given the years of savagely heavy bombing by both Nixon and Johnson. A more evident possibility was that even drawing back on some points previously insisted upon by North Vietnam and the Vietcong would still permit a slower but more productive political offensive. There was no evidence that bombing per se—or mining—brought about capitulation any more than it had the more industrialized nations of Britain or Germany. Although continued bombing obviously hurt both North and South Vietnam, the prime consideration was the ability to retain military forces in the South to protect the political strength which the Vietcong and the North Vietnamese were sure would end, or greatly modify, the Thieu regime in Saigon in a year not too distant from total American withdrawal. Mention of American aid in reconstruction of battered lands was a very secondary consideration to a people whose motivation far outweighed continuing casualties and destruction.

The Nixon administration faced at home increased congressional and public uneasiness and resentment in a military stalemate which could only be resolved by a politically impossible nuclear attack. Internationally, the United States was experiencing uniformly unfriendly attitudes which hampered its expected position of global leadership. A cease-fire and peace agreement in which the Thieu government was left with more than adequate forces of its own to sustain itself, which permitted the withdrawal of American prisoners of war, and which established the principle of internationally supervised elections was one which could be reconciled with previous American demands. If the Thieu government could no longer be retained in a protected position of sovereignty, it had at least been given a decent interval to establish such claims for itself.

Both the United States and its South Vietnamese ally and the Vietcong and their North Vietnamese ally thus gave up several points in order to effect a peace agreement. The Nixon administration had previously tried to insist that a cease-fire and a laying down of arms must precede political settlement, but had to relinquish what was a life and death matter for the National Liberation Front (NLF). The NLF gave in on the cease-fire coming before a political settlement, but retained both their own troops and 145,000 North Vietnamese allied troops in the field in South Vietnam to preclude another slaughter such as Diem carried out after the 1955 cease-fire. The United States promised total withdrawal of troops and the demining of North Vietnamese waters, but retained the possibility of stationing "civilian" advisers with President Thieu's forces. All American prisoners were to be released by the North Vietnamese. The North Vietnamese relented in their insistence upon one Vietnam, just as South Vietnam did on its own demand for two Vietnamese nations. As a compromise pending reunification efforts, they agreed to move back to the status of a provisional and nonterritorial demarcation line at the 17th parallel as set forth by the Geneva Accords of 1954. The North Vietnamese took the important step of recognizing a separation of military and political problems which was the key for an American extrication. An International Commission of Control and Supervision (ICCS), composed of Canadian, Hungarian, Indonesian, and Polish troops was to monitor the cease-fire. A National Council of National Reconciliation and Concord, combining Thieu's representatives with those of the NLF, was supposed to implement the agreements internally and organize elections under international supervision.

Thus an official count of 12 years and 26 days ended the longest war in American history. Most of the statistics involved were gargantuan. The United States dropped 7.2 million tons of bombs on this small Asian country over seven years, versus a total of 2 million tons dropped in all the theatres of war throughout World War II. The nation expended 46,000 American lives, 16,000 of them under the administration which promised to end the war, and the unable-to-be-comprehended sum of

$136 billion. In its persistent attempts to "save" Vietnam, it killed and wounded millions of Vietnamese, made refugees of other hundreds of thousands, and literally obliterated parts of its landscape. The war left behind it the example of the ineffectiveness of B-52s as weapons against revolutionary ideas in an age of resurgent nationalism. It left behind the strong impression that those three Presidents and their advisers most heavily involved militarily—Kennedy, Johnson, Nixon—never fully comprehended the character of Asian postcolonial revolutions or the fact of its inherently political rather than military nature. It also left behind it a badly distorted American economy, a torn society infected with a variety of unsolved problems, and an international image badly tarnished and sorely lacking in influence and world confidence. For this, the government claimed for its people a "peace with honor." A continued divisiveness persisted here. In behalf of the many Americans who considered the Vietnamese venture an immoral and unnecessary war far removed from American ideals and aspirations, the historian Henry Steele Commager aptly characterized it as one in which the nation had accrued "enough dishonor to last a thousand years." But to many other Americans, any war in which their government involved them and in which many fought and some died was an honorable proceeding regardless of its nature or necessity. The inability to reconcile opposing views of American ideals and American duties, this rift in the American culture itself, was a painful legacy of the Vietnamese War which might take longer to heal than the scars on the Vietnamese countryside.

The United States in the 1970s

As Americans looked ahead to their bicentennial year of 1976, many of them saw the quality of American life slowly declining. Some saw it in national attitudes of fear and hatred toward its young people and of indifference and neglect toward its indigent and old people. Some saw it in a headlong drive for material prosperity so obsessive on the part of many as to shrug at corruption, ignore the slaughter of Vietnam, and resent every tax dollar directed at the solution of persistent social problems. Others saw it in such diverse areas as the higher rate of crime and the growing fear of being on the streets at night, or in the increasing shoddiness of goods and services. In most cases, the dissatisfactions were analogous to revolutionary drives which historically gathered steam when the progress that was genuinely being made only revealed more clearly the enormous gap still remaining between reality and the goals of aspiration.

The young, and students in particular, were sure they could see a wide chasm readily visible between creed and deed, between principle

Comparative Social Statistics as of 1970

	1932	1945	1960	1970
Population	124,949,000	139,928,000	180,684,000	203,185,000
Percentage urban	NA	58.6	69.9	73.5
Percentage rural	NA	41.4	30.1	26.5
Percentage nonwhite	10.0	10.0	11.0	11.1
Birth Rate (per 1,000 live births)	19.5	20.4	23.7	18.2
Life expectancy:				
White	63.2	66.8	70.6	71.7
Nonwhite	53.7	57.7	63.6	64.6
High school graduates (as percentage of all persons over 16 years old	NA	NA	65.1	78.4
Labor union membership	3,226,000	14,796,000	18,117,000	20,752,000
Gross national product (billions of dollars)	58.5	213.6	503.7	976.8
Defense spending (millions of dollars)	1,688	84,311	51,334	78,013
As percentage of GNP	3.0	40.0	10.0	9.0
Advertising expenditures (millions of dollars)	1,627	2,874	11,932	19,600
Military personnel on active duty	244,902	12,123,455	2,476,435	3,065,508

Sources: *Statistical Abstract of the United States,* 1970; *Historical Statistics of the United States, Colonial Times to 1957;* and *Digest of Educational Statistics,* 1970.

and performance. Seeing more clearly the ideals for which America was supposed to stand by virtue of their educational experience, they also more surely saw the limited extent to which they were applied in practice. Their resistance and rebellion to these discrepancies, whether as the immorality of the Vietnamese War or as the failure of university administrations and faculty to take their views into account, was the heart of the campus disturbances of the late 1960s and at the end of the decade in 1970.

The wanton killings at Kent State in the latter year may have been a turning point. They alerted many young activists to the fact that repressive administrations, national or state, would not stop at shooting dissenters. But the incident also brought home sharply to government leaders and politicians, as did no other happening, the profound depth of feeling over the war and the divisions in society. In the early 1970s, the activism of the young simmered down to something approaching the apathy of two decades earlier. Campuses that had previously supported large chapters of the leftist SDS and the rightist YAF now found themselves without either one. As one comment had it regarding this apathetic trend: "If you liked the student 50s, you'll love the student 70s." The subduing of activism came in part from a despair over the absence of any credibility in the federal government and a failure to bring about needed changes by working within the system, but its sub-dued tones also reflected successes in student contribution to changed university procedures and student presence on faculty and administration bodies.

Militancy among blacks and other minority groups, like rebelliousness among the nation's young, was more subdued in the 1970s. Stokely Car-michael and Eldridge Cleaver, two earlier leaders of black dissent, had left the country. The Black Panthers were occupied by internal strivings. No black ghetto riots had taken place since 1968. The black population, which had risen slightly to 11 percent of the national census of 1970, revealed an increase of 50 percent in median black family income, al-though this still fell short by 40 percent of being on a par with white family income. In 1960, about 35 percent of young blacks finished high school. By 1970, the figure was up to 55 percent. As products of higher education, blacks had all but erased the large distinction between the white and the black male college graduate. Blacks with advanced de-grees were urgently sought after by the academic, professional, and business worlds. In politics, blacks were being elected to local office in states of the Deep South where their very existence was only tolerated once before. Black candidates in sophisticated urban communities like Atlanta were being elected to congressional office over white candidates by predominantly white constituencies.

The advantageous changes also showed more clearly the discrepancies still existing. Although black college graduates were sought after, blacks generally had far less education and opportunity than the average white American. Black unemployment consistently ran close to double the rate of white unemployment, and black teen-age unemployment fre-quently ran as high in the ghetto as the 1972 figure of 38 percent. Although it was true that more blacks escaped from poverty by the 1970s than ever before, it was also true that so many more whites were afforded the opportunity to do so that blacks were even more dispropor-tionately disadvantaged than before. According to a Commerce Depart-ment report of 1971, the poverty rate for blacks rose from 26 percent in 1960 to 32.1 percent by 1970. The rate for whites moved downward to 9.9 percent, or less than one third the black rate. A steady decline in poverty was noted since the Kennedy administration, with most noticeable improvements coming during the years of the Great Society programs of Johnson. By 1970, however, Nixon's fiscal policies sent the unemployment rate from 3.4 percent to 6.2 percent nationally, and his virtual obliteration of many urban improvement programs after 1972 was expected to help reverse the climb out of poverty for black families.

A national minority where rights were concerned—although an actual majority in numbers—was the wide basis for the active role in the 1970s of the women's liberation movement. Aided in good part by the earlier civil rights struggles of the 1960s, by women's sturdy role in them, and by the example of other groups striving to improve their demeaned status, militant women and their supporters moved to correct the economic and social discriminations practiced against them. Although they had earlier achieved the right to vote, the female resurgence in the economy and in government sparked by the Great Depression and World War II had died down in the postwar years.

Percent of Income Received by Each Fifth of Families and Individuals

Families and Individuals Ranked from Lowest to Highest	1929	1935	1941	1944	1961
Lowest fifth	13%	4%	4%	5%	5%
Second fifth		9	10	11	11
Middle fifth	14	14	15	16	16
Fourth fifth	19	21	22	22	23
Highest fifth	54	52	49	46	45
Top 5%	30	27	24	21	20

Source: U.S. Bureau of the Census, *Historical Statistics of the United States, Colonial Times to 1967*, p. 166.

The Commission on the Status of Women, set up by President Kennedy in 1961, found numerous examples of discrimination. Although women constituted 51 percent of the population, they accounted for only 7.6 percent of the nation's doctors, 2.8 percent of its lawyers, and 1 percent of its architects. More invidiously, their postcollege earnings were nowhere near those of male college graduates. Where 40 percent of working males earned more than $10,000 as of 1970, only 7 percent of female workers had reached this level. Perhaps even more shocking to many American men was the public revelation from Shirley Chisholm, the country's first black Congresswoman, that she was the subject of more discrimination as a woman than as a black.

The National Organization for Women (NOW), established in 1966, sought actively to erase the distinctions which automatically assumed for American women a secondary and subordinate role to men. Their statement of purpose insisted on a "true partnership of the sexes" which would call for "a different concept of marriage." More revolutionary views of feminists included the idea that many of the world's ills, whether war or imperialism, racism or authoritarianism, were the results of man's insistence in filling the role of master. While many American men were not willing to subscribe fully to this ideology, there was surprising willingness to accept "now" positions on equality in the professions, on birth control and abortion, and on a larger share of home-building tasks for men. The title of "Ms.," which concealed the fact of single or marital status as did the title of "Mr.," was widely approved. Legal barriers began slowly to give way in the 1970s with some state action to update and liberalize the laws covering abortion. The most general sign of approval was the action by the Senate in 1972 in passing the proposed 27th Amendment to the Constitution, which would deny any abridgement of equal rights under the law "on account of sex."

If, as Dostoevski wrote (and Emerson warmly seconded), "the degree of civilization in a society can be judged by entering its prisons," then Americans must have had some doubts regarding their own civilization in the wake of prison stories in the headlines of the early 1970s. Although there were inmate riots by desperate prisoners and shooting by their guards in a number of cases, the horror story of the decade was the massacre in September 1971 at Attica prison in upstate New York where 33 inmates and 10 guards were killed and many more injured. The report of the New York State Commission on Attica did not leave much doubt as to the uncivilized nature of the state prison system. Although it blamed the inmates for seizing hostages, it castigated the authorities for execrable conditions within the prison. Prisoners were almost entirely black or Puerto Rican, guards were white, and the sadistic and brutally demeaning conditions had never been reformed or changed as the authorities had promised. The nine-man commission found that the prison violence was a spontaneous and desperate answer to intolerable conditions, "the product of frustrated hopes and unfulfilled expectations after efforts to bring meaningful change had failed." The subsequent slaying by state police of all save one of the 43 killed was an unplanned resort to violence by the state which exceeded the violence of the inmates in this bloodiest prison uprising in American history.

Americans were more concerned over their crime rate, which mounted in less precipitous jumps in the decade of the 1970s but which still accounted for appalling statistics. Homicides had already increased nearly 75 percent during the preceding decade. In relation to other nations, the city of Philadelphia alone accounted for more homicides than were recorded in all of Great Britain with more than 20 times the population. Some 25 million handguns, which constituted the chief weapon in homicides, were readily accessible in spite of the weak Gun Control Act of 1968. Although other nations with strict handgun laws could show infinitely lower gun murder rates, the Nixon administration and the strong lobbies of the National Rifle Association opposed such legislation successfully. The urban riots of the mid-60s subsided, but crime in the larger cities moved steadily upward. Bus operators and taxi drivers, in order to slow down the wave of armed robbery, accepted only tokens and advertised that they carried no change. Neighborhoods sponsored dog patrols. People feared to walk at night, even in lighted areas. Manufacturers of lock devices and electronic protection were kept busy as a fearful nation moved toward a security-dominated state. The crime rate of 1960's 294 per 100,000 population surged up to a 773 per 100,000 ratio by 1970. A virtual epidemic of drug addiction furnished a growing basis for crimes committed in the inner city. Alienation among young radicalized whites found expression in the bombing and burning of public buildings in the end years of the 1960 decade. A new phenomenon of the 1970s was "skyjacking," in which disaffected whites or blacks commandeered commercial airliners at pistol point. Huge ransoms were demanded and paid rather than jeopardize hundreds of lives, or the air pirates were flown to various presumed refuges around the world. Many skyjackers were disturbed personalities who found some satisfaction in their temporary mastery over an increasingly dehumanized technological society and in seeing an account of their particular grievances spread across the nation's front pages. Nevertheless, so prevalent did skyjacking become that all airline passengers of the 70s found themselves subjected to mandatory searchings and electronic precautionary devices.

To many, the increased crime rate and riots and rebelliousness in any form could be found in what some considered a pernicious "permissiveness." Some political aspirants even sought (although unsuccessfully) to ride such public emotions into office. American society was indeed more permissive, but the permissiveness took a wide variety of forms. It did include a freer and more relaxed attitude toward sex, which could be seen in public attitudes, legislation, literature, and on stage and screen. Premarital sex found more public tolerance, whether its practice was up from the previous decade or not. Trial marriages were common. So was living together without bothering to go through the accepted formalities. Homosexuals mounted a "Gay Lib" Movement, and insisted that their rights as mutually consenting adults and as human beings should not be the target of law enforcement harassment. Musicals such as "Hair" and "Oh! Calcutta," with ample nudity visible on the stage, had stage runs of years in the United States and abroad. The movies burst out of their puritanical bonds to deal forthrightly with the realities of sex, and pornography in film and "literature" had its day in the released swing of the pendulum.

But permissiveness was also found in the condemnation of outdated laws and mores. The smoking of marijuana, many scientists insisted, was neither as harmful nor as addictive as alcohol or cigarette smoking, and older laws accounting it a crime were foolish and vindictive. Many parents disagreed, holding that this new and strange habit must be dealt with harshly lest it lead to further dissolution. Permissiveness could even be said to include a relaxed attitude where personal dress, habits, and life style were concerned. Young people led the way. The miniskirt, with a wealth of revealing leg, was a female contribution cheered by the males. In an amazing show of rare independence, women around the world finally rebuffed the annual attempt of the priests of high style to change to another skirt length. Young men sprouted hair in abandon, with beards, sweeping mustaches, and long hair flowing down to the shirt collar such as had not been seen for centuries. Finally, even business men agreed to somewhat longer hair, luxuriant sideburns, and even occasionally a neatly trimmed beard. The male also broke out of his penguin-like black and white dress to adopt extremes of brightly colored jackets and ties, ruffled and striped shirts, and gaudily striped trousers that would at least have earned the wearer some type of verbal or physical harassment ten years earlier. The new permissiveness drew upon a tolerance which to some extent came out of the rebellious mood and its partial successes of the 1960s. But the removal of inhibitions in the society of the 1970s may have been aided by erosions in some social institutions. The church, for example, showed a collective drop from the nearly 50 percent attendance in 1960 to only 40 percent in the early 70s. The Army and the large corporations declined in institutionalized influence, with more and more students rejecting careers in either one. A relative affluence spread into the ranks of youth, making for both less dependence and social inhibitions.

Above all other influences on the society of the 1970s loomed those of the Vietnamese War. The armed forces themselves suffered seriously from a decline in morality, integrity, prestige, and self-respect. Enlisted men "fragged" (killing by means of a fragmentation grenade) harshly discriminatory or overly demanding officers, and the drug addition during Vietnamese duty and bringing drugs back home created massive and continuing social problems. Atrocities in Vietnam were committed by American troops as never before in history. They were not only largely covered up or ignored, but most journalists knew of commanding officers who themselves frequently participated in wanton killing of "gooks" (any Vietnamese). In many cases, Army command seemed to have lost all control over forces in the field, and civilian control of the military was frequently either violated knowingly or was never exerted. To escape the shambles, young men went AWOL. The rate of such unofficial departures increased from 21.4 per thousand in 1967 to 73.5 in 1971. Thousands of others deserted in Germany or fled to Sweden or other refuges, but even more moved to Canada or went underground to avoid the draft. Returning veterans could also pose a threat to society, psychiatrists insisted, because of the dehumanizing effects of the all-pervasive feeling that "gooks" were a subhuman and essentially unnecessary form of life.

An extremely conservative dollar cost of the war reached beyond $400 billion, but this did not begin to include peripheral and less tangible costs. It could not include the costs of inflation or the resources wasted. It could not reconcile a war economy which generated unemployment on the one hand but which on the other used one of every five civilian electrical and mechanical engineers on war projects. Both Lyndon Johnson and Richard Nixon sought in varied ways to conceal the budgetary costs of the war from the public. When it finally became evident that both guns and costly social programs could not be afforded, the general mood suspiciously rejected the latter, particularly if tax increases were necessary to fund them. Such curtailment of programs in everything from pollution to urban renewal and from hospital care to hospital construction were, in good part, social costs of the war. An additional cost of the war was a turning away from politics as society's usual response to its problems, a "depoliticization" of society. A growing skepticism about politicians in general and the national government in particular arose during the late 1960s. Young people more than any other age group cynically switched from political activism or even traditional acceptance to dissent and alienation.

The war resulted in a widening gulf in American society. To many citizens, it was not a great source of satisfaction to know their nation was "No. 1" in the world in military power. More important to this group was the need to reverse such appalling statistics as those that showed the United States to be 8th in the world in infant mortality or 25th in life expectancy. The numbers of people who increasingly called for the war's end were vitally concerned with making the efforts necessary to raise the quality of American life. This might be aided by providing jobs for all who wanted to work, whether the government or private enterprise furnished the opportunities, by cleaning the environment and preventing urban decay; by eradicating poverty in the world's richest nation; by bringing about sufficient housing and hospital construction. There was a willingness to consider that some new taxes would be necessary and a hope that reduced military expenditure would not make such taxes excessive. To cut back on the pursuit of such aims while steadily increasing the armaments budget was, to this group, a perversion of American priorities.

An even larger part of American society disagreed. They held to the resurgent Puritan work-ethic of a half-century and more ago, as did President Nixon, that the unemployed or underemployed were some-

Gross National Product, 1929–70 (Billions of dollars, 1958 prices)

Year or Quarter	Total Gross National Product	Year or Quarter	Total Gross National Product	Year or Quarter	Total Gross National Product	Year or Quarter	Total Gross National Product
1929	203.6	1940	227.2	1950	355.3	1960	487.7
		1941	263.7	1951	383.4	1961	497.2
1930	183.5	1942	297.8	1952	395.1	1962	529.8
1931	169.3	1943	337.1	1953	412.8	1963	551.0
1932	144.2	1944	361.3	1954	407.0	1964	581.1
1933	141.5	1945	355.2	1955	438.0	1965	617.8
1934	154.3	1946	312.6	1956	446.1	1966	658.1
1935	169.5	1947	309.9	1957	452.5	1967	675.2
1936	193.0	1948	323.7	1958	447.3	1968	707.2
1937	203.2	1949	324.1	1959	475.9	1969	727.1
1938	192.9						
1939	209.4					1970*	724.3

* Preliminary.
Source: *Economic Report of the President*, 1971, p. 198.

how flawed in character and solely responsible for their predicament. They bitterly opposed social program expenditures and the taxes that went to support them. With considerable justification, they regarded with loathing and distrust the bureaucracy which administered such programs and grew even larger in the process. They were completely absorbed in their slow progress up the ladder to affluence, or with the struggles in the world of television sports. Expenditures for military hardware might not be the best of products, in this view, but they accounted for needed jobs and therefore must be continued. The Vietnamese bombing and destruction were readily rationalized, since the war was rapidly winding down. Middle America's values, polls showed, considered corruption high in political circles as the wholly acceptable name of the game. Traditional American ideals were stoutly defended against derogatory statistics. The office of the President, in Middle America values, must be supported without critical question. The war helped to produce an angry and alienated counter-culture among the young and disaffected, but that disaffection and its life style then produced a largely middle class counter-counter-culture which rejected all dissent as un-American and actively opted for noninvolvement rather than moral leadership. Regardless of what a widening gulf in American society might mean for the future, it was the confident Middle America which demonstrated its overwhelming majority in the presidential election of 1972.

The Election of 1972

President Nixon's renomination by his fellow Republicans was never in doubt, so that the front-page news of the spring and early summer was the infighting between Democratic contenders in the grueling presidential primaries. Senator Edmund Muskie, the 1968 vice presidential standard-bearer, was considered to be the front-runner and was clearly the favorite of the more conservative Democratic county chairmen. Senator Hubert Humphrey, the previous contender, with a base in labor and a sizeable black vote, was a strong possibility. Further down the list in the polls was the liberal antiwar Senator George McGovern of South Dakota, who had announced his candidacy in early 1971. Lesser possibilities were Senator Henry Jackson of Washington, who followed a hawkish line on Vietnam; Representative Wilbur D. Mills of Arkansas, who appealed to fiscal conservatives; Representative Shirley Chisholm of New York, who campaigned for the black vote and the Women's Lib vote and Mayor John Lindsay of New York City, who had recently changed his party allegiance from Republican to Democrat. Governor George Wallace of Alabama, who held to a "populist" and covertly racist platform, insisted he would forsake third parties and run as a Democrat.

Although Muskie won the early New Hampshire primary, he did so poorly that his candidacy went steadily downhill, and he soon withdrew. The great surprise was the McGovern primary campaign, which was extremely well organized on a largely volunteer basis. Students and young housewives, intellectuals, and liberal Democrats intent upon bringing the political process closer to a goal of full participation, all combined to knock party regulars out of control in state after state. They then went on to furnish the door-to-door grass-roots work that brought McGovern stunning victories in ten of twenty-three primaries and strong runner-up totals in such important states as Ohio and Michigan. Hubert Humphrey won Pennsylvania, Indiana, and West Virginia, and held a strong bloc of convention delegate votes. George Wallace used the appeal of antibusing and denunciation of heavy taxes and government bureaucracy to pile up primary votes in Florida, Tennessee, North Carolina, and Michigan. In a shocking attack by an assassin May 15 in a shopping center rally at Laurel, Maryland, Wallace was hit by two bullets and paralyzed from the waist down.

At the Democratic convention July 10–13 at Miami Beach, McGovern held a commanding lead in delegate votes, with the opposition candidates reduced to obstacle tactics to stave off quick victory. McGovern forces had also been instrumental in rule changes which eliminated such previous convention antics as interminable nomination speeches, placard-waving parades, and noisy demonstrations. McGovern, as chairman of a Democratic reform committee, played a leading role in liberalizing the rules under which convention delegates were chosen. The resultant switch away from appointed delegates to elected ones sent numbers of young people, women, and blacks to replace many old-line politicos for the first time. Two disputes over delegates were sharply divisive and had strongly negative effects upon the Democratic nominee's chances. In an effort to stop McGovern, Humphrey and other candidates got the convention to abrogate the California winner-take-all law, which gave McGovern a proportionate 151 votes for his plurality instead of the entire California vote of 271. A hasty decision by the U.S. Court of Appeals upheld the California law and gave the state's total back to McGovern. Independent Democrats were also able to challenge successfully and unseat the handpicked delegates of Mayor Richard J. Daley of Chicago, for many years the uncontested head of Illinois Democrats. Despite all efforts to block an early decision, McGovern took 1,865 votes and the Democratic nomination on the first ballot in an unusual come-from-behind upset victory.

The acclamation by Republicans of Richard Nixon as their nominee in the August 21–23 convention (also at 'Miami Beach) held few surprises. The President's early choice of his controversial Vice President, Spiro T. Agnew, for a second term confounded liberal Republicans and gratified the ultraconservative wing of the party. The Republican party platform, in contrast to the proposals of the Democrats, favored voluntary school prayers, and strongly opposed school busing, gun control laws, and amnesty for war resisters. The President's party, unlike their opposition, spoke only vaguely of tax reform and stoutly upheld the Nixon stand on the Vietnamese War.

The campaign began badly for the Democrats. Senator McGovern had picked the relatively little known Senator Thomas F. Eagleton of Missouri as his running mate after such party luminaries as Senators Edward Kennedy and Hubert Humphrey had declined. Eagleton, age 42, a liberal and a Catholic, had seemed an excellent choice from a strategic border state. It was soon disclosed, however, that Eagleton had voluntarily hospitalized himself several times over a period of six years for electric shock treatment of "nervous exhaustion." McGovern finally yielded to party pressures from critics fearing the use of such information in the campaign. His place was taken by R. Sargent Shriver, former Ambassador to France and head of the Peace Corps and the Office of Economic Opportunity under Kennedy and Johnson, and an articulate member, by marriage, of the potent Kennedy clan. McGovern, desperately trying to widen his base of support, sought the necessary electoral votes by making up with old-line Democratic chiefs who might be expected to profit more by his defeat than by liberal-reform leadership of the Democratic party. He mollified Mayor Daley and publicized reconciliations with Lyndon Johnson and party bosses around the country. In the process, he lost many of his younger, idealistic supporters who had originally accepted him as a "nonpolitician" type of candidate. Despite some back-pedalling on issues of defense cuts and welfare reform, McGovern was successfully tagged with the label of "radical," some of which arose from earlier statements on such nonissues as marijuana and abortion laws. McGovern's wavering on his stands and his inconsistency on a line of attack against the quite vulnerable Nixon made both McGovern and his advisers susceptible to glib accusations of ineptness and incompetency. Many Democrats forsook their party's candidate because of this image, and "Democrats for Nixon" organizations were common among conservative Southern Democrats.

President Nixon had some skilfully employed advantages for his candidacy besides the weight of his incumbency. The country was relatively tranquil and free of the riots of the late 1960s. Although unemployment was high and prices slowly rising, the economy appeared bullish. According to the Census Bureau, 1971 was the first time in history that more than 50 percent of all American families had incomes over $10,000, although inflation robbed this figure of some significance. President Nixon employed his Cabinet members as his surrogates in speaking and collecting funds to an extent new in American politics. Government agencies and their resources were put at the disposal of the President and the Republican party. Critics particularly pointed to information gathering by the FBI for White House use as something which had never been permitted while J. Edgar Hoover had been its head.

Financing the campaign and the administration campaign tactics came under fire as rarely before in history. Republican media joined in the condemnation of an election involving unparalleled sums of money, most of which found its way into Republican coffers, some by devious routes. Foremost among such revelations were the accounts of large sums which moved to Mexican banks and thence back through anonymous donors to Nixon election committees. Carried out before the April deadline of the Federal Campaign Election Act of 1971 took effect, Republican committees were not required to list the contributors. Unusual among those whose names were made public was Clement Stone, Chicago insurance magnate, who did not deny giving $2 million to each of Nixon's 1968 and 1972 campaigns. More controversial was the account of several hundred thousand dollars of "contributions" from lobbyists of International Telephone and Telegraph to hold the Republican convention in San Diego, California. Most disturbing of many incidents was the Watergate incident of June 17. Half a dozen persons, including former White House aides and ex-CIA personnel, employed by the Committee to Reelect the President (CREEP), crept into the Democratic National Committee's Watergate offices and were caught by police in the act of install-ing electronic listening devices. Most of those involved pled guilty in the trials which took place after the election, but the several trails lead-ing directly into the White House brought the question of high-level espionage into the history of presidential elections for the first time.

President Nixon's widely predicted landslide victory on November 7 reached historical proportions. The Republican nominee received a record-breaking 61.3 percent of the vote, eclipsing Lyndon Johnson's 61.1 percent against Goldwater in 1964 and Roosevelt's 60.8 percent over Landon in 1936. Although there were more eligible voters than ever before, only a disappointing 55 percent of Americans went to the polls.[2] Nixon swept 521 electoral votes against McGovern's 17, which were accounted for by Massachusetts and the District of Columbia. It was not the largest electoral margin in history, but it was the worst defeat ever suffered by a Democratic candidate. It was a great personal victory for Nixon, but not a party triumph. Republican leaders expressed widespread hostility over the refusal of the administration to include party congressional candidates in their electioneering, and results bore out their complaints. Republicans had hoped to gain six or eight seats in the Senate, but instead lost two. Ultraconservatives defeated Demo-cratic moderates in such states as Virginia and North Carolina, but "safe" Republican Senators in such states as Colorado, Iowa, Maine and Maryland were upset by liberal Democrats. In the House, the Re-publicans picked up twelve seats, many because of redistricting and reapportionment favoring the suburbs. Instead of a hoped-for majority, they remained a 191 to 244 minority. It marked the first time that a party capturing 60 percent or more of the votes failed to add seats in both houses of Congress.

Nixon achieved a paradox of sorts. He received a record-breaking percentage for himself, yet his party attained only negative records at the hands of the ticket-splitting electorate. Editorials that endorsed Nixon sometimes poorly concealed the low personal esteem in which he was held. Many voters made it plain that the Nixon administration was not considered highly trustworthy, but that McGovern and his ad-visers were distrusted even more. The record number of voters who stayed away from the polls supported the idea of a mutual nonaccep-tance. To gain the votes of Middle America and ethnic and labor groups, many traditionally Democratic, Nixon astutely blended nostalgia and covert racism. The 1960s and their continuing problems were largely ignored. The image that emerged in speeches was that of a nation still in the 1950s—calm, placidly content, unified, and blissfully crisis-free. It was evidently what a people too continuously assaulted by crises

---

[2] As compared, for example, with West Germany's 90 percent turnout.

wanted to hear. Vague fears concerning the turmoil and unrest in society were skilfully exploited. Code words readily comprehended by the President's audiences gave them needed assurance that violence in the streets, drugs, busing, campus upheavals, and the "welfare mess" were the work of blacks, the undeserving poor, and various dissidents, all of whom would be resolutely and sternly dealt with by the administration. Catholic voters were told by Nixon that they could "depend on him" to come to the aid of parochial schools, with McGovern then attempting similar vague assurances. Jewish voters were attracted by Nixon's strong pro-Israel stand, while McGovern's remonstrances regarding his own record of Israeli friendship were scarcely noted.

Although foreign policy did not play as prominent a role in the election as expected, the President profited greatly from current Soviet policy. After Nixon took the dangerous step of mining and bombing Haiphong harbor regardless of Russian, Chinese, and other nations' vessels, the Communist response was limply ineffectual. The Soviets, with severe economic difficulties and urgent needs for wheat trade, were obviously more intent upon consummating the prearranged summit meeting with the United States than on protests over Vietnam. To the man in the street, however, Nixon appeared as having pulled off a major gamble which presented him both as a statesman of reconciliation and a firm handler of Communist dangers. The President's campaign probably also profited from Henry Kissinger's excessively premature announcement of October 31 that "peace is at hand."

Undoubtedly Nixon benefitted most from Wallace's withdrawal. North and South, observers agreed, the Wallace vote shown in the primaries more likely went to Nixon in response to his antibusing and antiwelfare stands. A three-way race covering a wider spectrum of appeal would probably have furnished a more accurate picture of voter alignment. Nixon would still have won, but with a less persuasive mandate. It seemed equally apparent that no Democratic candidate could have defeated the incumbent President.

The race of '72 revealed an unusual growth of social callousness in the nation's voters. The vast majority of voters were indifferent to the bombing and destruction of Vietnam, so long as American casualties were reduced. Polls revealed that a majority of voters considered that "too much attention had been paid to blacks, and to welfare and urban decay problems." The Nixon administration was the first in history to indulge in such burglary, espionage, and sabotage at the presidential level. A *New York Times* editorial bluntly described the "sinister operation on the part of White House aides and the Nixon campaign organization" as having constituted "practice unprecedented in American politics." The Watergate affair, with its connections pointing clearly to the White House, would have brought down any parliamentary democracy in the Western world, yet in 1972 it was regarded by most voters as American as apple pie. Only in the year after, when confessions brought out clearly the extent of the Nixon administration involvement, were calls for impeachment heard from both voters and Republican Congressmen. The federal court investigation implicated H. R. Haldeman and John D. Erlichman, the President's top domestic aides. In April 1973 the President was pressured into requesting their resignations as well as that of Attorney General Kleindienst. John Dean III, the presidential counsel whose testimony was extremely damaging regarding White House participation in the sordid Watergate affair, was also discharged. Not only complicity in espionage and burglary, but the even more serious charge of criminal obstruction of justice through months of attemped cover-up threatened the entire structure of the White House organization and its principal occupant. In the televised investigative proceedings which soon followed, the Nixon staff and its spokesmen presented a spectacle of conflicting stories and memory lapses, amid the disclosure of additional hitherto unrevealed transgressions. The Nixon response was to "tough it out" with denials, and with refusal to acknowledge requests for information from the Senate Committee headed by Constitutional expert Senator Sam Ervin (D.No.Car.). Public opinion of President Nixon moved down to new lows in the first year of his second term, and national and international leadership stagnated from the resulting loss of confidence in the wake of Watergate.

A significant outcome for the Democrats was the emergence of a new political strata of the population. Young people, students, middle-class professional men and many suburban housewives exhibited a new willingness for political involvement. As the Republicans found out after Goldwater's crushing defeat, activists remain active. This definite threat to the power of the old pros was divisive within Democratic ranks but promised a hopeful new direction for the future. The Republicans could point to an amazing phenomenon in American politics—the defection of the entire South in less than three decades from the Democratic to the Republican party, and particularly in its right wing. Extending westward beyond the old Confederacy through the newer "Sun States" of Arizona and New Mexico its basis for presidential votes, even if not always for congressional votes, was encouraging to the GOP. To the rest of the world the American presidential election displayed a deeply troubled nation whose social rifts were still far from resolution.

Evaluation of the Nixon Administration

The Nixon actions in the field of foreign policy were more consequential and received more historical recognition than was the case with his essentially negative record in domestic affairs. The President's trip to Peking, ending decades of *de jure* policy which insisted that Chiang Kai-shek's Formosa was "China," opened the way for a more stabilized era of international and trade relations. The Nixon government did not go so far as to extend official recognition, but official "observers" and other ad hoc arrangements indicated its likelihood in the future. Nixon was both supported in and pushed towards an understanding with China. Both anti-Chinese and old Cold War reflexes were considerably subdued by the 1970s, as the earlier Ping Pong incident clearly showed. In the United Nations, the vote to admit the People's Republic was slowly but surely moving against the earlier U.S. position and toward a favorable majority. China herself, with increasing worries on her borders with the Soviet Union, was becoming less fractious and less belligerent rhetorically. She obviously wanted membership in the world body and was receptive to an accord with the United States. Finally, American lack of success in prior military objectives in Vietnam and the forthcoming presidential election of 1972 were other pressuring considerations. Nevertheless, impelled by whatever reasons, Nixon must be credited with turning around the United States' long and futile China policy. It may well have been only a Republican president who could have accomplished such an accord in the year 1971. Partisan discord over the China visit was virtually nonexistent, with only ultraconservative groups from Republican ranks objecting. Containment, however, was only abated and not renounced. The Nixon Doctrine and continued United States military presence in Southeast Asia gave evidence that this phase of American policy was slightly relaxed and more flexible, but scarcely discarded.

Having recognized the Chinese revolution of 1949, Nixon also sought for a further détente with the Soviet Union. There was more willingness (shown through revised Nixon-Kissinger policies) to accept the historical evidence that the Soviet Union had frequently sold out revolutionary movements around the globe and was primarily concerned with the great power needs of stability and profitable trade far more than with ideological global conspiracy. This reversed the official stand held through the Kennedy and Johnson administrations. In any case, the fact that the United States could no longer afford the varied costs of the Cold War was an influential pressure. The issues, the conflicts, and the competition, in Europe as in Asia, were increasingly centered in monetary policy and the damages of inflation, markets for trade, and the scarcity of basic resources. Confronting these factors became more important than irrational military confrontations. It also seemed likely that opposing ground forces in Europe would be slowly reduced. However, it did not appear that the Nixon administration intended any brake on the armaments race despite the SALT agreements. The military and their supporters were, in 1963, able to provide for the underground loophole in the Kennedy Test Ban Treaty which soon assumed gigantic proportions. In the same manner, the SALT agreements were vitiated by assurances to the Joint Chiefs which would allow for continued nuclear testing to "maintain weapons system technological superiority." Such testing of the effectiveness of "new and existing" systems precluded any halt in the insensate nuclear armaments race.

In Indochina, the war slowly and tortuously wound down, with only the frailest of guarantees against possible future American reinvolvement. The North Vietnamese were pressured by some impatience on the part of their Chinese and Russian suppliers and by years of bombing devastation. But evidently even more crucial was the forseeable possibility of eventually altering or modifying the Saigon government—always the ultimate issue of the internal Vietnamese struggle. That government, even given a neutralist basis, might lead in the indefinite future to a unifying of all of Vietnam with North Vietnamese and Vietcong domination that could never be possible so long as an American military presence remained. In a war which was clearly not winnable, even a long-term favorable prospect served to bring about a relaxation of the North Vietnamese grimly held principles. If the possibilities of unification and a people's government had not been present, those who fought against a series of foreign-dominated regimes would have fought 30 years in vain.

The Nixon administration found the war increasingly less winnable as measured against the rising costs of the war to the American economy and as regards Congressional difficulties. The White House abandoned winning by "decisive military action," moved back to "Vietnamization" and partial withdrawal, and thence to a cease-fire and total withdrawal. Nixon's 11-day resumption of Yuletide bombing alienated many Republicans and gave many supporters second thoughts. And after Nixon's cordial visits to China and Russia it became inescapably plain that the adversary was not a menacing "world communism," but only the small and remote country of Vietnam. Not since the Harding era, the retiring editor of *Foreign Affairs* pointed out, had the world had such a poor opinion of the United States or had its influence in world circles been at such a low ebb. Monetary and fiscal crises, however, were of even more consequence than protests, dissenters, or "a decent respect to the opinions of mankind." Nixon was also able to ignore the divisions in American society and the unmet social costs, although public pressure to bring back the POWs was making itself heard. But the continued pouring of funds into the war, when the American dollar was taking its worst beating of all time and inflation was moving supermarket prices to new highs, was more serious. And Congress, where even the most conservative members were becoming steadily angrier not only over the war's expenditures but particularly over Nixon's highhanded usurpation of congressional authority and prerogatives, was moving slowly but surely to cut off completely all funds for Indochinese use. Nixon and the business community were also keenly concerned with winning the race for lucrative trade relations with China and Russia against the stiff competition of Japan and West Germany. With the signing of the cease-fire agreement, congressional and historical argument could only center around Senator J. W. Fulbright's bitter question, "What have we gotten in this agreement that we couldn't have gotten four years ago?"

In any case, the Nixon administration showed no intention of removing the American military presence from other parts of Indochina such as Thailand and the coastal waters. It was considered that, in order to get President Thieu's reluctant consent to the cease-fire, Nixon had given some assurance of potential cause for American reintervention. The result was a tenuous truce rather than a genuine peace. As Frances Fitzgerald, author of the well-received work on American-Vietnamese relations, *Fire in the Lake,* commented in *Newsday,*

> In the future it (Thieu's regime) can be counted on to resist any and all steps that would lead the country toward a permanent end of the fighting. . . . Its efforts will also go into discovering, provoking, or inventing cease-fire violations by the other side in an attempt to bring the U.S. back into the war. . . . Its very survival depends on maintaining the state of hostility.

Nixon's first term domestically was one of dangerous paradox and negativism. The nation received many promises in everything from "six great goals" to a new welfare assistance program, and from unity to stepped-up antipollution drives, but the Nixon performance all too often moved in a direction opposite to the rhetoric. The President insisted he stood for a balanced budget, but the Nixon deficits actually exceeded the combined deficits of Eisenhower, Kennedy, and Johnson. Although arms agreement was reached with Russia and the Vietnamese War was being brought to a close, Nixon insisted that Congress must move upward by $4 billion an already bloated military budget. Although the President repeatedly vowed to get the unemployed off welfare rolls and into jobs, the jobless rate increased from 3.5 percent in 1969 to nearly 6 percent in 1972, and bills for job training and work making were vetoed. An avowed friend of antipollution, Nixon nevertheless vetoed the comprehensive Federal Water Pollution Control Act of 1972. When Congress passed it over his veto, he impounded and refused to allocate half of the funds voted, citing inflation. An outspoken advocate of health and education, Nixon vetoed bills for hospital construction, for the training of more doctors, for child day-care centers, and for Office of Education school lunch programs. He introduced the boldly innovative scheme for a modified version of guaranteed income, the Family Assistance Plan, but sensing the Middle America revolt against everything pertaining to welfare, he withdrew his support. Nixon undertook major changes in the U.S. economy with devaluations of the dollar and a wage-price freeze. But neither was directed against causative factors such as years of heavy military expenditures at home and around the world, or the shift from an export- to an import-oriented economy.

Throughout his career in government and into his first term in the presidency, Richard Nixon's political inclinations were restrained by the need to win the next election, whatever it happened to be. Given the final term of the ultimate office by a large mandate, the President took a number of deliberate steps which forecast the direction and policy of the final Nixon years. Resignations were demanded of most upper-level appointments, and those of independence of thought were replaced with men whose unswerving loyalties to the administration viewpoint were unquestioned. Changes in the administrative structure were made which centered powers and checkreins more firmly in the White House. Nixon turned a stony face toward the poor, the minority groups, and toward urban social problems. He made it abundantly clear that he intended to dismantle the Great Society of Johnson and reverse the antipoverty policies of Kennedy. Conversely, expenditures to the aerospace, defense, and shipbuilding industries were pushed steadily upward. Government servants who pointed out specific cases of appalling waste and continuing cost overruns in such areas were summarily discharged or transferred.

Nowhere was the aggressively negative stance of the second term more visible than in the earliest budgets. These cut $1.5 billion from welfare, $1.5 billion from Medicare and housing, and $1.0 billion from manpower programs. Health, education, and poverty programs were reduced by $1.0 billion, and environmental programs by the same amount. The President thus identified himself as an arch conservative on the issue of government spending for social purposes. He was able to muster widespread support for his position by insisting that such measures were not actually socially regressive but were saving the taxpayer from being robbed by welfare cases, criminals, chiselers and incompetent bureaucrats. Mayors of large cities, however, complained loudly in Washington meetings that such cutbacks meant new sewage systems had to be cancelled, slum housing phased out, and that some school systems lacking federal aid would have to close before the end of the school year. Governor Jimmy Carter of Georgia was representative of a number of states in pointing out that his state was losing more funds through federal program cutbacks than it was gaining from revenue sharing, which he labelled "a cruel hoax." As federal funds trickled out, heavy layoffs were predicted nationally in building and education, and the inner-city pressures which led to the riots of the 1960s were alleged to be rebuilding.

If the concentration of power over foreign affairs in the executive was a conspicuous feature of Nixon's first term, it was apparently to be matched in the second term by a similar concentration of power over domestic affairs. Controls were taken away from a variety of agencies and centered in the executive office under officials with greatly expanded responsibilities. One such example was also perhaps Nixon's most controversial second-term appointment. This was Roy L. Ash, former head of the floundering, defense-oriented conglomerate, Litton Industries, which had been accused by Vice Admiral Hyman Rickover of "misrepresentation, if not fraud" in cost overruns on nuclear submarine construction. Ash was named Director of the Office of Management and Budget (OMB), one of the most powerful of all government agencies, where Cabinet members were obliged to get permission to spend funds appropriated to them by Congress. Because of Ash's avowed intent to impound congressional appropriations and because of Litton Industries' dubious relationship with the Department of Defense, Congress introduced legislation requiring Senate confirmation of the directorship. Another new appointment was that of George P. Shultz as Secretary of the Treasury, with control over all national and international economic policy cutting across other departments and agencies. Schultz had formerly been Secretary of Labor and Director of OMB.

In the presidency, Nixon dismayed Congress and the media by increasing his isolation behind a small circle of advisers. His always thin-skinned reluctance to expose himself to press questioning and his use of prepared speeches instead had brought about, according to correspondents, the death of the open press conference as modern Presidents had developed it. Less and less information, the *Wall Street Journal* reported, emerged from the White House. Since several of the new Cabinet appointments also bore the dual title of Counselor to the President they, too, came under the doctrine of "executive privilege" by means of which Special Assistant Kissinger and others had refused to testify before Congress. Secrecy, impoundment, fund cutbacks, and usurpation of authority were issues increasingly focusing congressional anger and resentment on the White House as the second term began. An aroused Congress faced with a determined President was likely to result only in national problems politicized and solutions postponed.

Traditionally optimistic, Americans were nevertheless aware that their usual mood of confidence was shadowed by portents of frustration and divisiveness as the United States moved toward its bicentennial year.

Suggestions for Reading

For the close election of 1968 and its controversial conventions, see Mike Ryko, *Boss: Richard J. Daley of Chicago* (1971), and Norman Mailer, *Miami and the Siege of Chicago: An Informal History of the Republican and Democratic Conventions of 1968* (1968). On the nature of the Nixon campaign, see Joe McGinnis, *The Selling of the President* (1969). A comprehensive account is T. H. White, *The Making of the President 1968* (1969). For the opposition, see R. S. Anson, *McGovern* (1972), and Jeremy Larner, *Nobody Knows: Reflections on the McCarthy Campaign of 1968* (1970). For some reflections on the relationship between Vietnam and the events of 1968, see Richard Rovere, *Waist Deep in the Big Muddy* (1968).

Many of the works on Nixon deal primarily with the early years. A journalistic account is Rowland Evans, Jr., and R. D. Novak, *Nixon in the White House: The Frustration of Power*° (1971). The elusiveness of the Nixon character is reflected in H. D. Spalding, *The Nixon Nobody Knows* (1972), and Bruce Mazlish's "psychohistorical inquiry," *In Search of Nixon* (1972). A sympathetic biography is Earl Mazo and Stephen Hess, *Nixon: A Political Portrait* (1968). A critical analysis is Garry Wills, *Nixon Agonistes* (1970), and an account of his political comeback is Jules Witcover, *The Resurrection of Richard Nixon* (1970). John Osborne of *New Republic* keeps his eye on the White House in *The Nixon Watch* (1970), *The Second Year of the Nixon Watch* (1971), and *The Third Year of the Nixon Watch* (1972). Conservatives view Nixon in Allen Drury, *Courage and Hesitation: Inside the Nixon Administration* (1972), and R. J. Whalen, *Catch the Falling Flag* (1972). A laudatory work is Richard De Toledano, *One Man Alone: Richard Nixon* (1969). Comprehensive and critical is Leonard Lurie, *The Running of Richard Nixon* (1972). See also C. P. Henderson, *The Nixon Theology* (1972). Nixon has been a natural target for satire. See the comical Mark Harris, *Mark the Glove Boy* (1964) for the early years, and Philip Roth, for satire directed at the more recent years in *Our Gang* (1971). The paradoxes of Nixon's private enterprise philosophy and stern economic controls are cleverly examined in Leonard Silk, *Nixonomics* (1972), and in R. L. Miller and R. M. Williams, *The New Economics of Richard Nixon: Freezes, Floats, and Fiscal Policy* (1972). See also Jules Witcover, *White Knight: The Rise of Spiro Agnew* (1972), for an account of the Vice President.

On Vietnam, refer to the suggestions for the preceding chapters. See also Noam Chomsky, *At War with Asia: Essays on Indo-China* (1970), and Daniel Ellsberg, *Papers on the War* (1972). In summation, however, two comprehensive single-volume works are outstanding: G. M. Kahin and J. W. Lewis, *The United States in Vietnam*° (rev. ed. 1969), and Frances Fitzgerald, *Fire in the Lake: The Vietnamese and the Americans in Vietnam* (1972). *The Pentagon Papers*° (1971) remain an indispensable source. Consult also David Landau, *Kissinger: The Uses of Power* (1972) on the President's influential foreign policy adviser.

The last decade or so of American foreign policy has come increasingly under fire for its imperialistic activities. A foremost critic is Gabriel Kolko, *The Roots of American Foreign Policy: An Analysis of Power and Purpose* (1969). See also Ronald Steel, *Pax Americana*° (rev. ed. 1970); J. M. Swomley, Jr., *American Empire* (1970); and R. J. Barnet, *Intervention and Revolution: America's Confrontation with Insurgent Movements Around the World* (1968). A somewhat less critical view is found in M. J. Pusey, *USA Astride the Globe* (1972).

Increasingly of concern has been the rise of militaristic influence in American society and the perils and waste of the military-industrial complex. On the former see Col. J. A. Donovan, *Militarism, USA*° (1970), and Erwin Knoll and J. N. McFadden, eds., *American Militarism 1970* (1969). On the military-industrial complex, see Fred J. Cook, *The Warfare State*° (1962); Seymour Melman, *Pentagon Capitalism: The Political Economy of War* (1970); Sidney Lens, *The Military-Industrial Complex* (1970); William Proxmire, *Report from Wasteland: America's Military-Industrial Complex* (1970); J. W. Fulbright, *The Pentagon Propaganda Machine*° (1971); and C. R. Mollenhoff, *The Pentagon* (1967). See also R. J. Barnet, *The Economy of Death*° (1969); R. E. Lapp, *The Weapons Culture* (1968); and George Thayer, *The War Business: The International Trade in Armaments* (1969).

In the 60s and 70s America was also concerned with the rebelliousness and dissent of its youth and with the women's liberation movement. An outstanding writer on American youth is Kenneth Keniston, who has written *The Uncommitted*° (1965), *Young Radicals*° (1968), and *Youth and Dissent* (1971). A good analysis is found in Margaret Mead, *Culture and Commitment*° (1970); and an informative anthology is Alexander Klein, ed., *Natural Enemies: Youth and the Clash of Generations* (1970). Campus uprisings are covered in Nathan Glazer, *Remembering the Answers* (1970); Daniel Bell and Irving Kristol, eds., *Confrontation* (1969); Seymour Lipset and Sheldon Wolin, eds., *The Berkeley Student Revolt* (1965); and Jerry Avorn et al., *Up Against the Ivy Wall* (1968). For the counter culture, see Theodore Roszak, *The Making of a Counter Culture* (1969), and the idealistic Charles Reich, *The Greening of America* (1970). A biting review of the latter is that of Samuel McCracken in the periodical of higher education, *Change* (1971).

For recent history of the feminist movement, see W. H. Chafe, *The American Woman* (1972). See also Betty Friedan, *The Feminine Mystique* (1963). Social analyses are found in Elizabeth Janeway, *Man's World, Woman's Place: A Study in Social Mythology* (1971), and Juliet Mitchell, *Women's Estate* (1972). Useful collections are Judith Hole and Ellen Levine, eds., *Rebirth of Feminism* (1972); Robin Morgan, ed., *Sisterhood is Powerful*° (1970); and Jean Friedman and William Shades, eds., *Our American Sisters: Women in American Life and Thought.*°

Index

This book has been set in 10 and 9 point Caledonia, leaded 2 points. Chapter numbers are in 30 point Scotch Roman italic and chapter titles are in 18 point Scotch Roman italic. The size of the type page is 27 × 45½ picas.